Introduction to Behavioral Research Methods

Introduction to Behavioral Research Methods

Mark R. Leary
WAKE FOREST UNIVERSITY

WADSWORTH PUBLISHING COMPANY

Belmont, California

A Division of Wadsworth, Inc.

Psychology Editor: Ken King
Editorial Assistant: Cynthia Campbell
Production Editor: Gary Mcdonald
Managing Designer: Donna Davis
Print Buyer: Karen Hunt
Designer: Al Burkhardt
Copy Editor: Jeanne Woodward
Technical Illustrator: Alexander Teshin Associates
Cartoonist: Sidney Harris
Compositor: Bi-Comp, Inc.
Signing Representative: Tom Orsi
Cover Painting: Frank Stella: *Olkienniki I*, 1972. Felt, painted cardboard and canvas on chipboard, 92″ × 82″. Munson-Williams-Proctor Institute Museum of Art, Utica, New York.

Printed in the United States of America   50

1 2 3 4 5 6 7 8 9 10—94 93 92 91 90

Library of Congress Cataloging in Publication Data

Leary, Mark R.
  Introduction to behavioral research methods / Mark R. Leary.
     p.   cm.
  Includes bibliographical references and indexes.
  ISBN 0-534-13818-7
  1. Psychology—Research—Methodology.   I. Title.
BF76.5.L39 1990
150′.724—dc20   90-42536

Contents

CHAPTER **2**

Behavioral Variability and Research

24

CHAPTER **3**

The Measurement of Behavior

41

CHAPTER **6**
Correlational Research   **97**

CHAPTER **7**
Basics of Experimental Design   **120**

CHAPTER **8**

Experiments with One Independent Variable   **150**

CHAPTER **9**

The Design of Factorial Experiments   **175**

CHAPTER **10**

Analyzing Complex Experiments: The Analysis of Variance

194

CHAPTER **11**

Quasi-Experimental Designs

213

CHAPTER **12**
Single-Subject Designs

CHAPTER **13**
An Overview of Advanced Designs and Analyses

CHAPTER **14**
Ethical Issues in Behavioral Research   **259**

CHAPTER **15**
Disseminating Research Findings   **282**

Preface

If a nationwide poll were conducted of undergraduate psychology students, the consensus for the most difficult and least enjoyable course would undoubtedly be research methods. Students typically dread taking methods courses, find such courses difficult and dry, and often wonder, in retrospect, why such courses were required as part of their psychology major or minor.

A few years ago, I began to ponder why this should be so. After all, the individuals who teach research methods are generally quite enthusiastic about research, and most try to bring the topic alive for their students. Yet for some reason the research method course remains, in the students' eyes, the black sheep of the psychology curriculum. Although many factors converge to give the methods course this dubious distinction, I have concluded that three predominate.

First, most students major or minor in psychology either because they plan to enter a people-oriented profession in which knowledge of behavior is relevant (such as professional psychology, social work, or public relations) or because they are intrinsically interested in the subject matter of psychology. In either case, they seldom if ever enter psychology because they are enamoured by research. In fact, many students are initially surprised at the emphasis the discipline places on research. Although some students eventually come to appreciate the value of research to the science and profession of psychology, others continue to view it as an unnecessary curricular diversion imposed by misguided academicians. For most students, being required to take one or more courses in methodology supplants other courses in which they are more interested. To overcome these sentiments, the instructor and textbook must demonstrate the usefulness of understanding research methodology for the psychology student.

A second reason that the methods course is seldom a popular one is that students typically find it more difficult than most other courses in psychology. The concepts, principles, analyses, and ways of thinking central to methodology are new to most students and typically require effort to comprehend, learn, and retain. This problem is compounded by the fact that methods are often taught in a somewhat piecemeal fashion. Each topic—measurement, correlation, design, analysis, and so forth—is taught as an independent unit with little integration across topics. I maintain, however, that, with a few exceptions, the material is really not any more difficult to learn than that of other courses. It is, however, more difficult to *teach*.

Third, research methods courses are, on the whole—how can I put this delicately?—less interesting than most other courses in psychology. If the instructor and textbook do not make a special effort to make the material interesting and relevant, students are unlikely to dervive much enjoyment from studying research methods.

I wrote *Introduction to Behavioral Research Methods* because, as a teacher and as a researcher, I was frustrated by these and other shortcomings of the methods course. Although I have no delusion that this book will transform the methods course into the most popular course in the curriculum, I do think that it will help make research methodology more understandable, more palatable, and more interesting for many students.

My primary goal was to write a methodology text that was *readable*. I think that students should be able to understand most of the material in a book such as this without the course instructor having to serve as an interpreter. Enhancing comprehensibility can be achieved in two ways. The less preferred way is to simply dilute the material by omitting complex topics. The alternative, which I chose in this text, is to present the material with sufficient elaboration, explanation, and examples to render it understandable.

A second goal was to integrate the various topics in the book to a greater extent than is done in most texts, using the concept of variability as a unifying theme. From the development of a research idea, through measurement issues, to design and analysis, virtually the entire research process is an attempt to understand variability in behavior. Because the concept of variability is woven throughout the research process, I've used it as a framework to provide coherence to the various topics in the book.

I've tried to write a book that is interesting—presenting ideas in an engaging fashion and using examples of real and hypothetical research. (Unfortunately, a few topics, such as the calculation of a correlation coefficient, defied my best attempts.) Like most researchers, I am enthusiastic about the research process, and I hope that some of my enthusiasm will be contagious.

Methods courses differ widely in the degree to which statistics are incorporated into the course. My view is that statistics *are* research methods and that students' understanding of research methodology is enhanced by an elementary understanding of statistics. Thus, I've sprinkled statistical topics throughout the book. However, because I think it is more important that students develop a strong conceptual understanding of statistics than to learn to perform a wide array of analyses, I have emphasized the conceptual foundations of statistical analysis. I've included the analytical procedures for the most basic analyses—such as descriptive statistics, correlation coefficients, and *t*-tests—but I made no attempt to present a comprehensive coverage of statistics. However, knowing that some instructors will want coverage of more advanced analyses, I relegated more advanced material to Chapter 10 and Appendix B. Instructors who prefer to deemphasize statistics may omit Chapter 10 and Appendix B.

Many people contributed their time and effort to this book. Wendy McColskey critiqued most of the manuscript and listened to me obsess about it for nearly two years; it was quite helpful to have a spouse who holds her doctorate in research and evaluation. Robin Kowalski read, critiqued, and edited the entire manuscript and was always available when I needed to bounce ideas around. Throughout the entire process, Ken King and the production staff at Wadsworth provided expert encouragement and advice. I'm deeply indebted to all of these individuals.

Thanks also to these reviewers: Michael Berzonsky, SUNY, Cortland; Jim Blascovich, SUNY, Buffalo; Clarke A. Burnham, The University of Texas at Austin; Jerry L. Cohen, University of Rhode Island; Gary Gillund, College of Wooster; Valerie Greaud Folk, Educational Testing Service; David E. Hogan, Northern Kentucky University; Peter Mikulka, Old Dominion University; Margaret Thomas, University of Central Florida; and Paul A. Toro, SUNY, Buffalo.

My view is that research is an integral part of the search for knowledge about behavioral processes, as well as for the solution of psychological and social problems. I hope students will find this book useful in understanding and appreciating behavioral research.

Mark R. Leary
Winston-Salem, NC

Introduction to Behavioral Research Methods

1

Research in the Behavioral Sciences

Stop for a moment and imagine, as vividly as you can, a scientist at work. Let your imagination fill in as many details as possible regarding this scene. What does the imagined scientist look like? Where is the person working? What is the scientist doing?

When I recently asked a group of undergraduate students to imagine a scientist and to tell me what they imagined, their answers were quite interesting. First, virtually every student said that their imagined scientist was male. This in itself is interesting given that a high percentage of scientists are, of course, women.

Second, a great majority reported that they imagined the scientist to be wearing a white lab coat and to be working indoors in some kind of laboratory. The details regarding this laboratory differed from student to student, but the lab nearly always contained specialized scientific equipment of one kind or another. Some students imagined a chemist, surrounded by substances in test tubes and beakers. Other students thought of a biologist peering into a microscope. Still others conjured up a physicist working with sophisticated electronic equipment. One or two students even imagined an astronomer peering through a telescope. Most interesting to me was the fact that although these students were members of a psychology class (in fact, most were psychology majors), not one of them thought of a psychologist when I asked them to imagine a scientist.

Their responses were probably typical of what most people would say if asked to imagine a scientist. For most people, the prototypic scientist is a man wearing a white lab coat working in a laboratory filled with technical equipment. Most people do not think of psychologists as scientists in the same way they think of physicists, chemists, and biologists as scientists.

People tend to think of psychologists only in their roles as mental health professionals. If I had asked you to imagine a psychologist, you probably would have thought of a counselor talking with a client about his or her problems. You probably would *not* have imagined a behavioral researcher, such as a physiological psychologist studying startle responses, a social psychologist conducting an experiment on aggression, or an industrial psychologist interviewing the line supervisors at an automobile assembly plant.

Psychology, however is not only a profession that promotes human welfare through counseling, education, and other activities, but is also a scientific discipline that studies behavior and mental processes. Just as biologists study living organisms and astronomers study the stars, behavioral scientists conduct research involving behavior and mental processes.

Goals of Behavioral Research

Scientific research holds an important place within the discipline of psychology, as well as in society in general. Roughly speaking, behavioral research fulfills four interrelated functions: describing behavior, understanding behavior, predicting behavior, and solving applied problems.

Describing Behavior

Some behavioral researchers are interested primarily in describing behavior. Marketing researchers, for example, study consumers' preferences and buying practices. Similarly, public opinion polls, such as those that dominate the news during election years, attempt to describe people's attitudes. Other examples of descriptive studies include research in developmental psychology that describes age-related changes in behavior, and studies from industrial psychology that describe the behavior of effective managers.

Understanding Behavior

People have asked questions about the causes of behavior throughout written history. Aristotle was perhaps the first to systematically address basic questions about the nature of humans and why they behave as they do. For centuries, however, the approach to answering these questions was entirely speculative. People would simply concoct explanations of behavior based on everyday observation, creative insight, or religious doctrine. For several centuries, people who wrote about behavior tended to be philosophers or theologians, and their approach was not scientific. Even so, many of these early insights into behavior were, of course, quite accurate.

However, many of their explanations of behavior were completely wrong. They shouldn't be faulted for having made mistakes, for even modern researchers sometimes draw incorrect conclusions. Unlike behavioral scientists today, however, these early "psychologists" (to use the term loosely) did not rely on scientific research to provide answers about behavior. As a result, they had no way to test the validity of their explanations and, thus, no way to discover whether their interpretations were accurate.

Scientific psychology was born during the last quarter of the 19th century. Through the influence of early researchers such as Wilhelm Wundt, William James, John Watson, G. Stanley Hall, and others, people began to realize that basic questions about behavior could be addressed using many of the same approaches that were used in more established sciences, such as biology, chemistry, and physics.

Today, a great deal of behavioral research is devoted to providing a better understanding of behavior. **Basic research,** as it is often called, is aimed toward understanding behavior without regard for the immediate application of this knowledge. This is not to say that basic researchers are not interested in the applicability of their findings. They usually are. In fact, the results of basic research are often quite useful, often in ways that were not anticipated by the researchers themselves. For example, basic research involving brain function has led to the development of drugs that control some symptoms of mental illness, and basic research on cognitive development in children has led to educational innovations in schools. However, the immediate goal of basic research is to acquire knowledge rather than solve a particular problem.

Predicting Behavior

Many psychologists are interested in predicting people's behavior. For example, personnel psychologists try to predict employees' job performance from employment tests and interviews. Similarly, educational psychologists develop ways to predict academic performance from scores on standardized tests in order to identify students who might have learning difficulties in school. Likewise, some forensic psychologists are interested in predicting which criminals are likely to be dangerous if released from prison.

Developing ways to predict job performance, school grades, or violent tendencies requires considerable research. The tests to be used (such as employment or achievement tests) must be administered, analyzed, and refined to meet certain statistical criteria. Then, data are collected and analyzed to identify the best predictors of the target behavior. Prediction equations are calculated and validated on other samples of subjects to be sure they predict the target behavior well enough to be used. In brief, the scientific prediction of behavior involves behavioral research methods.

Solving Applied Problems

The goal of **applied research** is to provide solutions for current problems rather than to study basic psychological processes. For example, many industrial-organizational psychologists are hired by businesses to study and solve problems related to employee morale, satisfaction, and productivity. Similarly, community psychologists are sometimes asked to investigate social problems such as racial tension, littering, and teenage pregnancy. In such cases, researchers use behavioral research techniques to understand and solve some problem of immediate concern (such as employee morale or prejudice).

These four goals of behavioral research—description, understanding, prediction, and solving problems—overlap considerably. For example, much basic research is immediately applicable, and much applied research provides information regarding basic psychological processes. Furthermore, description and basic research often provide the foundation on which predictive and applied research rests, and applied research often provides questions for basic researchers. In addition, regardless of whether their goal is to describe, understand, predict, or improve behavior, researchers rely largely on the same general research strategies. Thus, you should regard these goals as four primary reasons that behavioral scientists conduct research rather than as four distinct types of research.

The Value of Research to the Student

Aside from the important role that research plays in psychology, a firm grasp of basic research methodology has advantages for students such as yourself. After all, many students have no intention of becoming researchers; indeed, many who major in psychology do not plan to become psychologists at all. Understandably, such students wonder what the benefits of studying research are for them.

A solid background in research has three important outcomes. First, knowledge about research methods is important because it allows people to understand research that is relevant to their professions. Many professionals who deal with people—not only psychologists, but also those in social work, nursing, teaching, management, public relations, communication, advertising, and the ministry—must keep up with advances in their fields. For example, those who become counselors and therapists are obligated to stay abreast of the research literature that deals with therapy and related topics. Most such information is published in professional research journals. However, as you may have already learned from personal experience, journal articles are often incomprehensible unless a person knows something about research and statistics. Thus, a background in research will provide you with knowledge and skills that you may find useful in professional life.

A second outcome of research training involves the development of critical thinking. Scientists are a critical lot, always asking questions, considering alternative explanations, insisting on hard evidence, refining their methods, and critiquing their own and others' conclusions. Many people have found a critical, scientific approach to solving problems is useful in areas other than research. For example, the Surgeon General of the United States and the tobacco industry have long been engaged in a debate regarding the dangers of cigarette smoking. The Surgeon General maintains that cigarettes are hazardous to your health, whereas cigarette manufacturers claim that no conclusive evidence exists that shows cigarette smoking to cause lung cancer and other diseases in humans. Furthermore, both sides present scientific data to support their arguments. Who is right? As you'll see later in the book, even a basic knowledge of research methods will allow you to resolve this controversy; we'll return to this debate in Chapter 6.

A third outcome of becoming involved in research activities is that it helps one become an authority, not only on research procedures, but in particular areas of psychology. In the process of reading about previous studies, wrestling with issues involving research strategy, collecting data, and interpreting the results, researchers grow increasingly familiar with their topics. For this reason, the faculty at many colleges urges students to become involved in research, such as class projects, independent research projects, or assisting with a faculty member's research. This is also one reason why many colleges and universities insist that their faculty maintain ongoing research programs. By remaining active as researchers, professors engage in an ongoing learning process that keeps them at the forefront of their fields.

CONTRIBUTORS TO BEHAVIORAL RESEARCH

Wilhelm Wundt and the Founding of Scientific Psychology

Wilhelm Wundt (1832–1920) was the first bonafide research psychologist. Most of those before him who were interested in behavior identified themselves primarily as philosophers, theologians, biologists, physicians, or physiologists. Wundt, on the other hand, was the first to view himself as a research psychologist.

Wundt, who was born near Heidelberg, Germany, began studying medicine, but switched to physiology after working with Johannes Müller, perhaps the leading physiologist of the time. His early research, then, was not in psychology, but in physiology. Wundt, however, became interested in applying the methods of physiology to the study of psychology. In 1874, Wundt published a landmark text, *Principles of Physiological Psychology*, in which he boldly stated his plan to "mark out a new domain of science."

In 1875, Wundt established one of the first two psychology laboratories in the world at the University of Leipzig. Although it has been customary to cite 1879 as the year in which his lab was founded, Wundt was actually given laboratory space by the university for his laboratory equipment in 1875 (Watson, 1978). William James established a laboratory at Harvard University at about the same time, thus establishing the first psychological laboratory in the United States (Bringmann, 1979).

Beyond establishing the Leipzig laboratory, Wundt made numerous other contributions to behavioral science. He founded a journal in 1881 for the publication of research in experimental psychology; this was the first journal to devote more space to psychology than to philosophy. (At the time, psychology was viewed as an area of philosophy.) He also conducted a great deal of research on a variety of psychological processes, including sensation, perception, reaction time, attention, emotion, and introspection. Importantly, he also trained many students who went on to make their own contributions to early psychology: G. Stanley Hall (who founded the American Psychological Association and is considered the founder of child psychology), Witmer Lightner (who established the first psychological clinic), Edward Titchener (who brought Wundt's ideas to the United States), and Hugo Münsterberg (a pioneer in applied psychology). Also among Wundt's students was James McKeen Cattell, who in addition to conducting early research on mental tests was the first to integrate the study of experimental methods into the undergraduate psychology curriculum (Watson, 1978). In part, you have Cattell to thank for the importance that psychology departments place on undergraduate courses in research methods.

The Scientific Approach

I noted earlier that it is more difficult for people to think of psychology as a science than to think of chemistry, biology, or astronomy as sciences. In part, this is because many people misunderstand what science is. Many people judge whether or not a discipline is scientific on the basis of the topics it studies. Research involving molecules, chromosomes, and sunspots seems more scientific than research involving emotions, memories, or social interactions, for example.

Whether an area is scientific has little to do with the topics it studies, however. Rather, science is defined in terms of the approaches used to study the topic. Specifically, three criteria must be met for an investigation to be regarded as scientific: systematic empiricism, public verification, and solvability (Stanovich, 1986).

Systematic Empiricism

Empiricism refers to the practice of relying on observation to draw conclusions. The phenomena studied in science must be objective and observable, and not the product of one person's imagination. Although most people today would agree that the best way to find out about something is to observe it directly, this was not always the case. Until the late 16th century, experts relied more heavily on reason, intuition, and religious doctrine than on observation to answer questions about the world.

But observation alone does not make something a science. After all, everyone draws conclusions about human nature from observing people in everyday life. Scientific observation is *systematic*. Scientists structure their observations in systematic ways so that they can draw conclusions about the nature of the world from them. For example, a behavioral researcher who is interested in the effects of exercise on stress is unlikely to simply chat with people who exercise about how much stress they feel. Rather, the researcher is likely to design a carefully controlled study in which people are assigned randomly to different exercise programs, then measure their stress using well-validated techniques. Data obtained through systematic empiricism allow researchers to draw more confident conclusions than they can draw from casual observation alone.

Public Verification

The second criterion for scientific investigation is that it be *publicly verifiable*. In other words, research must be conducted in such a way that the findings of one researcher can be observed, replicated, and verified by others.

There are two reasons for this. First, the requirement of public verification ensures that the phenomena scientists study are real and observable and not one person's fabrications. Scientists disregard claims that cannot be verified by others. For example, a person's claim that he or she was captured by Bigfoot makes interesting reading, but it is not scientific because it cannot be publicly verified.

Second, public verification makes science self-correcting. When research is open to public scrutiny, errors in methodology and interpretation can be discovered and corrected by other researchers.

Public verification requires that researchers report both their methods and their findings to the scientific community. Scientific reporting usually occurs in the form of journal articles or presentations of papers at professional meetings. In this way, their methods, results, and conclusions can be examined and, possibly, challenged by others. As long as the researcher reports his or her methods in full detail, other researchers can attempt to repeat, or replicate, the research. Not only does this replication catch errors, but it allows researchers to build upon and extend the work of others.

Solvable Problems

The third criterion for scientific investigation is that it deal only with *solvable problems*. Researchers can investigate only those questions that are answerable given current knowledge and research techniques. I heard two students recently debating whether rock musician Billy Joel would have been a greater composer than Beethoven had he lived in the 19th century. Such a question is, of course, unanswerable and thus not open to scientific investigation.

This means that many questions are out of the realm of science. For example, the question, Are there angels?, is not scientific: No one has yet devised a way of detecting angels that is empirical, systematic, and publicly verifiable. This does not necessarily imply that angels do not exist or that the question is unimportant. It simply means that this question is beyond the scope of scientific investigation.

IN DEPTH

Pseudoscience: Believing the Unbelievable

Many people are willing to believe in things for which there is little, if any, empirical proof. They readily defend their belief that extraterrestrials have visited Earth; that some people can read others' minds; that they have been visited by the dead; or that Bigfoot, the Abominable Snowman, and Elvis Presley have all been sighted recently.

From the perspective of science, such beliefs present a problem because the evidence that is marshalled to support them is nearly always pseudoscientific. Pseudoscientific evidence involves claims that masquerade as science but in fact violate the basic assumptions of scientific investigation (Radner & Radner, 1982). It is not so much that people believe things that have not been confirmed; even scientists do that. Rather, it is that the evidence that pseudoscientists offer in support of such ideas pretends to be scientific, but usually is not. Pseudoscience is easy to recognize because it violates the basic criteria of science discussed above: systematic empiricism, public verification, and solvability.

Nonempirical Evidence

To test their hypotheses, scientists rely on observation. Pseudoscientific evidence, however, is often not based on observation, but rather consists of myths and opinions. Some pseudoscientific belief systems are based in part on evidence provided by unsubstantiated myths. For example, in *Chariots of the Gods?* von Daniken (1970) uses biblical references to "chariots of fire" as evidence for ancient spacecrafts. Because biblical evidence is neither systematic nor verifiable, it cannot be considered scientific. This is not to say that such evidence is necessarily inaccurate; it is simply not permissible in scientific investigation because its veracity cannot be determined conclusively.

Similarly, pseudoscientists often rely on people's beliefs rather than on observation or accepted scientific fact to bolster their arguments. Scientists wait for the empirical evidence to come in rather than basing their conclusions on what others think might be the case.

Furthermore, unlike science, pseudoscience tends to be highly biased in the evidence presented to support its case. For example, those who believe in precognition—telling the future—point to specific episodes in which people seemed to know in advance that something was going to happen. In 1978 the *National Enquirer* invited its readers to send in their predictions of what would happen during the next year. When the 1500 submissions were opened a year later, one contestant was correct in all five of her predictions. The *Enquirer* called this a "stunning display of psychic ability." Was it? Isn't it just as likely that, out of 1500 entries, some people would, just by chance, make correct predictions? Scientific logic requires that the misses be considered as evidence along with the hits. Pseudoscientific logic, on the other hand, is satisfied with a single (perhaps random) occurrence.

Unverifiability

Much pseudoscience is based on individuals' reports of what they have experienced, reports that are essentially unverifiable. If Mr. Smith claims to have spent last Thursday in an alien spacecraft, how do we know whether he is telling the truth? If Ms. Brown says she "knew" beforehand that her uncle had been hurt in an accident, who's to refute her? Of course, Mr. Smith and Ms. Brown might be telling the truth. On the other hand, they might be playing a prank, mentally disturbed, trying to cash in on the publicity, or sincerely confused. Regardless, their claims, because they are unverifiable, cannot be used as scientific evidence.

Irrefutable Hypotheses

As we will discuss in detail below, scientific hypotheses must be potentially falsifiable. If a hypothesis cannot be shown to be false by empirical data, we have no way to determine its validity. Pseudoscientific beliefs, on the other hand, are often stated in such a way that they can never be disconfirmed. Those who believe in extrasensory perception (ESP), for example, sometimes argue that ESP cannot be tested empirically, because the conditions necessary for the occurrence of ESP are violated under controlled laboratory conditions. Thus, even though "not a single individual has been found who can demonstrate ESP to the satisfaction of independent investigators" (Hansel, 1980, p. 314), believers continue to believe. Similarly, some advocates of creationism claim that the Earth is much younger than it appears from geological evidence. When the Earth was created in the relatively recent past, they argue, God included in the ground fossils and geological formations that only make it *appear to be* millions of years old. In both these examples, the hypothesis is irrefutable and untestable, and thus is pseudoscientific.

The Role of Theory in Science

As we saw earlier, one primary purpose of scientific research is to advance our understanding of the world. Theories play an important role in this process. In essence, one primary purpose of science is to generate and test theories.

When you hear the word *theory*, you probably think of theories such as Darwin's theory of evolution or Einstein's theory of relativity. However, nothing in the concept of theory requires that it be as grand or all-encompassing as evolution or relativity. Most theories, both in psychology and other sciences, are much less ambitious, attempting to explain only a small and circumscribed range of phenomena.

A **theory** is a set of propositions that attempt to specify the interrelationships among a set of concepts. For example, Fiedler's (1967) contingency

THE
UNKNOWN
SCIENTIST
(WHO DID
SOME VERY
IMPORTANT
GROUNDWORK)

© 1990 by Sidney Harris, *American Scientist* Magazine.

theory of leadership specifies the conditions under which certain kinds of leaders will be more effective in group settings. Some leaders are predominately task oriented; they keep the group focused on its purpose, discourage socializing, and demand participation by members. Other leaders are predominately relationship oriented; these leaders are more concerned with fostering positive relations among group members and with group satisfaction. The contingency theory proposes that whether a task-oriented or relationship-oriented leader will be more effective depends on three factors: the quality of the relationship between the leader and group members, the degree to which the group's task is structured, and the leader's power within the group. In fact, the theory specifies quite precisely the conditions under which certain leaders are more effective than others. The contingency theory of leadership fits our definition of a theory because it attempts to specify the interrelationships among a set of concepts (the concepts of leadership effectiveness, task versus interpersonal leaders, leader–member relations, task structure, and leader power).

Occasionally, people use the word theory in everyday language to refer to hunches or unsubstantiated ideas. For example, in the debate on whether to teach creation in public schools, creationists dismiss evolution because it's *only* a theory. This use of the term *theory* can be misleading: Scientific theories are not wild guesses or unsupported hunches; on the contrary, theories are accepted as valid only to the extent that they are *supported by empirical findings.* Science insists that theories be consistent with the facts as they are currently known. Theories that are not supported by data are usually replaced by other theories.

You might imagine that scientific theories are discovered by diligent scientists poring over reams of data. On the contrary, theories in the behavioral sciences are constructed rather than discovered. Behavioral scientists construct theories to explain patterns of behavior they observe.

Theory construction is very much a creative exercise, and ideas for theories can come from virtually anywhere. Sometimes, researchers immerse themselves in the research literature and purposefully work toward developing a theory. In other instances, researchers construct theories to explain patterns they observe in data they have collected. Other theories have been developed on the basis of case studies or everyday observation. At other times, a scientist may get a fully developed theoretical insight at a time when he or she is not even working on research. (A friend of mine gets his best ideas during his daily 5-mile run.) Researchers are not constrained in terms of where they get their theoretical ideas. There is no single way to formulate a theory.

Research Hypotheses

On the whole, scientists are a skeptical bunch, and they are seldom inclined to accept theories that have not been supported by research. Thus, a great deal of their time is spent testing theories to determine their usefulness in explaining and predicting behavior. Although theoretical ideas may come from anywhere, scientists are much more constrained in the procedures they use to *test* their theories.

The process of testing theories is an indirect one. Theories themselves are not tested directly. The propositions in the theory are usually too broad and complex to be tested directly in a particular study. Rather, when researchers set about to test a theory, they do so indirectly by testing one or more hypotheses that are derived from the theory.

Hypotheses are specific propositions that logically follow from the theory. Deriving hypotheses from a theory involves **deduction,** a process of reasoning from a general proposition (the theory) to specific implications of that proposition (the hypotheses). Hypotheses, then, can be thought of as the logical implications of the theory. When deriving a hypothesis, the researcher asks, If the theory is true, what would we expect to observe? For example, one hypothesis that can be derived from the contingency model of leadership is that relationship-oriented leaders will be more effective when the group's task is moderately structured rather than unstructured. If we do an experiment to test the validity of this hypothesis, we are testing part, but only part, of the contingency theory of leadership.

You can think of hypotheses as if–then statements of the general form, If *a*, then *b*. Based on the theory, the researcher hypothesizes that *if* certain conditions occur, *then* certain other conditions should follow. Although not all hypotheses are actually expressed in this manner, virtually all hypotheses are reducible to an if–then statement.

Not all hypotheses are derived deductively from theory. Often, scientists arrive at hypotheses through **induction**—abstracting a hypothesis from a collection of facts. A researcher may develop hypotheses after puzzling over apparently contradictory findings, by thinking about what a group of behaviors may have in common, or by casually observing patterns of behavior in everyday life, for example.

Whether derived deductively from theory or inductively from observed facts, hypotheses must be formulated very precisely in order to be testable. Specifically, hypotheses must be stated in such a way that they are **falsifiable.** A hypothesis is of little use unless it has the potential to be found false (Popper, 1959). One criticism of Freud's psychoanalytic theory, for example, is that researchers have found it difficult to generate hypotheses that can be falsified by research. Although psychoanalytic theory can explain virtually any behavior after it has occurred, researchers have found it difficult to derive specific falsifiable hypotheses from the theory that will predict how people will behave under certain circumstances. Because parts of the theory do not easily generate falsifiable hypotheses, most behavioral scientists regard aspects of psychoanalytic theory as inherently nonscientific.

A Priori Predictions and Post Hoc Explanations

Most people can find reasons for nearly anything that happens. In fact, we often find it equally easy to explain completely opposite occurrences. Consider Jim and Marie, a couple I know who just got married. If I hear in 5 years that Jim and Marie are happily married, I'll be able to look back and find clear-cut reasons why their relationship worked out so well. If, on the other hand, I learn in 5 years that they're getting divorced, I'll undoubtedly be able to recall indications that all was not well even from the beginning. As the saying goes, Hindsight is 20/20. Nearly everything makes sense after it happens.

The ease with which we can retrospectively explain even opposite occurrences leads scientists to be skeptical of **post hoc** explanations—explanations made after the fact. In light of this, a theory's ability to explain occurrences in a post hoc fashion provides little evidence of its accuracy or usefulness. More telling is the degree to which a theory can successfully predict what will happen. Theories that accurately predict the outcomes of research are regarded more positively than those that can only explain the outcomes after the research or after the event.

This is one reason researchers seldom conduct studies just to see what happens. If they have no preconceptions about what should happen in their study, they can easily explain whatever pattern of results they obtain in a post hoc fashion. To provide a more convincing test of the theory, researchers usually make specific research hypotheses **a priori**—before collecting the data. By making specific predictions about what will occur in a study, researchers avoid the pitfalls associated with purely post hoc explanations.

Conceptual and Operational Definitions

I noted above that scientific hypotheses must be potentially falsifiable by empirical data. For a hypothesis to be falsifiable, the terms used in the hypothesis must be clearly defined. In everyday language, we usually don't worry about precisely how we define the terms we use. If I tell you "the baby is hungry," you understand what I mean without my specifying the criteria I'm using to conclude that the baby is, indeed, hungry. You are unlikely to ask detailed questions about exactly what I mean; you understand well enough for practical purposes.

More precision is required of the definitions we use in research, however. If the terms used in research are not defined precisely, we may be unable to determine whether or not the hypothesis was supported. Suppose that we are interested in studying the effects of hunger on attention. Our hypothesis is that people's ability to pay attention decreases as they become more hungry. We can study this topic only if we define clearly what we mean by *hunger* and *attention*. Without clear definitions, we won't know whether or not the hypothesis has been supported.

Researchers use two distinct kinds of definitions. On one hand, they use **conceptual definitions.** A conceptual definition is more or less like the definition we might find in a dictionary. For example, we might define hunger as *having a desire for food.*

Although conceptual definitions are necessary, they are seldom specific enough for research purposes. A second way of defining a concept is by an **operational definition.** An operational definition defines a concept by specifying precisely how the concept is measured or manipulated in a particular study. For example, we could operationally define hunger in our study as *being deprived of food for at least 12 hours.* An operational definition converts an abstract conceptual definition into concrete, situation-specific terms.

There are potentially many operational definitions of a single construct. For example, we could define hunger in terms of hours of food deprivation; a person who has been deprived of food for 12 (or 18 or 24) hours would be operationally defined as *hungry.*

Or, we could define hunger in terms of responses to the question:

How hungry are you at this moment?
1. Not at all
2. Slightly
3. Moderately
4. Very

We could classify a person as *hungry* if he or she indicated that he or she was *moderately* or *very* hungry on this scale.

A recent study of the incidence of hunger in America defined hungry people as those who were eligible for food stamps but who didn't get them. This particular operational definition is a poor one, however. Many people with low income living in a farming area would be classified as *hungry,* no matter how much food they raised on their own.

Operational definitions are essential so that researchers can replicate one another's studies. Without knowing *precisely* how hunger was measured or manipulated in a particular study, other researchers have no way of replicating the study in precisely the same manner that it was conducted originally. In addition, using operational definitions forces the researcher to clarify his or her concepts very precisely (Underwood, 1957), thereby allowing scientists to communicate clearly and unambiguously.

Occasionally, you will hear people criticize the use of of operational definitions. In most cases, they are not criticizing operational definitions per se but rather a perspective known as **operationism.** Proponents of operationism argue that operational definitions are the only legitimate definitions in science. According to this view, concepts can be defined only in terms of specific measures and operations. Conceptual definitions, they argue, are far too vague to serve the needs of a precise science. Most contemporary behavioral scientists reject the assumptions of strict operationism. Conceptual definitions do have their uses, even though they are admittedly vague and often refer to unobservable phenomena.

DEVELOPING YOUR RESEARCH SKILLS

Getting Ideas for Research

Researchers get their ideas from almost everywhere. Sometimes the ideas come easily, but at other times they are slower to emerge. Below are some suggestions of ways to stimulate ideas for research.

Read the research literature in an area that interests you   Be on the lookout for unanswered questions and conflicting findings. Often, the authors of research articles offer their personal suggestions for future research.

Deduce hypotheses from an existing theory   Read about a theory and ask yourself, If this theory is true, what are some implications for behavior? State your hypotheses in an if–then fashion. Traditionally, this has been the most common way for behavioral researchers to develop ideas for research.

Apply an old theory to an entirely new phenomenon   Often, a theory that was developed originally to explain one kind of behavior can be applied to an entirely different topic.

Perform an intensive case study of a particular animal, person, group, or event   Such case studies invariably raise interesting questions about behavior. For example, Irving Janis's study of the Kennedy administration's ill-fated Bay of Pigs invasion led to his theory of Groupthink (Janis, 1982). Similarly, when trying to solve an applied problem, researchers often talk to people who are directly familiar with the problem.

Reverse the direction of causality for a commonsense hypothesis   Think of some behavioral principle that you take for granted. Then, reverse the direction of causality to see whether you construct a plausible new hypothesis. For example, most people think that people daydream when they are bored. Is it possible that people become bored when they daydream?

Break a process down into its subcomponents   What are the steps involved in the process by which people learn to ride a bicycle? Decide to end a romantic relationship? Choose a career? Identify a sound?

Think about variables that might mediate a known cause-and-effect relationship   Most psychologists are interested in knowing more than that a particular effect occurs; they want also to understand the psychological processes that mediate the connection between the cause and the behavior. For example, we know that people are more likely to be attracted to others who are similar to them, but why? What mediating variables are involved?

Analyze a puzzling behavioral phenomenon in terms of its functions
Look around at all the seemingly incomprehensible things people do. Instead of studying, John got drunk the night before the exam. Gwen continues to date a guy who always treats her like dirt. The family dog keeps running into the street even though he's punished each time he does. Why do these behaviors occur? What function might they have?

Imagine what would happen if a particular factor were reduced to zero in a given situation   What if nobody ever cared what other people thought of them? What if there were no leaders? What if people had no leisure time? Such questions often raise provocative insights and questions about behavior.

Proof and Disproof in Science

As we have seen, the validity of scientific theories is assessed only indirectly by testing hypotheses. One consequence of this is that no theory can be proved or disproved by the data from research. In fact, scientists virtually never speak of *proving* a theory, although they often talk of theories being *confirmed* or *supported* by research.

The claim that theories cannot be proved may strike you as bizarre; what's the use of testing theories if we can't actually prove or disprove them anyway? Before answering this question, let me explain why theories cannot be proved or disproved.

The Logical Impossibility of Proof

Theories cannot be proved, because obtaining empirical support for a hypothesis does not necessarily mean that the theory from which it was derived is true. For example, imagine that we want to test Theory A. To do so, we logically deduce an implication of the theory that we'll call Hypothesis H. We then collect data to see whether Hypothesis H is, in fact, correct. If we find that Hypothesis H is supported by the data, can we conclude that Theory A is true? The answer is no. Hypothesis H may be supported even if the theory is completely wrong.

Suppose I have a theory that there are tiny invisible elves in the human body that are responsible for people's sensations of pain; when an elf is injured by an external stimulus, he causes the person to feel pain. One hypothesis that can be derived from this theory is that stabbing a person in the hand will produce pain (because the hand-elf will be injured). To test this, I could stab 30 people in the hand with a pin and record their responses. Sure enough, they experience pain. Does that prove my elf theory of pain transmission? Of course not. In logical terminology, it is invalid to prove the antecedent of an argument (the theory) by affirming the consequent (the hypothesis).

The Practical Impossibility of Disproof

Unlike proof, disproof is a *logically* valid operation. If I deduce Hypothesis H from Theory A, then find that Hypothesis H is not supported by the data, Theory A must be false by logical inference. If people don't feel pain when stabbed in the hand, then the elf theory of pain must be incorrect.

However, testing hypotheses in real-world research involves a number of practical difficulties that may lead a hypothesis to be disconfirmed even if the theory is true. Failure to find empirical support for a hypothesis can be due to a number of factors other than the fact that the theory is incorrect. For example, using poor measuring techniques may result in apparent disconfirmation of a hypothesis, even though the theory is actually valid. Similarly, obtaining an inappropriate or biased sample of subjects, failing to account for or control extraneous variables, and using improper research designs or statistical analyses can produce negative findings. Much of this book focuses on ways to eliminate problems that hamper a researcher's ability to produce strong, convincing evidence regarding the accuracy of a hypothesis.

Because there are many ways a research study can go wrong, the failure of a study to support a particular hypothesis seldom, if ever, means the death of a theory (Hempel, 1966). There are simply too many possible reasons that a study might fail to support a theory. This is the reason journals are reluctant to publish the results of studies that fail to support a theory. The failure to confirm one's research hypotheses can occur for many reasons.

If Not Proof or Disproof, Then What?

If proof is logically impossible and disproof is practically impossible, how does science advance? How do we ever decide which theories are good ones and which are not? This question has provoked considerable interest among philosophers and scientists alike (Feyerabend, 1965; Kuhn, 1962; Popper, 1959).

In practice, the merit of theories is judged, not on the basis of a single study, but on the accumulated evidence of several studies. Although any particular study that fails to support a theory may be disregarded, the failure to obtain support in many studies provides evidence that the theory has problems. Similarly, a theory whose hypotheses are repeatedly confirmed by research is regarded as *supported by the data.*

Primary Types of Behavioral Research

Roughly speaking, behavioral research can be classified into three broad categories: descriptive, correlational, and experimental. Although we will return to each of these types of research in later chapters, it will be helpful for you to understand the differences among them from the beginning.

Descriptive Research

Descriptive research describes the behavior, thoughts, or feelings of a particular group of subjects. Perhaps the most common example of purely descriptive research is public opinion polls that describe the attitudes of a particular group of people. Similarly, in developmental psychology, the purpose of some studies is to describe the typical behavior of children of a certain age. Along the same lines, naturalistic observation describes the behavior of animals or humans in their natural habitats.

The goal of descriptive research is, as its name indicates, primarily descriptive. There is little attempt in purely descriptive research to relate the behavior under study to other variables or to study its causes systematically.

Correlational Research

If behavioral researchers only described how people and animals behave, they would provide us with little insight into the complexities of psychological processes. Thus, most research goes beyond mere description to an examination of the correlates or causes of behavior.

Correlational research investigates the relationships among various psychological variables. Is there a relationship between self-esteem and shyness? Does parental neglect in infancy relate to particular problems in adolescence? Do certain personality characteristics predispose people to abuse drugs? Each of these questions asks whether or not there is a relationship—a *correlation*—between two variables. We'll return to correlational research in Chapter 6.

Experimental Research

Correlational research can only establish that certain variables are related to one another. It cannot tell us whether one variable actually causes the other. When researchers are interested in identifying variables that *cause* changes in behavior, thought, or emotion, they turn to **experimental research**. In an experiment, the researcher manipulates or changes one variable (called the *independent variable*) to see whether changes in behavior occur as a consequence (the *dependent variable*). If behavioral changes do occur, we can conclude that the independent variable caused changes in the dependent variable (assuming certain conditions are met).

For example, Terkel and Rosenblatt (1968) were interested in whether maternal behavior in rats is caused by hormones in the bloodstream. They injected virgin female rats with either blood plasma from rats who had just given birth or blood plasma from rats who were not new mothers. They found that the rats who were injected with the blood of mother rats began to show significantly more maternal behavior toward rat pups than those who were injected with the blood of nonmothers, suggesting that the presence of hormones in the blood of mother rats is partly responsible for maternal behavior. In this study, the nature of the injection (blood from mothers versus blood from nonmothers) was the independent variable and maternal behavior was the dependent variable. We'll spend four chapters (Chapters 7–10) on experimental designs like these.

Note that the term *experiment* applies to only one kind of research—that in which the researcher controls an independent variable to assess its effects on behavior. Thus, it is incorrect to use *experiment* as a synonym for *research* or *study*.

The Purpose of Statistics in Research

No matter what the topic being investigated or the research strategy being used, one aspect of the research process always involves the analysis of the data that are collected. Thus, the study of research methods necessarily involves an introduction to statistics. Unfortunately, many students are initially intimidated by statistics and often wonder why they are so important.

As we'll see in greater detail in later chapters, statistics serve two general purposes for researchers. **Descriptive statistics** are used to summarize and describe the behavior of subjects in a study. They are ways of reducing a large number of scores or observations down to interpretable numbers such as averages and percentages.

Inferential statistics, on the other hand, are used to draw conclusions about the reliability and generalizability of one's findings. They are used to help answer questions such as, How likely is it that my findings are due to random extraneous factors rather than to the variables of central interest in my study? How representative are my findings of the larger population from which my subjects came?

Descriptive and inferential statistics are simply tools that researchers use to interpret the behavioral data they collect. Beyond that, however, understanding statistics provides insight into what makes some research studies better than others. As you learn about basic statistical analyses throughout the book, you'll develop a keener sense of how to design powerful, well-controlled, tight studies.

IN DEPTH

APA Reference Citations

If you are new to psychology, you may be puzzled by the way I reference my sources in this book. Rather than putting the reference citations in footnotes (as you probably learned in English class), I put them either in the context of the sentence itself or in parentheses at the end of the sentence. For example, when discussing how science progresses, I wrote:

> This question has provoked considerable interest among philosophers and scientists alike (Feyerabend, 1965; Kuhn, 1962; Popper, 1959).

This reference format is known as the author–date system or, more commonly, **APA style.** In an attempt to standardize the style of research journal articles, the American Psychological Association has published a book entitled *Publication Manual of the American Psychological Association* (1983) that specifies the format for scientific papers. APA style has been nearly universally adopted by publishers of books and journals in the behavioral sciences. In addition, many psychology instructors require students to use APA style when they write reports and papers for class.

APA style incorporates reference citations into the body of the text. The full reference is then placed not in a footnote, but in a reference section at the end of the book, article, or paper.

Among other things, APA style eliminates the need to squeeze footnotes at the bottom of each page. In addition, by integrating the reference citation into the text itself, the reference can be used as a cue to help the reader remember a particular study. Psychologists are in the habit of referring to particular studies by the authors' last names (such as "My results perfectly replicate Festinger and Carlsmith's study"). Providing the authors' names in the text helps orient the reader to the specific work that is being cited without the need to refer back and forth between the text and footnotes.

You will learn more about APA style when we discuss how to write research reports in Chapter 15.

A Preview

The research process is a complex one. In every study researchers must address many questions:

- How should I measure subjects' behavior in this study?
- How do I obtain a sample of subjects for my research?
- Given my research question, what is the most appropriate research design?
- How can I be sure my study is as well designed as possible?
- What are the most appropriate and useful ways of analyzing the data?
- How should my findings be reported?
- What are the ethical issues involved in conducting this research?

Each chapter in this book deals with an aspect of the research process. Chapter 2 sets the stage by discussing what is perhaps the central concept in research design and analysis—variability. Armed with an understanding of variability, you will be better equipped to understand many of the issues we'll address in later chapters.

The quality of a research study depends heavily on how well the phenomena under study are measured: Chapter 3 deals with the issues one must consider when measuring behavior and psychological processes. Chapter 4 covers ways of describing and presenting data, and Chapter 5 addresses issues that are involved in obtaining samples of subjects for research.

The topics in Chapters 1 through 5 are relevant to all behavioral research. After covering these basic topics, we'll turn to specific research strategies. In Chapter 6, you'll learn about correlation and regression techniques, procedures that are used to investigate whether two variables are related and, if so, the nature of their relationship.

Chapter 7 will introduce you to the basics of experimentation, research that looks for causal relationships among variables. Chapters 8 through 10 then go into greater detail regarding the design and analysis of two-group and factorial experiments. In these chapters, you'll learn not only how to design experiments, but also how to analyze experimental data.

Chapter 11 deals with quasi-experimental designs, and Chapter 12 with single-subject designs. Then, Chapter 13 takes a quick look at some advanced designs and analyses. Because the topics covered in Chapter 13 involve advanced techniques, you'll learn what these techniques are, but not how to actually use them. The complex ethical issues involved in conducting behavioral research are discussed in Chapter 14. Finally, in Chapter 15 we'll take a close look at how to write research reports.

There are also two appendixes containing statistical tables and formulas we'll be needing later, along with a glossary and a list of references.

SUMMARY

1. Behavioral scientists conduct research to describe, understand, and predict behavior, as well as to solve applied problems.

2. Scientific psychology emerged in the late 1800s, stimulated in part by the laboratories established by Wundt in Germany and by James in the United States.

3. To be considered scientific, observations must be systematic and empirical, research must be conducted in a manner that is publicly verifiable, and the questions addressed must be potentially solvable given current knowledge.

4. Pseudoscience involves evidence that masquerades as science, but that fails to meet one or more of these three criteria.

5. Much research is designed to test the validity of theories. A theory is a set of propositions that attempts to specify the interrelationships among a set of concepts.

6. Researchers assess the usefulness of a theory by testing hypotheses—propositions that are deduced logically from the theory. To be tested, hypotheses must be stated in a manner that is potentially falsifiable.

7. By stating their hypotheses a priori, researchers avoid the risks associated with post hoc explanations.

8. Researchers use two distinct kinds of definitions in their work. Conceptual definitions are much like everyday, dictionary definitions. Operational definitions, on the other hand, define concepts by specifying precisely how they are measured or manipulated in the context of a particular study. Operational definitions are essential for replication, as well as for nonambiguous communication among scientists.

9. Strictly speaking, theories can never be proved or disproved by research. Proof is logically impossible because it is invalid to prove the antecedent

of an argument by showing that the consequent is true. Disproof, though logically possible, is impossible in a practical sense; failure to obtain support for a theory may reflect more on the research procedure than on the accuracy of the hypothesis.

10. Behavioral research falls into roughly three categories: descriptive, correlational, and experimental.

11. Statistics are used in research for two purposes: Descriptive statistics summarize data; inferential statistics provide information regarding the reliability and generalizability of the data.

12. When writing, behavioral researchers typically use the author–date system, also known as APA style.

KEY TERMS

basic research	post hoc explanation
applied research	conceptual definition
empiricism	operational definition
pseudoscience	operationism
theory	descriptive research
hypothesis	correlational research
deduction	experimental research
induction	descriptive statistics
falsifiability	inferential statistics
a priori prediction	APA style

REVIEW QUESTIONS

1. In what sense is psychology both a science and a profession?
2. What are the four basic purposes of behavioral research?
3. What was Wilhelm Wundt's primary contribution to behavioral research?
4. Briefly discuss the importance of systematic empiricism, public verification, and solvability to the scientific method.
5. In what ways does pseudoscience differ from true science?
6. Describe briefly the process by which hypotheses are developed and tested.
7. Why must hypotheses be falsifiable?
8. One theory suggests that people feel socially anxious or shy in social situations when two conditions are met: they are highly motivated to make a favorable impression on others who are present, but doubt that they will be able to do so. Suggest at least three research hypotheses that can be derived from this theory. Be sure your hypotheses are falsifiable.

9. Why are scientists skeptical of post hoc explanations?

10. Briefly discuss the importance of operational definitions in research.

11. Suggest three operational definitions for each of the following constructs:

   a. aggression
   b. patience
   c. test anxiety
   d. memory

12. What are some ways in which scientists get ideas for their research?

13. Why can theories not be proved or disproved by research? Given that proof and disproof are impossible in science, how does scientific knowledge advance?

14. Distinguish among descriptive, correlational, and experimental research.

15. For each of the research questions below, indicate which kind of research—descriptive, correlational, or experimental—would be most appropriate.

   a. What percentage of American women label themselves feminists?
   b. Does the artificial sweetener aspartame cause dizziness and confusion in some people?
   c. What personality variables are related to depression?
   d. What is the effect of a manager's style on employees' morale and performance?
   e. Do SAT scores predict college performance?

16. Why are statistics important in behavioral research?

QUESTIONS FOR THOUGHT AND DISCUSSION

1. Why do you think the science of psychology developed later than other sciences such as chemistry, physics, astronomy, and biology?

2. Why do you think many people have difficulty seeing psychologists as scientists and researchers?

3. How would the world be different if psychology had not developed as a science?

2

Behavioral Variability and Research

As we will examine in detail in a moment, behavioral research attempts to answer questions about behavioral variability—that is, how behavior varies across situations, differs among individuals, and changes over time. Thus, the concept of variability underlies many of the topics we will discuss in later chapters and provides the foundation on which much of this book rests. In this chapter, we will examine variability from both a conceptual and a statistical standpoint. We will see how researchers measure behavioral variability and what such measures of variability tell us about our data. The better you understand this basic concept now, the more easily you will grasp many of the topics we will discuss later in the book.

Variability and the Research Process

All aspects of the research process revolve around the concept of **variability**. The concept of variability runs through the entire enterprise of designing and analyzing research. To show what I mean, let me offer five propositions that involve the relationship between variability and psychological research.

PROPOSITION 1 *Psychology is the study of behavioral variability.* Psychology is often defined as the study of behavior and mental processes. Another way to say this is that psychologists are interested in understanding behavioral variability: They want to know why behavior varies—why it varies across situations, why it varies among people, and why it varies over time.

Think about the people you interact with each day and about the variation you see in their behavior. First, their behavior varies *across situations*. People act differently at a party than they do in class. College students are often more nervous when interacting with a person of the other sex than when interacting with a person of their own sex. Children behave more aggressively after watching violent movies than they did before watching them. A hungry pigeon who has been reinforced for pecking when a green light is on pecks more in the presence of a green light than a red light. In brief, people and animals behave differently in different situations. Behavioral researchers are interested in how and why situational factors cause this variability in behavior.

Second, behavior varies *among individuals*. Even in similar situations, not everyone acts the same. At a lively party, some people are talkative and outgoing, whereas others are quiet and shy. Some people are more conscientious and responsible than others. Some individuals generally appear confident and calm, while others seem nervous. And certain animals, such as dogs, display marked differences in behavior, depending on their breed. Thus, because of differences in their biological makeup and previous experience, people and animals behave differently. A great deal of behavioral research focuses on understanding this variability across individuals.

Third, behavior also varies *over time*. A baby who could barely walk a few months ago can run today. An adolescent girl who two years ago thought boys were "gross" now has romantic fantasies about them. A task that was interesting an hour ago has become boring. Even when the situation remains constant, behavior may change as time passes. Some of these changes, such as developmental changes that occur with age, are permanent; other changes, such as boredom or sexual drive, are temporary. Many psychologists are interested in understanding how and why behavior varies over time.

PROPOSITION 2 *Research questions in psychology are questions about behavioral variability.* Whenever behavioral scientists design research, they are interested in answering questions about behavioral variability. For example, suppose we want to know the extent to which sleep deprivation affects performance on cognitive tasks (such as deciding whether a blip on a radar screen is a flock of geese or an incoming enemy aircraft). In essence, we are asking how the amount of sleep people get causes their performance to change or vary. Or, imagine that we're interested in whether a particular form of counseling reduces family conflict. Our research centers on the question of whether counseling causes changes or variation in a family's interactions. Any specific research question we might develop can be phrased in terms of behavioral variability.

PROPOSITION 3 *Research should be designed in a manner that best allows the researcher to answer questions about behavioral variability.* Given that all behavioral research involves understanding variability, research must be designed in a way that allows us to identify, as unambiguously as possible, factors related to behavioral variability. A well-designed study is one that permits the researcher to accurately describe and account for the variability in the behavior of his or her research subjects. A poorly designed study is one in which the researcher has difficulty answering questions about the variability he or she observes.

As we'll see in later chapters, flaws in the design of a study can make it impossible for a researcher to determine why subjects behaved as they did. At each step of the design and execution of a study, researchers must be sure that their research will permit them to answer their questions about behavioral variability.

PROPOSITION 4   *The measurement of behavior involves the assessment of behavioral variability.* All behavioral research involves the measurement of some behavior. Our measures may involve the number of times a rat presses a bar, a subject's heart rate, the score a child obtains on an intelligence test, or a person's rating of how tired he or she feels on a scale of 1 to 7. In each case, we're assigning a number to a person or animal's behavior: 15 bar presses, 65 heartbeats per minute, an IQ score of 127, a tiredness rating of 5, or whatever.

No matter what is being measured, we want the number we assign to a subject's behavior to correspond in a meaningful way to the behavior being measured. Put another way, we would like the variability *in the numbers we assign* to correspond to the variability *in subjects' behaviors*. We must have confidence that the scores we use to capture subjects' behavior reflect the true variability in the behavior we are measuring. If the scores do not correspond, at least roughly, to the attribute we are measuring, the measurement technique is worthless and our research is doomed.

PROPOSITION 5   *Statistical analyses are performed to account for the observed variability in the behavioral data.* After a study is completed, all we have is a set of numbers that represent the behavior of our research subjects. The purpose of statistics is to summarize and answer questions about the behavioral variability we observe in our research. Assuming that the research was competently designed and conducted, statistics helps us account for or explain the behavioral variability we observed. Does a new treatment for depression cause an improvement in mood? Does a particular drug enhance memory in mice? Is self-esteem related to the variability we observe in how hard people try when working on difficult tasks? We use statistics to answer questions about the variability in our data.

In brief, the concept of variability follows us through the entire research process: Our research questions are about the causes and correlates of behavioral variability. We try to design studies that best let us describe and understand variability in a particular behavior. The measures we use attempt to capture numerically the variability we observe in subjects' behavior. And our statistics help us analyze the variability in our data to answer the questions we began with. Variability is truly the thread that runs throughout the research process. For this reason, we'll return to it repeatedly throughout the book.

Variance: A Statistical Index of Variability

Given the importance of the concept of variability in designing and analyzing behavioral research, researchers need a way of expressing how much variability there is in a set of data. Not only are researchers interested simply in knowing the amount of variability in their data, but they need a numerical index of the variability in their data to conduct certain statistical analyses that we'll examine in later chapters.

Researchers use a statistic known as **variance** to indicate the amount of observed variability in subjects' behavior. We will confront variance in a variety of guises throughout this book, so we need to understand it well. But before we look at variance from a statistical standpoint, let us look at it conceptually. You'll understand this important statistic better if you have an intuitive grasp of what it tells us about our data.

Let's imagine that you conducted a very simple study in which you asked 6 subjects to give their attitudes about capital punishment on a scale of 1 to 5 (where 1 indicates strong opposition and 5 indicates strong support for capital punishment). Suppose you obtained these responses:

Subject	Response
1	4
2	1
3	2
4	2
5	4
6	3

For a variety of reasons (that we'll discuss later), you may need to know how much variability there is in these data. Can you think of a way of expressing how much these responses, or scores, vary from one person to the next?

One possibility is simply to take the difference between the largest and the smallest scores. In fact, this number, the **range**, is sometimes used to express variability. If we subtract the smallest from the largest score above, we find that the range of these data is 3 (4 − 1 = 3). Unfortunately, the range has limitations as an indicator of the variability in our data. The problem is that the range tells us only how much the largest and smallest scores vary, but does not take into account the other scores and how much they vary from each other.

Consider the two distributions of data in Figure 2.1. These two sets of data have the same range. That is, the difference between the largest and smallest scores is the same in each set. However, the variability in the data in Figure 2.1(a) is much smaller than the variability in Figure 2.1(b), where the scores are more spread out. What we need is a way of expressing variability that includes information about all of the scores.

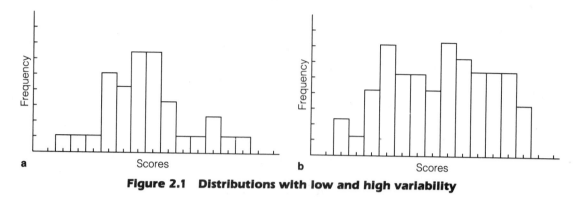

Figure 2.1   Distributions with low and high variability

Explanation: The two sets of scores shown in these graphs have the same range—the difference between the highest and lowest scores is the same in both graphs. However, the variability of the scores in (a) is smaller than the variability of the scores in (b). Overall, subjects' scores are more tightly clustered together—that is, less variable—in (a). By itself, the range fails to reflect the difference in the variability in these two sets of scores.

When we talk about things varying, we usually do so in reference to some standard. A useful standard for this purpose is the average or mean of the scores in our data set. Researchers use the term **mean** as a synonym for what you probably call the average—the sum of a set of scores divided by the number of scores you have.

The mean stands as a fulcrum around which all of the other scores balance. So, we can express the variability in our data in terms of how much the scores vary *around the mean.* If most of the scores in a set of data are tightly clustered around the mean (as in Figure 2.1(a)), then the variance of the data will be small. If, however, our scores are more spread out (as in Figure 2.1(b)), they will vary a great deal around the mean, and the variance will be large. So, the variance is nothing more than an indication of how tightly or loosely a set of scores clusters around the mean of the scores. As we will see, this provides a very useful indication of the amount of variability in a set of data.

Variance: The Statistical Approach

Now that we know conceptually what the variance is, let's see how it is calculated. Statistical formulas are typically written using **statistical notation.** Just as we commonly use symbols such as a plus sign to indicate *add* and an equal sign to indicate *is equal to,* we'll be using special symbols—such as Σ and s—to indicate statistical terms and operations. Although some of these symbols may be new to you, they are nothing more than symbolic representations of variables or mathematical operations, all of which are elementary.

We can calculate the variance of a set of numbers in five simple steps. We will refer here to the scores or observations obtained in our study of attitudes toward capital punishment.

STEP 1 As we saw above, variance refers to how much the scores are spread out around the mean of the data. So, to begin, we need to calculate the mean of the scores in our data set. Just sum the numbers (4 + 1 + 2 + 2 + 4 + 3 = 16) and divide by the number of scores you have ($^{16}/_6$ = 2.67).[1]

Statisticians use the symbol $\bar{y}$ (or $\bar{x}$) to represent the mean of a set of data, and represent the calculation of the mean this way:

$$\bar{y} = \Sigma y_i / n$$

The summation symbol is a large version of the uppercase Greek letter sigma (Σ) that in statistical notation tells us to add what follows. The symbol y_i is the symbol for each person's score. So the operation Σy_i simply tells us to add up all of the scores.

Then, the equation tell us to divide this sum by n. The symbol n is always used to indicate the number of subjects in a sample. In our survey, we obtained data from 6 people, so $n = 6$. In short, all we do on the first step is to calculate the mean of the six scores.

STEP 2 Now we need a way of expressing how much the scores vary around the mean. We do this by subtracting the mean from each score. Expressed in statistical notation, we perform the operation

$$y_i - \bar{y}$$

for each score. This formula tells us to subtract the mean ($\bar{y}$) from each person's score (y_i). This difference is called a *deviation score*.

Let's do this for our data involving people's attitudes toward capital punishment:

Subject	Deviation Score[1] $(y_i - \bar{y})$
1	4 − 2.67 = 1.33
2	1 − 2.67 = −1.67
3	2 − 2.67 = −0.67
4	2 − 2.67 = −0.67
5	4 − 2.67 = 1.33
6	3 − 2.67 = 0.33

STEP 3 By looking at these deviation scores, we can see how much each score varies or deviates from the mean. Subject 2's score falls furthest from the mean (1.67 units below the mean), whereas Subject 6 falls closest to

[1]In most instances, researchers round the results of their statistical calculations to two decimal places.

the mean (0.33 unit above it). Note that a positive number indicates that the person's score was above the mean, whereas a negative sign ($-$) indicates a score below the mean. (What would a deviation score of zero indicate?)

You might think we could add these six deviation scores to get a total variability score for the sample. However, if we sum the deviation scores for all of the subjects in a set of data, they always add to zero. So we need to get rid of the negative signs. We do this by squaring each of the deviation scores.

Subject	Deviation Score	Deviation Score Squared
1	1.33	1.77
2	-1.67	2.79
3	-0.67	0.45
4	-0.67	0.45
5	1.33	1.77
6	0.33	0.11

In statistical notation, what we're doing is this:

$$(y_i - \bar{y})^2$$

This says that we're squaring each of the deviation scores for each subject.

STEP 4   Now we add the squared deviation scores. The formula for this step is:

$$\Sigma(y_i - \bar{y})^2.$$

If we add all of the squared deviation scores obtained in step 3 above, we get

$$1.77 + 2.79 + 0.45 + 0.45 + 1.77 + 0.11 = 7.34.$$

As we'll see later, this number—the sum of the squared deviations of the scores from the mean—is central to the analysis of much research data. We have a shorthand way of referring to this important quantity; we call it the total **sum of squares.**

STEP 5   In step 4 we obtained an index of the total variability in our data—the total sum of squares. However, this quantity is affected by the number of scores we have; the more subjects in our sample, the larger the sum of squares will be. However, just because we have a larger number of subjects does not necessarily mean that the variability of our data will be greater.

Because we do not want our index of variability to be affected by the size of the sample, we divide the sum of squares by a function of the number of subjects in our sample. Although you might suspect that we would divide by the actual number of subjects from whom we obtained data, we usually divide by one less than the number of subjects. In statistical notation, the number of subjects is designated by the lowercase letter n, so we divide the sum of squares obtained in step 4 by $n - 1$.

This gives us the variance of our data, which is indicated by the symbol s^2. If we put the five steps above into a single formula for the variance, it looks like this:

$$s^2 = \Sigma(y_i - \bar{y})^2/(n - 1)$$

This formula simply tells us to (1) calculate the mean of the data, (2) subtract the mean from each score, (3) square these differences or deviation scores, (4) sum these squared deviation scores (this, remember, is the total sum of squares), and (5) divide by $n - 1$ (the number of scores minus 1). If we do this for our data, the variance is 1.47.

By following these steps, you should be able to calculate the variance of any set of data. But more importantly, you should understand precisely what the variance is. It is an index of the amount of variability in the data expressed in terms of how much the scores differ from the mean in squared units.

DEVELOPING YOUR RESEARCH SKILLS

A Shorthand Method for Calculating Variance

The formula in step 5 shows clearly what the variance is: It is an average of the sum of the squared deviations of the scores from the mean. However, when calculating the variance by hand, this formula has two shortcomings. First, it is very tedious when the data set is large. Second, because so many different calculations are involved as we subtract each score from the mean and square it, rounding errors decrease computational accuracy. For these reasons, researchers often use a different, slightly less tedious formula when calculating the variance by hand:

$$s^2 = \frac{\Sigma y_i^2 - [(\Sigma y_i)^2/n]}{n - 1}$$

To use this formula, you first square each score and add these squared scores together (Σy_i^2). Then, add up all of the original scores (Σy_i) and square the sum [$(\Sigma y_i)^2$]. Finally, plug these numbers into the formula, along with the sample size (n), to get the variance.

It simplifies the calculations if you set up a table with two columns—one for the raw scores and one for the square of the raw scores. If we do this for our data, we get

Subject	Raw Score (y_i)	Raw Score Squared (y_i^2)
1	4	16
2	1	1
3	2	4
4	2	4
5	4	16
6	3	9
	$\Sigma y_i = 16$	$\Sigma y_i^2 = 50$
	$(\Sigma y_i)^2 = 256$	

Then,

$$s^2 = \frac{50 - 256/6}{6 - 1} = \frac{50 - 42.67}{5} = 1.47.$$

This is the same answer that we obtained in step 5. However, as you can see, by using the shorthand formula you avoid calculating and squaring all of the deviation scores.

Standard Deviation

Variance is the most commonly used measure of variability for purposes of statistical analysis. However, when researchers simply want to *describe* how much variability exists in their data, it has a shortcoming. As you'll recall, we squared the deviation scores as we calculated s^2. As a result, the variance is expressed in terms of squared units and thus is difficult to interpret conceptually. Our example involved attitudes toward capital punishment, so the variance is expressed not in terms of the original attitude scores, but in terms of the attitude scores squared!

When researchers want to express behavioral variability in the original units of their data, they use the standard deviation. The **standard deviation** (for which we'll use the symbol *s*) is the square root of the variance. The standard deviation of the data for our 6 subjects is the square root of 1.47, or 1.21.

The standard deviation is very useful for describing how much the scores in a set of data vary. As we'll see in a moment, a great deal can be learned from only the mean and standard deviation of the data—much more than is apparent at first glance. For this reason, researchers often report the mean and standard deviation of their data as a matter of course.

Standard Deviation and the Normal Curve

In the 19th century, the Belgian statistician and astronomer Quételet demonstrated that many bodily measurements, such as height and chest circumference, showed identical distributions when plotted on a graph. Further, the shape of this distribution was identical to that obtained when one graphs the spread of gunshots around a bull's-eye (Watson, 1978). When plotted, such data form a curve, with most of the points on the graph falling near the center, and fewer and fewer points lying toward the extremes. Four such curves are shown in Figure 2.2.

Sir Francis Galton, an eminent British scientist and statistician, extended Quételet's discovery to the study of psychological characteristics. He found that no matter what attribute he measured, graphs of the data nearly always

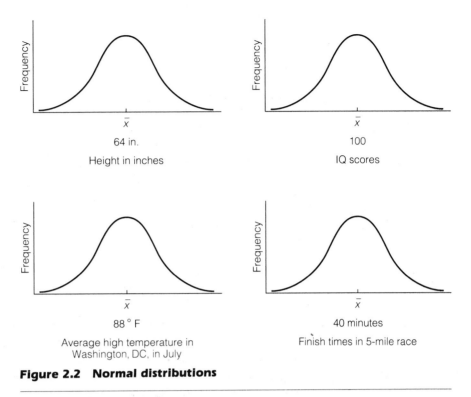

Figure 2.2   Normal distributions

Explanation: Figure 2.2 shows four idealized normal distributions. In normal distributions such as these, most scores fall toward the middle of the range, with the greatest number of scores falling at the mean of the distribution. As we move in both directions away from the mean, the number of scores tapers off symmetrically, indicating an equal number of low and high scores.

followed the same bell-shaped distribution. For example, Galton showed that scores on university examinations fell into this same pattern.

In fact, many of the variables in behavioral science fall, at least roughly, into a **normal distribution**. A normal distribution rises to a rounded peak at its center, then tapers off at both tails. This pattern indicates that most of the scores fall toward the middle of the range of scores, with fewer scores toward the extremes. That many data distributions approximate a normal curve is really not surprising because, regardless of what attribute is being measured, most people are about average, with few people having extreme scores.

Occasionally, however, our data distributions are skewed, such as those in Figure 2.3. In a **positively skewed distribution** such as Figure 2.3(a), there are more low scores than high scores in the set of data; if data are positively skewed, one observes a pileup of scores toward the lower, left-hand end of the scale, with the tail of the distribution extending to the right. A **negatively skewed distribution** (Figure 2.3(b)) is one in which there are more high scores than low scores; the hump is to the right of the graph, and the tail of the distribution extends to the left.

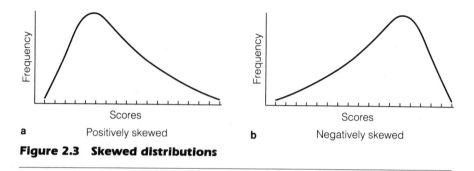

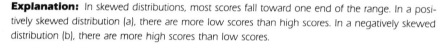

Figure 2.3 Skewed distributions

Explanation: In skewed distributions, most scores fall toward one end of the range. In a positively skewed distribution (a), there are more low scores than high scores. In a negatively skewed distribution (b), there are more high scores than low scores.

Assuming that we have a roughly normal distribution and a large enough sample size (one with $n > 30$), we can estimate the percentage of subjects who obtained certain scores just by knowing the mean and standard deviation of the data. For example, in any normally distributed set of data, approximately 68% of the scores (68.26%, to be exact) will fall in the range defined by ±1 standard deviation from the mean. In other words, roughly 68% of the subjects will have scores that fall between 1 standard deviation below the mean and 1 standard deviation above the mean.

Let's consider IQ scores, for example. One commonly used IQ test has a mean of 100 and a standard deviation of 15. The score falling 1 standard deviation below the mean is 85 (that is 100 − 15) and the score falling 1

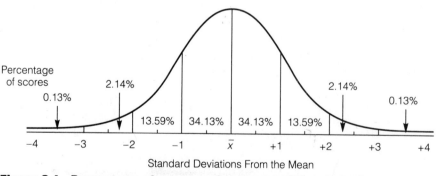

Figure 2.4 Percentage of scores under ranges of the normal distribution

Explanation: This figure shows the percentage of subjects who fall in various portions of the normal distribution. For example, 34.13% of the scores in a normal distribution will fall between the mean and 1 standard deviation above the mean. Similarly, 13.59% of subjects's scores will fall between −1 and −2 standard deviations below the mean.

standard deviation above the mean is 115 (that is, 100 + 15). Thus, approximately 68% of all people have IQ scores between 85 and 115.

Figure 2.4 shows this principle graphically. As you can see, 68.26% of the scores fall within 1 standard deviation (±1 s) from the mean. Furthermore, approximately 95% of the scores in a normal distribution fall ±2 standard deviations from the mean. On an IQ test with a mean of 100 and standard deviation of 15, 95% of people score between 70 and 130. Less than 1% of the scores fall further than 3 standard deviations below or above the mean. If you have an IQ score below 55 or above 145, you are quite unusual in that regard.

You can see now why the standard deviation is so useful. By knowing the mean and standard deviation of a set of data, we can tell not only how much the data vary, but how they are distributed across various ranges of scores. With real data, which are seldom perfectly normally distributed, these ranges are only approximate. Even so, researchers find the standard deviation very useful as they try to describe and understand the data they collect.

The z-Score

In some instances, researchers need a way to describe where a particular subject falls in the data distribution. Just knowing that a certain subject scored 47 on a test does not tell us very much. Knowing the mean of the data tells us whether the subject's score was above or below average, but without knowing something about the variability of the data, we still cannot tell how far above or below the mean the subject's score is, relative to other subjects.

The z-score, or *standard score*, is used to describe a particular subject's score relative to the rest of the data. A subject's z-score indicates how far the subject's score varies from the mean in terms of standard deviations. For example, if we find that a subject has a z-score of −1.00, we know that his or her score is 1 standard deviation below the mean. By referring to Figure 2.4, we can see that only about 16% of the other subjects scored lower than this person. Similarly, a z-score of +2.9 indicates a score nearly 3 s's above the mean—one that is in the uppermost ranges of the distribution.

If we know the mean and standard deviation of a sample, a subject's z-score is easy to calculate:

$$z = (y_i - \bar{y})/s$$

where y_i is the subject's score, $\bar{y}$ is the mean of the sample, and s is the standard deviation of the sample.

Sometimes researchers standardize an entire set of data by converting all of the subjects' raw scores to z-scores. This is a useful way to identify extreme scores or **outliers**. An outlier can be identified by a very low or very high z-score—one that falls below −3.00 or above +3.00, for example. Also, certain statistical analyses require standardization prior to the analysis. When a set of scores is standardized, the new set of z-scores always has a mean equal to 0 and a standard deviation equal to 1 regardless of the mean and standard deviation of the original data.

Systematic and Error Variance

So far, our discussion has dealt with the *total variance* in the responses of subjects in a research study. The formulas we learned for variance and standard deviation indicate the total amount of variability in our data.

However, the total variance in a set of data can be split into two parts:

Total variance = systematic variance + error variance

The distinction between systematic and error variance will follow us throughout the chapters of this book. Because systematic and error variance are important to the research process, developing a grasp of the concepts now will allow us to use them as needed throughout the book. We'll explore them in greater detail in later chapters.

Systematic Variance

Most research is designed to test the hypothesis that there is a relationship between two or more variables. For example, a researcher may wish to test the hypothesis that self-esteem is related to drug use or that changes in office illumination cause systematic changes in on-the-job performance. Put differently, researchers are usually interested in whether the variability in one variable (self-esteem, illumination) is related *in a systematic fashion* to variability in other variables (drug use, on-the-job performance).

Systematic variance is that part of the total variability in subjects' behavior that is related in an orderly, predictable fashion to the variables the researcher is investigating. If the subjects' behavior varies in a systematic way as certain other variables change, the researcher has evidence that those variables are related to behavior. Put differently, when some of the total variance in subjects' behavior is found to be associated with certain variables in an orderly, systematic fashion, we can conclude that those variables are related to subjects' behavior. Two examples may help clarify the concept of systematic variance.

Temperature and aggression   In an experiment that examined the effects of temperature on aggression, Baron and Bell (1976) led subjects to believe that they would administer electric shocks to another person. (In reality, that other person was an accomplice of the experimenter and was not actually shocked.) Subjects performed this task in a room in which the ambient temperature was 73°, 85°, or 95° F. To determine whether temperature did, in fact, affect aggression, the researchers needed to determine how much of the variance in subjects' aggression was related to temperature. That is, they needed to know how much of the total variance in aggression was systematic variance due to temperature. We wouldn't expect all of the variance in subjects' aggression to be a function of temperature. After all, subjects entered the experiment already differing in their tendencies to respond aggressively. In addition, other factors in the experimental setting may have affected aggressiveness. What the researchers wanted to know was whether *any* of the variance in aggression was due to differences in the temperatures in the three experimental conditions (cool, warm, and hot). If systematic variance related to temperature was obtained, they could conclude that changes in temperature affected aggressive behavior. Indeed, this and other research has shown that the likelihood of aggression is greater when the temperature is moderately hot than when it is cool, but that aggression decreases under extremely high temperatures (Anderson, 1989).

Optimism and health   In a correlational study of the relationship between optimism and health, Scheier and Carver (1985) administered subjects a measure of optimism. Four weeks later, the same subjects completed a checklist on which they indicated the degree to which they had been bothered by each of 39 symptoms. Of course, there was considerable variability in the number of symptoms that subjects reported experiencing. Some indicated that they were quite healthy, whereas others reported many symptoms. Interestingly, subjects who scored high on the optimism scale reported fewer symptoms than less optimistic subjects; that is, there was a correlation between optimism scores and the number of symptoms that subjects reported. In fact, approximately 7% of the total variance in reported symptoms was related to optimism; in other words, 7% of the variance in symptoms was *systematic* variance. Thus, optimism and symptoms were related in an orderly, systematic fashion.

As we'll see in detail in later chapters, researchers must design their studies so that they can tell how much of the total variance in subjects' behavior is systematic variance. If they don't, the study will fail to detect relationships among variables that are, in fact, related. Furthermore, researchers must design studies so that they know already the sources of systematic variance. Poorly designed studies do not permit researchers to conclude confidently which variables were responsible for the systematic variance they obtained. We'll return to this important point in later chapters.

Error Variance

Not all of the variance in subjects' behavior is systematic variance. Factors that the researcher is not investigating may also be related to subjects' behavior. In the Baron and Bell experiment, not all of the variability in aggression was due to temperature, for example. And, in the Scheier and Carver study, only 7% of the variance in the symptoms that subjects reported was related to optimism; the remaining 93% of the variance in symptoms was due to other factors.

Even after a researcher has determined how much of the total variance is related to the variables of interest in the study, some of the variance remains unaccounted for. Variance that remains unaccounted for is called **error variance**. Error variance is that portion of the total variance that is unrelated to the variables under investigation in the study.

Do not think of the term *error* as indicating errors or mistakes in the usual sense of the word. Although error variance may be due to mistakes in recording or coding the data, most often it is simply the result of factors that remain unidentified in a study. No study can investigate every factor that is related to the behavior of interest. Rather, a researcher chooses to investigate the impact of only a few variables on the target behavior. Baron and Bell chose to study temperature, for example, and ignored other variables that might influence aggression.

Even so, other factors are at work. For example, in the experiment on aggression, some subjects may have been in a worse mood than others, leading them to behave aggressively for reasons that had nothing to do with room temperature. Some may have come from aggressive homes, whereas others may have been raised by parents who were pacifists. The experimenter may have unconsciously treated some subjects more politely than others, thereby lowering their aggressiveness. A few subjects may have been unusually hostile because they had just failed an exam. Each of these factors may have contributed to variability in subjects' aggression, but none is related to the variable of interest in the study—temperature. These are the kinds of factors that contribute to error variance.

Error variance tends to mask or obscure the effects of the variables in which researchers are primarily interested. The more error variance there is, the more difficult it is to determine whether certain variables cause or predict behavior. For example, the more that subjects' aggression is affected by extraneous factors such as mood and weather, the more difficult it is to see whether temperature affects aggression. As we'll see later, a good research design is one that allows researchers to minimize error variance.

The first step toward minimizing the error variance in a study involves the use of good measures of the behavior being studied. In the next chapter we'll look at issues involved in measuring behavior in research settings.

SUMMARY

1. Psychology can be defined as the study of behavioral variability. Most aspects of behavioral research are aimed at explaining variability in behavior.

2. Variance is a statistical index of variability. Variance is the sum of the squared deviations of scores from the mean of the data.

3. The standard deviation, the square root of the variance, is used to express the variability in a set of data in the units of the original data.

4. Most behavioral data conforms, at least roughly, to a normal distribution or bell-shaped curve, although some data distributions are skewed.

5. Knowing the mean and standard deviation of a normally distributed set of data allows a researcher to estimate the percentage of scores that fall in certain ranges of scores. For example, approximately 68% of the scores will fall ±1 standard deviation from the mean.

6. The z-score, or standard score, indicates where a particular subject falls in a distribution of scores in terms of standard deviations from the mean of the data.

7. The total variance in a set of data can be broken into two components. Systematic variance is variance that is related to the variables under investigation. Error variance is variance that is due to unidentified sources. Throughout the research process, researchers try to minimize the error variance in their data.

KEY TERMS

variability

variance

range

mean

statistical notation

Σ

s^2

sum of squares

standard deviation

normal distribution

positively skewed distribution

negatively skewed distribution

z-score

outlier

systematic variance

error variance

REVIEW QUESTIONS

1. Discuss how the concept of behavioral variability relates to (a) the research questions that interest behavioral researchers, (b) the design of research studies, (c) the measurement of behavior, and (d) the analysis of behavioral data.

2. Conceptually, what does the variance tell us about a set of data?

3. What is the formula for variance?

4. Why do researchers prefer the standard deviation over the variance when describing the variability in a set of data?

5. How is a *z*-score calculated, and what does it tell you about a particular subject's score?
6. The total variance in a set of scores can be partitioned into two components. What are they, and how do they differ?
7. What are some factors that contribute to error variance in a set of data?
8. A researcher administered a test of political knowledge to 10 high school students. Their scores on the test (out of a possible 50 points) were as follows:

$$ s^2 = \frac{\Sigma y_i{}^2 - \left[(\Sigma y_i)^2 / N\right]}{N - 1} $$

3

48
25
30
38
40
44
40
38
42
22   367

Calculate the variance of the scores, using both the raw-score method and the shorthand method.

9. What is the standard deviation of these scores? Be sure you can state in words what the standard deviation tells you about the data.
10. Calculate the *z*-score for the subject who scored 30 on the test. What does the *z*-score tell you about the subject's performance on the test?

3

The Measurement of Behavior

In 1904, the French minister of public education decided that children of lower intelligence required special education, and he hired Alfred Binet to design a procedure to identify children in the Paris school system who needed special attention.

Binet faced a complicated task. Previous attempts to measure intelligence had been notably unsuccessful. Earlier in his career, Binet had experimented with craniometry, which involved estimating intelligence (as well as personality characteristics) from the size and shape of people's heads. Craniometry was an accepted practice at the time, but Binet was skeptical about its usefulness as a measure of intelligence. As he wrote in 1900, "The idea of measuring intelligence by measuring heads seemed ridiculous" (p. 403). Other researchers had tried using other aspects of physical appearance, such as facial features, to measure intelligence, but these were also unsuccessful. Still others had used tests of reaction time under the assumption that more intelligent people would show faster reaction times than less intelligent people. However, evidence for a link between intelligence and reaction time was also weak.

Thus, Binet rejected the previous methods and set about designing a new approach for measuring intelligence. The technique he developed involved a series of short tasks that involved basic cognitive processes such as comprehension and reasoning. For example, children would be asked to name objects, answer commonsense questions, and interpret pictures. Binet published the first version of his intelligence test in 1905 in collaboration with one of his students, Théodore Simon.

When he revised the test 3 years later, Binet proposed a new index of intelligence that was based on the age level of each task on the test. The various tasks were arranged sequentially in the order in which a child of average intelligence could pass them successfully. For example, an average 4-year-old knows his or her sex, can indicate which of two lines is longer, and can name familiar objects (such as a key), but cannot give differences between pairs of abstract terms (such as *pride* and *pretension*). By seeing which tasks a child could and could not complete, one could estimate the "mental age" of a child—the intellectual level at which the child is able to perform. Later, the German psychologist William Stern recommended dividing a child's mental age (as measured by Binet's test) by his or her chronological age to create the intelligence quotient, or IQ.

Binet's work provided the first useful measure of intelligence and set the stage for the widespread use of tests in psychology and education. Furthermore, it gave researchers the measurement tools they needed to conduct research on intelligence, a topic that continues to attract a great deal of research attention today. Although contemporary intelligence tests continue to have their critics, development of adequate measures was a prerequisite to the scientific study of intelligence.

All behavioral research involves the measurement of some behavioral or mental event. It would be inconceivable to conduct a study in which nothing is measured. Importantly, the success of a particular piece of research depends heavily on the quality of the measures used. Measures of behavior that are flawed in some way can distort our results and lead us to draw erroneous conclusions about the data.

Because measurement is so important to the research process, an entire speciality known as **psychometrics** is devoted to the study of psychological measurement. Psychometricians investigate the properties of the measures used in behavioral research and work toward improving psychological measurement.

In this chapter, we will look at how researchers measure behavioral and mental events. Along the way, we will examine the types of measures that behavioral researchers commonly use, discuss the numerical properties of such measures, highlight the characteristics that distinguish good measures from bad ones, and consider ways of improving behavioral measurement.

Measures Used in Behavioral Research

The measures used in behavioral research fall roughly into three categories: behavioral measures, physiological measures, and self-reports.

Behavioral Measures

Behavioral measures involve the direct observation of behavior. Behavioral measures can therefore be used to measure anything an animal or person does that researchers can observe—a rat pressing a bar, eye contact between people in conversation, fidgeting by a person giving a speech, aggression in children on the playground, the time it takes a worker to complete a task. In each case, researchers observe and record the subject's behavior directly or from tape recordings.

To measure behaviors such as these, researchers typically use a **behavioral coding system** to record the behaviors they observe. A coding system is used to convert observed behavior to numerical data for purposes of analysis. In a very simple coding system, a researcher may simply count the number of times a particular behavior occurs (such as bar presses or head nods) or measure the duration of certain behaviors (such as how long it takes to complete a task). In more complex coding systems, researchers classify behaviors into categories. For example, a researcher interested in decision making in groups might classify subjects' comments during a group discussion into one of several categories, such as *gives opinion, agrees, disagrees, asks for information, seems unfriendly,* and so on (Bales, 1970). Many standardized behavioral coding systems have been developed, although researchers often must create their own coding systems for use in a particular study.

Occasionally, researchers recruit **knowledgeable informants**—people who know the subjects well—to observe and rate their behavior (Moscowitz, 1986). Typically, these individuals are people who play a significant role in the subjects' lives, such as best friends, parents, romantic partners, co-workers, or teachers. For example, in a study of factors that affect the congruence between people's perceptions of themselves and others' perceptions of them, Cheek (1982) obtained ratings of 85 college men by three of their fraternity brothers.

Because people often behave unnaturally when they know they are being watched, researchers sometimes measure behavior indirectly rather than observing it directly. For example, to measure alcohol consumption, Sawyer (1961) counted the number of empty liquor bottles in neighborhood garbage cans rather than asking residents how much alcohol they drink. **Unobtrusive measures** such as this are useful when direct observation would lead to unnatural behavior.

Physiological Measures

Many behavioral researchers are interested in the relationships between bodily processes and behavior. Most such internal processes are not directly observable, but can be measured with sophisticated equipment. Other physiological processes, such as certain reflexes, are observable, yet specialized equipment is needed to measure them accurately.

Physiological measures can be classified into four general types.

First, measures of neural activity are used to investigate activity within the nervous system. For example, researchers who study sleep and dreaming use the electroencephalogram (EEG) to measure brain wave activity. Electrodes are attached to the outside of the head to record the brain's patterns of electrical activity. Other researchers *implant* electrodes directly into areas of the nervous system to measure the activity of specific neurons or groups of neurons.

Second, other physiological techniques are used to measure activity in the autonomic nervous system, that portion of the nervous system that controls involuntary responses of the visceral muscles and glands. For example, measures of heart rate, respiration, blood pressure, skin temperature, and electrodermal response all reflect activity in the autonomic nervous system.

Third, some researchers study physiological processes by drawing and analyzing subjects' blood. For example, certain hormones, such as adrenaline and cortisol, are released in response to stress, and other hormones, such as testosterone, are related to activity level and aggression. Of course, analyzing blood samples requires sophisticated equipment and extensive technical knowledge.

Finally, other physiological measures are used to measure precisely bodily reactions that, though observable, require specialized equipment for quantification. For example, electromyographs are used to measure muscular reactions, such as reflexes. And to measure sexual arousal, researchers use a plethysmograph (for women) and a penile strain gauge (for men).

Self-Reports

Types of self-report measures   Self-report measures involve the replies subjects give in response to questionnaires and interviews. The information that self-reports provide may involve cognitive, affective, or behavioral events.

Cognitive self-reports measure what subjects *think* about something. For example, a developmental psychologist may ask a child which of two chunks of clay is larger—one rolled into a ball or one formed in the shape of a hot dog. Or a political pollster may ask voters about their preferences regarding candidates for President. As we'll see, researchers cannot always trust people's statements about what they think; a man who is prejudiced toward those of another race may be reluctant to admit it, for example. Even so, self-report measures are the only direct way to access a person's thoughts.

Affective self-reports involve subjects' responses regarding how they *feel*. Behavioral researchers are often interested in emotional reactions such as depression, anxiety, stress, grief, and happiness, and in people's evaluations of themselves and others. The most straightforward way of assessing these kinds of reactions is to ask subjects to report on them.

Behavioral self-reports involve subjects' reports of how they *act*. Subjects may be asked how often they read the newspaper, go to the dentist, or have sex, for example. Similarly, many personality inventories ask subjects to indicate how frequently they engage in certain behaviors. Like other self-report measures, behavioral self-reports are open to reporting bias. When possible, researchers prefer to observe subjects' behaviors directly rather than to rely on subjects' reports about how they behave. However, because this is often not practically or ethically possible, self-reports are used.

BEHAVIORAL RESEARCH CASE STUDY

Self-Reported Reactions to Divorce

With the climbing divorce rate in the seventies and eighties, psychologists have become increasingly interested in understanding people's reactions to divorce and in developing ways to help people cope with the breakup of their marriages.

In a study involving factors related to people's reactions to divorce, Berman (1988) used self-report measures that assessed cognitive, affective, and behavioral responses. Berman asked women to recall a pleasant or an unpleasant memory about their ex-husbands and to describe their thoughts in a sentence or two. In addition to this cognitive self-report measure, subjects completed affective self-report measures where they rated how depressed they had felt during the divorce process as well as their current mood. Finally, he used behavioral self-report measures to ask about the women's current relationships with their ex-partners, such as how much contact they had had with their ex-husbands during the last 2 weeks.

His results showed that women who reported affection and respect for an ex-husband were more bothered by thoughts about him, and were more likely to become depressed after recalling positive memories about him. Berman concluded that divorced women who dwell on the positive aspects of their previous marriages experience more depression and stress.

Questionnaires and Interviews Self-reports are obtained either on questionnaires or in interview settings. On **questionnaires**, subjects respond to written questions or statements. In **interviews**, an interviewer asks the questions and the subject responds orally.

Each of these techniques has advantages and disadvantages. Questionnaires are usually less expensive to administer than interviews. Also, because it is easier to administer a questionnaire than an interview, questionnaires require less training of researchers. And, because questionnaires can usually be administered to groups of people, they take less time than interviews with one respondent at a time. Furthermore, if the topic is a sensitive one, subjects can be assured that their responses to a questionnaire will be anonymous, whereas anonymity is impossible in a face-to-face interview. Thus, subjects may be more honest on questionnaires than in interviews.

On the other hand, if respondents are drawn from the general population, questionnaires are inappropriate for those who are illiterate—approximately 10% of the adult population of the United States. Similarly, young children are incapable of completing questionnaires on their own. Unlike questionnaires, interviews can be administered to both literate and illiterate respondents. Also, interviews allow the researcher to be sure respondents understand each question before answering. We have no way of knowing whether respondents understand all of the questions on a questionnaire. Perhaps the greatest advantage of interviews is that detailed information can be obtained about complex topics. A skilled interviewer can probe respondents for elaboration of details in a way that is impossible on a questionnaire.

Table 3.1 presents a comparison of the advantages of questionnaires and interviews.

Table 3.1	**Questionnaires Versus Interviews**

Questionnaires:
   Less expensive
   Easier to administer
   May be administered in groups
   Less training of researchers
   Anonymity can be assured
Interviews:
   More appropriate for illiterate respondents
   More appropriate for children and persons with low IQ
   Can ensure that respondents understand questions
   Allows for follow-up questions
   Can explore complex issues more fully

DEVELOPING YOUR RESEARCH SKILLS

Designing Questionnaires and Interviews

Questionnaires are perhaps the most ubiquitous of all psychological measures. Not only are they widely used by behavioral researchers, but questionnaires are used by clinical psychologists to obtain information about their clients, by companies to collect data on applicants and employees, by members of Congress to poll their constituents, by restaurants to assess the quality of their food and service, and by colleges to obtain students' evaluations of their teachers. You have undoubtedly completed many questionnaires, and you may even have designed a questionnaire for use in a class, club, church, or other activity.

Designing a good questionnaire involves much more than writing a few questions. Below I offer several guidelines for designing a useful questionnaire.

Use precise terminology in phrasing the questions Be certain that your respondents will interpret each question exactly as you intended. What reply would you give, for example, if I asked you on a questionnaire, What kinds of drugs do you take? One person might list the recreational drugs he or she has tried, such as marijuana or cocaine. Other respondents, however, might interpret the question to be asking what kinds of *prescription* drugs they are taking and list things such as penicillin or insulin. Still others might try to recall the brand names of the various over-the-counter remedies in their medicine cabinets.

Write the questions as simply as possible, avoiding difficult words, unnecessary jargon, and cumbersome phrases Many subjects would stumble over instructions such as, Rate your self-relevant affect on the following scales. Why not just say, Rate how you feel about yourself? Also, keep the questions short and uncomplicated. Testing experts recommend limiting each question to no more than 20 words.

Don't make unwarranted assumptions about the respondents There is a tendency to assume that most other people are just like us and to write questions that make unjustified assumptions based on our own experiences. The question, How do you feel about your mother?, for example, assumes that the subject knows his or her mother, which might not be the case.

Choose an appropriate response format The **response format** refers to the manner in which the subject indicates his or her answer to the question. There are four basic response formats.

In a *free-response format*, the subject fills in a blank or writes an unstructured response to the question. For example, a respondent might be asked, Describe your perceptions of the Soviet Union.

When a *true-false response format* is used, the subject indicates whether a statement is true or false. A subject might be asked to indicate true or false in response to the statement, I am nearly always punctual. Although a true–false format is useful for questions of fact (for example, I attended church last week), they are not recommended for measuring attitudes and feelings. In many cases, people's subjective reactions are not clear-cut enough to fall neatly into a true or false category. For example, if asked to respond true or false to the statement, I feel nervous in social situations, most people would have difficulty answering either true or false and would probably say, It depends.

When questions are asked about things that vary in frequency or intensity, a *rating scale response format* should be used. Often, a 5-point scale is used. For example:

How do you feel about capital punishment?
_____ Strongly oppose
_____ Moderately oppose
_____ Neither oppose nor support
_____ Moderately support
_____ Strongly support

However, other length scales are also used, as in this example of a 4-point rating scale:

How nervous do you feel when you must speak in front of a group?

_____ Not at all

_____ Slightly

_____ Moderately

_____ Very

Finally, sometimes respondents are asked to choose one response from a set of possible alternatives—the *multiple choice* or *fixed-alternative response format*. For example:

What is your attitude toward abortion?

_____ Disapprove under all circumstances

_____ Approve only under special circumstances, such as when the woman's life
        is in danger

_____ Approve whenever a woman wants one

Pretest the questionnaire   When possible, researchers pretest their questionnaires before using them in a study. Questionnaires are often pretested by asking a few people to complete the questionnaire as they tell the researcher what they think each question is asking, report on difficulties they have in understanding the questions or using the response formats, and express other reactions to the items. Based on subjects' responses during pretesting, the questionnaire can be revised before it is actually used in research.

Each of these guidelines for designing questionnaires is equally relevant for designing an **interview schedule**—the series of questions that are used in an interview. In addition, the researcher must consider how the interview process itself—the interaction between the interviewer and respondent—will affect the quality of the data obtained.

Below are a few suggestions for interviewers:

Create a friendly atmosphere   The interviewer's first goal should be to put the respondent at ease. Respondents who like and trust the interviewer will be more open and honest in their responses than those who are angered or intimidated by the interviewer's style.

Maintain an attitude of friendly interest   The interviewer should appear truly interested in the respondent's answers, rather than mechanically recording the responses in a disinterested manner.

Order the sections of the interview to facilitate rapport building and to create a logical sequence   Start the interview with the most basic and least threatening topics, then move slowly to more specific and sensitive questions as the respondent becomes more relaxed.

Conceal personal reactions to the respondent's responses   The interviewer should never show surprise, approval, disapproval, or other reactions to the respondent's answers.

Ask questions exactly as they are worded　In most instances, the interviewer should ask the question in precisely the same way to all respondents. Impromptu wordings of the questions introduce differences in how various respondents are interviewed.

Don't lead the respondent　In probing the respondent's answer—asking for clarification or details—one must be careful not to put words in the respondent's mouth.

Contemporaneous Versus Archival Research

In most studies, measurement is *contemporaneous*—it occurs at the time the research is conducted. A researcher designs a study, recruits subjects, then collects data about those subjects using a predesigned behavioral, physiological, or self-report measure.

However, some research is conducted using data that were collected *prior* to the time the research was designed. In **archival research,** researchers analyze data pulled from existing records, such as census data, court records, personal letters, newspaper reports, government documents, and so on. In most instances, archival data were collected for purposes other than research. Like contemporaneous measures, archival data may involve data about behavior (such as immigration records, school records, and marriage statistics), physiological processes (such as hospital records), or self-reports (such as personal letters and diaries).

Scales of Measurement

Regardless of what kind of measure is used—behavioral, physiological, or self-report—the goal of measurement is to assign numbers to subjects' responses so that they can be summarized and analyzed. For example, a researcher may convert subjects' marks on a questionnaire to a set of numbers (from 1 to 5, perhaps) that meaningfully represents the subjects' responses. These numbers are then used to describe and analyze subjects' answers.

However, in analyzing and interpreting research data, not all numbers can be treated the same. As we'll see, some numbers used to represent subjects' behaviors are, in fact, "real" numbers that can be added, subtracted, multiplied, and divided. Other numbers, however, have special characteristics and require special treatment.

Researchers distinguish between four different scales of measurement. These scales of measurement differ in the degree to which the numbers that researchers use to represent subjects' behaviors correspond to the real number system. Differences between these scales of measurement are important because they have implications for what a particular number indicates about a subject and how one's data may be analyzed.

(1)   The simplest type of scale is a **nominal scale**. With a nominal scale, the numbers that are assigned to subjects' behaviors or characteristics are really just labels. For example, for purposes of analysis, we may assign all boys in a study the number 1 and all girls the number 2. Or, we may indicate whether a student was late for class by giving punctual students a 0 and late students a 1. Numbers on a nominal scale indicate things about our subjects, but they are labels or names rather than real numbers (nominal means *name*). Thus, it usually makes no sense to perform mathematical operations on them.

(2)   An **ordinal scale** involves the rank ordering of a set of behaviors or characteristics and conveys more information than a nominal scale. For example, we might rank subjects according to their test scores, from highest to lowest. Measures that use ordinal scales tell us the relative order of our subjects on a particular dimension, but do not indicate the distance between subjects. The difference in scores between students who ranked 3rd and 4th on a test may not be the same as the difference between students who ranked 11th and 12th, for example.

(3)   When an **interval scale** of measurement is used, equal differences between the numbers reflect equal differences between subjects in the characteristic being measured. On an IQ test, for example, the difference between scores of 90 and 100 (10 points) is the same as the difference between scores of 130 and 140 (10 points). However, an interval scale does not have a true zero point that indicates the absence of the quality being measured. An IQ score of 0 does not necessarily indicate that no intelligence is present. Similarly, on the Fahrenheit thermometer, which is an interval scale, a temperature of 0° does not indicate the absence of temperature. Because it has no true zero point, numbers on an interval scale can not be multiplied or divided. It makes no sense to say that a temperature of 100° is twice as hot as a temperature of 50°, or that a person with an IQ of 60 is one third as intelligent as one with an IQ of 180.

(4)   The highest level of measurement is the **ratio scale**. Ratio measurement involves real numbers that can be added, subtracted, multiplied, and divided. This is because a ratio scale has a true zero point. Many measures of physical characteristics, such as weight, are on a ratio scale. Weight has a true zero point (indicating no weight) so it makes sense to talk about 100 pounds being twice as heavy as 50 pounds.

Scales of measurement are important to the researcher for two reasons. First, the measurement scale used determines the amount of information provided by a particular measure. Nominal scales provide less information than ordinal, interval, or ratio scales. When asking people about their opinions, for example, simply asking whether they agree or disagree with particular statements (which is a nominal scale) does not capture as much information as an interval scale that asks *how much* they agree or disagree. In many cases, choice of a measurement scale is determined by the characteristic being measured; it would be difficult to measure gender on anything other than a nominal scale, for example. However, if given a choice, researchers prefer to use measures that are at a higher level of measurement because they provide more information about subjects' responses or characteristics.

The second important implication of scales of measurement involves the kinds of statistical analyses that can be performed on the data. As we've seen, certain mathematical operations can be performed only on numbers that conform to the properties of a particular measurement scale. The more useful and powerful statistical analyses, such as *t*-tests and *F*-tests (which we'll meet in later chapters) generally require that numbers be on interval or ratio scales. As a result, researchers try to use scales that allow them to use the most informative statistical tests.

Now that we've learned about the kinds of measures that behavioral researchers use, we'll turn our attention to characteristics that distinguish good from bad measures.

Estimating the Reliability of a Measure

The goal of measurement is to assign numbers to objects or events (such as behaviors) in such a way that the numbers we assign correspond in some meaningful way to the attribute we are trying to measure. But how do we know whether a particular measurement technique does, in fact, give us scores that are meaningful and useful reflections of whatever we want to measure?

The first characteristic that any good measure must possess is reliability. **Reliability** refers to the consistency or dependability of a measuring technique. If you weigh yourself on a bathroom scale three times in a row, you expect to obtain the same weight each time. If, however, you weigh 140 pounds the first time, 98 pounds the second time, and 167 pounds the third time, then the scales are *unreliable*—they can't be trusted to provide consistent weights. Similarly, measures used in research must be reliable. When they aren't, we can't trust them to provide meaningful data regarding the behavior of our subjects.

Measurement Error

A subject's score on a particular measure consists of two components: the true score and measurement error. We can portray this by the equation:

$$\text{Observed score} = \text{true score} + \text{measurement error}$$

The **true score** is the score that the subject would have obtained if our measure were perfect and we were able to measure without error. If researchers were omniscient beings, they would know exactly what a subject's score should be—that Susan's IQ was *exactly* 138 or that the rat pressed the bar *precisely* 52 times, for example.

However, the measures used in research are never that precise. Virtually all measures contain **measurement error.** This component of the observed score is the result of factors that distort the subject's score so that it isn't precisely what it should be. If Susan was anxious and preoccupied when she took the IQ test, for example, her observed IQ score might be lower than 138. If the counter on the bar in a Skinner box malfunctioned, it might record only 50 bar presses instead of 52.

Although many factors can contribute to measurement error, these can be broken down into five categories. First, measurement error is affected by *transient states* of the subject. For example, the subject's mood, health, level of fatigue, and anxiety level can all contribute to measurement error.

Second, *stable attributes* of the subject can lead to measurement error. Paranoid or suspicious subjects may distort their answers, and less intelligent subjects may misunderstand certain questions, for example. Furthermore, individual differences in motivation can affect test scores; on tests of ability, motivated subjects will score more highly than unmotivated subjects regardless of their real level of ability. Both transient and stable characteristics of subjects can give us scores that are lower or higher than their true score would be.

Third, *situational factors* in the testing situation can create measurement error. If the researcher is particularly friendly, a subject might try harder; if the researcher is stern and aloof, subjects may be intimidated, angered, or unmotivated. Handling animals roughly can introduce changes in behavior. Room temperature, lighting, and crowding can also artificially affect scores.

Fourth, *aspects of the measure* itself can create measurement error. For example, ambiguous questions that can be interpreted in more than one way create error. And measures that induce fatigue (such as tests that are too long) or fear (such as intrusive or painful physiological measures) can affect scores.

Finally, actual *mistakes* in recording subjects' responses can make the observed score different from the true score. If a researcher sneezes while counting the number of times a rat presses a bar, he may lose count. A careless researcher may write her 3s so that they look like 5s.

Whatever its source, measurement error undermines the reliability of the measures researchers use. In fact, the reliability of a measure is an inverse function of measurement error: The more measurement error present in a measuring technique, the less reliable the measure is.

Reliability as Systematic Variance

Unfortunately, researchers never know for certain precisely how much measurement error is contained in a particular subject's score, nor what the subject's true score really is. However, researchers have ways of estimating the reliability of the measures they use. If they find that a measure is not acceptably reliable, they can take steps to increase its reliability. If that doesn't work, they may decide not to use it at all.

Assessing a measure's reliability involves an analysis of the variability in a set of scores. We saw above that each subject's observed score is composed of a true-score component and a measurement error component. If we combine the scores of several subjects and calculate the variance, the total variance of the *set* of scores is composed of the same two components:

$$\text{Total variance} = \text{variance due to true scores} + \text{variance due to measurement error}$$

In assessing the reliability of measures, researchers estimate the proportion of the total variance that is true-score variance versus measurement error. Statistically, then, reliability is the proportion of the total variance that is true-score variance:

$$\text{Reliability} = \frac{\text{true-score variance}}{\text{total variance}}$$

The reliability of a measure can range from .00 (indicating no reliability) to 1.00 (indicating perfect reliability). As the equation above shows, the reliability is .00 when none of the total variance is true-score variance. When the reliability is zero, the scores reflect nothing but measurement error and the measure is totally worthless. At the other extreme, a reliability of 1.00 would be obtained if all of the total variance is true-score variance. A measure is perfectly reliable if there is no measurement error. As a rule of thumb, a measure is considered sufficiently reliable if at least 50% of the total variance in scores is systematic, true-score variance.

Assessing Reliability

Researchers use three ways to estimate the reliability of their measures: test–retest reliability, interitem reliability, and interrater reliability. All three methods are based on the same general logic. To the extent that two measurements of the same object or event yield similar scores, we can assume that both measurements are tapping into the same true score. However, if two measurements of the same thing yield very different scores, the measures must contain a high degree of measurement error.

Thus, by statistically testing the degree to which the two measurements yield similar scores, we can estimate the proportion of the total variance that is systematic true-score versus error variance, thereby estimating the reliability of the measure.

Test–retest reliability   Test-retest reliability refers to the consistency of subjects' responses on a measure over time. Assuming that the characteristic being measured is relatively stable, subjects should obtain approximately the same score each time they are measured. If a person takes an intelligence test twice, we would expect his or her two test scores to be similar, for example. Because there is some measurement error in even well-designed tests, the scores won't be exactly the same, but they should be close.

Test–retest reliability is determined by measuring subjects on two occasions, usually separated by a few weeks. Then the two sets of scores are correlated to see how closely related the second set of scores is to the first. (We'll cover details regarding correlation in Chapter 6.) If the scores correlate highly (at least .70), the measure has good test–retest reliability. If they do not correlate highly, the measure contains too much measurement error, is unreliable, and should not be used. Low and high test–retest reliability is shown pictorially in Figure 3.1.

Assessing test–retest reliability makes sense only if the attribute being measured would not be expected to change between the two measurements. We would expect high test–retest reliability on an intelligence or personality test, but not on a measure of hunger or fatigue, for example.

Interitem reliability   A second kind of reliability is relevant only for measures that consist of more than one item. Personality inventories, for example, typically consist of several questions that are summed to provide a single score. Similarly, on a scale used to measure depression, subjects may be asked to rate themselves on several mood-related items (sad, unhappy, blue, helpless) that are then added together to provide a single mood score.

When several questions or items are summed to provide a single score, researchers are interested in interitem reliability. **Interitem reliability** refers to consistency among the items on a scale. Ideally, we would like all of the questions on a scale to measure the same construct (such as a personality trait or mood). On an inventory to measure extraversion, we want all of the items to be measuring some aspect of extraversion, for example. Including items in a test score that don't measure the construct of interest increases measurement error.

Researchers examine interitem reliability by looking at item-total correlations, split-half reliability, and by computing Cronbach's alpha coefficient. These three approaches are described below.

First, they look at the **item-total correlation** for each question or item on the scale. Does each item correlate with the sum of all other items? If the item measures the same construct as the rest of the items, it should correlate with them. If not, the item adds only measurement error to the test score and doesn't belong on the scale.

Researchers also use **split-half reliability** as an index of interitem reliability. With split-half reliability, the researcher divides the items on the scale into two sets. Sometimes the first and second halves of the scale are used, sometimes the odd-numbered items form one set and even-numbered items form the other, or sometimes items are randomly put into one set or the other. Then, a total score is obtained for each set by adding the items within each set. The

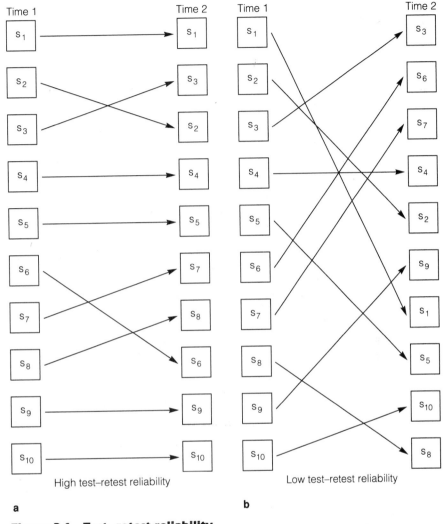

Figure 3.1 Test–retest reliability

Explanation: High test–retest reliability indicates that subjects' scores are consistent across time. In Figure 3.1(a), for example, subjects' scores were relatively consistent from time 1 to time 2. If they are not consistent across time, as in Figure 3.1(b), test–retest reliability is low.·

correlation between these two sets of scores is then calculated. If the items on the scale hang together well and estimate the true score consistently, scores obtained on the two halves of the test should correlate highly. If the split-half correlation is small, however, it indicates that the total score contains a great deal of measurement error.

There is one drawback to the use of split-half reliability. The reliability one obtains depends on how the items are split. Using a first-half/second-half split is likely to provide a slightly different estimate of reliability than an even/

odd split. What, then, is the *real* interitem reliability? To get around this ambiguity, researchers often use **Cronbach's alpha coefficient** (Cronbach, 1970). Cronbach's alpha is equivalent to the average of all possible split-half reliabilities.

Interrater reliability   Interrater reliability (also called interjudge or interobserver reliability) involves the consistency among two or more researchers who observe and record subjects' behavior. Obviously, when two or more observers record subjects' behaviors, we would like them to be consistent among themselves. If one observer records 15 bar presses and another observer records 18 bar presses, the difference between their observations represents measurement error.

For example, Gottschalk, Uliana, and Gilbert (1988) analyzed recent presidential debates for evidence that the candidates were cognitively impaired at the time of the debates. They coded what the candidates said during the debates using the Cognitive Impairment Scale. In their report of the study, the authors presented data to support the interrater reliability of their procedure. The reliability analysis demonstrated that the raters agreed sufficiently among themselves, and that measurement error was acceptably low. (By the way, their results showed that Ronald Reagan showed significantly more evidence of impairment than Jimmy Carter, in 1980, or Walter Mondale, in 1984, and that Reagan showed more impairment during the 1984 debates than he did 4 years earlier.)

Researchers use two general ways of assessing interrater reliability. If the raters are simply recording whether or not a behavior occurred, we can calculate the percentage of times they agreed. Alternatively, if the raters are rating the subjects' behavior along a scale (an anxiety rating from 1 to 5, for example), we can correlate their ratings across subjects. If the observers are making similar ratings, we should obtain a relatively high correlation between them.

DEVELOPING YOUR RESEARCH SKILLS

Increasing the Reliability of Measures

Unfortunately, it is not always possible to assess the reliability of measures used in research. For example, if we ask a person to rate how happy he or she feels right now on a scale of 1 to 7, we have no direct way of testing the reliability of the response. Test–retest reliability is inappropriate because the state we are measuring changes over time. Interitem reliability is irrelevant because there is only one item. And, because others cannot observe and rate the subject's feelings of happiness, we cannot assess interrater reliability. Even though researchers assess the reliability of their techniques whenever possible, the reliability of some measures cannot be determined.

In light of this, often the best a researcher can do is to make every effort to maximize the reliability of his or her measures. This is done by eliminating possible sources of measurement error. A few ways of increasing the reliability of behavioral measures are listed below.

Standardize administration of the measure   Ideally, every subject should be measured under precisely the same conditions. Differences in how the measure is taken can contribute to measurement error. If possible, have the same researcher administer the measure to all subjects in precisely the same setting.

Clarify instructions and questions   When some subjects do not fully understand the instructions or questions, measurement error results. When possible, questions to be used in interviews or questionnaires should be pilot tested to be sure they are understood properly.

Train observers   If subjects' behavior is being observed and rated, train the observers carefully. Observers should also be given the opportunity to practice using the rating technique.

Minimize errors in coding data   No matter how reliable a measuring technique is, error is introduced if researchers make mistakes in recording, coding, tabulating, or computing the data.

Summary

Reliable measures are a prerequisite of good research. A reliable measure is one that is relatively unaffected by sources of measurement error and thus is consistent and dependable. More specifically, reliability reflects the proportion of the total variance in a set of scores that is systematic, true-score variance. The reliability of measures is estimated in three ways: test–retest reliability, interitem reliability, and interrater reliability. Even in instances in which the reliability of a technique cannot be determined, steps should be taken to minimize sources of measurement error.

Estimating the Validity of a Measure

Not only must the measures used in research be reliable, but they must also be valid. **Validity** refers to the extent to which a measurement procedure actually measures what it is intended to measure rather than something else. Validity is the degree to which variability in subjects' scores on a particular measure reflects variability in the characteristic we want to measure. Do scores on the measure relate to the attribute of interest? Are we measuring what we think we are measuring?

If a researcher is interested in the effects of a new drug on depression, for example, the measure of depression he or she uses must reflect actual differences in subjects' depression. The measure must actually measure depression rather than something else (or nothing at all).

It is important to note that a measure can be highly reliable, but not valid. For example, the cranial measurements that early psychologists such as Binet used to assess intelligence were reasonably reliable. When measuring a person's skull, two researchers would arrive at similar, though not always identical, measurements—that is, interrater reliability was quite high. Furthermore, skull size also demonstrates high test–retest reliability; it can be measured consistently over time with little measurement error.

However, no matter how reliable skull measurements may be, they are not a *valid* measure of intelligence. They are not valid because they do not measure the construct of intelligence. Thus, researchers need to know whether measures are reliable *and* whether they assess what they're supposed to measure.

Assessing Validity

When researchers refer to a measure as valid, they do so in terms of a particular scientific or practical purpose. Validity is not a property of a measuring technique per se, but an indication of the degree to which the technique measures a particular entity *in a particular context*. Thus, a measure may be valid for one purpose, but not for another. Cranial measurements, for example, are valid measures of hat size, but they are not valid measures of intelligence.

Researchers often refer to three different types of validity: face validity, construct validity, and criterion validity.

Face validity   Face validity refers to the extent to which a measure *appears* to measure what it's supposed to measure. Rather than being a technical or statistical procedure, face validation involves the judgment of the researcher or of subjects recruited by the researcher.

Face validity can be important for three reasons. The first and most obvious is that a researcher is more likely to have faith in an instrument whose content obviously taps into the construct he or she is interested in measuring than a measure that is not face valid.

A second reason is less obvious. If a measuring technique, such as a test, does not have face validity, subjects, clients, job applicants, and other laypeople are likely to doubt its relevance and importance (Cronbach, 1970). Furthermore, they are likely to feel resentful if they are affected by the results of a test whose validity they doubt. Thus, all other things being equal, it is usually better to have a measure that is face valid than one that is not. It simply engenders greater confidence by the public at large.

Although face validity is often desirable, three qualifications must be kept in mind. First, just because a measure has face validity doesn't necessarily mean that it is actually valid. There are many cases of face-valid measures that did not measure what they appeared to measure. To researchers of the 19th century, skull size was a face-valid measure of intelligence.

Second, there are many measures that lack face validity that are, in fact, valid. Many items from the Minnesota Multiphasic Personality Inventory (MMPI)—a measure of personality that is used widely both in practice and in research—do not appear face valid, yet predict various psychological problems. For example, expressing a preference for Washington over Lincoln as president, or for corn over peas, is a valid indicator of certain attributes, although these items are by no means face valid.

Third, researchers sometimes want to disguise the purpose of their tests. If they think that respondents will be hesitant to answer sensitive questions honestly, they may design instruments that lack face validity and thereby conceal the purpose of the test.

"You can't build a hut, you don't know how to find edible roots, and you know nothing about predicting the weather. In other words, you do terribly on our IQ test."

© 1990 by Sidney Harris, *American Scientist* Magazine.

Construct validity   Much behavioral research involves the measurement of **hypothetical constructs**—entities that cannot be directly observed, but are inferred on the basis of empirical evidence. Psychology abounds with hypothetical constructs such as anxiety, intelligence, satiation, attraction, status, schema, self-concept, and so on. None of these entities can be observed directly, but they are hypothesized to exist on the basis of indirect evidence. In studying these kinds of constructs, researchers must use valid measures. But how does one go about validating the measure of a hypothetical (and invisible) construct?

In an important article, Cronbach and Meehl (1955) suggested that the validity of measures of such constructs can be assessed by studying the relationship between the measure of the construct and scores on other measures. For any measure, we can specify what the scores on the measure should be related to if the measure is valid. For example, scores on a measure of self-esteem should be positively related to scores on measures of confidence and optimism, but negatively related to measures of insecurity and anxiety. We can correlate scores on the test with scores from other measures to see whether the relationships are as predicted. Evidence that the measure is related to other measures as it should be supports its construct validity.

For example, Hart, Leary, and Rejeski (1989) developed a measure of physique anxiety—the tendency to become apprehensive when others scrutinize one's body (at the beach, for example). The researchers needed to know whether the scale actually measured people's concerns about others' evaluations of their physiques. To examine construct validity, the researchers asked themselves what physique anxiety should be associated with. They reasoned that physique anxiety should be related to negative ratings of one's bodily attractiveness, with weight and skin-fold measurements (heavier and fatter people should be more physique-anxious), with a fear of being negatively evaluated by others, and with self-consciousness. Indeed, their data showed that people who scored high on the physique anxiety scale judged their attractiveness lower, weighed more, had a higher percentage of body fat, scored higher in fear of negative evaluation, and were more self-conscious. These data supported the construct validity of the physique anxiety measure. If some of the predicted relationships with other measures had not been obtained, the validity of the scale would have been questioned.

Criterion-related validity   A third type of validity is criterion-related validity. **Criterion-related validity** refers to the extent to which a measure allows a researcher to distinguish among subjects on the basis of some behavioral criterion. For example, do scores on the Scholastic Aptitude Test (SAT) permit us to distinguish people who will do well in college from those who will not? Note that the issue is not one of assessing the link between the measure and other constructs (as in construct validity), but in assessing the relationship between the measure and a relevant *behavioral* criterion.

Researchers distinguish between two kinds of criterion validity: concurrent and predictive validity. A measure that allows a researcher to distinguish between people at the present time is said to have **concurrent validity**. In the study of physique anxiety described above, women who scored high on the physique anxiety scale showed significantly higher increases in heart rate when their physiques were being examined than did women who scored low (Hart et al., 1989). Thus, the scale successfully distinguished among women at the present time.

Predictive validity refers to a measure's ability to distinguish between people on a relevant behavioral criterion at some time in the future. Does the measure predict future behavior? For the SAT, for example, the issue is one of predictive validity. No one really cares whether high school seniors who score high on the SAT are better prepared for college *at the time they take the test* than low scorers (concurrent validity). Instead, college admissions officers want to know whether SAT scores predict academic performance 1 to 4 years later (predictive validity).

Criterion-related validity is most often of interest to researchers in applied research settings. In educational research, for example, researchers are often interested in the degree to which tests predict academic performance. Similarly, before using tests to select new employees, personnel psychologists must demonstrate that the tests predict future on-the-job performance.

IN DEPTH

The Reliability and Validity of College Admission Exams

Most colleges and universities use applicants' scores on one or more entrance examinations as one criterion for making admissions decisions. By far the most frequently used exam for this purpose is the Scholastic Aptitude Test (SAT), developed by the Educational Testing Service.

Many students are skeptical of the SAT and similar exams. Many claim, for example, that they don't test well on standardized tests and that their scores indicate little, if anything, about their ability to do well in college. No doubt, there are many people for whom the SAT does not predict performance well. Like all tests, the SAT contains measurement error and thus underestimates and overestimates some people's true aptitude scores. (Interestingly, I've never heard anyone derogate the SAT because they scored *higher* than they should have on it.) However, a large amount of data attests to the overall reliability and validity of the SAT. The psychometric data regarding the SAT are extensive, based on tens of thousands of scores over a span of many years.

The reliability of the SAT is impressive in comparison with most psychological tests. The SAT possesses high test–retest reliability, as well as high interitem reliability. Reliability coefficients average around .90. (Kaplan, 1982), which means that over 80% of the total variance in SAT scores is systematic, true-score variance. Recall that the minimum criterion for reliability is that at least 50% of the total variance in test scores be true-score variance.

In the case of the SAT, *predictive* validity is of paramount importance. Many studies have examined the relationship between SAT scores and college grades. These studies have shown that the criterion-related validity of the SAT depends, in part, on one's major in college. SAT scores predict college performance better for some majors than for others. In general, however, the predictive validity of the SAT is fairly good. On the average, about 16% of the total variance in first-year college grades is systematic variance accounted for by SAT scores (Kaplan, 1982). Sixteen percent may not sound like a great deal until one considers all of the other factors that contribute to college grades, such as motivation, health, personal problems, the difficulty of one's courses, the prestige of one's college or university, and so on. Given everything that affects performance in college, it is not too surprising that a single test score does not predict with greater accuracy.

Of course, most colleges and universities also use criteria other than entrance exams in the admissions decision. The Educational Testing Service advises admissions offices to consider high school grades, activities, and awards, for example. Using these other criteria further increases the validity of the selection process.

This is not to suggest that the SAT and other college entrance exams are infallible or that certain people do not obtain inflated or deflated scores. But such tests are not as unreliable or invalid as many students suppose.

Counteracting Common Sources of Invalidity

Measures may lack validity for many reasons. However, some sources of invalidity are common to many different measures.

Socially desirable responding   Research subjects are often concerned with how they are perceived by the researcher and by other subjects. As a result, they sometimes respond in a socially acceptable fashion rather than naturally and honestly. People are hesitant to admit certain problems or to express certain attitudes, for example. Similarly, people may not act naturally when they know they are being observed because they are concerned with how their behavior will appear.

Socially desirable response biases can lower the validity of some measures. When people bias their answers or behaviors in a socially desirable direction, the instrument no longer measures what it was supposed to measure. Instead, it measures subjects' proclivity for behaving in a socially desirable fashion.

Social desirability biases can never be eliminated entirely. However, steps can be taken to reduce their effect upon subjects' responses. First, questions should be worded as neutrally as possible so that concerns with social desirability do not occur. Second, when possible, subjects should be assured that their responses are anonymous, thereby lowering their concern with others' evaluations. Third, in observational studies, observers should be as unobtrusive as possible to minimize subjects' concerns about being watched.

Researchers sometimes examine the degree to which a particular measure is contaminated by social desirability bias by using the Social Desirability Scale. Items on the Social Desirability Scale (Crowne & Marlowe, 1964) involve 33 behaviors that are desirable but unlikely ("No matter who I'm talking to, I'm always a good listener") or undesirable but common ("There have been times when I have been jealous of the good fortune of others"). People who indicate that the uncommon, desirable statements are true of them, but the common, undesirable statements are not true of them are particularly likely to behave in a socially desirable fashion in research settings. Thus, researchers correlate scores on the Social Desirability Scale with the measures they are using. If their measures correlate highly with scores on the Social Desirability Scale, the validity of their measures is being affected by the social desirability response bias.

Other response sets   Certain people have other response tendencies, or sets, that create problems with validity. Some individuals tend to agree with statements regardless of their content—the **acquiescence response set**. Others tend to disagree with statements (**naysaying**). Still others show a **response deviation set** in which they try to respond in an unusual, deviant fashion. Steps must be taken to minimize the impact of these response tendencies on subjects' behavior.

Observer biases   Other biases can undermine the validity of observers' ratings of subjects' behavior. A **halo bias** occurs when observers' ratings are affected by their overall positive or negative evaluation of the subject. For example, an observer who forms a positive impression of a subject may interpret his or her behavior differently than an observer who forms a negative impression of the same subject. If the observers are counting how many times the subject interrupts another person during a conversation, an observer who views the subject negatively may "count" more interruptions than the first.

Summary

Validity refers to the degree to which a measuring technique measures what it's intended to measure. Although face-valid measures are often desirable, construct and criterion validity are much more important. Construct validity is assessed by seeing whether scores on a measure are related to other measures as they should be. A measure has criterion-related validity if it correctly distinguishes between people on the basis of a relevant behavioral criterion either at present (concurrent validity) or in the future (predictive validity).

SUMMARY

1. Measurement lies at the heart of all research. Behavioral researchers have a wide array of measures at their disposal, including behavioral measures, physiological measures, and self-report measures.

2. Whatever type of measure they use, researchers must consider whether the measure is at a nominal, ordinal, interval, or ratio scale of measurement. A measure's scale of measurement has implications for the kind of information that the instrument provides, as well as for the statistical analyses that can be performed.

3. Reliability refers to the consistency or dependability of a measuring technique.

4. All scores consist of two components—the true score and measurement error. The true-score component reflects the score that would have been obtained if the measure were perfect; measurement error reflects the effects of factors that distort the true score. The more measurement error, the less reliable the measure.

5. Three types of reliability can be assessed: test–retest reliability (consistency of the measure across time), interitem reliability (consistency among a set of items intended to assess the same construct), and interrater reliability (consistency between two or more researchers who have observed and recorded the subject's behavior).

6. Validity refers to the extent to which a measurement procedure measures what it's supposed to measure.

7. Three types of validity were discussed: face validity (does the measure appear to measure the construct of interest), construct validity (does the measure correlate with measures of other constructs as it should), and criterion-related validity (does the measure correlate with measures of current or future behavior as it should).

8. Researchers must ensure that the measures they use are adequately reliable and valid, and take steps to improve the reliability and validity of their measures. Ways of doing so were discussed.

KEY TERMS

psychometrics
behavioral measure
behavioral coding system
knowledgeable informant
unobtrusive measure
physiological measure
self-report measure

questionnaire
interview
response format
free-response format
true–false response format
rating scale response format
fixed–alternative response format

interview schedule

archival research

nominal scale

ordinal scale

interval scale

ratio scale

reliability

true score

measurement error

test–retest reliability

interitem reliability

item-total correlation

split-half reliability

Cronbach's alpha coefficient

interrater reliability

validity

face validity

construct validity

hypothetical construct

criterion-related validity

concurrent validity

predictive validity

social desirability bias

acquiescence response set

naysaying

response deviation set

halo bias

REVIEW QUESTIONS

1. Distinguish between behavioral, physiological, and self-report measures.
2. Discuss briefly the relative advantages and disadvantages of questionnaires versus interviews as ways of obtaining self-report data.
3. What are some of the things a researcher must consider when designing a questionnaire?
4. What are the four major types of response format that behavioral researchers use?
5. What are some considerations that must be kept in mind when an interview is used to collect data?
6. Distinguish between nominal, ordinal, interval, and ratio scales of measurement. Why do researchers prefer to use interval and ratio scales when possible?
7. What is the relationship between the reliability of a measure and the degree of measurement error it contains?
8. What factors can contribute to measurement error?
9. What are the three primary ways in which researchers assess the reliability of their measures?
10. Distinguish between item-total correlation, split-half reliability, and Cronbach's alpha coefficient as ways to assess interitem reliability.
11. What steps can a researcher take to increase the reliability of his or her measuring techniques?
12. Distinguish between face validity, construct validity, and criterion-related validity. In general, which kind of validity is least important to researchers?
13. What are some common sources of invalidity, and how can they be minimized?

QUESTIONS FOR THOUGHT AND DISCUSSION

1. Many students experience a great deal of anxiety whenever they take tests. Imagine that you are conducting a study involving test anxiety. Suggest three behavioral measures, three physiological measures, and three self-report measures you might use in such a study.

2. Design a questionnaire that assesses people's eating habits. Your questions could address such questions as when they eat, what they eat, how much they eat, who they eat with, where they eat, how health-conscious their eating habits are, and so on. In designing your questionnaire, be sure to consider the issues discussed throughout this chapter.

3. Pretest your questionnaire by administering it to three people. Ask for their reactions to each question, looking for confusing questions and inappropriate response formats.

4. If you wanted to examine the criterion-related validity of your questionnaire, how might you do it? Briefly discuss possible ways of looking at both concurrent and predictive validity.

5. Do you think that people's responses on your questionnaire might be affected by response biases? If so, what steps could you take to minimize them?

4

Describing and Presenting Data

After a study is completed, one of the first tasks a researcher faces is to summarize the data that were collected. No matter what topic is investigated or which research design is used, researchers must find meaningful ways to summarize their data. Not only is summarizing the data essential for analyzing the results of a study, but researchers must describe and present the data so that it is easily comprehended by others.

In descriptive studies, the sole purpose of the research is to describe patterns of behavior. Survey research, for example, aims to describe the attitudes of a particular group of people. Likewise, studies of sexual response, such as those conducted by Masters and Johnson (1966), involved observing and describing the sexual response cycle in more than 700 people.

In correlational and experimental studies, researchers are not interested in simply describing what their subjects do, but rather in exploring variables that cause or are related to subjects' behavior. Even when description is not the primary goal, however, researchers must always find ways to summarize and describe their data in the most meaningful and useful fashion possible.

Criteria of a Good Description

To be useful, the description of data should meet three criteria: accuracy, conciseness, and understandability.

Accuracy

Obviously, data must be summarized and described accurately in order to be useful. Some ways of describing the findings of a study are more accurate than others. For example, as we'll see below, certain ways of graphing data may be misleading. Similarly, depending on the nature of the data (whether or not it is skewed, for example), certain descriptive statistics may summarize and describe the data more accurately than others. Researchers should always present their data in ways that represent the data most accurately.

Conciseness

Unfortunately, the most accurate descriptions of data are often the least useful because they overwhelm the reader with information. Strictly speaking, the most accurate description of a set of data would involve a list of the **raw data**—all subjects' scores on all measures. Only when dealing with raw data is there no possibility that the data will be distorted by condensing and summarizing. However, imagine trying to make sense out of a table that contained the raw data for a study that collected 20 measures on 160 subjects. The table would contain 3200 entries! To be interpretable, data must be summarized in a concise and meaningful form. At the same time, the summary should sacrifice as little information as possible.

Understandability

Third, the description must be easily understood. Overly complicated tables, graphs, or statistics can obscure the findings of a study and lead to confusion. Researchers must be selective in the data they choose to present, presenting only the data that most clearly describe the results. Having decided which aspects of the data best portray the findings of a study, researchers must then choose the clearest, most straightforward manner of describing the data.

The Raw Data

All descriptions of behavioral data begin with a **raw data matrix**. The raw data matrix is a table in which each subject is represented by a row and each dependent variable is represented by a column.

I recently asked 24 undergraduates to tell me at what age they thought they would die. Table 4.1 shows the raw data matrix for their answers.

Although researchers find it useful to construct a raw data matrix as they begin to analyze their data, the information in the raw data matrix must usually be summarized and presented in a more concise manner. It is difficult to make much sense out of a raw data matrix, even a small one such as Table 4.1, by just eyeballing the data.

Methods of summarizing and describing sets of numerical data can be classified as either **graphical methods** or **numerical methods**. Graphical methods involve the presentation of data in graphical or pictorial form, such as

Table 4.1	A Raw Data Matrix

Subject	Estimated age of death
1	70
2	75
3	82
4	72
5	72
6	81
7	78
8	75
9	87
10	72
11	70
12	68
13	75
14	75
15	85
16	72
17	80
18	74
19	75
20	88
21	82
22	78
23	76
24	80

graphs. Numerical methods summarize data in the form of numbers such as percentages or means. As we'll see, often such numbers are presented in a table.

Frequency Distributions

The basis of many data descriptions is the frequency distribution. A **frequency distribution** summarizes the information in a raw data matrix by showing the number of scores that fall within each of several categories.

Simple Frequency Distributions

One way to summarize a raw data matrix is to construct a **simple frequency distribution** of the data. A simple frequency distribution is a table that indicates the number of subjects who obtained each score. The possible scores are

Table 4.2	**A Simple Frequency Distribution**		
Age	Frequency	Age	Frequency
68	1	79	0
69	0	80	2
70	2	81	1
71	0	82	2
72	4	83	0
73	0	84	0
74	1	85	1
75	5	86	0
76	1	87	1
77	0	88	1
78	2		

arranged from lowest to highest. Then, in a second column, the number of scores, or **frequency** of each score, is shown. Table 4.2 shows the simple frequency distribution for the raw data matrix in Table 4.1.

Constructing a simple frequency distribution makes it easier to describe the data. For example, from looking at Table 4.2 it is easy to see the range of scores (88 − 68 = 20) and to see which scores occur most frequently (72 and 75).

Grouped Frequency Distributions

In many instances, a simple frequency distribution provides a meaningful, easily comprehended summary of the raw data. However, in other cases it is less useful. Imagine, for example, that instead of having a range of 20 (as do the data in Table 4.2), the range of the data was much greater. If the scores in the table had been IQ scores rather than the ages at which subjects expected to die, for example, the range would be larger, perhaps spanning 100 points or more. If the range had been this large, our simple frequency distribution would contain 100 rows instead of 21. Such a table would be difficult to summarize and interpret.

In cases such as this, researchers use a **grouped frequency distribution**. Rather than presenting the frequency of each individual score, a grouped frequency distribution shows the frequency of subsets of scores. To make a grouped frequency distribution, you first break the range of scores into several subsets, or **class intervals**, of equal size. For example, for the data in Table 4.2 we could clump the scores together in class intervals of three scores. Subjects who indicated they would die at ages 68, 69, and 70 could be grouped together into a single class interval, those who expected to die at 71, 72, and 73 could be grouped together, and so on. We could then indicate the frequency of scores in each of the class intervals, as shown in Table 4.3.

Table 4.3 | **A Grouped Frequency Distribution**

Class interval	Frequency
68–70	3
71–73	4
74–76	7
77–79	2
80–82	5
83–85	1
86–88	2

If you'll compare the grouped frequency distribution (Table 4.3) to the simple frequency distribution (Table 4.2), I think you'll agree that the grouped frequency distribution provides a clearer picture of the data.

You should notice three things about the grouped frequency distribution. First, the class intervals are mutually exclusive. A person could not fall into more than one class interval. Second, the class intervals capture all possible responses; there are no data in the raw data matrix that cannot be included in one of the class intervals of the grouped frequency distribution. Third, all of the class intervals are the same size. In this example, each class interval spans 3 years. All grouped frequency distributions must have these three characteristics.

Relative Frequency Distributions

In some instances, researchers include relative frequencies in a table such as this. The **relative frequency** of each class is the *proportion* of the total number of scores that falls in each class interval. It is calculated by dividing the frequency for a class interval by the total number of scores. For example, the relative frequency for the class interval 68–70 in Table 4.3 is 3/24, or .13. A relative frequency distribution is shown in Table 4.4.

Table 4.4 | **A Relative Frequency Distribution**

Class interval	Frequency	Relative frequency
68–70	3	.13 —(3 ÷ 24)
71–73	4	.17 —(4 ÷ 24)
74–76	7	.29 —(7 ÷ 24)
77–79	2	.08
80–82	5	.21
83–85	1	.04
86–88	2	.08

24 Scores

Frequency Histograms and Polygons

Simple and grouped frequency distributions provide useful summaries of data. In many cases, however, the information given in a frequency distribution is more easily grasped by others if it is presented graphically rather than in a table.

Frequency distributions are often portrayed graphically in the form of **histograms** and **bar graphs**. The horizontal *x*-axis of histograms and bar graphs presents the class intervals, and the vertical *y*-axis shows the frequency in each class interval. Bars are drawn to a height that indicates the frequency of cases in each response category. For example, if we graphed the data in Table 4.3, the histogram would look like the graph in Figure 4.1.

Although histograms and bar graphs look similar, they differ in an important way. A histogram is used when the variable on the *x*-axis is on an interval or ratio scale of measurement. Because the variable is continuous and equal differences in the scale values represent equal differences in the attribute being measured, the bars on the graph touch one another (as in Figure 4.1). However, when the variable on the *x*-axis is on a nominal or ordinal scale (and, thus, equal differences in scale values do not reflect equal differences in the characteristic being measured), the bars are separated to avoid any implication that the categories of the variable are on a continuous scale.

More commonly, researchers present frequency data as a **frequency polygon** or *line graph*. The axes on the frequency polygon are labeled just as they are for the histogram, but rather than using bars (as in the histogram), lines are drawn to connect the frequencies of the class intervals. Typically, this type of graph is used only for data that are on an interval or ratio scale. The data from Table 4.3, which was shown in Figure 4.1 as a histogram, looks like Figure 4.2 when illustrated as a line graph.

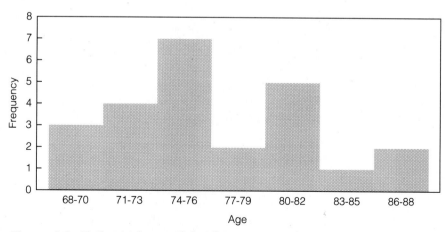

Figure 4.1   Estimated age of death

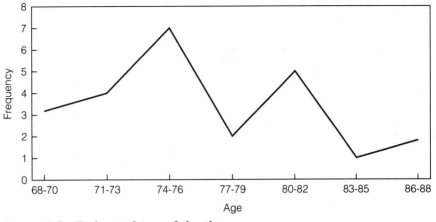

Figure 4.2 Estimated age of death

How to Lie with Statistics: Part I—Bar Charts and Line Graphs

In 1954, Darrell Huff's humorous look at the misuse of statistics, entitled *How to Lie with Statistics,* was published. Among the topics Huff discussed was what he called the "gee-whiz graph." A gee-whiz graph is a graph that, although technically accurate, is constructed in such a way as to give a misleading impression of the data, usually to catch the reader's attention or to make the data appear more striking than they really are.

Consider the graph in Figure 4.3, which shows the percentage of households in the United States that were touched by crime between 1976 and 1985. From just glancing at the graph, it is obvious that the crime rate has dropped sharply over these years. Or has it?

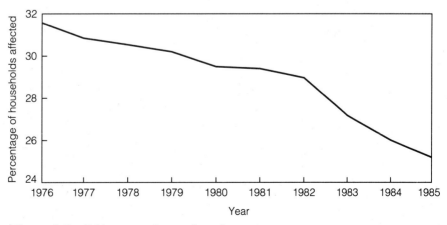

Figure 4.3 Crime rate drops sharply

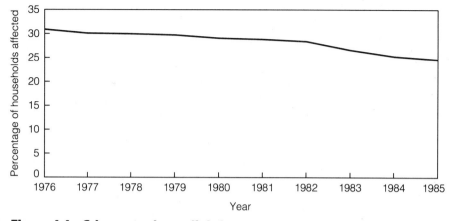

Figure 4.4   Crime rate drops slightly

Let's look at another graph of the same data. In the graph in Figure 4.4, we can see that the crime rate has indeed declined between 1976 and 1985. However, its rate of decline is nowhere as great as the one implied by the first graph.

If you'll look closely, you'll see that the two graphs present *exactly the same data*; technically speaking, they both portray the data accurately. The only difference in these graphs involves the units along the *y*-axis. The first graph used very small units and no zero line, to give the impression of a large change in the crime rate. The second graph provided a more accurate perspective by using a zero line.

A similar tactic for misleading readers employs bar graphs. Again, the *y*-axis can be adjusted to give the impression of more or less difference between categories than actually exists.

For example, the bar graph in Figure 4.5(a) shows the effects of two different antianxiety drugs on people's ratings of anxiety. From this graph it appears that subjects who took drug B expressed much less anxiety than those who took drug A.

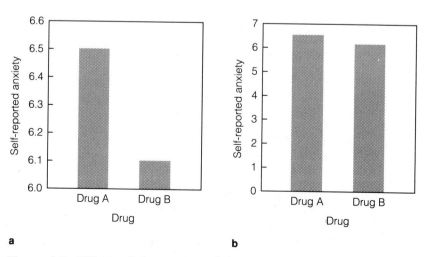

a   b

Figure 4.5   Effects of drugs on anxiety

Note, however, that the actual difference in anxiety ratings is quite small. This fact is seen more clearly when the scale on the *y*-axis is extended (Figure 4.5(b)).

Misleading readers with such graphs is common in advertising. However, the goal of research is to express the data as accurately and as honestly as possible. Rather than using gee-whiz graphs, researchers should present their data in ways that most clearly and accurately portray their findings.

Measures of Central Tendency

Frequency distributions, however they are portrayed, convey important information about subjects' responses. However, researchers are typically interested in summarizing the data for an entire group of subjects. To do this, they use descriptive statistics—numbers that summarize an entire distribution of data.

Much information can be obtained about a distribution of scores by knowing only the average or typical score in the distribution. For example, rather than presenting you with a detailed table showing you the number of hospitalized mental patients per state last year, I might simply tell you that there were an average of 4,282 patients per state. Or, rather than drawing a frequency polygon of the distribution of students' IQ scores in my city's school system, I might simply tell you that the average IQ is 104.6.

Measures of central tendency convey information about a distribution by providing information about the average or most typical score. In many instances, such descriptive statistics are all that are needed to describe the important characteristics of the data for a particular study.

Three measures of central tendency are used most often, each of which tells us something different about the data.

The mean By far, the most commonly used measure of central tendency is the **mean**, or average. As we saw in Chapter 2, the mean is calculated by summing the scores for all cases, then dividing by the number of cases:

$$\bar{y} = \Sigma y_i / n.$$

In general, the mean is the most common and useful measure of central tendency. On occasion, however, it can be misleading. Consider the raw data matrix in Table 4.5.

The mean of the the distribution in Table 4.5 is 25.3. However, as you can see, the mean overshoots all of the ages except one (an older student who was returning to college later in life). In a case such as this, the mean does not accurately represent the average or typical case. When the data are skewed such as this, researchers also report the median and the mode of the distribution.

Table 4.5	Ages of Students in a Senior Seminar
	21
	20
	21
	22
	54
	21
	20
	24
	25

The median   The **median** is the middle score of a distribution. If we rank-order the scores according to their magnitude, the median is the score that falls in the middle. Put another way, it is the score below which 50% of the measurements fall. For example, we can rank-order the 9 ages in Table 4.6.

The middle score, or median, of this distribution is 21, which more closely represents the typical score than the mean of 25.3.

The advantage of the median over the mean is that it is less affected by extreme scores, or **outliers**. In the data shown in Table 4.6, the 54-year-old student is an outlier.

The median is easy to identify when there is an odd number of scores; it is, as we said, the middle score. When there are an even number of scores, however, there is no middle score. In this case, the median falls halfway between the two middle scores. For example, if the two middle scores in a distribution were 48 and 50, the median would be 49, even though no subject actually obtained that score.

The mode   The **mode** is the most frequent score. The mode of the distribution in Table 4.6 is 21; more students were 21 years old than any other age. In this instance the mode is the same as the median, but this is not always the case.

Table 4.6	Rank-Ordered Ages
	20
	20
	21
	21
	21 ← Median
	22
	24
	25
	54

If all of the scores in the distribution are different, there is no mode. Occasionally, a distribution may have more than one mode. Such distributions are called bimodal (two modes) or trimodal (three modes).

DEVELOPING YOUR RESEARCH SKILLS

How to Lie with Statistics: Part II—Central Tendency

In *How to Lie with Statistics*, Huff also discussed the misleading uses of measures of central tendency. He pointed out that, in everyday language, the word *average* has a loose meaning and can be used to indicate mean, median, or mode. If the reader does not know which use is meant, he or she may be misled.

Imagine that you own a business and that you have 10 employees. Five of them earn $25,000 a year, 4 earn $35,000 a year, and 1 earns $50,000 a year. As owner, your salary is approximately $100,000. Your employees want to know the average salary in the company (including yours) for last year. What do you tell them?

On the one hand, you could report the *mean* salary, which would be $37,727.27. This might create some hostility among your employees, however, because all but one of them would perceive they are being paid less than average.

Alternatively, you could report that the *modal* salary was $25,000. Although perfectly accurate, such a statement distorts the true distribution, ignoring the higher salaries.

Finally, you could tell them that the *median* salary was $35,000: In this instance, the median seems to distort the true picture least. Even so, it hides the extreme range of salaries in the company.

Although behavioral researchers generally prefer the mean over the median and mode as a measure of central tendency, they are alert to instances in which the mean fails to describe the data accurately. In many cases, researchers report all three measures of central tendency to provide the fullest and clearest picture of their data.

Measures of Variability

In the example above, your employees would have learned additional information about company salaries if given information about the *variability* in the salaries. In addition to knowing the average or typical score in a data distribution, it is helpful to know how much the scores in the distribution vary.

Among other things, knowing about the variability in a distribution tells us how typical the mean is of the scores as a set. If the variability in a set of data is very small, the mean is representative of the scores as a whole. When variability is small, the mean tells us a great deal about the typical subject's score. On the other hand, if the variability is large, the mean is not very representative of the scores as a set.

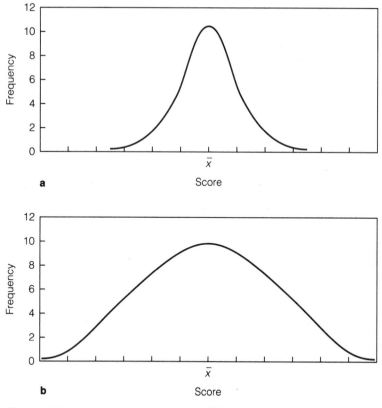

Figure 4.6   Small and large variability

This principle is shown by the two graphs in Figure 4.6. Both of the distributions have the same mean, median, and mode. However, as you can see, the variability of the distribution on the top (Figure 4.6(a)) is much less than the variability of the distribution on the bottom (Figure 4.6(b)). This indicates that the mean is a better indicator of subjects' scores in the upper distribution. In fact, if asked to guess what any particular subject's score was in Figure 4.6(a), we would not be too far off if we guessed the mean. Because the variability in Figure 4.6(b) is much greater, the mean is not a good indicator of the scores as a set. Guessing the mean for a particular subject would probably miss his or her score by a wide margin.

Put another way, the variability tells us how homogeneous versus heterogeneous the subjects are on the attribute being measured. Large variability indicates that the subjects are heterogeneous, whereas low variability indicates that the subjects are more homogeneous. To examine the extent to which scores in a distribution vary from one another (and, thus, the degree to which the scores are homogeneous versus heterogeneous), researchers use **measures of variability**—descriptive statistics that convey information about the spread or variability of a set of data.

We discussed the most commonly used measures of variability in Chapter 2, but will review them briefly here.

The range   We saw that the **range** was the difference between the largest and smallest scores in a distribution. The range is the least useful of the measures of variability because it is based entirely on the two extreme scores and does not take the variability of the remaining scores into account.

The variance and standard deviation   The variance and standard deviation are much more useful. When we learned how to calculate these important descriptive statistics in Chapter 2, we learned that they are based on the sum of the squared differences between each score and the mean. (You may want to quickly review the material on the variance and standard deviation in Chapter 2.)

The standard deviation is more often used as a descriptive statistic than is the variance because the standard deviation is expressed in the same units as the original measurements, whereas the variance is expressed in squared units.

SUMMARY

1. Researchers attempt to describe their data in ways that are accurate, concise, and easily understood.

2. Some methods of describing data are graphical, such as histograms and line graphs, whereas other methods, such as the mean and variance, are numerical.

3. A simple frequency distribution is a table that indicates the number (frequency) of subjects who obtained each score.

4. A grouped frequency distribution indicates the frequency of scores that fall in each of several mutually exclusive class intervals. Often, the proportion of scores falling in each class interval is also presented—a relative frequency distribution.

5. Histograms, bar graphs, and frequency polygons (line graphs) are common graphical methods of describing data.

6. A full statistical description of a set of data usually involves both measures of central tendency (mean, median, mode) as well as measures of variability (range, variance, standard deviation).

7. The mean is the numerical average of a set of scores, the median is the middle score when a set of scores is rank ordered, and the mode is the most common score. The mean is the most commonly used measure of central tendency, but it can be misleading if the data are very skewed.

8. The range is the difference between the largest and smallest scores. The variance and its square root (the standard deviation) indicate the total

variability in a set of data. Among other things, the variability in a set of data indicates how representative the mean is of the scores as a whole.

KEY TERMS

raw data	bar graph
raw data matrix	frequency polygon
graphical method	measures of central tendency
numerical method	mean
frequency distribution	median
simple frequency distribution	outlier
frequency	mode
grouped frequency distribution	measures of variability
class interval	range
relative frequency	variance
histogram	standard deviation

REVIEW QUESTIONS

1. What three criteria characterize good descriptions of data?
2. Why might it be said that the raw data matrix is the most accurate, but least useful, way of describing data?
3. Distinguish between graphical and numerical methods of describing data.
4. Under what conditions is a grouped frequency distribution more useful as a means of describing a set of scores than a simple frequency distribution? Why do researchers often add relative frequencies to their tables?
5. What three rules govern the construction of a grouped frequency distribution?
6. What are the most commonly used measures of central tendency? What are the most commonly used measures of variability?
7. Discuss the conditions under which the median is a more meaningful measure of central tendency than the mean.
8. Why do researchers prefer the standard deviation over the range as a measure of variability?

EXERCISES

Imagine that you have collected the following set of IQ scores:

110	124	100	125	104	119
98	130	76	95	143	90
132	102	125	96	99	78

100	80	112	112	103	88
94	108	88	132	87	119
109	104	104	100	119	99
135	128	92	110	90	92
120	95	110	78		

1. Construct a simple frequency distribution of these scores.
2. Construct a grouped frequency distribution of these scores that includes both frequencies and relative frequencies.
3. Construct a frequency polygon, using the grouped frequency data.
4. Find the mean, median, and mode of the data. Does one of these measures of central tendency represent the data better than the others?

Sampling in Behavioral Research

Among the decisions behavioral scientists face when they design research is the selection of subjects to participate in the study. Researchers can rarely examine every individual in the population that is relevant to their interests—all newborns, all paranoid schizophrenics, all color-blind adults, all registered voters in California, all female porpoises, or whatever. Rather than trying to study every subject in the relevant population, researchers collect data from a subset, or **sample,** of subjects in the population. **Sampling** is the process by which a researcher selects a sample of subjects for a study from the population of interest.

Samples are of two types: probability samples and nonprobability samples.

Probability Samples

The purpose of much research is to accurately describe the thoughts, feelings, or behavior of a larger population on the basis of data collected from a smaller sample. In survey research, for example, the goal is to estimate the attitudes or behavior of a large group from the answers of a small number of respondents. When accurate description is the goal, researchers must ensure that the sample they select is representative of the population. A **representative sample** is one from which we can draw accurate, unbiased estimates of the characteristics of the larger population. Only if we have a representative sample can we draw accurate inferences about the population from data obtained on the sample.

Unfortunately, samples rarely mirror their parent populations in every respect. The characteristics of the individuals selected for the sample almost always differ somewhat from the characteristics of the general population.

This difference, called **sampling error,** leads to results that differ from what would have been obtained had the entire population been studied.

Fortunately, when certain sampling procedures—known as probability sampling techniques—are used, researchers can estimate how much error is in their sample data. The **error of estimation** (also called the *margin of error)* specifies the degree to which the data obtained from the sample would be expected to deviate from the population as a whole. For example, you may have heard television newscasters report the results of a political opinion poll, then add that the results "are accurate within 3 percentage points." What this means is that if 45% of the respondents in the sample endorsed Smith for President, we know that there is a 95% probability that the true percentage of people in the population who support Smith is between 42% and 48% (that is, 45% ±3%).

Researchers can calculate the error of estimation only if they know the probability that a particular individual in the population was included in the sample. Probability samples are used for this purpose. When a **probability sample** is used, the researcher can specify the probability that any individual in the population will be included in the sample. Typically, for example, researchers use an **epsem design,** which specifies that all cases in the population have an equal probability of being chosen for the sample (Schuman & Kalton, 1985). (Epsem stands for *equal-probability selection method.*) Knowing the probability that a particular case will be included in the sample tells the researcher how representative the sample is of the population and allows him or her to estimate the sampling error.

Probability samples may be obtained in several ways, but the three basic methods involve simple random sampling, stratified random sampling, and cluster sampling.

Simple Random Sampling

When a sample is chosen in such a way that every possible sample of the desired size has the same chance of being selected from the population, the sample is a **simple random sample.** For example, suppose we want to select a sample of 200 subjects from a school district that has 5,000 students. If we wanted a simple random sample, we would select our sample in such a way that every possible combination of 200 students has the same probability of being chosen.

To obtain a simple random sample, the researcher must have a **sampling frame**—a listing of the population from which the sample will be drawn. Then subjects are chosen randomly from this list.

You might think that you could simply take every 25th name from the list to get your sample of 200. Although this procedure, called **systematic sampling,** is sometimes used, it is not a truly random procedure; after all, the names may be listed in some particular order. If the names were in alphabetical order, for example, most children from the same family (that is, those with the same last name) would be listed together. Taking every 25th name would preclude the possibility of obtaining any siblings in the sample, thereby introducing a systematic bias into the sample.

Generally, researchers prefer to use a truly random procedure. If the population is small, one approach is to write the name of each case in the population on a slip of paper, shuffle the slips of paper, then pull slips out until a sample of the desired size is obtained. For example, we could have each of the 5,000 students' names typed on cards, shuffle the cards, then randomly pick 200.

However, with larger populations, pulling names "out of a hat" becomes unwieldy. One common procedure is to use a **table of random numbers**. A portion of such a table is shown in Table 5.1, along with an explanation of how to use it.

Table 5.1	**Random Numbers**

54	83	80	53	90	50	90	46	47	12	62	68	30	91	21	01	37	36	20
36	85	49	83	47	89	46	28	59	02	87	98	10	47	22	67	27	33	13
60	98	76	53	02	01	82	77	45	12	68	13	09	20	73	07	92	53	45
62	79	39	83	88	02	60	92	82	00	76	30	77	98	45	00	97	78	16
43	32	31	21	10	50	42	16	85	20	74	29	64	72	59	58	96	30	73

DEVELOPING YOUR RESEARCH SKILLS

Using a Table of Random Numbers

When researchers want to obtain a random sample from a larger population, they often use a table of random numbers. The numbers on such a table are generated randomly, usually by a computer, such that there is absolutely no order to the sequence of numbers in the table. A small portion of a table of random numbers is shown below for demonstrational purposes. A complete table of random numbers appears in Appendix A-1.

You will note that the table consists of two-digit numbers (54, 83, 80 . . .). These are arranged in columns to make them easier to read and use. In practice, you should disregard the two-digit numbers and columns and think of the table as a very long list of single-digit numbers (5, 4, 8, 3, 8, 0, 5, 3, 9, 0 . . .).

To use the table to select a random sample, you would first number the cases in your population. For example, if the school system from which you were sampling had 5,000 students, you would number the students from 0001 to 5000.

Then, beginning anywhere in the table, you would take 200 sets of four-digit numbers. For example, let's say you randomly entered the table at the fifth digit in the second row:

36 85 49 83 47 89 46 28 59 02 87 98 10 47 22 67 27 33 13

↑

Imagine you selected this digit as your starting point.

Starting with this number, you would take the next four digits, which are 4983. Thus, the first subject you would select for your sample would be the student who was no. 4983 in your original list of 5000. The next four digits are 4789, so you would take student no. 4789 for your sample. The third subject to be taken from the population would be no. 4628 because the next four digits on the table are 4628.

The next four digits are 5902. However, there were only 5,000 students in the population, so student no. 5902 does not exist. Similarly, the next four digits, 8798, are out of the range of your population size. You would ignore numbers on the table that exceed the size of the population, such as 5902 and 8798. However, the next four digits, 1047, do represent a student in the population—no. 1047—and this student would be included in the sample.

You would continue this process until you reached your desired sample size. In our example, in which we wanted a sample of 200, we would continue until we obtained 200 four-digit random numbers between 0001 and 5000, inclusive. (Obviously, to draw a sample of 200, you would need to use the full table in Appendix A-1 rather than the small portion of the table shown here.) The cases in the population that correspond to these numbers would then be used in the sample.

Tables of random numbers are used for purposes other than selecting a sample. For example, when using an experimental design, researchers must assign subjects to the various experimental conditions in a random fashion. A random numbers table can be used to ensure that the manner in which subjects are assigned to conditions is truly random. We'll return to this use of random numbers in a later chapter.

Stratified Random Sampling

Stratified random sampling is a variation of simple random sampling. Rather than selecting cases directly from the population, we first divide the population into two or more strata. A **stratum** is a subset of the population that shares a particular characteristic. For example, we might divide the population into men and women, or into six age ranges (20–29, 30–39, 40–49, 50–59, 60–69, over 69). Then, cases are randomly sampled from each of the strata.

By first dividing the population into strata, we sometimes increase the probability that the subjects we select will be representative of those in the population. In addition, stratification ensures that the researcher has an adequate number of subjects from each strata so that he or she can analyze differences in responses among the various strata. For example, the researcher might want to compare younger respondents (20–29 years old) with older respondents (60–69 years old). By first stratifying the sample, the researcher ensures that there will be an ample number of both young and old respondents in the sample.

Cluster Sampling

Although they provide us with the most accurate pictures of the population, simple and stratified random sampling have a major drawback. To use random sampling, we must have a sampling frame of all of the cases in the population; only then can we specify the probability than any particular case will be included in the sample and be assured that our sample was selected truly at random. Obtaining the listing for small, easily identified populations is no problem. You would find it relatively easy to obtain a list of all students in your college or all members of the American Psychological Society, for example.

Unfortunately, not all populations are easily identified. Could we, for example, obtain a list of every person in the United States or, for that matter, in New York City? Could we get a sampling frame of all Hispanic 3-year-olds, all retired persons in California, or all single-parent families in Canada headed by the father? In cases such as these, random sampling is not possible, because without a listing we cannot locate potential subjects or specify the probability that a particular case will be included in the sample.

In such instances, **cluster sampling** is typically used. To obtain a cluster sample, the researcher first samples not subjects, but groupings or **clusters** of subjects. These clusters are often based on naturally occurring groupings, such as geographical areas or particular institutions. For example, if we wanted a sample of elementary school children in West Virginia, we might first randomly sample from the 55 county school systems in West Virginia. Perhaps we would pick 15 counties at random. Then, after selecting this small random sample of counties, we could get lists of students for those counties and obtain random samples of students from the selected counties.

Often, cluster sampling involves a **multistage sampling** process in which we begin by sampling large clusters, then we sample smaller clusters from within the large clusters, then we sample even smaller clusters, and finally we obtain our sample of subjects. For example, we could randomly pick counties, then randomly choose several particular schools from the selected counties. We could then randomly select particular classrooms from the schools we selected, and finally randomly sample students from each classroom.

Cluster sampling has two distinct advantages. First, a sampling frame of the population is not needed to begin, only a listing of the clusters. In this example, all we would need to start is a list of counties in West Virginia—a list that would be far easier to obtain than a census of all children enrolled in West Virginia schools. Then, after sampling the clusters, we can get lists of students within each cluster (that is, county) that was selected, which is much easier than getting a census for the entire population of students in West Virginia.

The second advantage is that, if each cluster represents a grouping of subjects that are close together geographically (such as students in a certain county or school), less time and effort are required to contact the subjects. Focusing on only 15 West Virginia counties would require considerably less time, effort, and expense than sampling students from all 55 counties in that state.

BEHAVIORAL RESEARCH CASE STUDY

A Survey Researcher's Nightmare

In 1936, the magazine *Literary Digest* polled a sample of more than 2 million voters regarding their preference for Alfred Landon versus Franklin Roosevelt in the upcoming presidential election. Based on the responses they received, the *Digest* predicted that Landon would defeat Roosevelt by approximately 15 percentage points. When the election was held, however, Roosevelt was elected President by a wide margin—62% versus 38% of the popular vote! What happened?

The problem was purely one of sampling. The names of the respondents contacted for the poll were taken from telephone directories and automobile registration lists. This sampling procedure had yielded accurate predictions in the presidential elections of 1920, 1924, 1928, and 1932. However, the problem was that in 1936 people who had telephones and automobiles were not representative of voters in the country at large. In the aftermath of the Great Depression, many voters had neither cars nor phones, and those voters overwhelmingly supported Roosevelt. Because the sample was not representative, the results of the survey were biased.

Today, many surveys are conducted by telephone. The bias encountered in the *Literary Digest* poll of 1936 is less of a problem today, however, because over 90% of American households have telephones (Schuman & Kalton, 1985). Even so, a slight bias is introduced when only telephone owners are polled.

Sample Size and the Error of Estimation

Probability samples allow researchers to estimate the error in their sample data and to specify how confident they are that the sample results accurately reflect the behavior of the population. Their confidence is expressed in terms of the error of estimation.

The smaller the error of estimation, the more closely the results from the sample estimate the behavior of the larger population. For example, if the limits on the error of estimation are only ±1%, the sample data are a better indicator of the population than if the limits on the error of estimation are ±10%. Obviously, researchers prefer the error of estimation to be as small as possible.

The error of estimation is a function of sample size, population size, and variance of the data.

Most important is the size of the sample. The larger a probability sample, the more similar to the population the sample tends to be (that is, the smaller the sampling error) and the more accurately the data estimate the population. In light of this, you might expect that researchers always obtain as large a sample as possible. This is not the case, however. Rather, researchers opt for an **economic sample**—one that provides a reasonably accurate estimate of the population (within a few percentage points, for example) at reasonable effort and cost. After a sample of a certain size is obtained, collecting additional data does little to add to the accuracy of the results.

For example, if we are trying to estimate the percentage of voters in a population of 10,000 who will vote for a particular candidate in a very close election, interviewing a sample of 500 will allow us to estimate the percentage of voters in the population who will support each candidate within nine percentage points. Increasing the sample size to 1,000 (an increase of 500 respondents) lowers the error of estimation to only 3%. However, adding an additional 500 subjects to the sample beyond that helps relatively little; with 1,500 respondents in the sample, the error of estimation drops only to 2.3%. From a practical standpoint, it may make little sense to increase the sample size beyond 1,000 in this instance. Formulas have been developed for determining the most economical sample size.

The error of estimation also is affected by the size of the population from which the sample was drawn. Imagine we have two samples of 200 respondents. The first was drawn from a population of 400, the second from a population of 10 million. In which sample would we expect the results to more closely mirror the behavior of the population? I think you can guess that the error of estimation will be lower when the population contains 400 cases than when it contains 10 million cases.

The third factor that affects the error of estimation is the variance of the data. The greater the variability in the data, the more difficult it is to estimate the population accurately. We saw in earlier chapters that the larger the variance, the less representative the mean is of the scores as a whole. As a result, the larger the variance in the data, the larger the sample must be to draw accurate inferences about the population.

DEVELOPING YOUR RESEARCH SKILLS

Calculating the Error of Estimation

Formulas have been developed for calculating the error of estimation for various kinds of probability samples. The details of these formulas go beyond the scope of this book, but one example will show how they work.

For our example, let's return to the data we collected from 6 respondents regarding attitudes toward capital punishment (Chapter 2). Let's assume that the 6 respondents were a random sample chosen from a class of 40 students, and that we want to estimate the average attitude toward capital punishment in the class (the population) from the sample.

To refresh your memory, the scores for the 6 subjects were 4, 1, 2, 2, 4, and 3. (Recall that these were responses on a 5-point scale, where 1 indicates opposition and 5 indicates support for capital punishment.) The mean of the six scores was 2.67 and the variance was 1.47.

To calculate the error of estimation, we use the following formula:

$$\text{Error of estimation} = 2\sqrt{\left(\frac{s^2}{n}\right)\left(\frac{N-n}{N}\right)}$$

where s^2 is the variance of the data (1.47), n is the size of the sample (6), and N is the size of the population (40).

Entering the appropriate numbers, we get

$$E = 2\sqrt{(1.47/6)\,(40-6/40)}$$
$$= 2\sqrt{(0.25)(0.85)}$$
$$= 2\sqrt{(0.21)}$$
$$= 2\,(0.46)$$
$$= 0.92$$

The error of estimation is 0.92. This means there is a 95% probability that the true average attitude toward capital punishment in the population is 2.67 (the mean of the sample) ± 0.92.

Nonprobability Samples

Sometimes, it is impossible, impractical, or unnecessary for a researcher to obtain a probability sample. In such cases, nonprobability samples are used. With a **nonprobability sample,** the researcher has no way of knowing the probability that a particular case will be chosen for the sample. As a result, there is no way to determine precisely how representative the sample is of the population at large or to calculate the error of estimation.

Three primary types of nonprobability samples include convenience, quota, and purposive samples.

Convenience Sampling

In **convenience sampling,** the researcher simply uses whatever subjects are readily available. Subjects are chosen until a sample of the desired size is obtained without regard to its representativeness. For example, we could stop the first 150 shoppers we encounter on a downtown street. Or we could sample people waiting in an airport or bus station, or patients at a local hospital.

Most commonly, behavioral researchers use convenience samples of introductory psychology students as subjects for their experiments. No one argues that students are representative of people in general or even of 18-to-22-year-olds. Even so, such samples are often used because they are convenient.

Although using students as subjects does not necessarily invalidate the results of a study, researchers should be aware of the potential biases involved in student samples. For example, college students tend to be more intelligent than the general population. They also tend to come from middle- and upper-class backgrounds, and to hold slightly more liberal attitudes than the population-at-large.

Further sampling biases are introduced when students are asked to *volunteer* to participate in research. Volunteers tend to differ in systematic ways from students who choose not to volunteer. Volunteers tend to be more unconventional, more self-confident, more extroverted, and higher in need for achievement (Bell, 1962).

Quota Sampling

A **quota sample** is a convenience sample in which the researcher takes steps to ensure that certain kinds of subjects are obtained in particular proportions. The researcher specifies in advance that the sample will contain certain percentages of particular kinds of subjects. For example, if a researcher wanted to obtain an equal proportion of male and female subjects, he or she might decide to obtain 75 women and 75 men in a sample obtained on a downtown street.

Purposive Sampling

In **purposive sampling,** the researcher uses his or her judgment to decide which respondents to include in the sample. The researcher tries to choose respondents that are typical of the population. Unfortunately, researchers' judgments are not a trustworthy way of selecting a sample.

One area in which purposive sampling has been used successfully involves forecasting the results of national elections. Based on previous elections, it is possible to identify particular areas of the country that tend to vote like the country as a whole. Voters from these areas are then interviewed and their political preferences used to predict the outcome of an upcoming election.

IN DEPTH

Sampling and Gender Differences

The nature of one's sample has a direct impact on the results that are obtained in a study. If the sample is biased or nonrepresentative, erroneous conclusions may be drawn from the data.

A case in point involves the use of samples that consist entirely of one sex or the other (Grady, 1981). In the early days of psychology, when a disproportionate number of college students were men, researchers commonly used only male subjects in research. For example, early work on achievement motivation (McClelland, Atkinson, Clark, & Lowell, 1953) used only male subjects. Even as late as 1968, an analysis of articles in the *Journal of Personality and Social Psychology*—one of the leading journals in behavioral science—showed that all-male samples were used twice as frequently as all-female samples (31% versus 15%; Carlson, 1971). Interestingly, this trend may have reversed during the 1970s. A study by Reardon and Prescott (1977) found more all-female than all-male samples.

Either way, at least one fourth of behavioral research uses only one sex or the other. In many instances, single-sex samples are justified by the researcher's interest; a study of postpartum depression necessarily involves a female sample, for example. The problem is that the vast majority of the studies that use only one sex generalize their findings to the population as a whole (Reardon & Prescott, 1977).

Are findings obtained with members of one sex generalizable to the other? Often they are. Studies that look for potential sex differences often find none; men and women respond similarly in many respects. However, many findings are specific to one sex or the other. A researcher is never justified in generalizing from the behavior of one sex to the behavior of people in general. Only by using samples composed of both men and women can conclusions be drawn about ways in which the sexes do or do not differ from one another.

Probability Versus Nonprobability Samples

Few behavioral researchers question the superiority of probability over nonprobability samples. Without a doubt, probability samples provide the most valid picture of the population of interest. However, it may surprise you to learn that relatively little psychological research uses probability samples.

When a researcher is interested in accurately describing the typical attitudes, feelings, or behavior of a particular population, probability sampling is a necessity. Without probability sampling, we cannot be sure of the degree to which the data provided by the sample approximate the behavior of the larger population. Thus, in survey research, such as political opinion polls, probability sampling is essential.

The difficulty with probability sampling, however, is that it is time-consuming, expensive, and difficult, if not impossible in many instances. For example, a developmental psychologist who was interested in studying language development would have a difficult time obtaining a probability sample of all preschool children in the United States. Similarly, a psychophysiologist who was interested in hearing loss would not be able to obtain a probability sample of all deaf people.

Although probability samples are desirable, they are virtually never used in experimental research. As we've seen, much psychological research is conducted on convenience samples of college students, samples that are not representative of all people or even of college-age students as a whole. Similarly, the animals used in behavioral research are never sampled randomly from all animals of that species, but rather consist of particular species that were raised for laboratory use. You might wonder, then, about the validity of research that does not use probability samples.

Although probability samples are preferable, nonprobability samples are useful as long as researchers keep three considerations in mind.

First, although the results of a particular experiment may be suspect because a nonprobability sample was used, the generalizability of the findings can be assessed through replication. The same experiment can be conducted using other samples of subjects who differ in age, education level, socioeconomic status, region of the country, and so on. If similar findings are obtained using several different samples, we have increased faith in the validity of the results. Unfortunately, most studies are never systematically replicated.

Second, the goal of much research is not to describe how a particular population behaves. In most experimental research, for example, the purpose is to test hypotheses regarding the effects of particular variables on behavior. Hypotheses are derived from theories, then research is conducted to see whether the predicted effects of the independent variables are obtained. To the extent that many of the processes studied in experimental research are basic, there is often little reason to expect different samples to respond differently. If this is true, then it matters little what kind of sample one uses. The processes involved will be similar. Of course, we cannot blithely assume that certain psychological processes are, in fact, universal; only replication can show whether findings generalize across samples. But it is erroneous to automatically assume that research conducted on nonprobability samples tells us nothing about people in general.

Finally, although the nature of one's sample is important, other considerations sometimes outweigh sampling as researchers design their studies. For example, experimental psychologists are willing to risk sampling bias to increase their control over experimental variables. Furthermore, the time and expense involved in obtaining a representative sample would prohibit much important research from being done at all. Researchers must weigh the advantages of probability samples against other considerations.

BEHAVIORAL RESEARCH CASE STUDY

Sampling and Sex Surveys

People are understandably interested in how they compare with others. One dimension that people are often interested in is sexual behavior. Am I more or less sexually active than other people my age? How do my attitudes about sex compare to most other people's? Do I have more or fewer anxieties about sex than others do?

The first major surveys of sexual behavior were published by Kinsey, Pomeroy, and Martin in 1948 (*Sexual Behavior in the Human Male*) and by Kinsey et al. in 1953 (*Sexual Behavior in the Human Female*). Kinsey's researchers interviewed over 10,000 American men and women, asking about their sexual histories and current sexual practices. You might think that with such a large sample, Kinsey would have obtained valid data regarding sexual behavior in the United States. Unfortunately, although Kinsey's data are often cited as if they reflect the typical sexual experiences of Americans, his sampling techniques do not permit us to draw confident conclusions about sexual behavior in this country.

Rather than using a probability sample that would have allowed him to calculate the error of estimation in his data, Kinsey relied upon what he called "100 percent sampling." His researchers would contact a particular group, such as a professional organization or sorority, then obtain responses from 100% of its members. Although 100% samples were obtained, the groups were not selected at random. As a result, there were a disproportionate number of respondents from Indiana in the sample, as well as an overabundance of college students, Protestants, and well-educated people (Kirby, 1977). In an analysis of Kinsey's sampling technique, Cochran, Mosteller, and Tukey (1953) concluded that because he had not used a probability sample, Kinsey's results "must be regarded as subject to systematic errors of unknown magnitude due to selective sampling" (p. 711).

Recent surveys of sexual behavior have encountered similar difficulties. For example, in the Hunt (1974) survey, 24 American cities were selected. Then names were chosen at random from the phone books for these cities. This technique produced three sampling biases. First, the cities were not selected randomly. Second, by selecting names from the phone book, the survey overlooked people without phones and those with unlisted numbers (approximately one fourth of the population). Third, only 20% of the people who were contacted agreed to participate in the study; how these respondents differed from those who declined is impossible to judge.

Several popular magazines—such as *McCall's, Psychology Today,* and *Redbook*— have also conducted large surveys of sexual behavior. Again, probability samples were not obtained and thus the accuracy of their data is questionable. The most obvious sampling bias in these surveys is that only people who can read responded to the questionnaire in the magazines, thereby eliminating the estimated 10% of the adult population that is illiterate. Also, readers of particular magazines are unlikely to be representative of the population at large.

In fairness to all of these studies, obtaining accurate information about sexual behavior is a difficult and delicate task. Aside from the problems associated with obtaining any probability sample, the fact that a high percentage of people will refuse to answer questions about sexuality biases the findings. The bottom line is that although the results of such surveys are interesting, we should not regard them as true indicators of sexual behavior in the general population.

S U M M A R Y

1. Sampling is the process by which a researcher selects a group of subjects for research (the sample) from a larger population.
2. When a probability sample is used, the researcher can specify the probability that any individual in the population will be included in the sample. In a probability sample, the degree to which the data obtained from the sample accurately reflect the population—the error of estimation—can be estimated.
3. Most probability samples are selected by epsem—an equal-probability selection method. Simple random samples, for example, are selected in such a way that every possible sample of the desired size has an equal probability of being chosen.
4. Researchers often use a table of random numbers to select random samples.
5. A stratified random sample is chosen by first dividing the population into subsets or strata that share a particular characteristic. Then subjects are sampled randomly from each stratum.
6. In cluster sampling, the researcher first samples groupings or clusters of subjects, then samples subjects from the selected clusters. In multistage sampling, the researcher sequentially samples clusters from within clusters before choosing the final sample of subjects.
7. Error of estimation is a function of the size of the sample, the size of the population, and the variance of the data. Researchers usually opt for an

economical sample that provides an acceptably low error of estimation at reasonable cost and effort.

8. When nonprobability samples—such as convenience, quota, and purposive samples—are used, the researcher has no way of determining the degree to which they are representative of the population, nor of calculating the error of estimation. Even so, nonprobability samples are used far more often in behavioral research than probability samples.

KEY TERMS

sample
sampling
representative sample
sampling error
error of estimation
probability sample
epsem design
simple random sample
sampling frame
systematic sampling
table of random numbers

stratified random sample
stratum
cluster sampling
cluster
multistage sampling
economic sample
nonprobability sample
convenience sample
quota sample
purposive sample

REVIEW QUESTIONS

1. Why are probability samples generally preferred over nonprobability samples?
2. What is the central difficulty involved in obtaining simple random samples from large populations?
3. How does cluster sampling solve the practical problems involved in simple random sampling?
4. What is the difference between a stratum and a cluster?
5. What is the drawback of obtaining random samples by telephone?
6. What does the error of estimation tell us about the results of a study conducted using probability sampling?
7. What happens to the error of estimation as one's sample size increases?
8. What factors affect the error of estimation?
9. What type of sample is used most frequently in behavioral research?
10. What are the advantages and disadvantages of using convenience samples?
11. Why do behavioral researchers tend to use nonprobability samples more frequently than probability samples despite the obvious advantages of probability sampling?

EXERCISES

1. Suppose that you wanted to obtain a simple random sample of lawyers in your state. How would you do it?

2. Suppose that you wanted to study children who have Down's syndrome. How might you use cluster sampling to obtain a probability sample of children with Down's syndrome in your state?

3. Using the table of random numbers in Appendix A-1, draw a stratified random sample of 10 boys and 10 girls from the population below:

Tom	Ed	Jenny
Jerry	Dale	David
Kevin	Erin	Ashley
Chris	Eleanor	Stacey
Collin	Tom	Ryan
Allison	Bryce	Andrew
Shannon	Gary	Patrick
Daniel	Ann	Rick
Susan	Robert	Kelly
Robin	Taylor	Sam
Mark	Greg	Teresa
Wendy	Pam	Marilyn
Bill	Jack	Richard
Vincent	Jim	Barry
Anne	Kathy	Paul
Brenda	Philip	Elvis
Rowland	Debbie	Elisha
Gail	Patsy	Mike
Jon	Julie	Betsy

4. Imagine that you are a researcher employed by a local board of education. The board wants to know the average IQ of the 2,500 seventh-grade students in your school district. You administer an IQ test to a simple random sample of 350 students and find that the mean IQ score for this group is 103.7 and the variance is 196. Calculate the error of estimation and tell how you would explain your findings to the members of the school board (who we will imagine know nothing about research or sampling).

6

Correlational Research

My grandfather, a farmer for over 50 years, has told me on several occasions that the color and thickness of a caterpillar's coat is related to the severity of the coming winter. When "woolly worms" have dark, thick furry coats, he says, we can expect an unusually harsh winter.

Whether this common bit of folk wisdom is true, I don't know. But like my grandfather, we all hold many beliefs about associations between events in the world. Some of our beliefs are true; others are undoubtedly false. Many people believe, for instance, that hair color is related to personality—that people with red hair have fiery tempers and that blondes are of less-than-average intelligence. Others think that geniuses are particularly likely to suffer from mental disorders or that people who live in large cities are apathetic and uncaring. Those who believe in astrology claim that the date on which a person is born is associated with the person's personality later in life. Sailors capitalize on the relationship between the appearance of the sky and approaching storms, as indicated by the old saying: Red sky at night, sailor's delight; red sky at morning, sailors take warning. You probably hold many such beliefs about things that tend to go together.

Like all of us, behavioral researchers are also interested in whether certain variables are related to each other. Are SAT scores related to college grades? Is outside temperature related to the incidence of urban violence? To what extent are children's IQ scores related to the IQs of their parents? Is shyness associated with low self-esteem? Each of these questions asks whether two variables (such as SAT scores and grades) are related and, if so, how strongly they are related.

When researchers are interested in such questions, they often conduct **correlational research.** Correlational research is used to describe the relationship between two or more naturally occurring variables. Before delving into details regarding correlational research, let's look at an example of a correlational study that we'll return to throughout the chapter.

Personality Resemblance Between Children and Parents

Since the earliest days of psychology, researchers have debated the relative importance of genetic versus environmental influences on behavior—often dubbed the nature–nurture controversy. Scientists have disagreed regarding whether people's behaviors are affected more by their inborn biological makeup or by their experiences in life. Most psychologists now agree that the debate is a complex one—that behavior and mental ability are a product of *both* inborn and environmental factors. So rather than discuss whether a particular behavior should be classified as *innate* or *acquired,* researchers have turned their attention to studying the interactive effects of nature and nurture on behavior, and to identifying aspects of behavior that are more affected by nature than nurture, and vice versa.

Part of this work has focused on the relationship between the personalities of children and their parents. Common observation tells us that children display many of the characteristics of their parents. But is this due to genetic factors or to the fact that the parents raised their children in a particular way? Is this resemblance due to nature or to nurture?

If we only study children who were raised by their natural parents, we cannot answer this question; both genetic and environmental influences can explain similarities between children and their biological parents. For this reason, many researchers have turned their attention to children who were adopted in infancy. Because any resemblance between children and their adoptive parents is unlikely to be due to genetic factors, it must be due to environmental variables.

In one such study, Sandra Scarr and her colleagues administered several personality measures to 120 adolescents and their natural parents, and to 115 adolescents and their adoptive parents (Scarr, Webber, Weinberg, & Wittig, 1981). These scales measured a number of personality traits, including introversion–extraversion (the tendency to be inhibited versus outgoing) and neuroticism (the tendency to be anxious and insecure). The researchers wanted to know whether children's personalities were related more closely to their natural parents' personalities or to their adoptive parents' personalities.

This study produced a wealth of data, a small portion of which is shown in Table 6.1. This table shows **correlation coefficients** that indicate the nature of the relationships between the children's and parents' personalities. As we'll learn in detail below, these correlation coefficients indicate both the strength and direction of the relationship between parents' and children's scores on the two personality measures. In one column are the correlations between children

| Table 6.1 | **Correlations Between Children's and Parents' Personalities** | |

Personality measure	Biological parents	Adoptive parents
Introversion–extraversion	.19	.00
Neuroticism	.25	.05

and their biological parents, and in the other column are correlations between children and their adoptive parents.

This table can tell us a great deal about the relationship between children's and parents' personalities, but first we must learn how to interpret correlation coefficients.

The Correlation Coefficient

A **correlation coefficient** is a statistic that indicates the degree to which two variables are related to one another. In the study just described, the researchers were interested in the relationship between children's personalities and those of their parents. Any two variables can be correlated: self-esteem and shyness, enjoyment of rock music and hearing acuity, marijuana use and scores on a test of memory, and so on. We could even do a study that looked at the correlation between the thickness of caterpillars' coats and winter temperatures. The only requirement for a correlational study is that we obtain scores on two variables for all subjects.

The **Pearson correlation coefficient,** designated by the letter r, is the most commonly used measure of correlation. There are other kinds of correlations, but they are alternative approximations of the Pearson correlation coefficient.

The numerical value of a correlation coefficient always ranges between -1.00 and $+1.00$. When interpreting a correlation coefficient, a researcher considers two things: its sign and its magnitude.

The *sign* of a correlation coefficient ($+$ or $-$) indicates the *direction* of the relationship between the two variables. Variables may be either positively or negatively correlated. A **positive correlation** indicates a direct, positive relationship between the two variables. If the correlation is positive, scores on one variable tend to increase as scores on the other variable increase. For example, the correlation between SAT scores and college grades is a positive one. People with higher SAT scores tend to have higher grades, whereas people with lower SAT scores tend to have lower grades. Similarly, the correlation between educational attainment and income is positive: Better educated people tend to make more money.

A **negative correlation** indicates an inverse, negative relationship between two variables. As values of one variable increase, values of the other variable decrease. For example, the correlation between self-esteem and shyness is negative. People with higher self-esteem tend to be less shy, whereas people with lower self-esteem tend to be more shy. The correlation between alcohol consumption and college grades is also negative. On the average, the more alcohol a student consumes in a week, the lower his or her grades are likely to be.

The *magnitude* of the correlation—its numerical value, ignoring the sign—expresses the strength of the relationship between the variables. A correlation of zero ($r = .00$) indicates that the variables are not at all related—there is absolutely no relationship between them. As the numerical value of the coefficient increases, so does the strength of the relationship. Thus, a correlation of $+.78$ indicates that the variables are more strongly related than does a correlation of $+.30$.

Keep in mind that the sign of a correlation coefficient indicates only the direction of the relationship and tells us nothing about its strength. Thus, a correlation of $-.78$ indicates a larger correlation (and a stronger relationship) than a correlation of $+.40$. But the first relationship is negative, whereas the second one is positive.

A Graphic Representation of Correlations

The relationship between any two variables can be portrayed graphically on an *x*- and *y*-axis. For each subject, we can plot a point that represents his or her combination of scores on the two variables (which we can designate X and Y). When scores for an entire sample are plotted, the resulting graphical representation of the data is called a **scatter plot.**

Figure 6.1 shows several scatter plots of relationships between two variables. Positive correlations can be recognized by their upward slope to the right, which indicates that high values on one variable are associated with high values on the other; whereas low values on one variable are associated with low values on the other. Negative correlations slope downward to the right.

The stronger the correlation, the more tightly the data are clustered around an imaginary line running through them. When we have a **perfect correlation** (-1.00 or $+1.00$), all of the data fall in a straight line, as in Figure 6.1(e). At the other extreme, a zero correlation appears as a random array of dots because the two variables bear no relationship to one another (see Figure 6.1(f)).

Interpreting the Example

You should now be able to make sense out of the correlation coefficients in Table 6.1.

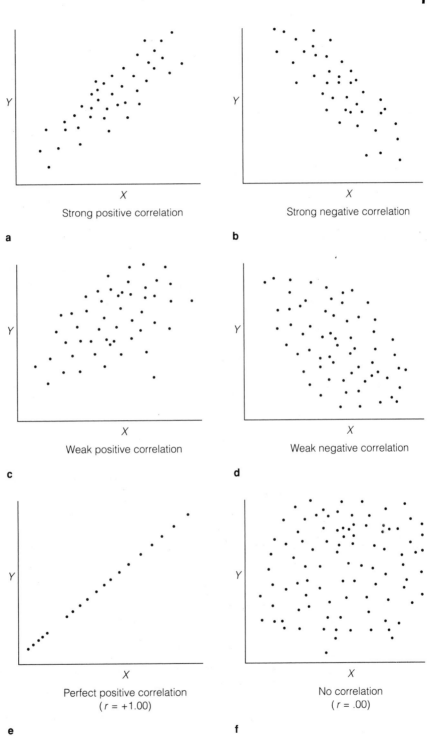

Figure 6.1 Scatter plots and correlations

First, we see that the correlation between the introversion–extraversion scores of children and their natural parents is +.19. This is a positive correlation, which means that children who scored high in introversion–extraversion tended to have natural parents whose introversion–extraversion scores were also high. Conversely, children with lower scores tended to have natural parents whose scores were low. The correlation is only .19, however, which indicates a relatively weak relationship between the scores of children and their natural parents.

The correlation between the introversion–extraversion scores of children and their adoptive parents, however, was .00; there was no relationship. Taking these two correlations together suggests that a child's level of introversion–extraversion is more closely related to that of his or her natural parents than to that of his or her adoptive parents.

The same appears to be true of neuroticism. The correlation for children and their natural parents was +.25, whereas the correlation for children and adoptive parents was only +.05. Again, these positive correlations are small, but they are stronger for natural than for adoptive parents.

The Coefficient of Determination

We've seen that the correlation coefficient, r, expresses the direction and strength of the relationship between two variables. But what, precisely, does the value of r indicate? If children's neuroticism scores correlate +.25 with the scores of their parents, we know there is a positive relationship, but what does the number itself tell us?

To interpret a correlation coefficient fully, we must first square it. This is because r is not on a ratio scale. As a result, we can't add, subtract, multiply, or divide correlation coefficients. Nor can we compare them directly. Contrary to how it appears, a correlation of .8 is *not* twice as large as a correlation of .4!

To make r more easily interpretable, we square it to obtain the **coefficient of determination**. The coefficient of determination is on a ratio scale of measurement and is easily interpretable. What does it show? To answer this question, let us return momentarily to the concept of variance.

We learned in Chapter 2 that variance indicates the amount of variability in a set of data. We learned also that the total variance in a set of data can be partitioned into systematic variance and error variance. Systematic variance is that part of the total variability in subjects' responses that is related to variables the researcher is investigating. Error variance is that portion of the total variance that is unrelated to the variables under investigation in the study.

When two variables are uncorrelated—when r is .00—they are totally independent. The scores on one variable are unrelated to scores on the other variable; the two sets of scores do not covary. Another way to say this is that the variability within one set of scores is not related to the variability within the other set of scores. Changes in the variance of one set of scores would not affect the variance of the other set. Because none of the variance of one variable is related to scores on the other variable, *there is no systematic variance.* In statistical terms, when r (and r-squared) is .00, we cannot account for any of the variance in one of our variables by the other variable.

However, to the extent that two variables are correlated with one another, scores on one variable *are* related to scores on the other variable. The variance of one variable is related to the variance of the other variable, indicating that systematic variance is present. The existence of a correlation (and systematic variance) means that we can account for some of the variance in one variable by the other variable.

The squared correlation coefficient (or coefficient of determination) tells us *the proportion of variance in one of our variables that is accounted for by the other variable.* Viewed another way, the coefficient of determination is the proportion of the total variance in one variable that is systematic variance shared with the other variable. For example, if we square the correlation between children's neuroticism scores and those of their biological parents (.25 × .25), we obtain a coefficient of determination of .0625. This tells us that 6.25% of the variance in children's neuroticism scores can be accounted for by their parents' scores. Or, put differently, 6.25% of the total variance in children's scores is systematic variance that is related to the parents' scores.

If we were all-knowing beings who knew everything there was to know about neuroticism, we would know *all* of the factors that account for the variance in our neuroticism scores. Thus, we would be able to account for 100% of the variance in children's neuroticism. What are some of the things that might make some people more neurotic than others? Some possibilities include genetic factors, the absence of a secure home life as a child, neurotic parents who provide models of neurotic behavior, low self-esteem, exploitation by other people, and so on. If we knew everything about neuroticism, we could account for *all* of the variance in children's neuroticism scores. In other words, armed with omniscience, we could account for or explain all of the variability we observed in neuroticism—100% of it.

However, we are not all-knowing. The best we can do is to conduct research that looks at the relationship between neuroticism and a handful of other variables. In the case of the research conducted by Scarr et al. (1981) discussed earlier, we can account for only a relatively small portion of the variance in children's neuroticism scores—that portion that is associated with the neuroticism of their natural parents. Given the myriad of factors that influence neuroticism, it is really not surprising that one particular factor, such as parental neuroticism, is related only weakly to children's neuroticism.

In summary, the square of a correlation coefficient—its coefficient of determination—indicates the proportion of variance in one variable that can be accounted for by another. If r is zero, we account for none of the variance. If r equals −1.00 or +1.00, we can perfectly account for 100% of the variance.

Table 6.2   **Correlation Coefficients and Their Corresponding Coefficients of Determination**

Correlation coefficient (r)	Coefficient of determination (r^2)	Percentage of variance accounted for (%)
.10	.01	1
.20	.04	4
.30	.09	9
.40	.16	16
.50	.25	25
.60	.36	36
.70	.49	49
.80	.64	64
.90	.81	81
1.00	1.00	100

And if r is in between, the more variance we account for, the stronger the relationship. Again, it is important to square a correlation coefficient to get the clearest picture of the strength of the relationship between the variables. As shown in Table 6.2, the true size of the relationship between two variables as indicated by the coefficient of determination is nearly always smaller than that implied by the correlation coefficient itself.

DEVELOPING YOUR RESEARCH SKILLS

Calculating the Pearson Correlation Coefficient

Now that we understand what a correlation coefficient tells us about the relationship between two variables, let's take a look at how it is calculated. To calculate the Pearson correlation coefficient (r), we must sample several individuals and obtain two measures on each.

The Formula

The equation for calculating r is

$$r = \frac{\Sigma xy - \frac{\Sigma x \Sigma y}{n}}{\sqrt{\left(\Sigma x^2 - \frac{(\Sigma x)^2}{n}\right)\left(\Sigma y^2 - \frac{(\Sigma y)^2}{n}\right)}}$$

In this equation, x and y represent subjects' scores on the two variables of interest, for example shyness and self-esteem, or neuroticism scores for oneself and one's parents. The term Σxy indicates that we multiply each subject's x- and y-scores together, then sum these products across all subjects. Likewise, the term $\Sigma x \Sigma y$ indicates that we sum all subjects' x-scores, sum all subjects' y-scores, then multiply these two sums. The rest of the equation should be self-explanatory. Although calculating r may be time-consuming with a large number of subjects, the math involves only simple arithmetic.

An Example

Many businesses use ability and personality tests to help them hire the best employees. Before they may legally use such tests, however, employers must demonstrate that scores on the tests are, in fact, related to job performance. Psychologists are often called upon to validate employment tests by showing that test scores correlate with performance on the job.

Suppose we are interested in whether scores on a particular test relate to job performance. We obtain employment test scores for 10 employees. Then, 6 months later, we ask these employees' supervisors to rate their employees' job performance on a scale of 1 to 10, where a rating of 1 represents extremely poor job performance and a rating of 10 represents superior performance.

Table 6.3 shows the test scores and ratings for the 10 employees, along with some of the products and sums we need to calculate r. In this example, two scores have been obtained for 10 employees: an employment test score (x) and a job performance rating (y). We wish to know whether the test scores correlate with job performance.

Table 6.3   **Calculating the Pearson Correlation Coefficient**

Employee	Test score (x)	Job performance Rating (y)	x^2	y^2	xy
1	85	9	7,225	81	765
2	60	5	3,600	25	300
3	45	3	2,025	9	135
4	82	9	6,724	81	738
5	70	7	4,900	49	490
6	80	8	6,400	64	640
7	57	5	3,249	25	285
8	72	4	5,184	16	288
9	60	7	3,600	49	420
10	65	6	4,225	36	390

$\Sigma x = 676$ $\Sigma y = 63$ $\Sigma x^2 = 47{,}132$ $\Sigma y^2 = 435$ $\Sigma xy = 4451$
$(\Sigma x)^2 = 456{,}976$ $(\Sigma y)^2 = 3{,}969$

The formula for r is:

$$\frac{\Sigma xy - \frac{(\Sigma x)(\Sigma y)}{n}}{\sqrt{\left(\Sigma x^2 - \frac{(\Sigma x)^2}{n}\right)\left(\Sigma y^2 - \frac{(\Sigma y)^2}{n}\right)}}$$

Entering the appropriate numbers into the formula yields:

$$r = \frac{4451 - (676)(63)/10}{\sqrt{(47,132 - 456,976/10)(435 - 3,969/10)}}$$

$$= \frac{4451 - 4258.8}{\sqrt{(47,132 - 45,697.6)(435 - 396.9)}}$$

$$= \frac{192.2}{\sqrt{(1,434.4)(38.1)}} = \frac{192.2}{\sqrt{54,650.64}} = \frac{192.2}{233.77} = .82$$

As you can see, we've obtained x^2, y^2, and the product of x and y (xy) for each subject, along with the sums of x, y, x^2, y^2, and xy. Once we have these numbers, we simply substitute them for the appropriate terms in the formula for r. The obtained correlation for the example in Table 6.3 is +.82.

Can you interpret this number? First, the sign of r is positive, indicating that test scores and job performance are directly related. Employees who score higher on the test tend to be evaluated more positively by their supervisors, whereas employees with lower scores tend to be rated less positively.

The value of r is .82, which is a strong correlation. To see precisely how strong the relationship is, we square .82 to get the coefficient of determination, .67. This indicates that 67% of the variance in employees' job performance ratings can be accounted for by knowing their test scores. The test seems to be a valid indicator of job performance.

CONTRIBUTORS TO BEHAVIORAL RESEARCH

The Invention of Correlation

The development of correlation as a statistical procedure began with the work of Sir Francis Galton. Intrigued by the ideas of his cousin, Charles Darwin, regarding evolution, Galton began investigating human heredity. One aspect of his work on inheritance involved measuring various parts of the body in hundreds of people and their parents. In 1888, Galton introduced the "index of co-relation" as a method of describing the degree to which two such measurements were related. Rather than being a strictly mathematical formula, Galton's original procedure for estimating co-relation (which he denoted by the letter r) involved inspecting data that had been graphed on x- and y-axes (Stigler, 1986).

Galton's seminal work provoked intense excitement among three British scientists who further developed the theory and mathematics of correlation. W. R. R. Weldon, a Cambridge zoologist, began using Galton's ideas regarding correlation in his research on shrimps and crabs. In the context of this work, Weldon first introduced the concept of *negative correlation.*

In 1893 Francis Edgeworth published the first mathematical formula for calculating the coefficient of correlation directly. Unfortunately, Edgeworth did not initially recognize the importance of his work, which was buried in a more general paper on statistics (Stigler, 1986).

Thus, when one of Galton's students, Karl Pearson, derived a formula for calculating *r* in 1895, he didn't know that Edgeworth had obtained an essentially equivalent formula 2 years earlier. Edgeworth himself notified Pearson of this fact in 1896. Unlike Edgeworth, however, Pearson recognized the importance of the discovery and went ahead to make the most of it, applying his formula to research problems in both biology and psychology (Pearson & Kendall, 1970; Stigler, 1986). Because Pearson was the one to popularize the formula for calculating *r*, the coefficient became known as the *Pearson* correlation coefficient, or Pearson *r.*

Considerations in Interpreting *r*

Researchers must keep several matters in mind when they calculate and interpret correlation coefficients.

Correlation Is an Index of Linear Relationships

Correlation is a measure of the **linear relationship** between two variables. If the variables are plotted on an axis as in Figure 6.1, do the scores relate to one another in a straight line?

When *r* is zero, we know that the variables are not linearly related. However, it is possible that they are related in a *curvilinear* fashion. Look, for example, at Figure 6.2. This graph shows the relationship between arousal and performance. It shows that people perform better when they are moderately aroused than when arousal is very low or very high.

If we calculate a correlation coefficient for these data, *r* will be nearly zero. Can we conclude that arousal and performance are unrelated? No, for as Figure 6.2 shows, they are closely related. But the relationship is curvilinear, and correlation tells us only about linear relationships. There are statistics for measuring the degree of curvilinear relationship between two variables, but those statistics don't concern us here. Simply remember that correlation coefficients tell us only about linear relationships between variables. Many research-

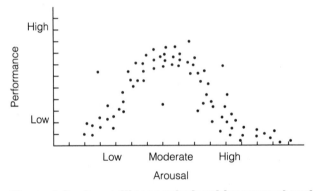

Figure 6.2   **A curvilinear relationship: arousal and performance**

Explanation. This is a scatter plot of 60 subjects' scores on a measure of arousal (*x*-axis) and a measure of performance (*y*-axis). The relationship between arousal and performance is curvilinear—subjects with moderate arousal performed better than those with low or high arousal. Because *r* is a measure of linear relationships, calculating a correlation coefficient for these data would yield a value of *r* that was approximately zero. Obviously, this cannot be taken to indicate that arousal and performance are unrelated.

ers regularly examine a scatter plot of their data to be sure the variables are not curvilinearly related.

Artificially Large and Small Correlations Are Possible

Correlation coefficients are not always what they appear to be. Many factors can result in coefficients that either underestimate or overestimate the true degree of relationship between two variables. Therefore, when interpreting correlation coefficients, one must be on the lookout for three factors that may artificially inflate or deflate the magnitude of correlations.

Restricted range   Look for a moment at Figure 6.3(a). From this scatter plot, do you think SAT scores and grade point averages are related? There is an obvious positive linear trend to the data, which reflects a moderate positive correlation.

Now look at Figure 6.3(b). In this set of data, are SAT scores and grade point average (GPA) correlated? In this case, the pattern, if indeed there is one, is much less pronounced. It is difficult to tell whether there is a relationship or not.

If you'll now look at Figure 6.3(c), you'll see that Figure 6.3(b) is actually taken from a small section of Figure 6.3(a). However, rather than representing the full range of possible SAT scores and grade point averages, the range of the data shown in Figure 6.3(b) is quite narrow, or **restricted**. Instead of ranging from 200 to 1600, for example, the entrance exam scores fall only in the range from 1000 to 1150.

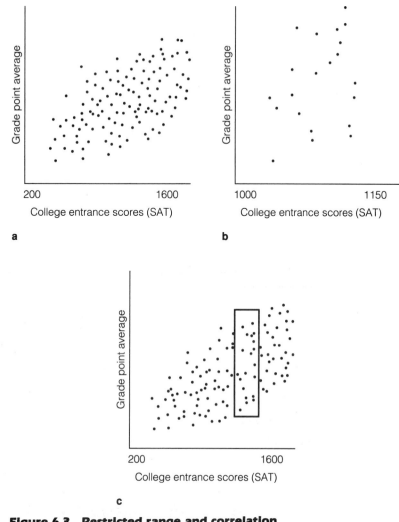

Figure 6.3   Restricted range and correlation

Explanation: *Scatter plot (a) shows a distinct positive correlation between SAT scores and grade point averages when the full range of SAT scores (from 200 to 1600) is included. However, when a more restricted range of scores is examined (those from 1000 to 1150), the correlation is less apparent (b). This displays graphically the effects of restricted range (c) on correlation.*

These figures show graphically what happens to correlations when the range of one's data is restricted. Correlations obtained on a relatively homogeneous group of subjects whose scores fall in a narrow range are smaller than those obtained from a heterogenous sample with a wider range of scores. If the range of scores is restricted, a researcher may be misled into concluding that the two variables are only weakly correlated, if at all. However, had a broader range of scores been sampled, a strong relationship would have emerged. The

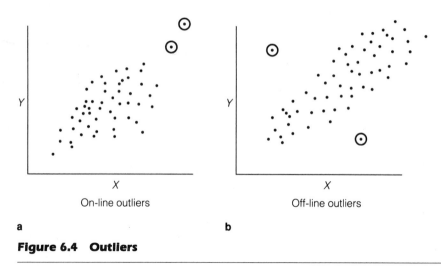

a   **b**

Figure 6.4   Outliers

Explanation. Two on-line outliers are circled in Figure 6.4(a). On-line outliers lead to inflated correlation coefficients. Off-line outliers, such as those circled in Figure 6.4(b), tend to artificially deflate the magnitude of r.

lesson here is to examine one's raw data to be sure the range of scores is not artificially restricted.

Outliers   Outliers are scores that are obviously deviant from the remainder of the data—so much so that one can question whether they belong in the data set at all. Many researchers consider a score to be an outlier if it is farther than 3 standard deviations from the mean of the data. You may remember from Chapter 2 that, assuming we have a roughly normal distribution, scores that fall more than 3 standard deviations below the mean are smaller than more than 99% of the scores; a score that falls more than 3 standard deviations above the mean is larger than more than 99% of the scores. Clearly, scores that deviate from the mean by more than ±3 standard deviations are very unusual.

Figure 6.4 shows two kinds of outliers. Figure 6.4(a) shows two *on-line* outliers. Two subjects' scores, while falling in the same pattern as the rest of the data, are extreme on both variables. On-line outliers tend to artificially inflate correlation coefficients, making them larger than is warranted by the rest of the data.

Figure 6.4(b) shows two *off-line* outliers. Off-line outliers tend to artificially deflate the value of r. The presence of even a few off-line outliers will cause r to be smaller than indicated by most of the data.

Because outliers can lead to erroneous conclusions about the strength of the correlation between variables, one should examine scatter plots to look for outliers. Some researchers exclude outliers from their analyses, arguing that such extreme scores are flukes that don't really belong in the data. Other researchers change outliers' scores to the value of the variable that is 3 standard deviations from the mean. By making the outlier less extreme, the researcher can include the subject's data in the analysis while minimizing the degree to which it distorts the correlation coefficient.

Reliability of measures   Unreliable measures attenuate the magnitude of correlation coefficients. All other things being equal, the less reliable our measures, the lower the correlation coefficients we will obtain. (You may wish to review the section on reliability in Chapter 3.)

To understand why this is so, let us again imagine that we are all-knowing. In our infinite wisdom, we know that the real correlation between a child's neuroticism and the neuroticism of his or her parents is, say, +.45. However, let's also assume that a poorly trained, fallible researcher uses a measure of neuroticism that is totally unreliable. That is, it has absolutely no internal consistency or test–retest reliability. If the researcher's measure is completely unreliable, what value of *r* will he or she obtain between parents' and children's scores? Not +.45 (the true correlation), but rather .00. Of course, researchers seldom use measures that are totally unreliable. Even so, the less reliable the measure, the lower the correlation will be.

Correlation Does Not Imply Causality

I've saved perhaps the most important consideration regarding correlational research until last: Often people will conclude that two things that go together must be causally related in some way. This is not necessarily so; one variable can be strongly related to another, yet not cause it. Even if the thickness of a caterpillar's coat correlates closely with the severity of winter weather, we wouldn't conclude that caterpillars *cause* blizzards, ice storms, and freezing temperatures.

This principle is important when doing correlational research. A correlation can never be used to conclude that one of the variables causes or influences the other—no matter how large the correlation may be. Put simply, *correlation does not imply causality*.

For us to conclude that one variable *causes* another variable, three criteria must be met: covariation, directionality, and elimination of extraneous variables. However, most correlational research satisfies only the first of these criteria unequivocally.

Covariation   To conclude that two variables are causally related, they first must be found to covary, or correlate. If one variable causes the other, then changes in the values of one variable should be associated with changes in values of the other variable. Of course, this is what correlation is by definition, so if two variables are found to be correlated, this first criterion for inferring causality is met.

Directionality   Second, to infer that two variables are causally related, we must show that the presumed cause precedes the presumed effect in time. However, in most correlational research, both variables are measured at the same time. For example, if a researcher correlates subjects' scores on two personality measures that were collected at the same time, there is no way for him or her to determine the direction of causality. Does variable X cause variable Y, or does variable Y cause variable X (or, perhaps, neither)?

In some instances, one possible direction of causality is more plausible than the other. If we find that room temperature and aggression are correlated, only one causal direction makes sense. It would be reasonable to assume that temperature causes changes in aggression, but not to conclude that aggressive behavior causes temperature to rise.

BEHAVIORAL RESEARCH CASE STUDY

Cross-Lagged Panel Correlation: Television and Aggression

Questions about directionality can be addressed in part by **cross-lagged panel correlation design** (Cook & Campbell, 1979). In this design, the correlation between two variables, X and Y, is calculated at two different points in time. Then, correlations are calculated between measurements of the two variables across time. For example, we would correlate the scores on X taken at time 1 with the scores on Y taken at time 2. Likewise, we would calculate the scores on Y at time 1 with those on X at time 2. If X causes Y, we should find that the correlation between X at time 1 and Y at time 2 is larger than the correlation between Y at time 1 and X at time 2. This is because the relationship between a cause (variable X) and its effect (variable Y) should be stronger if the causal variable is measured before rather than after its effect.

A cross-lagged panel design was used, for example, to study the link between violence on television and aggressive behavior. Nearly 30 years of research has demonstrated that watching violent television programs is associated with aggression. For example, the amount of violence a person watches on TV correlates positively with the person's level of aggressiveness. However, we should not infer from this correlation that television violence *causes* aggression. It is just as plausible to conclude that people who are naturally aggressive simply like to watch violent programs.

Eron, Huesmann, Lefkowitz, and Walder (1972) used a cross-lagged panel correlation design to disentangle the direction of the relationship between television violence and aggressive behavior. These researchers studied a sample of 427 subjects twice: once when the subjects were in the third grade and again 10 years later. On both occasions, subjects provided a list of their favorite TV shows, which were later rated for violence. In addition, each subject's aggressiveness was rated by his or her peers.

Correlations were calculated between TV violence and subjects' aggressiveness across the two time periods. The results for the male subjects are shown in Figure 6.5.

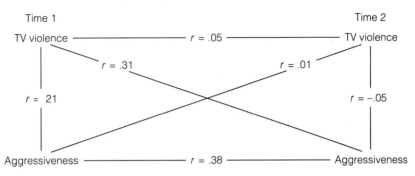

Figure 6.5 Correlations obtained in the Eron et al. study

From "Does television violence cause aggression?," by L. Eron, L. R. Huesmann, M. A. Lefkowitz, and L. O. Walder, 1972, *American Psychologist, 27,* p. 26. Adapted with permission of Leonard Eron.

Explanation: The important correlations in this cross-lagged panel correlation design are on the diagonals. The correlation between the amount of TV violence watched by the children at time 1 and aggressiveness 10 years later was larger than the correlation between aggressiveness at time 1 and TV watching 10 years later. This pattern is more consistent with the notion that watching TV violence causes aggressive behavior than with the idea that being aggressive disposes children to watch TV violence. Strictly speaking, however, we can never infer causality from correlational data.

The important correlations are on the diagonals of Figure 6.5—the correlations between TV violence at time 1 and aggressiveness at time 2, and between aggressiveness at time 1 and TV violence at time 2. As you can see, the correlation between earlier TV violence and later aggression (*r* = .31) is larger than that between earlier aggressiveness and later TV violence (*r* = .01). This pattern is consistent with the idea that watching televised violence causes subjects to become more aggressive rather than the other way around.

Elimination of extraneous variables The third criterion for inferring causality is that all extraneous factors that might influence the relationship between the two variables be eliminated. Correlational research never satisfies this requirement completely. Two variables may be correlated not because they are causally related to one another, but because they are both related to a third variable.

For example, Levin and Stokes (1986) were interested in correlates of loneliness. Among other things, they found that loneliness correlated +.60 with depression. Does this mean that being lonely makes people depressed or that being depressed makes people feel lonely? Perhaps neither. Another option is that both loneliness and depression are due to a third variable, such as the quality of a person's social network. Having a large number of friends and acquaintances, for example, may reduce both loneliness and depression.

Researchers can statistically control for the effects of such third variables through **partial correlation**. A partial correlation is the correlation between two variables with the influence of one or more other variables removed. When Levin and Stokes calculated the partial correlation between loneliness and depression, removing the influence of subjects' social networks, the correlation dropped from .60 to .39. This suggests that some of the relationship between loneliness and depression is mediated by social network. However, even with the social network factor removed, loneliness and depression were still correlated, which suggests that other factors than social network contribute to the relationship between them.

IN DEPTH

Correlation, Cigarettes, and Cancer

The inability to draw conclusions about causality from correlational data is the basis of the tobacco industry's insistence that no research has produced evidence of a causal link between smoking and cancer in humans. Plenty of research shows that smoking and the incidence of cancer are *correlated* in humans; more smoking is associated with a greater likelihood of getting lung cancer. But because the data are correlational, we cannot, strictly speaking, infer a causal link between smoking and health.

Research *has* established that smoking causes cancer in laboratory animals, however. This is because animal research involves experimental studies that allow us to infer cause-and-effect relationships. Such research on humans, which would require a randomly assigned group of subjects to smoke heavily, would be unethical, however. (Would you volunteer to participate in a study that might give you cancer?) Thus we are unable to conduct the kind of study that could show whether smoking causes cancer in human beings.

Although research that conclusively documents that smoking causes cancer in humans has not been conducted, the animal experimental data, in combination with the human correlational data, have resulted in the Surgeon General's warning that smoking may be hazardous to your health.

Linear Regression

Imagine again that you are an industrial-organizational psychologist who works for a large company. One of your responsibilities is to develop better ways of selecting employees from the large number of people who apply for jobs with this company. You have developed a job aptitude test that is administered to everyone who applies for a job. Furthermore, when you looked at the relationship between scores on this test and how employees were rated by their supervisors after working for the company for 6 months, you found that scores on the aptitude test correlated positively with ratings of job performance.

Armed with this information, you should be able to *predict* applicants' future job performance, allowing you to make better decisions about whom to hire. One consequence of two variables being correlated is that if we know a person's score on one variable, we can predict his or her score on the other variable. Our prediction is seldom perfectly accurate, but if the two variables are correlated, we can predict their scores within limits.

This is accomplished through **linear regression analysis**. The goal of regression analysis is to develop a **regression equation** from which we can predict one score on the basis of one or more other variables. This procedure is quite useful in situations where psychologists must make predictions. For example, regression equations are used to predict students' college performance from entrance exams and high school grades. They are also used in business and industrial settings to predict potential job performance on the basis of a job applicant's test scores and other factors. Regression analysis is also used in basic research settings to describe mathematically the relationships between sets of variables.

The precise manner in which a regression equation is calculated need not concern us here. What is important is that you know what a regression analysis is and the rationale behind it should you encounter one.

Remember that a correlation indicates a linear relationship between two variables. If the relationship between two variables is linear, a straight line can be drawn through the data to represent the relationship between the variables. For example, Figure 6.6 shows the scatter plot for the relationship between the

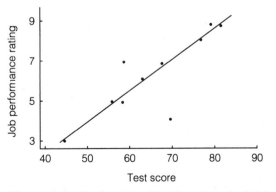

Figure 6.6   Regression line for data in Table 6.3

Explanation: This is a scatter plot of the relationship between scores on an employment test (*x*-axis) and job performance ratings 6 months later (*y*-axis). The line running through the scatter plot is the regression line for the data—the line that best represents, or fits, the data. A regression line such as this can be described mathematically by the equation for a straight line. The equation for this particular regression line was $y = -2.76 + .13x$.

employees' test scores and job performance ratings that we analyzed earlier. (Remember that we found that the correlation between the test scores and job performance was +.82.) The line drawn through the scatter plot portrays the nature of the relationship between test scores and performance ratings. In following the trend in the data, this line reflects how test scores and job performance tend to be related.

The goal of regression analysis is to find the equation for the line that best fits the data. If we can find the equation for the line that best portrays the relationship between the two variables, this equation will provide us with a mathematical description of how the variables are related.

You may remember from high school geometry that a line can be represented by the equation $y = mx + b$, where m is the slope of the line and b is the y-intercept. In linear regression, the symbols are different and the order of the terms is reversed, but the equation is the same:

$$Y = \beta_0 + \beta_1 X$$

In a regression equation, Y is the variable we would like to predict. This is usually called the *outcome variable*, or **criterion variable**. X is the variable we are using to predict Y; X is called the **predictor variable.** β_0, called the **regression constant** or beta-zero, is the y-intercept of the line that best fits the data in the scatter plot. It is equivalent to b in the formula you learned in geometry class. The **regression coefficient,** β_1, is the slope of the line that best represents the relationship between the predictor variable (X) and the criterion variable (Y).

The regression equation for the line for the data in Figure 6.6 is

$$Y = -2.76 + .13 X$$

or

$$\text{Job performance rating} = -2.76 + .13(\text{test score}).$$

If X and Y represent any two variables that are correlated, we can predict a person's y-score by plugging his or her x-score into the equation. For example, suppose a job applicant obtained a test score of 75. Using the regression equation for the scatter plot in Figure 6.6, we can solve for Y (job performance rating):

$$Y = -2.76 + .13 (75) = 6.99$$

On the basis of knowing how well he or she performed on the test, we would predict this applicant's job performance rating after 6 months to be 6.99. Thus, if job ability scores and job performance are correlated, we can, within limits, predict an applicant's job performance from the score he or she obtains on the employment test.

We can extend this idea to include more than one predictor variable. For example, you might decide to predict job performance on the basis of three variables: aptitude test scores, a measure of work motivation, and an index of physical strength. Using **multiple regression analysis,** you might develop a regression equation that includes three predictors. Once the equation is determined, you can predict job performance from an applicant's scores on the three predictor variables.

When we use linear regression, we usually want to know how well X predicts Y. After all, if our predictors did a poor job of predicting the outcome variable, we wouldn't want to use the equation to make decisions about job applicants. To express the usefulness of a regression equation for predicting, we calculate the **multiple correlation coefficient,** symbolized by the letter R. R describes the degree of relationship between the criterion variable (Y) and the *set* of predictor, or X, variables. Unlike the Pearson r, multiple correlation coefficients range only from .00 to 1.00. The larger R is, the better job the equation does of predicting the outcome variable from the predictor variables.

SUMMARY

1. Correlational research is used to describe the relationship between two variables. A correlation coefficient (r) expresses both the direction and magnitude of the relationship.
2. If the scores on the two variables tend to increase and decrease together, the variables are positively correlated. If the scores are inversely related, the variables are negatively correlated.
3. The magnitude of a correlation coefficient ranges from 0 to ± 1.00 and indicates the strength of the relationship between the variables.
4. The square of the correlation coefficient, the coefficient of determination (r^2), reflects the proportion of the variance in one variable that can be accounted for by the other variable.
5. When interpreting correlations, researchers consider the possibility that the variables are curvilinearly related. They are also on the lookout for factors that may artificially inflate and deflate the magnitude of the correlation—restricted range, outliers, and reliability.
6. Correlational research seldom if ever meets all three criteria for inferring causality—covariation, directionality, and elimination of extraneous variables. Thus, correlation does not imply causality.
7. If two variables are correlated, one variable may be predicted from the other. Linear regression analysis is used to calculate an equation to predict subjects' scores on an outcome variable from one or more predictor variables.
8. When using regression, the multiple correlation coefficient, R, expresses the degree of relationship between the predictor and outcome variables and indicates how well the regression equation predicts subjects' scores.

KEY TERMS

correlational research	cross-lagged panel correlation
correlation coefficient	design
Pearson correlation coefficient	partial correlation
positive correlation	linear regression analysis
negative correlation	regression equation
scatter plot	criterion variable
perfect correlation	predictor variable
coefficient of determination	regression constant
linear relationship	regression coefficient
restricted range	multiple regression analysis
outlier	multiple correlation coefficient

REVIEW QUESTIONS

1. The correlation between self-esteem and shyness is −.50. Interpret this correlation.

2. Which is larger—a correlation of +.45 or a correlation of −.60? Explain.

3. Why do researchers often examine scatter plots of their data when doing correlational research?

4. The correlation between self-esteem and shyness is −.50, and the correlation between self-consciousness and shyness is +.25. How much stronger is the first relationship than the second? (Be careful on this one.)

5. Why do researchers calculate the coefficient of determination?

6. Why can it be argued that the formula for calculating *r* should be named the Edgeworth, rather than the Pearson, correlation coefficient?

7. Discuss the effects of restricted range and outliers on correlation coefficients. How would you detect and correct these two problems in your data?

8. Why can't we infer causality from correlation?

9. How does a cross-lagged panel design provide evidence to support a causal link between two variables?

10. If you think two variables are correlated because both are related to a third variable, what procedure would you use to test your hypothesis?

11. Describe the rationale behind regression analysis.

12. What is the general form of a regression equation? Explain.

13. How can a researcher determine how well a set of predictor variables predicts a criterion variable?

EXERCISES

Imagine that you are a college professor. You notice that fewer students appear to attend class on Friday afternoons when the weather is warm than when it is cold outside. To test your hunch, you collect data regarding outside temperature and attendance for several randomly selected weeks during the academic year.

Your data are as follows:

Temperature (°F)	Attendance (number of students)	Σxy	Σx^2	x^2
1. 58	85	4930	3364	7225
2. 62	83	5146	3844	6889
3. 78	64	4992	6084	4096
4. 77	62	4774	5929	3844
5. 67	66	4422	4489	4356
6. 50	86	4300	2500	7396
7. 80	60	4800	6400	3600
8. 85	82	6970	7225	6724
9. 70	65	4550	4900	4225
10. 75	62	4650	5625	3844

1. Draw a scatter plot of the data.
   (a) Do the data appear to be roughly linear?
   (b) Do you see any evidence of outliers?
   (c) Does there *appear* to be a correlation between temperature and attendance? If so, is it positive or negative?
2. Calculate and interpret r for these data.
3. The regression equation for predicting attendance from temperature for these data is

$$\text{Attendance} = 114.35 - .61 \text{ (temperature)}$$

Imagine that the weather forecaster predicts that next Friday's temperature will be 82°F. How many students would you expect to attend class?

7

Basics of Experimental Design

Students in one of my courses recently asked whether I would postpone for 1 week an exam that was scheduled for the next Monday. From my perspective as instructor, postponing the exam would have disrupted the course schedule, and I felt that postponing the test a week was too much to ask. So, I told them, "No, I think it would be better to have the test as scheduled." After a moment of silence, a student asked, "Well, if you won't postpone the test a week, will you postpone it at least until next Friday?" I was still reluctant, but finally agreed.

In retrospect, I think I was a victim of the "door-in-the-face" phenomenon. The door-in-the-face effect works like this: By first making an unreasonably large request, a person increases the probability that a second, smaller request will be granted. Refusing the students' request to postpone the test until Monday increased the chance that I would agree to postpone it until the preceding Friday.

This interesting phenomenon has been studied in a series of experiments by Robert Cialdini and his colleages (Cialdini, Vincent, Lewis, Catalan, Wheeler, & Darby, 1975). In one such experiment, researchers approached people walking on the campus of Arizona State University and made one of three requests. Subjects in one group were first asked whether they would be willing to work as a nonpaid counselor for the County Juvenile Detention Center for 2 hours a week for 2 years. Not surprisingly, no one agreed to such an extreme request. However, after the subject had turned down this request, the researcher asked whether the subject would be willing to chaperone a group of children from the Juvenile Detention Center for a 2-hour trip to the zoo.

Subjects in a second group were asked only the smaller request—to chaperone the trip to the zoo—without first being asked the more extreme request. For a third group of subjects, researchers described both the extreme and the small request, then asked subjects whether they would be willing to perform either one.

Which subjects should have been most likely to volunteer for the small request? According to the door-in-the-face effect, they should have been the ones who first heard and rejected the extreme request. The results of the experiment are shown in Table 7.1. As you can see, compliance to the small request was greatest when subjects had already turned down the extreme request. Fifty percent of the subjects in that condition agreed to go to the zoo. This was twice the number of those who complied after hearing both requests before responding (25%). In contrast, only 16.7% of those who were asked only about the small request agreed to be a chaperone. In short, making an extreme request that was certain to be rejected increased the probability that the person agreed to the subsequent smaller request.

So far, we have discussed two kinds of research in this book: descriptive and correlational. Descriptive and correlational studies are important, but they have a shortcoming when it comes to understanding behavior: They do not allow us to test directly hypotheses about the *causes* of behavior. Descriptive research allows us to describe how our subjects think, feel, and behave; and correlational research allows us to see whether certain variables are related to one another. Although descriptive and correlational research provide hints about possible causes of behavior, we can never be sure from such studies that a particular variable does, in fact, cause changes in behavior. Experimental designs, on the other hand, allow researchers to draw conclusions about cause-and-effect relationships. Thus, when Cialdini and his colleagues wanted to know whether refusing an extreme request *causes* people to comply more frequently with a smaller request, they conducted an **experiment**.

Does the presence of other people at an emergency deter people from helping the victim? Does eating sugar increase hyperactivity and hamper school performance in children? Do stimulants affect the speed at which peo-

| **TABLE 7.1** | **Results of the Door-in-the-Face Experiment** |

Experimental condition	Percentage of subjects who agreed to the small request
Large request, followed by small request	50.0
Small request only	16.7
Simultaneous requests	25.0

From Cialdini, R. B., et al. (1975), "Reciprocal Concessions Procedure for Inducing Compliance: The Door-in-the-Face Technique," *Journal of Personality and Social Psychology, 31*, 206–215. Adapted with permission of Robert Cialdini.

ple learn? Does observing cartoon violence cause children to behave more aggressively? Does making an extreme request cause people to comply with smaller requests? These kinds of questions about causality are ripe topics for experimental investigations.

This chapter delves into the ingredients of a good experimental design. A well-designed experiment has three essential properties: (1) The researcher must *vary at least one independent variable* to assess its effects on subjects' behavior, (2) the researcher must have the power to *assign subjects to the various experimental conditions*, and (3) the researcher must *control extraneous variables* that may influence subjects' behavior. We will discuss each of these elements of an experiment below.

Manipulating the Independent Variable

The logic of experimentation stipulates that the researcher vary conditions that are under his or her control to assess the effects of those different conditions on subjects' behavior. By seeing how subjects' behavior varies with changes in the conditions controlled by the experimenter, we can then determine whether those variables affect subjects' behavior.

Independent Variables

In every experiment, the researcher varies or manipulates one or more **independent variables** to assess their effects on subjects' behavior. For example, a researcher interested in the effects of caffeine on memory would vary how much caffeine subjects receive in the study; some subjects might get capsules containing 100 milligrams (mg) of caffeine, some might get 300 mg, some 600 mg, and others might get capsules that contained no caffeine. After allowing time for the caffeine to enter the bloodstream, the subjects' memory for a list of words could be assessed. In this experiment the independent variable is the amount of caffeine subjects received.

An independent variable must have two or more **levels**. The levels refer to the different values of the independent variable. For example, the independent variable in the experiment described in the preceding paragraph had four levels: Subjects received doses of 0, 100, 300, or 600 mg of caffeine. Often researchers refer to the different levels of the independent variable as the experimental **conditions**. There were four conditions in this experiment. Cialdini's door-in-the-face experiment, on the other hand, had three experimental conditions (see Table 7.1).

Sometimes the levels of the independent variable involve *quantitative* differences in the independent variable. In the experiment on caffeine and memory, for example, the four levels of the independent variable reflect differences in the *quantity* of caffeine subjects received: 0, 100, 300, or 600 mg. In other experiments, the levels involve *qualitative* differences in the independent variable. In the experiment involving the door-in-the-face effect, subjects were treated qualitatively differently by being given different sequences of requests.

Independent variables in behavioral research can be classified into roughly three types: environmental, instructional, and invasive. **Environmental manipulations** involve experimental modifications of the subject's physical or social environment. For example, a researcher interested in visual perception might vary the intensity of illumination, a study of learning might manipulate the amount of reinforcement a pigeon receives, and an experiment investigating attitude change might vary the characteristics of a persuasive message. In social and developmental psychology, **confederates**—accomplices of the researcher who pose as other subjects or as uninvolved bystanders—are sometimes used to manipulate the subject's social environment.

Instructional manipulations vary the independent variable through verbal information provided to subjects. For example, subjects in a study of creativity may be given one of several different instructions regarding how they should go about solving a particular task. In a study of how people's expectancies affect their performance, subjects may be led to expect to do either well or poorly on a test.

Third, **invasive manipulations** involve creating physical changes in the subject's body through surgery or the administration of drugs. When testing the effects of chemicals on emotion and behavior, for example, the independent variable is the amount of drug given to the subject. In physiological psychology, surgical procedures may be used to modify subjects' nervous systems.

Experimental and Control Groups

In some experiments, one level of the independent variable involves the absence of the variable of interest. In the caffeine-and-memory study above, for example, some subjects received doses of caffeine, whereas other subjects received no caffeine at all. Subjects who receive a nonzero level of the independent variable compose the **experimental groups,** and those who receive a zero level of the independent variable make up the **control group**. In this study, there were three experimental groups (those subjects who received 100, 300, or 600 mg of caffeine) and one control group (those subjects who received no caffeine).

Although control groups are useful in many experimental investigations, they are not always necessary. For example, if a researcher is interested in the effects of audience size on performers' stage fright, she may have subjects perform in front of audiences of 1, 3, or 9 people. In this example, there is no control group in which subjects perform without an audience. The door-in-the-face study also had no control group—one in which some subjects did not receive any sort of request.

Researchers must decide whether a control group will help them interpret the results of a particular study. Control groups are particularly important when the researcher wants to know the baseline level of a behavior. For example, if we are interested in the effects of caffeine on memory, we would probably want a control group to determine how well subjects remember words when they do not have any caffeine in their systems.

Dependent Variables

In an experiment, the researcher is interested in the effect of the independent variable on one or more **dependent variables**. A dependent variable is the response being measured in the study. In psychological research, this is typically a measure of subjects' thoughts, feelings, overt behavior, or physiological reactions. In the experiment involving caffeine, the dependent variable might involve how many words subjects remember. In Cialdini's study of the door-in-the-face phenomenon, the dependent variable was whether or not the subject agreed to chaperone the trip to the zoo. Most experiments have several dependent variables. Few researchers are willing to expend the effort needed to conduct an experiment, then collect data regarding only one behavior.

DEVELOPING YOUR RESEARCH SKILLS

Identifying Independent and Dependent Variables

Are you a good or a poor speller? Research suggests that previous experience with misspelled words can undermine a person's ability to spell a word correctly. For example, teachers report that they sometimes become confused about the correct spelling of certain words after grading the spelling tests of poor spellers.

To study this effect, Brown (1988) used 44 university students. In the first phase of the study, the subjects took a spelling test of 26 commonly misspelled words (such as *adolescence, convenience,* and *vacuum*). Then, half of the subjects were told to purposely generate two incorrect spellings for 13 of these words. (For example, a subject might write *vacume* and *vaccum* for *vacuum*.) The other half of the subjects were not asked to generate misspellings; rather they performed an unrelated task. Finally, all subjects took another test of the same 26 words as before, but presented in a different order.

As Brown had predicted, subjects who generated the incorrect spellings subsequently switched from correct to incorrect spellings on the final test at a significantly higher frequency than subjects who performed the unrelated task.

1. What was the independent variable in this experiment? How many levels did it have? How many conditions were there and what were they?
2. What did subjects in the experimental group(s) do? Was there a control group?
3. What was the dependent variable?

The answers to these questions appear at the end of the chapter.

Assignment of Subjects to Conditions

We've seen that, in an experiment, subjects in different conditions receive different levels of the independent variable. At the end of the experiment, the responses of subjects in the various experimental and control groups are compared, to see whether there is any evidence that their behavior was affected by the manipulation of the independent variable.

Such a strategy for testing the effects of independent variables on behavior makes sense only if we can assume that our groups of subjects were roughly equivalent at the beginning of the study. If we see differences in the behavior of subjects in various experimental conditions at the end of the study, we want to have confidence that these differences were produced by the independent variable. The possibility exists, however, that the differences we observe at the end of the study were due to the fact that the groups of subjects differed at the start of the experiment—even before they received one level or another of the independent variable.

For example, in our study of caffeine and memory, perhaps the group of subjects who received no caffeine was, on the average, simply more intelligent than the other groups, and thus they remembered more words than subjects in the other groups. For the results of the experiment to be interpretable, we must be able to assume that subjects in our various experimental groups did not differ from one another before the experiment began. We would want to be sure, for example, that subjects in the four experimental conditions did not differ markedly in average intelligence as a group.

Simple Random Assignment

The easiest way to be sure that the experimental groups are roughly equivalent before manipulating the independent variable is to use a procedure known as **simple random assignment**. Simple random assignment involves placing subjects in conditions in such a way that every subject has an equal probability of being placed in any experimental condition. For example, if we had an experiment with only two conditions—the simplest possible experiment—we could flip a coin to assign each subject to one of the two groups. If the coin came up heads, the subject would be assigned to one experimental group; if it came up tails, the subject would be placed in the other experimental group.

Random assignment ensures that, on the average, subjects in the groups do not differ. No matter what personal attribute we might consider, subjects with that attribute have an equal probability of being assigned to both groups. So, on average, the groups should be equivalent in intelligence, personality, age, attitudes, appearance, self-confidence, anxiety, and so on. When random assignment is used, researchers have confidence that their experimental groups are roughly equivalent at the beginning of the experiment.

Matched Random Assignment

Research shows that simple random assignment is very effective in equating experimental groups at the start of an experiment, particularly if the number of subjects assigned to each experimental condition is sufficiently large. However, there is always a small possibility that random assignment will not produce roughly equivalent groups.

Researchers sometimes try to maximize the similarity among the experimental groups by using **matched random assignment**. When matched random assignment is used, the researcher obtains subjects' scores on a measure known to be relevant to the outcome of the experiment. Typically, this matching variable is a pretest measure of the dependent variable. For example, if we were doing an experiment on the effects of a counseling technique on math anxiety, we could pretest our subjects using a math anxiety scale.

Then, subjects are ranked on this measure from highest to lowest. The researcher then matches subjects by putting them in clusters or blocks of size *k*, where *k* is the number of conditions in the experiment. The first *k* subjects with the highest scores are matched together into a cluster, the next *k* subjects are matched together, and so on. Then, the researcher randomly assigns the *k* subjects in each cluster to each of the experimental conditions.

For example, assume we wanted to use matched random assignment in our study of caffeine and memory. We might obtain pretest scores on a memory test for 40 individuals, then rank these 40 subjects from highest to lowest. Because our study has four conditions, *k* = 4. We would take the 4 subjects with the highest memory scores and randomly assign each subject to one of the four conditions (0, 100, 300, or 600 mg of caffeine). We would then take the 4 subjects with the next highest scores and randomly assign each to one of the conditions, followed by the next block of four subjects, and so on until all 40 subjects were assigned to an experimental condition. This procedure ensures that each experimental condition contains subjects who possess comparable levels of memory ability.

Repeated Measures Designs

When different subjects are assigned to each of the conditions in an experiment, as in simple and matched random assignment, the design is called a **randomized groups design**. This kind of study is also sometimes called a **between-subjects** or **between-groups design** because we are interested in differences in behavior between different groups of subjects.

In some studies, however, a single group of subjects serves in all conditions of the experiment. For example, rather than randomly assigning subjects into four groups, each of which receives one of four dosages of caffeine, a researcher may test a single group of subjects under each of the four dosage levels. Such an experiment uses a **within-subjects design** in which we are interested in differences in behavior across conditions within a single group of subjects. This is also commonly called a **repeated measures design** because each subject is measured more than once.

Using a repeated measures design eliminates the need for random assignment because every subject is tested under every level of the independent variable. What better way is there to be sure the groups do not differ than to use the same subjects in every experimental condition? In essence, each subject in a repeated measures design serves as his or her own control.

Advantages of within-subjects designs The primary advantage of a within-subjects design is that it is more powerful than a between-subjects design. In statistical terminology, the **power** of a research design refers to its ability to detect effects of the independent variable. A powerful design is able to detect effects of the independent variable more easily than less powerful designs.

Within-subjects designs are more powerful because the subjects in all experimental conditions are identical in every way (after all, they are the same subjects). When this is the case, none of the observed differences in responses to the various conditions can be due to preexisting differences between subjects in the groups. Because we have repeated measures on every subject, we can more easily detect the effects of the independent variable on subjects' behavior.

A second advantage of within-subjects designs is that they require fewer subjects. Because each subject is used in every condition, fewer are needed.

Disadvantages of within-subjects designs Despite their advantages, within-subjects designs create some special problems. The first involves **order effects**. Because each subject receives all levels of the independent variable, the possibility arises that the order in which the levels are received affects subjects' behavior.

For example, imagine that all subjects in our memory study are first tested with no caffeine, then with 100, 300, and 600 mg (in that order). Because of the opportunity to practice memorizing lists of words, subjects' performance may improve as the experiment progresses. Because all subjects receive increasingly higher doses of caffeine during the study, it may appear that their memory is best when they receive 600 mg of caffeine when, in fact, their memory may have improved as the result of practice alone.

To guard against this possibility, researchers use **counterbalancing**. Counterbalancing involves presenting the levels of the independent variable in different orders to different subjects. When feasible, all possible orders are used.

In the caffeine-and-memory study, for example, there were 24 possible orders in which the levels of the independent variable could be presented:

	| Order			
	1st	2nd	3rd	4th
1	0 mg	100 mg	300 mg	600 mg
2	0 mg	100 mg	600 mg	300 mg
3	0 mg	300 mg	100 mg	600 mg
4	0 mg	300 mg	600 mg	100 mg
5	0 mg	600 mg	100 mg	300 mg
6	0 mg	600 mg	300 mg	100 mg
7	100 mg	0 mg	300 mg	600 mg
8	100 mg	0 mg	600 mg	300 mg
9	100 mg	300 mg	0 mg	600 mg
10	100 mg	300 mg	600 mg	0 mg
11	100 mg	600 mg	0 mg	300 mg
12	100 mg	600 mg	300 mg	0 mg
13	300 mg	0 mg	100 mg	600 mg
14	300 mg	0 mg	600 mg	100 mg
15	300 mg	100 mg	0 mg	600 mg
16	300 mg	100 mg	600 mg	0 mg
17	300 mg	600 mg	0 mg	100 mg
18	300 mg	600 mg	100 mg	0 mg
19	600 mg	0 mg	100 mg	300 mg
20	600 mg	0 mg	300 mg	100 mg
21	600 mg	100 mg	0 mg	300 mg
22	600 mg	100 mg	300 mg	0 mg
23	600 mg	300 mg	0 mg	100 mg
24	600 mg	300 mg	100 mg	0 mg

If you look closely, you'll see that all possible orders of the four conditions are listed. Furthermore, every level of the independent variable appears in each order position an equal number of times.

In this example, all possible orders of the four levels of the independent variable were used. However, complete counterbalancing becomes unwieldy when the number of conditions is greater than four, because of the large number of possible orders. Instead, researchers randomly choose a smaller subset of these possible orderings. For example, a researcher might randomly choose orders 2, 7, 9, 14, 19, and 21 from the whole set of 24, then assign each subject randomly to one of these six orders.

Even when counterbalancing is used, the results of a repeated measures experiment can be affected by **carryover effects**. Carryover effects occur when the effects of one level of the independent variable are still present when another level of the independent variable is introduced. In the experiment involving caffeine, for example, a researcher would have to be sure that the caffeine from one dosage wears off before giving subjects a different dosage.

BEHAVIORAL RESEARCH CASE STUDY

A Within-Subjects Design: Sugar and Behavior

Parents and teachers have become increasingly concerned in recent years about the effects of sugar on children's behavior. The popular view is that excessive sugar consumption results in behavioral problems ranging from mild irritability to hyperactivity and attention disturbances. Interestingly, few studies have tested the effects of sugar on behavior, and those that have studied its effects have obtained inconsistent findings.

Against this backdrop of confusion, Rosen, Booth, Bender, McGrath, Sorrell, and Drabman (1988) used a within-subjects design to examine the effects of sugar on 45 preschool and elementary school children. All 45 subjects served in each of three experimental conditions. In the high-sugar condition, the children drank an orange-flavored breakfast drink that contained 50 g of sucrose (approximately equal to the sucrose in two candy bars). In the low-sugar condition, the drink contained only 6.25 g of sucrose. And in the control group, the drink contained aspartame (Nutrasweet), an artificial sweetener.

Each child was tested five times in each of the three conditions. Each morning for 15 days each child drank a beverage containing 0, 6.25, or 50 g of sucrose. To minimize order effects, the order in which subjects participated in each condition was randomized across those 15 days.

Several dependent variables were measured. Subjects were tested on several measures of cognitive and intellectual functioning. In addition, their teachers (who did not know what each child drank) rated each student's behavior every morning. Observational measures were also taken of behaviors that may be affected by sugar, such as activity level, aggression, and fidgeting.

The results showed that high amounts of sugar caused a slight increase in activity, as well as a slight decrease in cognitive performance for girls. Contrary to the popular view, however, the effects of even excessive consumption of sugar were quite small in magnitude. The authors concluded that "the results did not support the view that sugar causes major changes in children's behavior" (Rosen et al., 1988, p. 583). Interestingly, parents' expectations about the effects of sugar on their child were uncorrelated with the actual effects.

Summary

One requirement for all experiments is that subjects in the various conditions be roughly equivalent prior to manipulation of the independent variable. Only then can observed effects be confidently attributed to the independent variable as opposed to preexisting differences between the groups. Three basic procedures are used to equate the groups: simple random assignment, matched random assignment, and repeated measures.

Experimental Control

The third critical ingredient of a good experiment is **experimental control.** Experimental control refers to eliminating or holding constant extraneous factors that might affect the outcome of the study. If the effects of such factors are not eliminated, it will be difficult, if not impossible, to determine whether the independent variable had an effect on subjects' responses.

Systematic Variance

To understand why experimental control is important, let's return to the concept of variance. You will recall from Chapter 2 that variance is an index of how much subjects' scores differ or vary from one another's. Furthermore, you may recall that the total variance in a set of data can be broken into two components—systematic variance and error variance.

In the context of an experiment, **systematic variance** (often called **between-groups variance**) is that part of the total variance that reflects differences among the experimental groups. The question to be addressed in any experiment is whether any of the total variability we observe in subjects' scores is systematic variance due to the independent variable. If the independent variable affected subjects' responses, then we should find that some of the variability in subjects' scores is associated with the manipulation of the independent variable.

Put differently, if the independent variable had an effect on behavior, we should observe *systematic differences* between the scores in the various experimental conditions. If scores differ systematically between conditions—if subjects remember more words in some experimental groups than in others, for example—systematic variance exists in the scores. This systematic or between-groups variability in the scores may come from two sources: the independent variable (in which case it is called treatment variance) and extraneous variables (in which case it is called confound variance).

Treatment variance   The portion of the variance in subjects' scores that is due to the independent variable is called **treatment variance** (or sometimes **primary variance**). If nothing other than the independent variable affected subjects' responses in an experiment, then all of the variance in the data would be treatment variance. This is rarely the case, however. As we will see, subjects' scores typically vary for other reasons as well. Specifically, we can identify two other sources of variability in subjects' scores: confound variance (which we must eliminate from the study) and error variance (which we must minimize).

Confound variance   Ideally, all subjects in the various experimental conditions should be treated in precisely the same way, other than the fact that subjects in different conditions receive different levels of the independent variable. The only thing that may differ between the conditions is the independent variable. Only if this is so can we conclude that changes in the dependent variable were caused by manipulation of the independent variable.

Unfortunately, researchers sometimes design faulty experiments in which something other than the independent variable differs among the conditions. For example, if in a study of the effects of caffeine on memory, all subjects who received 600 mg of caffeine were tested at 9:00 a.m. and all subjects who received no caffeine were tested at 3:00 p.m., the groups would differ not only in how much caffeine they received, but in the time at which they participated in the study. In this experiment, we would be unable to tell whether differences in memory between the groups were due to the fact that one group ingested caffeine and the other one didn't, or to the fact that one group was tested in the morning and the other in the afternoon.

When a variable other than the independent variable differs between the groups, **confound variance** is produced. Confound variance, which is sometimes called **secondary variance**, is that portion of the variance in subjects' scores that is due to extraneous variables that differ systematically between the experimental groups.

Confound variance must be eliminated at all costs. The reason is clear: It is impossible for researchers to distinguish treatment variance from confound variance. Although we can easily determine how much systematic variance is present in our data, we cannot tell how much of the systematic variance is treatment variance and how much, if any, is confound variance. As a result, the researcher will find it impossible to tell whether differences in the dependent variable between conditions were due to the independent variable or to this unwanted, confounding variable. As we'll discuss in greater detail later, confound variance is eliminated through careful experimental control in which all factors other than the independent variable are held constant or allowed to vary nonsystematically between the experimental conditions.

Error Variance

Error variance (also called **within-groups variance**) is the result of *unsystematic* differences among subjects. Not only do subjects differ at the time they enter the experiment in terms of ability, personality, mood, past history, and so on, but chances are that the experimenter will treat individual subjects in slightly different ways. In addition, measurement error contributes to error variance by introducing random variability into the data (see Chapter 3).

In our study of caffeine and memory, we would expect to see differences in the number of words recalled by subjects who were in the same experimental condition. This variability in scores within an experimental condition is not due to the independent variable, because all subjects in a particular condition receive the same level of the independent variable. Nor is this within-groups variance due to confounding variables, because all subjects within a group would experience the same confound. Rather, this variability—the error variance—is due to individual differences among subjects within the group, to random variations in the experimental setting and procedure (time of testing, weather, researcher's mood, and so forth), and to other unsystematic influences.

Unlike confound variance, error variance does not invalidate an experiment. This is because, unlike confound variance, there are statistical ways to distinguish between treatment variance (due to the independent variable) and error variance (due to unsystematic extraneous variables).

Even so, the more error variance, the more difficult it is to detect effects of the independent variable. (We'll return to the reason for this later.) Because of this, researchers take steps to control the sources of error variance in an experiment, although they recognize that error variance will seldom be eliminated.

An Analogy

To summarize, the total variance in subjects' scores at the end of an experiment may be composed of three components:

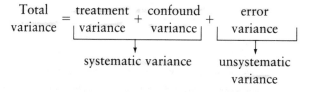

Together, the treatment and confound variance constitute systematic variance (creating systematic differences among experimental conditions), and the error variance is unsystematic variability within the various conditions.

In an ideal experiment, researchers maximize the treatment variance, eliminate confound variance, and minimize error variance. To understand this more fully, we'll use the analogy of watching television.

When you watch television, the image on the screen constantly varies or changes. In the terminology we have been using, there is variance in the picture on the set. Three sets of factors can affect the image on the screen.

The first is the signal being sent from the transmitting tower of the television station. This, of course, is the only source of image variance that you're really interested in when you watch TV. Ideally, you would like the image on the screen to change only as a function of the signal being received from the station. Systematic changes in the picture that are due to changes in the signal from the TV station are analogous to treatment variance due to the independent variable.

Unfortunately, the picture on the tube may be altered in one of two ways. First, the picture may become systematically distorted. The image may be shifted to the right or left, or shifted upwards so that the tops of people's heads appear at the bottom of the screen. Or, the picture may roll. These distortions are much like confound variance because they distort the primary image in a *systematic* fashion. In fact, if you were watching a bizarre rock music video, you might not know whether something was wrong with your set or whether the distortions were intentional. That is, you might not be able to distinguish the true signal (treatment variance) from the distortion (confound variance).

The primary signal can also be weakened by static, fuzz, or snow. Static produces *unsystematic* changes in the TV picture. It dilutes the image without actually distorting it. If the static is extreme enough—because someone in the house is running an electrical appliance, for example—you may not be able to recognize the real picture at all. Similarly, error variance in an experiment clouds the signal produced by the independent variable.

To really enjoy TV, then, you want the primary signal to be as strong as possible; in fact, you might buy a better antenna, connect to your local cable system, or buy a satellite dish. You also want to eliminate systematic distortions entirely; if your picture shifts or rolls, you might have the set repaired or buy a new one. And, you want to minimize static. Only then will the true program come through loud and clear.

In an analogous fashion, researchers want to maximize treatment variance, eliminate confound variance, and reduce error variance. The remainder of this chapter deals with the ways researchers use experimental control to eliminate confound variance and minimize error variance.

Eliminating Confounding

Internal Validity

At the end of an experiment, we would like to have confidence that any differences we observe between the experimental and control groups resulted from our manipulation of the independent variable rather than from extraneous variables. **Internal validity** is the degree to which a researcher draws accurate conclusions about the effects of the independent variable. An experiment is internally valid when it eliminates all potential sources of confound variance. When an experiment has internal validity, a researcher can confidently conclude that observed differences were due to variation in the independent variable.

To a large extent, internal validity is achieved through experimental control. The logic of experimentation requires that nothing can differ systematically between the experimental conditions other than the independent variable. If something other than the independent variable differs in some systematic way, we say that **confounding** has occurred. When confounding occurs, there is no way to know whether the results were due to the independent variable or to the extraneous variable. Confounding is a fatal flaw in experimental designs, one that makes the findings nearly worthless. As a result, possible threats to internal validity must be eliminated at all costs.

One well-publicized example of confounding involved the "Pepsi Challenge" (see Huck & Sandler, 1979). The Pepsi Challenge was a taste test in which people were asked to taste two cola beverages and indicate which they preferred. As it was originally designed, glasses of Pepsi were always marked with a letter M, and glasses of Coca-Cola were marked with a Q. People seemed to prefer Pepsi over Coke in these tests, but a confound was present. Do you see it? The letter on the glass was confounded with the beverage in it. Thus, we don't know for certain whether people's preference was for Pepsi over Coke or for M over Q. As absurd as this possibility may sound, later tests demonstrated that subjects' preferences *were* affected by the letter on the glass. No matter which cola was in which glass, people tended to indicate a preference for the drink marked M over that marked Q.

Before discussing some common threats to the internal validity of experiments, see if you can find the threat to internal validity in the hypothetical experiment described in the accompanying box.

DEVELOPING YOUR RESEARCH SKILLS

Confounding: Can You Find It?

A researcher was interested in how people's perceptions of others are affected by the presence of a physical handicap. Earlier research had suggested that people may rate those with physical disabilities less positively than those without disabilities. Because of the potential implications of this bias for job discrimination against disabled persons, the researcher wanted to see whether subjects responded less positively to disabled applicants.

The subject was asked to play the role of an employer who wanted to hire a computer programmer, a job in which physical disability is irrelevant. Subjects were shown one of two sets of bogus job application materials prepared in advance by the experimenter. Both sets of application materials included precisely the same information about the applicant's qualifications and background (such as college grades, extracurricular activities, test scores, and so on.) The only difference in the two sets of materials was in the photograph attached to the application. In one picture he was shown seated in a wheelchair, thereby making his disability obvious to subjects. The other photograph did not show that he was disabled; in this picture, only his head and shoulders were shown. Other than the degree to which the applicant's disability was apparent, the content of the two applications was identical in every respect.

In the experiment, 20 subjects saw the photo in which the disability was apparent, and 20 subjects saw the photo in which the applicant did not appear disabled. Subjects were randomly assigned to one of these two experimental conditions. After viewing the application materials, including the photograph, each subject completed a questionnaire on which he or she rated the applicant on several dimensions. For example, subjects were asked how qualified the applicant was for the job, how much they liked the applicant, and whether they would hire him.

1. What was the independent variable in this experiment?
2. What was the dependent variable?
3. The researcher made a critical error in designing this experiment, one that introduced confounding and compromised the internal validity of the study. Can you find the researcher's mistake?
4. How would you design the experiment differently to eliminate this problem?

Answers to these questions appear at the end of the chapter.

Threats to Internal Validity

The reason that threats to internal validity, such as in the Pepsi Challenge taste test, are so bad is that they introduce **alternative rival explanations** for the results of a study. Instead of confidently concluding that differences among the conditions are due to the independent variable, the researcher must concede that there are alternative explanations for the results. When this happens, the results are highly suspect, and no one is likely to take them seriously. Although it would be impossible to list all potential threats to internal validity, a few of the more common threats are discussed below.

Biased assignment of subjects to conditions We've already discussed one common threat to internal validity. If the experimental conditions were not equated before subjects received the independent variable, the researcher may conclude that the independent variable caused differences between the groups when, in fact, those differences were due to **biased assignment**. Biased assignment of subjects to conditions (which is often referred to as the *selection* threat to internal validity) introduces the alternative explanation that the effects were due to nonequivalent groups rather than to the independent variable. We've seen that this problem is eliminated through simple or matched random assignment or use of within-subjects designs.

Experimental confounds Ideally, every subject in an experiment should be treated in precisely the same way, except that subjects in different conditions will receive different levels of the independent variable. Of course, it is virtually impossible to treat each subject exactly the same. Even so, it is essential that no *systematic* differences be imposed other than the different levels of the independent variable. When subjects in one group are treated differently than those in another group, confounding destroys our ability to identify effects of the independent variable and introduces an alternative rival explanation of the results. The study involving reactions to disabled job applicants provided a good example of an experimental confound, as did the case of the Pepsi Challenge.

Differential attrition   Attrition refers to the loss of subjects during a study. For example, some subjects may be unwilling to complete the experiment because they find the procedures difficult, objectionable, or embarrassing. In medical research and some animal studies (but rarely in human psychological research), attrition may occur because some subjects die.

When attrition occurs in a random fashion and affects all experimental conditions equally, it is only a minor threat to internal validity. However, when the rate of attrition differs across the experimental conditions, a condition known as **differential attrition,** internal validity is weakened. If attrition occurs at a different rate in different conditions, the independent variable may have caused the loss of subjects. The consequence is that the experimental groups are no longer equivalent; differential attrition has destroyed the benefits of random assignment.

For example, suppose we are interested in the effects of physical stressors on intellectual performance. To induce physical stress, subjects in the experimental group will be asked to immerse their right arm to the shoulder in a container of ice water for 15 minutes, a procedure that is painful but not damaging. Subjects in the control condition will put their arms in water that is at room temperature. While their arms are immersed, subjects in both groups will complete a set of mental tasks. For ethical reasons, we must give subjects the choice of whether or not to participate in this study. Let's assume, however, that whereas all of the subjects who were assigned to the room-temperature condition agree to participate, 15% of those assigned to the experimental, ice-water condition decline. Differential attrition has occurred and the two groups are no longer equivalent. If we assume that subjects who dropped out of the ice-water condition were more fearful than those who remained, then the average subject who remains in the ice-water condition is probably less fearful than the average subject in the room temperature condition, creating a potential bias.

Pretest sensitization   In some experiments, subjects are pretested to obtain a measure of their behavior before receiving the independent variable. Although pretests provide useful baseline data, they have a drawback. Taking a pretest may sensitize subjects to the independent variable so that they react differently to the independent variable than they would have had they not been pretested. When **pretest sensitization** occurs, the researcher may conclude that the independent variable had an effect when, in reality, the effect was a combined result of the pretest and the independent variable.

For example, imagine that a teacher has designed a program to raise students' degree of cultural literacy—their knowledge of common facts that are known by most literate, educated people within a particular culture (for example, what happened in 1492 or who Thomas Edison was). To test the effectiveness of this program, the teacher administers a pretest of such knowledge to 100 students. Fifty of these students then participate in a 2-week course designed to increase their cultural literacy, whereas the remaining 50 students take another course. Both groups are then tested again, using the same test they completed during the pretest.

Assume that the teacher finds that students who took the cultural-literacy course showed a significantly greater increase in knowledge than students in the control group. Was the course responsible for this change? Possibly, but pretest sensitization may also have been involved. When students took the pretest, they undoubtedly encountered questions they couldn't answer. When this material was covered during the course itself, they may have been more attentive to it because of their experience on the pretest. As a result, they learned more than they would have had they not taken the pretest. Thus, the pretest sensitized them to the experimental treatment and thereby affected the results of the study.

History The results of some studies are affected by extraneous events that occur outside of the research setting. As a result, the obtained effects are due not to the independent variable itself but to an interaction of the independent variable and **history effects**.

For example, imagine that we are interested in the effects of filmed aggression toward women on attitudes toward sexual aggression. Subjects in one group watch a 30-minute movie that contains a realistic depiction of rape, whereas subjects in another group watch a film about wildlife conservation. We then measure both groups' attitudes toward sexual aggression. Let's imagine, however, that a female student was brutally raped on campus the week before we conducted the study. It is possible that subjects who viewed the aggressive movie would be reminded of the rape and that their subsequent attitudes would be affected by the *combination* of the film and their thoughts about the campus rape. That is, the movie may have produced a different effect on attitudes given the fact that a real rape had occurred recently. Subjects who watched the wildlife film, however, would not be prompted to think about rape for 30 minutes. Thus, differences we obtain between the two groups could be due to this interaction of history (the real rape) and treatment (the film).

Maturation In addition to possible outside influences, changes within the subjects themselves can create confounds. If the experiment occurs over a long span of time, for example, developmental **maturation** may occur in which subjects go through age-related changes. If this occurs, we don't know whether the differences we observed between experimental conditions are due to the independent variable, or to the independent variable in combination with age-related changes. Obviously, maturation is more likely to be a problem in research involving children.

These by no means exhaust all of the factors that can compromise the internal validity of an experiment, but they should give you a feel for unwanted influences that can undermine the results of experimental studies.

Experimenter Expectancies, Demand Characteristics, and Placebo Effects

The validity of researchers' interpretations of the results of a study are also affected by the researcher's and subjects' beliefs about what *should* happen in the experiment. In this section, I'll discuss three potential problems in which people's expectations affect the outcome of an experiment.

Experimenter expectancy effects   Researchers usually have some idea about how subjects will respond. Indeed, they usually have an explicit hypothesis regarding the results of the study. Unfortunately, experimenters' expectations can distort the results of an experiment by affecting how they interpret subjects' behavior.

A good example of the **experimenter expectancy effect** (sometimes called the Rosenthal effect) is provided in a study by Cordaro and Ison (1963). In this experiment, psychology students were taught to classically condition a simple response in planaria (a flatworm). Some students were told that the planaria had been previously conditioned and should show a high rate of response. Other students were told that the planaria had not been conditioned; thus they thought their worms would show a low rate of response. In reality, both groups of students worked with identical planaria. Despite the fact that their planaria did not differ in responsiveness, the students who expected responsive planaria recorded 20 times more responses than the students who expected unresponsive planaria!

Did the student experimenters in this study intentionally distort their observations? Perhaps; but more likely, their observations were affected by their expectations. People's interpretations are often affected by their beliefs and expectations; people often see what they expect to see. Whether such effects involve intentional distortion or an unconscious bias, experimenters' expectancies may affect their perceptions, thereby compromising the validity of an experiment.

Demand characteristics   Subjects' assumptions about the nature of a study can also affect the outcome of research. If you have ever participated in research as a subject, you probably tried to figure out what the study was about and how the researcher expected you to respond.

Demand characteristics are aspects of a study that indicate to subjects how they should behave. Because many people want to be good subjects who do what the experimenter wishes, their behavior is affected by demand characteristics rather than by the independent variable itself. In some cases, experimenters unintentionally communicate their expectations in subtle ways that affect subjects' behavior. In other instances, subjects draw assumptions about the study from the experimental setting and procedure.

A good demonstration of demand characteristics was provided by Orne and Scheibe (1964). These researchers told subjects they were participating in a study of stimulus deprivation. In reality, subjects were not deprived of stimulation at all, but simply sat alone in a small, well-lit room for 4 hours.

To create demand characteristics, however, subjects in the experimental group were asked to sign forms that released the researcher from liability if the experimental procedure harmed the subject. They also were shown a panic button they could push if they could stand the deprivation no longer. Such cues would likely raise in subjects' minds the possibility that they might have a severe reaction to the study. (Why else would release forms and a panic button be needed?) Subjects in the control group were told that they were serving as a control group, were not asked to sign release forms, and were not given a panic button. Thus, the experimental setting would not lead control subjects to expect extreme reactions.

As Orne and Scheibe expected, subjects in the experimental group showed more extreme reactions during their deprivation period than subjects in the control group even though they all underwent precisely the same experience of sitting alone for four hours. The only difference between the groups was the presence of demand characteristics that led subjects in the experimental group to expect more severe reactions. Given that early studies of stimulus deprivation were plagued by demand characteristics such as these, Orne and Scheibe concluded that many so-called effects of deprivation were, in fact, the result of demand characteristics rather than of stimulus deprivation per se.

To eliminate demand characteristics, experimenters often conceal the purpose of the experiment from subjects. In addition, they try to eliminate any cues in their own behavior or in the experimental setting that would lead subjects to draw inferences about the hypotheses or about how they should act.

Perhaps the most effective way to eliminate both experimenter expectancy effects and demand characteristics is to use a **double-blind procedure**. With a double-blind procedure, neither the subjects nor the experimenters who interact with them know which experimental condition a subject is in at the time the study is conducted. The experiment is supervised by another researcher, who assigns subjects to conditions and keeps other experimenters "in the dark." This procedure ensures that the experimenters who interact with the subjects will not subtly and unintentionally influence subjects to respond in a particular way.

"Find out who set up this experiment. It seems that half of the patients were given a placebo, and the other half were given a different placebo."
Copyright © 1982 by Sidney Harris—*American Scientist* magazine.

Placebo effects   Conceptually related to demand characteristics are placebo effects. A **placebo effect** is a physiological or psychological change that occurs as a result of the mere suggestion that the change will occur. In experiments that test the effects of drugs or therapies, for example, changes in health or behavior may occur because subjects *think* that the treatment will work.

Imagine that you are testing the effects of a new drug, Mintovil, on headaches. One way you might design the study would be to administer Mintovil to one group of subjects (the experimental group), but not to another group of subjects (the control group). You could then measure how quickly the subjects' headaches disappear.

Although this may seem to be a reasonable research strategy, this design leaves open the possibility that a placebo effect will occur, thereby jeopardizing internal validity. The experimental conditions differed in two ways. Not only did the experimental group receive Mintovil, but they *knew* they were receiving some sort of drug. Subjects in the control group, in contrast, received no drug and knew they had received no drug. If differences are obtained in headache remission for the two groups, we do not know whether the difference is due to Mintovil itself (a true treatment effect) or to the fact that the experimental group received a drug they expected might reduce their headaches (a placebo effect).

When a placebo effect is possible, researchers use a **placebo control group**. Subjects in a placebo control group are administered an ineffective treatment. For example, in the study above, a researcher might give the experimental group a pill containing Mintovil and the placebo control group a pill that contains an inactive substance. Then, both groups would believe they were receiving medicine, although only the experimental group would receive a pharmaceutically active drug. The children who received the aspartame-sweetened beverage in Rosen et al.'s (1988) study of the effects of sugar on behavior were in a placebo control group.

The presence of placebo effects can be detected by using both a placebo control group and a true control group in the experimental design. Whereas subjects in the placebo control group receive an inactive substance (the placebo), subjects in the true control group receive no pill and no medicine. If subjects in the placebo control group (who received the inactive substance) improve more than those in the true control group (who received nothing), a placebo effect is operating. If this occurs, the researcher must demonstrate that the experimental group improves more than the placebo control group to conclude that the treatment was effective.

Error Variance

Although a less "fatal" problem than confound variance, error variance creates its own set of difficulties. Error variance decreases the power of an experiment, reducing the researcher's ability to detect effects of the independent variable on the dependent variable. Error variance is seldom eliminated from experimental designs. However, researchers try hard to minimize it.

Sources of Error Variance

Individual differences   The most common source of error variance is preexisting individual differences among subjects. When subjects enter an experiment, they already differ in a variety of ways—cognitively, physiologically, emotionally, and behaviorally. As a result of their preexisting differences, even subjects who are in the same experimental condition respond differently to the independent variable, creating error variance.

Of course, nothing can be done to eliminate individual differences among people. However, one partial solution to this source of error variance is to use **homogeneous samples** of subjects. The more alike subjects are, the less error variance is produced by their differences, and the easier it is to detect effects of the independent variable.

This is one reason that researchers who use animals as subjects prefer samples composed of littermates. Littermates are genetically similar, are of the same age, and have usually been raised in the same environment. As a result, they differ little among themselves. Similarly, researchers who study human behavior often prefer homogeneous samples. For example, whatever other drawbacks they may have as research subjects, college sophomores at a particular university are often a relatively homogeneous group.

Transient states   In addition to differing on relatively stable dimensions such as those above, subjects differ in terms of *transient states*. At the time of the experiment, some are healthy whereas others are ill. Some are tired; others are well rested. Some are happy; others are depressed. Some are enthusiastic about participating in the study; others resent having to participate. Subjects' current moods, attitudes, and physical conditions can affect their behavior in ways that have nothing to do with the experiment.

About all a researcher can do to reduce the impact of these factors is to avoid creating different transient reactions in different subjects during the course of the experiment itself. If the experimenter is friendlier toward some subjects than toward others, for example, error variance will increase.

Environmental factors   Error variance is also affected by differences in the environment in which the study is conducted. For example, subjects who appear for the study drenched to the skin are likely to respond differently than those who sauntered to the experiment under clear skies. External noise may distract some subjects. Collecting data at different times during the day may create extraneous variability in subjects' responses.

To reduce error variance, researchers try to hold the environment as constant as possible as they test different subjects. Of course, little can be done about the weather, and it may not be feasible to conduct the study at only one time each day. However, factors such as laboratory temperature and noise should be held constant. Experimenters try to be sure that the experimental setting is as invariant as possible as different subjects are tested.

Differential treatment   Ideally, researchers should treat each and every subject within each condition exactly the same in all respects. However, as hard as they may try, experimenters find it difficult to treat all subjects in precisely the same way during the study.

For one thing, the experimenter's mood and health is likely to differ across subjects. As a result, he or she may respond more positively toward some subjects than toward others. Furthermore, the experimenter is likely to act differently toward different kinds of subjects. Experimenters are likely to respond differently toward subjects who are pleasant, attentive, and friendly than toward subjects who are unpleasant, distracted, and belligerent. Even the subjects' physical appearance can affect how he or she is treated by the researcher. Furthermore, the experimenter may inadvertantly modify the procedure slightly, by using slightly different words when giving instructions, for example. Also, male and female subjects may respond differently to male and female experimenters, and vice versa.

Unfortunately, even slight differences in how subjects are treated introduce error variance into their responses. One solution is to automate the experiment as much as possible, thereby removing the influence of the researcher to some degree. To eliminate the possibility that the experimenter will vary in how he or she treats subjects, many researchers tape-record the instructions for the study rather than deliver them live. Similarly, animal researchers often automate their experiments, using programmed equipment to deliver food, manipulate variables, and measure behavior, thereby minimizing the impact of the human factor on the results.

Measurement error   We saw in Chapter 3 that nearly all behavioral measures contain some degree of measurement error. Measurement error contributes to error variance because it causes subjects' scores to vary in unsystematic ways. Researchers should make every effort to use only reliable techniques, and should take steps to minimize the influence of factors that create measurement error (see Chapter 3).

DEVELOPING YOUR RESEARCH SKILLS

Tips for Minimizing Error Variance

1. Use a homogeneous sample.
2. Aside from differences in the independent variable, treat all subjects precisely the same at all times.
3. Hold all laboratory conditions (heat, lighting, noise, and so on) constant.
4. Standardize all research procedures.
5. Use only reliable measurement procedures.

Summary   Each of these factors can create extraneous variability in behavioral data. Because the factors that create error variance are spread across all conditions of the design, they do not create confounding or produce problems with internal validity. Rather, they simply add static to the picture produced by the independent variable. They produce unsystematic, yet unwanted changes in subjects' scores that can cloud the effects the researcher is studying. After reading Chapter 8, you'll understand more fully why error variance makes it more difficult to detect effects of the independent variable. For now, simply understand what error variance is, the factors that cause it, and how it can be minimized through experimental control.

The Shortcomings of Experimentation

Because they allow us to determine causal relationships, experimental designs are preferred by many behavioral scientists. However, there are many topics in psychology for which experimental designs are inappropriate. Sometimes, researchers are not interested in cause-and-effect relationships. Survey researchers, for example, often want only to *describe* people's attitudes and aren't interested in *why* people hold the attitudes they do.

In other cases, researchers are interested in causal effects but find it impossible or infeasible to conduct a true experiment. As we've seen, experimentation requires that the researcher be able to carefully control aspects of the research setting. For example, to do an experiment on the effects of people's names on their self-concepts (Do men named Jock see themselves differently than men named Siegfried?) would require the researcher to randomly assign names to people! Obviously, this can't be done.

In other instances, experimentation is possible, but ethically questionable. To conduct an experiment on the effects of oxygen deprivation during the birth process on later intellectual performance would require researchers to deprive newborns of oxygen for varying lengths of time. Despite the fact that experiments can provide clear evidence of causal processes, descriptive and correlational studies, as well as quasi-experimental designs (which we'll examine in Chapter 11), are sometimes more appropriate and useful.

Experimental Control and Generalizability: The Experimenter's Dilemma

We've seen that experimental control involves treating all subjects precisely the same, with the exception of giving subjects in different conditions different levels of the independent variable. The tighter the experimental control, the more internally valid the experiment will be. And the more internally valid the experiment, the stronger, more definitive conclusions we can draw about the causal effects of the independent variables.

However, experimental control is a two-edged sword. Tight experimental control means that the researcher has created a highly specific and often artificial situation. The effects of extraneous variables that affect behavior in the real world have been eliminated or held at a constant level. The result is that the more controlled a study is, the more difficult it is to generalize the findings.

External validity refers to the degree to which the results obtained in one study can be replicated or generalized to other samples, research settings, and procedures. External validity refers to the *generalizability* of the research results to other settings (Campbell & Stanley, 1966).

To some extent the internal validity and external validity of experiments are inversely related; high internal validity tends to produce lower external validity, and vice versa. The conflict between internal and external validity has been called the **experimenter's dilemma** (Jung, 1971). The more tightly the experimenter controls the experimental setting, the more internally valid the results, but the lower the external validity. Thus, researchers face the dilemma of choosing between internal and external validity.

When faced with this dilemma, virtually all experimental psychologists opt in favor of internal validity. After all, if internal validity is weak, then they cannot draw confident conclusions about the effects of the independent variable, and the findings should not be generalized anyway.

Furthermore, in experimental research, the goal is seldom to obtain results that generalize to the real world. The goal is not to make generalizations, but to test them (Mook, 1983). As we saw in Chapter 1, most research is designed to test hypotheses about the effects of certain variables on behavior. This approach is particularly pervasive in experimental research. Researchers develop tentative hypotheses, then design studies to determine whether those hypotheses are supported by the data. If they are supported, evidence is provided that supports the theory. If they are not supported, the theory is called into question.

The purpose of most experiments, then, is not to discover what people do in real-life settings, or to create effects that will necessarily generalize to other settings or to the real world. In fact, the findings of any single experiment should *never* be generalized—no matter how well the study was designed, who its subjects were, or where it was conducted. The results of any particular study are too highly dependent on the context in which it was conducted to allow us to generalize its findings.

Rather, the purpose of most experimentation is to test general propositions about the determinants of behavior. If the theory is supported by data, we may then try to generalize the theory, not the results, to other contexts. We determine the generalizability of a theory through replicating experiments in other contexts, with different subjects, and using modified procedures. Replication tells us about the generality of our hypotheses.

In brief, although important, external validity is not a crucial consideration in all research (Mook, 1983). Of course in some cases, external validity is very important. In survey research, for example, we want to be sure that our findings are representative of the population at large. Such studies aim to describe what people in the real world actually think or do. We want to predict from our sample to the population. In most experimental research, however, this is not the goal.

SUMMARY

1. Of all research designs, only experiments directly allow researchers to provide conclusive evidence regarding causal relationships.

2. In all experiments, the researcher manipulates one or more independent variables to determine their effects on aspects of subjects' behavior (the dependent variable).

3. The logic of the experimental method requires that the various experimental and control groups be equivalent before the independent variable is manipulated.

4. This is accomplished in one of two ways. In a between-subjects or randomized groups design, subjects are randomly assigned to experimental conditions. This ensures that, on the average, subjects in the various conditions are equivalent. Alternatively, in within-subjects or repeated measures designs, all subjects serve in all experimental conditions, thereby ensuring their equivalence.

5. A second requirement for experimental research is that nothing other than the independent variable may vary systematically across conditions.

6. When something other than the independent variable differs across groups, confounding occurs. Confounding destroys the internal validity of the experiment, making it difficult, if not impossible, to draw conclusions about the effects of the independent variable. This is the most serious flaw in any experiment.

7. Researchers try to minimize sources of error variance. Error variance is produced by unsystematic differences between subjects within experimental conditions. Although error variance does not undermine the validity of an experiment, it makes it more difficult to detect effects of the independent variable.

8. Attempts to reduce the error variance in an experiment often lower the study's external validity—the degree to which the results can be generalized. However, the so-called experimenter's dilemma is a problem primarily when the purpose of the experiment is to draw inferences about how people will behave in other settings.

9. Most experiments are designed to test hypotheses about the causes of behavior. If the hypotheses are supported, then they—not the particular results of the study—are generalized.

KEY TERMS

experiment

independent variable

level

condition

environmental manipulation

confederate

instructional manipulation
invasive manipulation
experimental group
control group
dependent variable
simple random assignment
matched random assignment
randomized groups design
between-subjects design
within-subjects design
repeated measures design
power
order effects
counterbalancing
carryover effects
experimental control
systematic variance
between-groups variance
treatment variance
confound variance

error variance
within-groups variance
internal validity
confounding
alternative rival explanation
biased assignment
attrition
differential attrition
pretest sensitization
history effects
maturation
experimenter expectancy effect
demand characteristics
double-blind procedure
placebo effect
placebo control group
homogeneous sample
external validity
experimenter's dilemma

REVIEW QUESTIONS

1. What advantage do experiments have over descriptive and correlational studies?
2. A well-designed experiment possesses what three characteristics?
3. Distinguish between qualitative and quantitative levels of an independent variable.
4. Must all experiments include a control group? Explain.
5. Why must researchers ensure that their experimental groups are roughly equivalent before manipulating the independent variable?
6. Explain how a within-subjects design equates the experimental conditions.
7. Discuss the relative advantages and disadvantages of within-subjects designs relative to between-subjects designs.
8. Distinguish between treatment, confound, and error variance.
9. Why is it essential to eliminate sources of confound variance?
10. What is confounding, and what effect does it have on the outcome of an experiment?
11. Discuss the primary factors that reduce internal validity. What can be done to minimize the effects of each of these factors on the outcome of an experiment?

12. What are experimenter expectancy effects, and how do researchers minimize them?

13. How do researchers detect and eliminate placebo effects?

14. What effect does error variance have on the results of an experiment? What things can a researcher do to minimize error variance?

15. Discuss the trade-off between internal and external validity. Which is more important? Explain.

QUESTIONS FOR THOUGHT AND DISCUSSION

1. Psychology developed primarily as an experimental science. However, during the past 20 to 25 years, nonexperimental methods have become increasingly popular. Why do you think this change has occurred? Do you think an increasing reliance on nonexperimental methods is beneficial or detrimental to the field?

2. Imagine you are interested in the effects of background music on people's performance at work. Design an experiment in which you test the effects of classical music (played at various decibels) on employees' job performance. In designing the study, you will need to decide: how many levels of loudness to use, whether to use a control group, how to assign subjects to conditions, how to eliminate confound variance and minimize error variance, and how to measure job performance.

3. The text discusses the trade-off between internal and external validity, known as the *experimenter's dilemma*. Speculate on things a researcher can do to simultaneously increase internal and external validity, thereby designing a study that ranks high on both.

ANSWERS TO PROBLEMS

A. Identifying Independent and Dependent Variables (page 124)

1. The independent variable involved generating misspellings of words. There were two conditions: subjects either did or did not generate two misspellings for each of 13 words.

2. Subjects in the experimental group generated two incorrect spellings of 13 words. Yes, there was a control group; subjects in the control group performed a task unrelated to spelling.

3. The dependent variable was the number of words for which subjects switched from correct to incorrect spellings.

B. Confounding: Can You Find It? (page 134)

1. The independent variable was the physical disability of the job applicant.

2. The dependent variables involved subjects' ratings of the applicant on several dimensions.

3. The two conditions differed not only in the fact that the applicant appeared to be disabled in one photograph and not in the other, but in the fact that one photograph showed the applicant's whole body, whereas the other photo showed only his head and shoulders. If differences are obtained in subjects' average ratings of the applicant in these two conditions, the researcher will be unable to tell whether the difference was due to the disability variable or to the amount of the applicant's body that was shown. (Perhaps people's ratings of others are affected by whether or not they can see their bodies.) Thus, an extraneous variable (amount of body shown in the picture) is confounded with the independent variable.

4. One way to correct this problem would be to use full-body pictures of the applicant in both conditions, but to show the applicant seated in a wheelchair in the experimental condition, but seated in a normal chair in the control condition. In this way, nothing varies between the conditions other than the independent variable.

8

Experiments with One Independent Variable

P eople are able to remember verbal material better if they understand what it means. For example, people find it difficult to remember seemingly meaningless sentences such as "the notes were sour because the seams had split." However, once they comprehend the sentence (it refers to a bagpipe), they remember it easily.

Bower, Karlin, and Dueck (1975) were interested in whether comprehension aids memory for pictures as it does for verbal material. These researchers designed an experiment to test the hypothesis that people remember pictures better if they comprehend them than if they don't comprehend them.

In this experiment subjects were shown a series of "droodles." A droodle is a picture that, on first glance, appears meaningless but that has a funny interpretation. An example of a droodle is shown in Figure 8.1. Subjects were assigned randomly to one of two conditions. Half of the subjects were given an interpretation of the droodle as they studied each picture. The other half simply studied each picture without being told what it was supposed to be.

After viewing 28 droodles for 10 seconds each, subjects were asked to draw as many droodles as they could remember. Then, 1 week later, the subjects returned for a recognition test. They were shown 24 sets of three pictures. Each of these sets contained one droodle that the subjects had seen the previous week, plus two pictures they had not seen previously. Subjects rated the three pictures in each set according to how similar each was to a picture they had seen the week before. The two dependent variables in the experiment, then, were the number of droodles the subjects could draw immediately after seeing them and the number of droodles that subjects correctly recognized the following week.

Did the results of this experiment support the researchers' hypothesis? We'll postpone discussion of the results of the experiment until later in the

Figure 8.1 Example of a droodle

From "Comprehension and Memory for Pictures" by G. H. Bower, M. B. Karlin, and A. Dueck, 1975, *Memory and Cognition, 3,* p. 217.

Explanation: What is it?

Answer: An early bird who caught a very strong worm.

chapter. For now, we'll use the droodles study to discuss the most basic experimental designs—those that involve the manipulation of a single independent variable. In the experiment described above, only one independent variable—whether an interpretation was attached to the pictures—was manipulated by the researchers. Some subjects were given an interpretation of the droodles, while others were not. As we'll see in Chapter 9, experimental designs may be considerably more complex than this, involving the simultaneous manipulation of two or more independent variables.

Basic One-Way Designs

Experimental designs involving only one independent variable are called **one-way designs**. The simplest one-way design is a **two-group experimental design**, in which there are only two levels of the independent variable (and thus two conditions). A minimum of two conditions is needed so that we can compare subjects' responses in one experimental condition with those in another condition. Only then can we determine whether the different levels of the independent variable led to differences in subjects' behavior. (A study that had only one condition would not be classified as an experiment at all, because no independent variable was manipulated.) The droodles study was a two-group experimental design.

Although at least two conditions are necessary in an experiment, experiments often involve more than two levels of the independent variable. These are called **multilevel experimental designs**.

One-way designs come in three basic varieties, each of which we discussed briefly in Chapter 7: the randomized groups design, the matched-subjects design, and the within-subjects or repeated measures design.

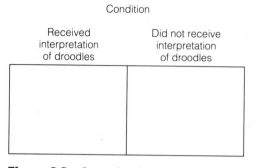

Figure 8.2   A randomized two-group design
(Bower, Karlin, & Dueck, 1975)

Explanation: In a randomized groups design such as this, subjects are randomly assigned to one of the experimental conditions.

Randomized Groups Design

As we learned in Chapter 7, the **randomized groups design** is a between-subjects design in which subjects are randomly assigned to one of two or more groups. In the randomized two-group design, subjects in one group receive one level of the independent variable and those in another group receive another level of the independent variable. In some cases, one group is an experimental group (that receives a nonzero level of the independent variable) and the other is a control group (that receives a zero level of the independent variable). This was true in the droodles experiment: As seen in Figure 8.2, subjects in one condition received interpretations, and those in the other condition did not. In other experiments, both groups are experimental groups that receive different nonzero levels of the independent variable and there is no control group.

In multilevel randomized groups designs, subjects are randomly assigned to one of three or more groups, each of which receives a different level of the independent variable. For example, in a study designed to examine the effectiveness of weight-loss programs, Mahoney, Moura, and Wade (1973) randomly assigned 53 obese adults to one of five conditions: (a) one group rewarded themselves when they lost weight, (b) another punished themselves when they didn't lose weight, (c) a third group used both self-reward and self-punishment, (d) a fourth group monitored their weight but did not reward or punish themselves, and (e) a control group did not monitor their weight. This study involved a randomized groups design with a single independent variable that had five levels (the various weight-reduction strategies). (In case you're interested, the results showed that self-reward resulted in significantly more weight loss than the other strategies.)

Matched-Subjects Design

You will recall from Chapter 7 that **matched random assignment** is sometimes used in between-subjects designs to increase the similarity of the experimental groups prior to an experiment. Subjects are first matched into blocks on the basis of a variable the researcher believes relevant to the experiment. Then subjects in each matched block are assigned randomly to one of the experimental or control conditions.

Although the researchers did not use a **matched-subjects design** in the study of weight loss above, they could have. They could have obtained subjects' weights before the experiment, then ranked the subjects from heaviest to lightest. Then the 5 subjects who weighed the most would be matched, the next 5 heaviest subjects would be matched, and so on until all subjects were matched into blocks with others who weighed approximately the same. Then each of the 5 subjects in each matched group would be randomly assigned to one of the five experimental conditions. This procedure would ensure that the five experimental groups contained subjects with the same range of weights, thereby more closely equating the groups.

Repeated Measures Design

As we learned earlier, in a **repeated measures** (or **within-subjects**) **design**, each subject serves in all experimental conditions. Blumenthal and Gescheider (1987) used a one-way repeated measures design to study the acoustic startle response. Sudden noises evoke a startle response that involves an eye-blink reaction, among other things. Interestingly, the intensity of this response to a sudden sound can be affected by stimulating skin on the hand. This phenomenon is of interest to psychophysiologists because it provides information about the structure of the nervous system.

In their experiment, Blumenthal and Gescheider presented an acoustic startle stimulus—a short blast of noise—to 27 subjects. Their design had five conditions that varied according to how soon before the startle stimulus the skin on the subject's hand was stimulated with a vibrator contactor. The stimulation of the hand occured 50, 100, 200, or 300 ms before the acoustic startle stimulus; in a fifth, control condition, the hand was not stimulated at all. Thus, the independent variable was the length of lead time between hand stimulation and startle stimulus. What makes this a repeated measures design is the fact that each of the 27 subjects served in *all five of the conditions* (see Figure 8.3).

In Chapter 7 we saw that when researchers use a within-subjects design, they must vary the order in which subjects receive the levels of the independent variable through either counterbalancing or randomization. In the startle experiment, subjects received the five levels of the independent variable in one of five random orders, thereby controlling for order effects.

Results of this study showed that the various lead times affected the startle response in different ways. With a short lead time (50 ms), the tactile stimulation increased the amplitude of the acoustic startle response. With longer lead times (200 and 300 ms), the tactile stimulation decreased the startle response.

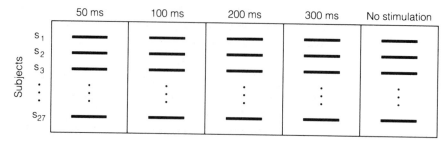

Figure 8.3   A repeated measures design

Adapted from "Modification of the Acoustic Startle Response by a Tactile Prepulse: Effects of Stimulus Onset Synchronicity and Prepulse Intensity" by T. D. Blumenthal and G. A. Gescheider, 1987, *Psychophysiology, 24,* 320–327.

Explanation: In this repeated measures design, each of the 27 subjects served in all five experimental conditions. To control for order effects, the order in which subjects received each level of the independent variable was counterbalanced.

DEVELOPING YOUR RESEARCH SKILLS

Design Your Own Experiments

Below are three research questions. For each, design an experiment in which you manipulate a single independent variable. Your independent variable may have as many conditions as necessary to address the research question.

1. Timms (1980) suggested that if a person who is embarrassed tries to keep him- or herself from blushing, the person may actually blush more than if he or she doesn't try to stop blushing. Design an experiment to determine whether this is true.

2. Have you ever wondered why stoplights are red? Why not blue, or yellow, or green? One possibility is that the human nervous system is structured in such a way that people react more quickly to the color red than to other colors. Design an experiment to determine whether people's reaction times are shorter to red stimuli than to stimuli of other colors.

3. In some studies, subjects are asked to complete a large number of questionnaires over the span of an hour or more. Researchers sometimes worry that completing so many questionnaires may make subjects tired, frustrated, or angry. If so, the process of completing the questionnaires may actually change subjects' moods. Design an experiment to determine whether subjects' moods are affected by completing lengthy questionnaires.

In designing each experiment, did you use a randomized groups, matched-subjects, or repeated measures design? Why? Whichever design you chose for each research question, redesign the experiment using each of the other two kinds of one-way designs. Consider the relative advantages and disadvantages of using each of the designs to answer the research questions.

Posttest and Pretest–Posttest Designs

The three basic one-way experimental designs described above are diagrammed in Figure 8.4. Each of these three designs is called a **posttest-only design** because, in each instance, the dependent variable is measured only *after* the experimental manipulation has occurred.

In some cases, however, researchers measure the dependent variable twice—once before the independent variable is manipulated and again afterward. Such designs are called **pretest–posttest-designs**. Each of the three posttest-only designs described above can be converted to a pretest–posttest design by measuring the dependent variable both before and after manipulating the independent variable. Figure 8.5 shows the pretest–posttest versions of the randomized groups, matched-subjects, and repeated measures designs.

In pretest–posttest designs, subjects are pretested to obtain their scores on the dependent variable at the outset of the study. Pretesting subjects offers three possible advantages over the posttest-only designs. First, by obtaining

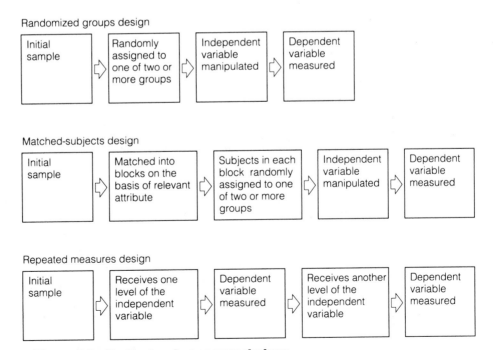

Figure 8.4   Posttest-only one-way designs

Randomized groups design

Matched-subjects design

Repeated measures design

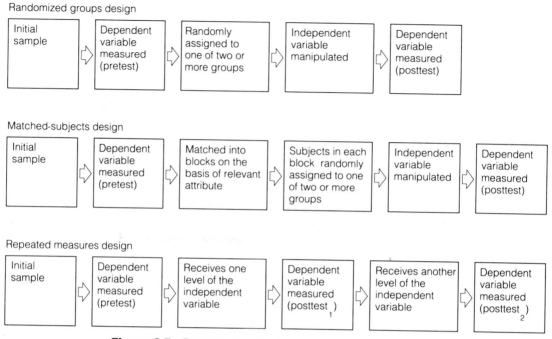

Figure 8.5   Pretest–posttest one-way designs

pretest scores on the dependent variable, the researcher can determine that subjects in the various experimental conditions did not differ with respect to the dependent variable at the beginning of the experiment. In this way, the effectiveness of random or matched assignment can be documented. In addition, by comparing pretest and posttest scores on the dependent variable, researchers can see exactly how much the independent variable changed subjects' behavior. Pretests provide useful baseline data for judging the size of the independent variable's effect. Third, pretest–posttest designs are more powerful, that is, they are more likely than a posttest-only design to detect the effects of an independent variable on behavior.

Although pretest–posttest designs are useful, they are by no means necessary. A posttest-only design provides all of the information needed to determine whether the independent variable had an effect on the dependent variable. Assuming that subjects were assigned to conditions in a random fashion or that a repeated measures design was used, posttest differences between conditions indicate that the independent variable had an effect.

One possible drawback of using pretests is **pretest sensitization**. Administering a pretest may sensitize subjects to respond to the independent variable differently than they would have responded had they not been pretested. For example, imagine we are conducting an experiment to study the effects of social interaction on reducing racial stereotypes. We pretest subjects' stereotypes about other races, then have subjects talk with persons of another race for an hour. Afterward, we posttest subjects' stereotypes. In such a study, the pretest may prompt subjects to think about their racial beliefs, thereby sensitizing them to the subsequent interaction with others of another race. Thus, we may be misled into believing that the independent variable (talking to people of another race) changed subjects' stereotypes, when the effect was actually caused by the combination of the pretest and social interaction.

When subjects are pretested on the dependent variable, researchers sometimes add conditions to their design to look for pretest effects. For example, half of the subjects in each experimental condition could be pretested before receiving the independent variable, whereas the other half would not be pretested. By comparing posttest scores for subjects who were and were not pretested, the researcher could then see whether the pretest had any effects on the results of the experiment.

Summary

We have identified three basic one-way designs: the randomized groups design, the matched-subjects design, and the repeated measures (or within-subjects) design. Each of these designs can be employed as a posttest-only design or a pretest–posttest design, depending on the requirements of a particular experiment. When a pretest–posttest design is used, researchers must be on the lookout for pretest sensitization effects.

Analyzing Experimental Data: An Intuitive Approach

After an experiment is conducted, the researcher must analyze the data to determine whether the independent variable did, in fact, have the predicted effect on the dependent variable(s). Did the manipulation of the independent variable cause systematic changes in subjects' responses? Was memory for pictures affected by providing subjects with interpretations of the droodles they saw? Did different patterns of self-reward and self-punishment result in different amounts of weight loss? Did the length of the lead time between stimulation of the hand and the acoustic startle stimulus affect startle responses?

Examining Group Means

At the most general level, we can determine whether the independent variable had an effect by determining whether the data contain any treatment variance (see Chapter 7). Specifically, the presence of treatment variance is indicated by comparing the means on the dependent variable for the various experimental groups. If the independent variable had an effect on the dependent variable, we would expect to find that the means for the two groups differ. Different group averages would suggest that the independent variable did have an effect—it created differences in the behavior of subjects in the various conditions and thus resulted in treatment variance. Assuming that subjects who were assigned to the experimental conditions did not differ systematically before the study and assuming that no confounds were present (see Chapter 7), the only thing that could have caused the means to differ at the end of the experiment is the independent variable.

In the droodles experiment, for example, subjects who were given an interpretation of the droodles recalled an average of 19.6 of the pictures immediately afterwards. Subjects in the control group (who received no interpretation) recalled an average of only 14.2 of the pictures (Bower et al., 1975). Furthermore, on the recognition test administered a week later, subjects who received interpretations identified an average of 22.0 of the pictures correctly, whereas subjects who did not receive interpretations recognized only 20.1 of the droodles they had seen. On the surface, then, subjects who were given an interpretation remembered more pictures than those who were not given an interpretation.

The Problem: Error Variance Can Affect Mean Differences

This conclusion is not as straightforward as it may appear, however, because the means of the experimental conditions may differ even if the independent variable did *not* have an effect. We discussed one possible cause of such differences in Chapter 7—confound variance. Recall that if something other than the independent variable differs in a systematic fashion between experimental conditions, the differences between the means may be due to this confounding variable rather than to the independent variable. When confounding occurs, the researcher has no way of determining whether the independent variable contributed to the observed differences between the means.

However, even assuming that the researcher successfully eliminates confound variance, the means may differ for yet another reason that is unrelated to the independent variable. Suppose for a moment that the independent variable did *not* have an effect in the droodles experiment described above—that providing an interpretation did not enhance subjects' memory for the droodles. What would we expect to find when we calculated the average number of pictures remembered by subjects in the two groups? Would we expect the means for the two experimental groups to be exactly the same? Probably not. Even if the independent variable did not have an effect, it is unlikely that the means would be identical.

In fact, even if we measured the dependent variable *without* manipulating the independent variable, we would be unlikely to obtain perfectly identical means. Imagine that we randomly assigned subjects to two groups, then showed them droodles while giving interpretations of the droodles to all subjects in both groups. Then we asked subjects to recall as many of the droodles as possible. Would the average number of pictures recalled be exactly the same in both groups even if they both received interpretations? Probably not.

Because of error variance in the data, the recall of the two groups is likely to differ even if they are treated the same. You will recall that error variance reflects the random influences of factors that remain unidentified in the study, such as individual differences and slight variations in how the researcher treats different subjects. These uncontrolled and unidentified variables lead subjects to respond differently whether or not the independent variable has an effect. As a result, the means of experimental groups typically differ even when the independent variable itself did not affect subjects' responses.

But if the means of the two experimental conditions would be expected to differ somewhat even if the independent variable did *not* have an effect, how can we tell whether the difference between the means of the conditions was due to the independent variable (treatment variance) or due to random differences between the groups (error variance)? How big a difference between the means of our conditions must we observe to conclude that the independent variable had an effect?

The Solution: Inferential Statistics

The solution to this problem is simple, in principle. If we can estimate how much the means of the conditions would be expected to differ *even if the independent variable had no effect*, we can then determine whether the difference we obtained exceeds this amount. Put another way, we can conclude that the independent variable had an effect when the difference between the means of the experimental conditions is larger than we would expect it to be if the difference were due only to the effects of error variance.

Unfortunately, we can never be absolutely certain that the difference we obtain between group means is not just the result of error variance. Even large differences between the means of the groups could be due to error variance rather than to the independent variable. We can, however, specify the *probability* that the difference we observed between the means is due to error variance.

Researchers use **inferential statistics** to determine whether observed differences between the means of the experimental groups are greater than what would be expected on the basis of error variance alone. If the observed difference between the group means is larger than we would expect given the amount of error variance in the data, we can conclude that the independent variable caused the difference.

Hypothesis Testing

The Null Hypothesis

Specifically, researchers use inferential statistics to examine the effects of the independent variable by testing something known as the null hypothesis. The **null hypothesis** for an experiment states that the independent variable *did not have an effect on the dependent variable*. Of course, this is usually the opposite of the researcher's actual **experimental hypothesis**, which states that the independent variable *did* have an effect. For statistical purposes, however, we test the null hypothesis rather than the experimental hypothesis. The null hypothesis for the droodles experiment was that subjects provided with interpretations of droodles would remember the same number of droodles as those not provided with an interpretation. Stated another way, the null hypothesis says that the mean number of droodles that subjects remembered would be equal in the two experimental conditions.

Based on the results of statistical tests, the researcher will make one of two decisions about the null hypothesis. On the one hand, if the data show there is a high probability that the null hypothesis is false, the researcher will **reject the null hypothesis** and conclude that the independent variable did indeed have an effect. The researcher will reject the null hypothesis if statistical analyses show that the difference between the means of the experimental groups is larger than would be expected on the basis of how much error variance there is in the data.

On the other hand, if the analyses show an unacceptably low probability of the null hypothesis being false, the researcher will **fail to reject the null hypothesis**. Failing to reject the null hypothesis means that the researcher will conclude that the independent variable had no effect. This would be the case if the statistical analyses indicated that the difference between the group means was about the same as would be expected on the basis of the amount of error variance in the data. Put differently, the researcher will fail to reject the null hypothesis if analyses show a high probability that the difference between the group means reflects nothing more than the influence of error variance.

I said that when there is a low probability of the null hypothesis being false, the researcher would *fail to reject* the null hypothesis—not that the researcher would *accept* the null hypothesis. We use this terminology because, strictly speaking, we cannot obtain data that allow us to truly accept the null hypothesis as confirmed or verified. Although we can determine that an independent variable probably had an effect on the dependent variable (and thus reject the null hypothesis), we cannot conclusively determine that an independent variable did not have an effect (and thus we cannot accept the null hypothesis).

An analogy may clarify this point. In a murder trial, the defendant is assumed not guilty (a null hypothesis) until the jury becomes convinced by the evidence that he or she is, in fact, the murderer. If the jury remains unconvinced of the defendant's guilt, it does not necessarily mean the defendent is innocent. It may simply mean there isn't enough conclusive evidence to convict. When this happens, the jury returns a verdict of not guilty. This verdict does not mean the defendant is innocent. Rather, it means only that the current evidence isn't sufficient to pronounce him or her guilty.

Similarly, if we find that the means of our experimental conditions are not different, we cannot logically conclude that the null hypothesis is true. We can only conclude that the current evidence isn't sufficient to reject it. Strictly speaking, then, the failure to obtain differences between the means of the experimental conditions leads us to *fail to reject* the null hypothesis rather than to *accept* it.

Thus, based on the results of statistical tests, the researcher will either reject or fail to reject the null hypothesis but can never be certain that he or she made the correct decision. We can never know for sure whether the differences between the means of the experimental conditions represent a true difference caused by the independent variable or a spurious difference resulting from error variance. Fortunately, inferential statistics allow us to specify the probability that the difference is due to error variance. By using inferential statistics, we can specify the probability that we would have obtained a particular pattern of results if the null hypothesis had been true.

Type I and Type II Errors

Figure 8.6 shows the decisions that a researcher may make about the null hypothesis and the outcomes that may result. Four outcomes are possible. First, the researcher may correctly reject the null hypothesis, thereby identifying a true effect of the independent variable. Second, the researcher may correctly fail to reject the null hypothesis, accurately concluding that the independent variable had no effect. In both cases, a correct conclusion was reached.

We may also make two kinds of error when deciding whether to reject the null hypothesis. These other two possible outcomes are known as Type I and Type II error. A **Type I error** occurs when a researcher erroneously concludes that the null hypothesis is false and, thus, rejects it. More straightforwardly, a

Researcher's decision

	Reject null hypothesis	Fail to reject null hypothesis
Null hypothesis is false	Correct decision	Type II error
Null hypothesis is true	Type I error	Correct decision

Figure 8.6 Statistical decisions and outcomes

Type I error occurs when a researcher concludes that the independent variable had an effect on the dependent variable when, in fact, the difference between the means of the experimental conditions was actually due to error variance.

The probability of making a Type I error—of rejecting the null hypothesis when it is true—is called the **alpha level**. As a rule of thumb, researchers set the alpha level at .05. In other words, researchers usually reject the null hypothesis when there is less than a .05 chance (that is, fewer than 5 chances out of 100) that the difference they obtained between the means of the experimental groups was due to error variance rather than to the independent variable. If statistical analyses indicate that there is less than a 5% chance that the difference between the means of our experimental conditions was due to error variance, we reject the null hypothesis, knowing there is only a small chance that our decision was mistaken.

When we reject the null hypothesis with a low probability of making a Type I error, we refer to the difference between the means as **statistically significant**. A statistically significant finding is one that has a low probability (usually < .05) of occurring as a result of error variance alone. We'll return to the important concepts of alpha level and statistical significance below.

On the other hand, the researcher may fail to reject the null hypothesis when, in fact, it is false—a **Type II error**. In this case, the researcher concludes that the independent variable did not have an effect when, in fact, it did. The probability of making a Type II error is called **beta**.

Several factors can lead to Type II errors. If the researcher did not measure the dependent variable properly or if the measurement technique was unreliable, he or she might not detect effects of the independent variable that occurred. Or mistakes may have been made in collecting, coding, or analyzing the data. Alternatively, the researcher may have used too few subjects to detect the effects of the independent variable.

IN DEPTH

Publishing Null Findings

Students are often surprised to learn that scientific journals are reluctant, if not downright unwilling, to publish studies that fail to obtain effects of the independent variable. You might think that such **null findings** tell us that certain independent variables do *not* affect behavior. After all, if we predict that comprehension increases memory for droodles, but our data show that subjects who do and do not receive interpretations of the droodles don't differ in their recall of the pictures, haven't we learned that comprehension does *not* affect memory?

The answer is no, for as we have seen, we may fail to obtain differences between our experimental conditions for reasons that have nothing to do with the truth of a particular hypothesis. As a result, null findings are uninformative regarding the hypothesis being tested. Was the hypothesis disconfirmed, or did we simply design a lousy experiment and make a Type II error? Because we can never know for certain, journals generally will not publish studies that fail to obtain effects.

Keep in mind that although researchers cannot be sure they drew the correct conclusion about the validity of their hypothesis, they can specify the probability that they made a Type I error if they rejected the null hypothesis. This will become clearer below.

Summary

In analyzing data collected in experimental research, researchers attempt to determine whether the means of the various experimental conditions differ above and beyond what they would if the differences were due only to error variance. If the difference between means is large relative to the error variance, the researcher rejects the null hypothesis and concludes that the independent variable had an effect. The researcher makes this conclusion with the understanding that there is less than a .05 probability that he or she has made a Type I error. If the difference in means is no larger than one would expect simply on the basis of the amount of error variance in the data, the researcher fails to reject the null hypothesis and concludes that the independent variable had no effect.

Analysis of Two-Group Experiments: The *t*-test

Two statistical tests are often used to analyze the results of experiments that have a single independent variable. If an independent variable has only two levels and the scores are at an interval or ratio level of measurement, the *t*-test is typically used. When the experiment has more than two conditions (and the scores are at the interval or ratio level), researchers analyze their data using the *F*-test, which we'll discuss in Chapter 10.

Both of these tests are based on the same rationale. The error variance in the data is calculated to obtain an estimate of how much the means of the conditions would be expected to differ if the differences were due only to random error variance (and the independent variable had no effect). Then the observed differences between the means are compared with this estimate. If the observed differences between the means are so large, relative to this estimate, that they are highly unlikely to be the result of error variance alone, the null hypothesis is rejected. As we saw above, the likelihood of erroneously rejecting the null hypothesis is held at less than whatever alpha level the researcher has stipulated, usually .05.

Conducting a *t*-test

Although the rationale behind inferential statistics may seem complex and convoluted, conducting a *t*-test to analyze data from a two-group randomized groups experiment is straightforward. To conduct a *t*-test, you calculate a value for *t* using a simple formula. You then see whether this calculated value of *t* exceeds a certain critical value in a table. If it does, the group means differ by more than what we would expect on the basis of error variance alone.

The formula for a *t*-test is

$$t = \frac{\bar{x}_1 - \bar{x}_2}{s_p \sqrt{1/n_1 + 1/n_2}}.$$

Conducting a *t*-test is accomplished in five steps:

Step 1. Calculate the means of the two groups.
Step 2. Calculate the standard error of the difference between the two means.
Step 3. Find the calculated value of *t*.
Step 4. Find the critical value of *t*.
Step 5. Determine whether the null hypothesis should be rejected by comparing the calculated value of *t* to the critical value of *t*.

We will describe each of these steps in detail.

STEP 1 To test whether the means of two experimental groups are different, we obviously need to know the means. These means will go in the numerator of the formula above. Thus, first we must calculate the means of the two groups, $\bar{x}_1$ and $\bar{x}_2$.

STEP 2 To determine whether the means of the two experimental groups vary more than we would expect on the basis of error variance, we need an estimate of how much the means would be expected to differ on the basis of error variance alone. The *standard error of the difference between two means*, which is the quantity in the denominator of the formula for *t*, provides an index of this.

As you will see in a moment, this quantity is based directly on the amount of error variance in the data. As we saw in Chapter 7, error variance is estimated from the variability *within* the experimental groups. Any variability we observe in the responses of subjects in the same experimental condition cannot be due to the independent variable, because they all received the *same* level of the independent variable. Rather this variance reflects extraneous variables, chiefly individual differences in how subjects responded to the independent variable and unsystematic differences in how subjects were treated during the study (that is, poor experimental control).

Calculating the standard error of the difference is accomplished in 4 steps. (2a) First, calculate the variances of the two experimental groups. You may want to review the section in Chapter 2 that dealt with the variance. The variance for each group is calculated from one of these formulas:

$$s^2 = \frac{\Sigma x^2 - \frac{(\Sigma x)^2}{n}}{n-1} \quad \text{or} \quad \frac{\Sigma(x-\bar{x})^2}{n-1}$$

You'll calculate this twice, once for each experimental group.

(2b) Then, calculate the pooled variance—s_p^2. This is the average of the variances for the two groups:

$$s_p^2 = \frac{(n_1 - 1)s_1^2 + (n_2 - 1)s_2^2}{n_1 + n_2 - 2}$$

In this formula, n_1 and n_2 are the sample sizes for groups 1 and 2, and s_1^2 and s_2^2 are the variances that you calculated in Step 2a.

(2c) Then take the square root of the pooled variance, which gives you the pooled standard deviation. Insert this quantity for s_p in the formula for t.

(2d) Also insert the values for n_1 and n_2 into the formula. These are the sample sizes for the two groups.

STEP 3 With values for the means of the two groups ($\bar{x}_1$ and $\bar{x}_2$), the pooled standard deviation (s_p), and the sample sizes (n_1 and n_2), you are ready to calculate t.

$$t = \frac{\bar{x}_1 - \bar{x}_2}{s_p\sqrt{1/n_1 + 1/n_2}}$$

STEP 4 Then, you must locate the critical value of t in a table designed for that purpose. Appendix A-2 shows the critical values of t. To find the critical value of t, you need to know two things.

(4a) First, calculate the degrees of freedom for the t-test. For a two-group randomized design, the degrees of freedom (abbreviated df) is equal to the number of subjects minus 2 (that is, $n_1 + n_2 - 2$).

(4b) Second, you need to specify the alpha level for the test. As we saw earlier, the alpha level is the probability we are willing to accept for making a Type I error—rejecting the null hypothesis when it is true. Usually, researchers set the alpha level at .05.

With these two numbers, you consult the table in Appendix A-2 to find the critical value of t. For example, let's assume we have 10 subjects in each group. The degrees of freedom would be $10 + 10 - 2 = 18$. Then, assuming the alpha level is set at .05, we look down the column marked 1-tailed .05 until we reach df = 18. Here we find that the critical value of t is 1.734.

STEP 5 Finally, you compare your calculated value of t to the critical value of t obtained in the table of t-values. If the absolute value of the calculated value of t (step 3) exceeds the critical value of t obtained from the table (step 4), you reject the null hypothesis. The difference between the two means is large enough, relative to the error variance, that you can conclude that the difference is due to the independent variable and not to error variance. A difference that is so large that it is very unlikely to be due to error variance is called **statistically significant.**

However, if the absolute value of the calculated value of t obtained in step 3 is less than the critical value of t, you do not reject the null hypothesis. You conclude that the probability that the difference between the means is due to error variance is unacceptably high. In such cases, the difference between the means is called *nonsignificant.*

DEVELOPING YOUR RESEARCH SKILLS

Computational Example of a *t*-test

To those of us who are sometimes inclined to overeat, anorexia nervosa is a puzzle. The anorexic exercises extreme control over her eating (virtually all anorexics are women) so that she loses a great deal of weight, often to the point that her health, if not life, is threatened. Why would a person restrict her intake of food so drastically? One theory suggests that anorexics restrict their eating to maintain a sense of control over the world. When everything else in one's life seems out of control, one can always exercise control over what and how much one eats. One implication of this theory is that anorexics should respond to a feeling of low control by reducing the amount they eat.

To investigate this hypothesis, imagine that we selected college women who scored high on a measure of anorexic tendencies. We assigned these subjects randomly to one of two experimental conditions. Subjects in one condition were led to experience a sense of having high control, whereas subjects in the other condition experienced a loss of control. Subjects were then given the opportunity to sample sweetened breakfast cereals under the guise of a taste test. The dependent variable is the amount of cereal each subject eats.

The number of pieces of cereal for 12 subjects in this study are shown below:

High control condition	Low control condition
13	3
39	12
42	14
28	11
41	18
58	16

The question to be addressed is whether subjects in the low control condition ate significantly less cereal than subjects in the high control condition. We can conduct a *t*-test on these data by following the five steps above:

STEP 1   Calculate the means of the two groups.

High control $= \bar{x}_1 = (13 + 39 + 42 + 28 + 41 + 58)/6 = 36.8$

Low control $= \bar{x}_2 = (3 + 12 + 14 + 11 + 18 + 16)/6 = 12.3$

STEP 2 (2a) Calculate the variances of the two groups, using either of the formulas we have learned. Here we use the formula $s^2 = \Sigma(x - \bar{x})^2/(n - 1)$.

High control group			Low control group		
x	$(x - \bar{x})$	$(x - \bar{x})^2$	x	$(x - \bar{x})$	$(x - \bar{x})^2$
13	−23.8	566.44	3	−9.3	86.49
39	2.2	4.84	12	−0.3	.09
42	5.2	27.04	14	1.7	2.89
28	−8.8	77.44	11	−1.3	1.69
41	4.2	17.64	18	5.7	32.49
58	21.2	449.44	16	3.7	13.69

$$\Sigma = 1{,}142.84$$
$$s_1^2 = 1142.84/5 = 228.57$$

$$\Sigma = 137.34$$
$$s_2^2 = 137.34/5 = 27.47$$

(2b) Calculate the pooled variance, using the formula

$$s_p^2 = \frac{(n_1 - 1)s_1^2 + (n_2 - 1)s_2^2}{n_1 + n_2 - 2}$$

$$= \frac{(6 - 1)(228.57) + (6 - 1)(27.47)}{6 + 6 - 2}$$

$$= \frac{(1{,}142.85) + (137.35)}{10}$$

$$s_p^2 = 128.02$$

$$s_p = \sqrt{128.02} = 11.31.$$

STEP 3 Solve for the calculated value of t:

$$t = \frac{\bar{x}_1 - \bar{x}_2}{s_p\sqrt{1/n_1 + 1/n_2}}$$

$$= \frac{36.8 - 12.3}{11.31\sqrt{1/6 + 1/6}}$$

$$= \frac{24.5}{11.31\sqrt{.333}}$$

$$= \frac{24.5}{11.31\,(.577)}$$

$$= \frac{24.5}{6.53}$$

$$t = 3.75.$$

STEP 4   Find the critical value of *t* in Appendix A-2. The degrees of freedom equal 10 (6 + 6 − 2); we'll set the alpha level at .05. Looking down the column for a one-tailed test, we see that the critical value of *t* is 1.812.

STEP 5   Comparing the calculated value of *t* to the critical value, we see that the calculated value exceeds the critical value. Thus, we conclude that the average amount of cereal eaten in the two conditions differed significantly.

Back to the Droodles Experiment

To analyze the data from their droodles experiment, Bower and his colleagues conducted two *t*-tests—one on the number of droodles that subjects recalled immediately after seeing them, and a second on the number of droodles that subjects were able to identify 1 week later.

Immediate recall of droodles   As we saw earlier in this chapter, subjects who received an interpretation of the droodles recalled an average of 19.6 droodles immediately afterward, whereas those who did not receive an interpretation recalled an average of 14.2. When the authors conducted a *t*-test on these means using the above formula, they obtained a calculated value of *t* of 3.43. They then referred to a table of the critical values of *t* (such as that in Appendix A-2). The degrees of freedom were $n_1 + n_2 - 2$, or $9 + 9 - 2 = 16$. Rather than setting the alpha level at .05, the researchers were more cautious and used an alpha level of .01. (That is, they were willing to risk only a 1-in-100 chance of making a Type I error.) The critical value of *t* when df = 16 and alpha level = .01 is 2.583. Because the calculated value of *t* (3.43) was larger than the critical value (2.583), the means differed more than would be expected if only error variance were operating. Thus, the two means were significantly or reliably different. Put differently, the researchers rejected the null hypothesis that comprehension does not aid memory for pictures, knowing that the probability that they made a Type I error was less than 1 in 100.

As the authors themselves put it:

> The primary result of interest is that an average of 19.6 pictures out of 28 (70%) were accurately recalled by the label group . . . , whereas only 14.2 pictures (51%) were recalled by the no-label group. . . . The means differ reliably in the predicted direction [$t(16) = 3.43, p < .01$]. Thus, we have clear confirmation that "picture understanding" enhances picture recall (Bower et al., 1975, p. 218).

Recognition of droodles 1 week later   The data regarding how many droodles subjects recognized accurately 1 week later were also analyzed using a *t*-test. Although subjects who received an interpretation of the droodles recognized 22 droodles whereas those who did not receive an interpretation recognized 20.1 droodles, the *t*-test showed that this difference was *not* larger than what we might expect from error variance alone. Because the calculated value of *t* did not exceed the critical value of *t*, the null hypothesis was not rejected.

I N   D E P T H

One-Tailed and Two-Tailed Tests

A hypothesis about the outcome of a two-group experiment can be stated in one of two ways. A **directional hypothesis** states explicitly which of the two condition means is expected to be larger. That is, the researcher predicts the specific direction of the anticipated effect. A **nondirectional hypothesis** merely states that the two means are expected to differ, but no prediction is ventured regarding which mean will be larger. ~ 2 TAILED

When a researcher's prediction is directional—as is most often the case—a one-tailed *t*-test is used. Each of the examples above involved one-tailed tests because the direction of the difference between the means was predicted. Because the hypotheses were directional, we used the value for a one-tailed test in the table of *t* values (Appendix A-2). In the droodles experiment, for example, the researchers predicted that the number of droodles remembered would be *greater* in the condition in which the droodle was explained than in the control condition. Because this was a directional hypothesis, they used the critical value for a one-tailed *t*-test. Had their hypothesis been nondirectional, a two-tailed test would have been used.

Analyses of Matched-Subjects and Within-Subjects Designs

The procedure for conducting a *t*-test we just described is for a two-group randomized groups design. A slightly different formula, the **paired *t*-test**, is used when the experiment involves a matched-subjects or a within-subjects design. The paired *t*-test takes into account the fact that the subjects in the two conditions are similar, if not identical, on an attribute related to the dependent variable. In the matched-subjects design we have randomly assigned matched pairs of subjects to the two conditions; in the within-subjects design the same subjects serve in both conditions.

Either way, each subject in one condition is matched with a subject in the other condition (again, in a within-subjects design the matched subject is the subject him- or herself). As a result of this matching, aside from whatever effects the independent variable may have, the matched scores in the two conditions should be correlated. In a matched-subjects design the matched partners of subjects who score high on the dependent variable in one condition (relative to the other subjects) should score relatively high on the dependent variable in the other condition. And the matched partners of subjects who scored low in one condition should tend to score low in the other. Similarly, in a within-subjects design subjects who score high in one condition should score relatively high in the other condition, and vice versa. Thus, a positive correlation should be obtained between the matched scores in the two conditions.

The paired *t*-test takes advantage of this correlation to reduce the estimate of error variance used to calculate *t*. In essence, we can account for the source of some of the error variance in the data: It comes from individual differences among the subjects. Given that we have matched pairs of subjects, we can use the correlation between the two conditions to estimate the amount of error variance that is due to these differences. Then we can remove this component of the error variance—just throw it away—when we test the difference between the condition means.

Reducing error variance leads to a more *powerful* test of the null hypothesis—one that is more likely to detect the effects of the independent variable than the randomized groups *t*-test. The paired *t*-test is more powerful because we have reduced the size of s_p in the denominator of the formula for *t*. And as s_p gets smaller, the calculated value of *t* gets larger.

We will not go into the formula for the paired *t*-test here. However, a detailed explanation of this test can be found in most introductory statistics books. Two are listed at the end of this chapter.

CONTRIBUTORS TO BEHAVIORAL RESEARCH

Statistics in the Brewery: W. S. Gosset

One might imagine that the important advances in research design and statistics came at the hands of statisticians hidden away in stuffy offices at noted universities. Indeed, many of those who provided the foundation for behavioral science, such as Wilhelm Wundt and Karl Pearson, were academicians. However, many methodological and statistical approaches were developed while solving real-world problems, notably in industry and agriculture.

A case in point involves the work of William Sealy Gosset (1876–1937), whose contributions to research included the *t*-test. With a background in both chemistry and mathematics, Gosset was hired by Guinness Brewery in Dublin, Ireland, in 1899. Among his duties, Gosset investigated how the quality of beer is affected by various raw materials (such as different strains of barley and hops) and by various methods of production (such as variations in brewing temperature).

During 1906–07, Gosset spent a year in specialized study in London, where he studied under Karl Pearson (see Chapter 6). During this time, Gosset worked on developing solutions to statistical problems he encountered at the brewery. Based on this work, in 1908 he published a paper that laid out the principles for the *t*-test. Interestingly, he published his work under the pen name Student, and to this day, this test is often referred to as the Student's *t*.

SUMMARY

1. The simplest experiment is the one-way experimental design, an experiment in which there is a single independent variable.

2. Researchers use three general versions of the one-way design—the randomized groups design (in which subjects are assigned randomly to two or more groups), the matched-subjects design (in which subjects are first matched into blocks then randomly assigned to conditions), and the repeated measures design (in which each subject serves in all experimental conditions).

3. Each of these designs may involve a single measurement of the dependent variable after the manipulation of the independent variable, or a pretest and a posttest.

4. Experimental data are analyzed by comparing the difference between the condition means to the amount we would expect the means to differ if the independent variable did not affect subjects' responses.

5. If the means differ more than expected based on the amount of error variance present, researchers reject the null hypothesis and conclude that the independent variable had an effect. If the means do not differ by more than error variance would predict, researchers fail to reject the null hypothesis.

6. Because the decision to reject or fail to reject the null hypothesis is a probabilistic one, researchers may make one of two kinds of errors. A Type I error occurs when the researcher rejects the null hypothesis when it is true; a Type II error occurs when the researcher fails to reject the null hypothesis when it is false.

7. The *t*-test is used to analyze the data from two-group experiments. A value for *t* is calculated; then it is compared with a critical value of t. If the calculated value exceeds the critical value, the null hypothesis is rejected.

8. Hypotheses about the outcome of two-group experiments may be directional or nondirectional. Whether the hypothesis is directional or nondirectional has implications for whether the critical value of *t* used in the *t*-test is one-tailed or two-tailed.

FOR MORE INFORMATION

Details regarding *t*-tests, including paired *t*-tests, may be found in:

Statistics for the Behavioral Sciences: A First Course for Students of Psychology and Education by F. J. Gravetter and L. B. Wallanu, 1982, St. Paul, MN: West Publishing.

Elementary Statistics (4th ed.) by J. T. Spence, J. W. Cotton, B. J. Underwood, and C. P. Duncan, 1983, Englewood Cliffs, NJ: Prentice-Hall.

KEY TERMS

one-way design
two-group experimental design
multilevel experimental design
randomized groups design
matched random assignment
matched-subjects design
repeated measures design
posttest-only design
pretest–posttest design
pretest sensitization
inferential statistics
null hypothesis
experimental hypothesis

rejecting the null hypothesis
failing to reject the null hypothesis
Type I error
Type II error
alpha level
beta
null findings
t-test
F-test
statistically significant
directional versus nondirectional hypothesis
paired *t*-test

REVIEW QUESTIONS

1. How many conditions are there in the simplest possible experiment?
2. Contrast how subjects are assigned to conditions in a randomized groups, a matched-subjects, and a repeated measures design.
3. What are the relative advantages and disadvantages of posttest-only designs versus pretest–posttest experimental designs?
4. In analyzing the data from a two-group experiment, why is it not sufficient to simply examine the condition means to see whether they differ?
5. Why do researchers use inferential statistics?
6. When analyzing data, why do researchers test the null hypothesis rather than the experimental hypothesis?
7. Discuss the two decisions a researcher may make about the null hypothesis on the basis of statistical analyses.
8. Why are journal editors reluctant to publish null findings?

9. Explain the rationale behind the *t*-test.

10. Distinguish between one-tailed and two-tailed tests.

11. What was W. S. Gosset's contribution to behavioral research?

EXERCISES

1. This question is to help you gain experience using the table of the critical values of *t* in Appendix A-2.

a. Find the critical value of *t* for an experiment in which there were 28 subjects, using an alpha level of .05 for a one-tailed test.

b. Find the critical value of *t* for an experiment in which there were 28 subjects, using an alpha level of .01 for a one-tailed test.

c. You will notice that, given the same degrees of freedom, the critical value of *t* is larger when the alpha level is .01 than when it is .05. Can you figure out why?

2. With the increasing availability of computers, many students now type their class papers using word processors rather than typewriters. Because it is so much easier to edit and change text with word processors, we might expect word-processed papers to be better than those simply typed. To test this hypothesis, imagine that we instructed 30 students to write a 10-page term paper. We randomly assigned 15 students to type their papers on a typewriter and the other 15 students to type their papers on a word processor. (Let's assume all of the students were at least mediocre typists with some experience on a word processor.)

After receiving the students' papers, we then retyped all of the papers to be uniform in appearance (to eliminate the confound that would occur because typed and word-processed papers *look* different). Then, a professor graded each paper on a 10-point scale. The grades were as follows:

Typed papers	Word-processed papers
6	9
3	4
4	7
7	7
7	6
5	10
7	9
10	8
7	5
4	8
5	7
6	4
3	8
7	7
6	9

Conduct a *t*-test to determine whether the quality of papers written using a word processor was higher than that of papers typed on a typewriter.

ANSWERS TO EXERCISES

1. a. If there are 28 subjects, the degrees of freedom are 26. The critical value of a one-tailed *t*-test with df = 26 and an alpha level of .05 is 1.706.

   b. The critical value for a one-tailed *t*-test with df = 26 and an alpha level of .01 is 2.479.

   c. The critical value of *t* is larger when the alpha level is .01 than .05 because by setting the alpha level at .01, we require greater certainty that the difference between the condition means was not due to error variance. To achieve this greater certainty, the difference between the means, relative to the error variance, must be greater. Thus, the critical value of *t* is larger.

2. The calculated value of *t* for these data is −2.08, which exceeds the critical value of 1.701 (alpha level = .05, df = 28, one-tailed *t*-test). Thus, the average grade for the papers written on a word processor (mean = 7.2) was significantly higher than the average grade for typed papers (mean = 5.8).

The Design of Factorial Experiments

With the growth of urban areas during the 1960s, psychologists became interested in the effects of crowding on behavior, emotion, and health. In early work on crowding, researchers assumed that increasing the density of a situation—decreasing the amount of space or increasing the number of people in it—typically leads to negative effects such as aggressiveness and stress.

Jonathan Freedman (1975) questioned this view, proposing that rather than always evoking negative reactions, high-density situations simply intensify whatever reactions people are experiencing at the time. If people are in an unpleasant situation, increasing density will make their experience even more unpleasant. Feeling crowded during a boring lecture only makes things worse, for example. But if people are enjoying themselves, Freedman predicted, higher density will intensify their positive reactions. The larger the crowd at an enjoyable concert, the more you might enjoy it (within reasonable limits, of course).

Think for a moment about how you might design an experiment to test Freedman's density–intensity hypothesis. According to this hypothesis, people's reactions to social settings are a function of two factors: the density of the situation and the pleasantness of people's reactions in it. Thus, testing this hypothesis requires studying the combined effects of two independent variables simultaneously.

The one-way experimental designs we discussed in Chapter 8 would not be particularly useful in this regard. A one-way design allows us to examine the effects of only one independent variable. What is needed is a design that involves two or more variables simultaneously. Such a design, in which two or more independent variables are manipulated, is called a **factorial design**. Often the independent variables are referred to as **factors**.

To test his density–intensity hypothesis, Freedman (1975) designed an experiment in which he manipulated two independent variables: the density of

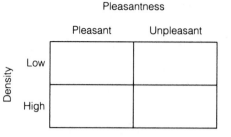

Figure 9.1   A factorial design: Freedman's density–intensity experiment

---

Explanation: *Freedman manipulated two independent variables: the density of the setting (low versus high density) and the pleasantness of the situation (pleasant versus unpleasant). In this design, four conditions reflect all possible combinations of density and pleasantness.*

the room and the pleasantness of the situation. In his study, subjects delivered a brief speech to a small audience. The audience was instructed to provide the speaker with either positive or negative feedback about the speech. Thus, for subjects in one condition the situation was predominately pleasant, whereas for subjects in the other condition the situation was predominately unpleasant.

In addition, Freedman varied the size of the room in which subjects gave their speeches. Some subjects spoke in a large room (150 square feet) and some gave their speeches in a small room (70 square feet). Thus, although audience size was constant in both conditions, the density was higher for some subjects than for others.

After giving their speeches and receiving either positive or negative feedback, subjects completed a questionnaire on which they indicated their reactions to the situation, including how much they liked the members of the audience and how willing they would be to participate in the study again.

The experimental design for Freedman's experiment is shown in Figure 9.1. As you can see, two variables were manipulated: density and pleasantness. There were four conditions in the study that represented the four possible combinations of these two variables. The density–intensity theory predicts that high density will increase positive reactions in the pleasant condition and increase negative reactions in the unpleasant condition. As we'll see below, the results of the experiment clearly supported these predictions.

Factorial Designs

Like the density–intensity theory, many theories stipulate that behavior is a function of two or more variables. Researchers use factorial designs to study the individual and combined effects of two or more factors within a single experiment.

To understand factorial designs, you need to become familiar with the nomenclature researchers use to describe the size and structure of such designs. First, just as a one-way design has only one independent variable, a two-way factorial design has two independent variables, a three-way factorial design has three independent variables, and so on. Freedman's test of the density–intensity hypothesis was a two-way factorial design because two independent variables were involved.

The structure of a factorial design is often specified in a way that immediately indicates to a reader how many independent variables were manipulated and how many levels there were of each variable. For example, Freedman's experiment was an example of what researchers call a 2 × 2 (pronounced

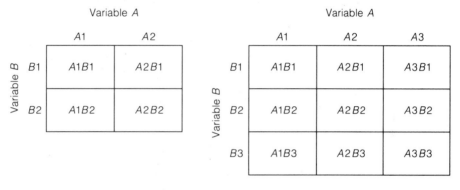

a 2 × 2 design   **b** 3 × 3 design

c 4 × 2 design

Figure 9.2   Examples of two-way factorial designs

Explanation (a): A 2 × 2 design has two independent variables, each with two levels, for a total of four conditions.

Explanation (b): In this 3 × 3 design, there are two independent variables, both of which have three levels. Because there are nine possible combinations of variables A and B, the design has nine conditions.

Explanation (c): In this 4 × 2 design, independent variable A has four levels and independent variable B has two levels, resulting in eight experimental conditions.

"2 by 2") factorial design. The phrase 2 × 2 tells us that the design had two independent variables, each with two levels (see Figure 9.2(a)). A 3 × 3 factorial design also involves two independent variables, but each variable has three levels (see Figure 9.2(b)). A 2 × 4 factorial design has two independent variables, one with two levels and one with four levels (see Figure 9.2(c)).

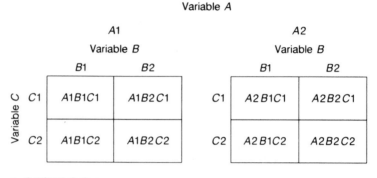

a   2 × 2 × 2 design

b   2 × 2 × 4 design

Figure 9.3   Examples of higher-order designs

Explanation (a): A three-way design such as this one involves the manipulation of three independent variables—*A, B,* and *C.* In a 2 × 2 × 2 design, each of the variables has two levels, resulting in eight conditions.

Explanation (b): This is a 2 × 2 × 4 (three-way) design. Variables *A* and *B* each have two levels, and variable *C* has four levels. There are 16 possible combinations of the three variables and therefore 16 conditions in the experiment.

So far, our examples have involved two-way factorial designs, that is, designs with two independent variables. However, experiments can have more than two. For example, a $2 \times 2 \times 2$ design has three independent variables; each of the variables has two levels (see Figure 9.3(a)). A $2 \times 2 \times 4$ factorial design also has three independent variables; two of the independent variables have two levels each and the other variable has four levels. (see Figure 9.3(b)). A four-way factorial design, such as a $2 \times 2 \times 3 \times 3$ design, would have four independent variables—two would have two levels and two would have three levels. The size and structure of every factorial design can be described using this system.

We can tell how many experimental conditions a factorial design has simply by multiplying the numbers in a design specification. For example, a 2×2 design has four different cells or conditions, that is four possible combinations of the two independent variables ($2 \times 2 = 4$). A $3 \times 4 \times 2$ design has 24 different experimental conditions ($3 \times 4 \times 2 = 24$), and so on.

Types of Factorial Design

Like the one-way designs we discussed in Chapter 8, factorial designs may include randomized groups, matched-subjects, or repeated measures designs. In addition, as we will see, the split-plot or between-within design combines features of the randomized groups and repeated measures designs.

Randomized Groups Factorial Design

In a **randomized groups factorial design** (which is also called a *completely randomized factorial design*) subjects are assigned randomly to one of the possible combinations of the independent variables. In Freedman's (1975) test of the density–intensity hypothesis, subjects were assigned randomly to one of four combinations of density and pleasantness.

Matched-Subjects Factorial Design

As in the matched-subjects one-way design we discussed in Chapter 8, the **matched-subjects factorial design** involves first matching subjects into blocks on the basis of some variable that correlates with the dependent variable. There will be as many subjects in each matched block as there are experimental conditions. In a 3×2 factorial design, for example, 6 subjects would be matched into each block. Then the subjects in each block are randomly assigned to one of the six experimental conditions. As before, the primary reason for using a matched-subjects design is to more closely equate the subjects in the experimental conditions before introducing the independent variable.

Repeated Measures Factorial Design

A **repeated measures** (or *within-subjects*) **factorial design** requires all subjects to participate in every experimental condition. Although repeated measures designs are feasible with small factorial designs (such as a 2 × 2 design), they become unwieldy with larger designs. For example, in a 2 × 2 × 2 × 4 repeated measures factorial design, each subject would serve in 32 different conditions! With such large designs, order and carryover effects can become a problem.

Split-Plot Factorial Design

Because one-way designs involve a single independent variable, they must involve random assignment, matched-subjects, or repeated measures. Because factorial designs involve more than one independent variable, they can combine features of both randomized groups designs and repeated measures designs in a single experiment. Some independent variables in a factorial experiment may involve random assignment while other variables involve a repeated measure. A design that combines one or more between-subjects variables with one or more within-subjects variables is called a **split-plot factorial design** or a **between-within design**. The name *split-plot*, which was adopted from agricultural research, actually refers an area of ground that has been subdivided for research purposes.

Walk (1969) used a split-plot design to study depth perception in infants, using a "visual cliff" apparatus. The visual cliff consists of a clear Plexiglas platform with a checkerboard pattern underneath. On one side of the platform, the checkerboard is directly under the Plexiglas. On the other side of the platform, the checkerboard is farther below the Plexiglass, giving the impression of a sharp drop-off, or cliff. In Walk's experiment, the deep side of the cliff consisted of a checkerboard design 5 inches below the clear Plexiglas surface. On the shallow side, the checkerboard was directly beneath the glass.

Walk experimentally manipulated the size of the checkerboard pattern. In one condition the pattern consisted of ¾-inch blocks, and in the other condition the pattern consisted of ¼-inch blocks. Subjects (who were 6½-to-15 month-old babies) were randomly assigned to *either* the ¼-inch or ¾-inch condition just as in a randomized groups design.

Walk manipulated a second independent variable just as in a repeated measures or within-subjects design. He had each infant tested on the cliff more than once. Each was placed on the board between the deep and shallow sides of the cliff and beckoned by its mother from the shallow side; then the procedure was repeated on the deep side. Thus, each infant served in both the shallow and deep conditions.

This is a split-plot or between-within factorial design because one inde-

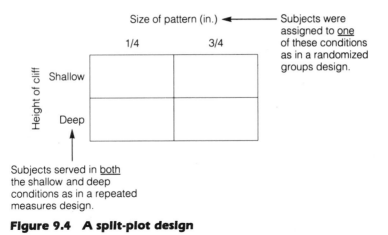

Figure 9.4   A split-plot design
(after Walk, 1969)

Explanation: In this 2 × 2 split-plot design, one independent variable (size of the block design) was a between-subjects factor in which subjects were assigned randomly to one condition or the other. The other independent variable (height of the visual cliff) was a within-subjects factor. All subjects were tested at both the shallow and deep sides of the visual cliff.

pendent variable (size of pattern) involved randomly assigning subjects to conditions, whereas the other independent variable (shallow versus deep side) involved a repeated measure. This design is shown in Figure 9.4.

Main Effects and Interactions

The primary advantage of factorial designs over one-way designs is that they provide information not only about the separate effects of each independent variable but about the effects of the independent variables when they are combined.

Put another way, assuming we have eliminated all experimental confounds (see Chapter 7), a one-way design allows us to identify only two sources of the total variability we observe in subjects' responses: Either the behavioral variability was treatment variance due to the independent variable or it was error variance (see Chapter 8). A factorial design allows us to identify other possible sources of the variability we observe in the dependent variable. When we use factorial designs, we can examine whether the variability in scores was due (1) to the individual effects of each independent variable, (2) to the combined or interactive effects of the independent variables, or (3) to error variance. Thus, factorial designs give researchers a fuller, more complete picture of how behavior is affected by sets of independent variables acting together.

Main Effects

The effect of a single independent variable in a factorial design is called a **main effect**. A main effect reflects the effect of a particular independent variable and ignores the effects of other independent variables. A factorial design will have as many main effects as there are independent variables. For example, because a 2 × 3 design has two independent variables, we can examine two main effects.

In Freedman's (1975) density–intensity experiment, two main effects were tested: the effects of density (ignoring pleasantness) and the effects of pleasantness (ignoring density). The test of the main effect of density asked whether subjects' responses differed in the high- and low-density conditions (ignoring whether they were in the pleasant or unpleasant condition). Analysis of the data showed no differences between subjects' responses in the low- and high-density conditions. That is, averaging across the pleasant and unpleasant conditions, Freedman found that subjects in the low- and high-density conditions did not differ significantly. The means for the low- and high-density conditions were 2.06 and 2.07, respectively. As Freedman expected, high density by itself had no discernible effect on subjects' reactions.

Not surprisingly, Freedman did find a main effect of the pleasantness variable. Subjects who received positive reactions to their speeches rated the situation as more pleasant (mean rating = 2.12) than those who received negative reactions (mean rating = 2.01). Of course, this main effect is not particularly surprising or interesting, but it serves as a manipulation check by showing that subjects perceived the pleasant situation to be more pleasant than the unpleasant situation.

Interactions

In addition to providing information about the main effects of the independent variables, a factorial design provides information about interactions between the independent variables. An **interaction** is present when the effect of one independent variable differs across the levels of other independent variables. For example, if the effect of variable *A* is different under one level of variable *B* than it is under another level of variable *B*, an interaction is present.

Consider, for example, what happens if you mix alcohol and certain drugs, such as sedatives. The effects of drinking a given amount of alcohol are quite different depending on whether you've taken no sleeping pills, one sleeping pill, or four sleeping pills, for example. Two mixed drinks that may result in only slight inebriation under normal circumstances may create pronounced changes in behavior if you've taken four sleeping pills. Alcohol and sleeping pills *interact* to affect behavior.

Similarly, the density–intensity hypothesis predicted an interaction of density and pleasantness on subjects' reactions. High density should have a different effect on subjects who received positive feedback than on those who

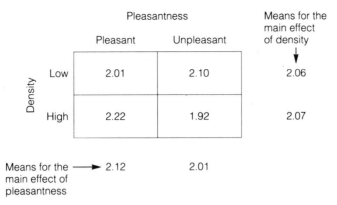

Figure 9.5   Effects of density and pleasantness on subjects' liking for other participants in study

From *Crowding and Behavior* (p. 150) by J. L. Freedman, 1975, San Francisco: W. H. Freeman and Company. Copyright 1975 by J. L. Freedman. Adapted by permission of Jonathan Freedman and the publisher.

Explanation: These numbers are subjects' average ratings of how much they liked the members of the audience who observed their speeches. Higher numbers indicate greater liking. As the density-intensity hypothesis predicted, high density increased liking more than low density did when the situation was pleasant. However, high density decreased liking more than low density did when the situation was unpleasant. The fact that density had a different effect depending on whether the situation was pleasant or unpleasant indicates the presence of an interaction.

received negative feedback. Freedman's data, shown in Figure 9.5, revealed the predicted interaction. High density resulted in more positive reactions for subjects in the pleasant condition, but in less positive reactions for subjects in the unpleasant condition. Density and pleasantness *interacted* to affect subjects' responses to the situation.

Interpreting Main Effects and Interactions

When an interaction is present, main effects must be interpreted with caution. In fact, under certain circumstances main effects cannot be interpreted meaningfully if the independent variables interact. The presence of an interaction indicates that the effect of one independent variable on behavior is a function of another independent variable. Knowing that the effect of one variable depends on another makes researchers reluctant to make generalizations about the effects of either variable alone.

Whether an interaction precludes interpreting the main effects depends on whether the interaction *qualifies* the main effects. An interaction qualifies a main effect if the effects of one variable *disappear or reverse* depending on the level of the other independent variable. If the main effect is qualified by the interaction, the main effect cannot be interpreted.

Figure 9.6 shows five possible results from a 2 × 2 factorial design. This design involved two independent variables, which we'll call *A* and *B*, each of which had two levels. In Figure 9.6, five sets of hypothetical means for the four experimental conditions have been plotted on graphs.

Figure 9.6(a) shows what the pattern of condition means might look like in a case in which there are main effects of both *A* and *B*, but no interaction. The main effect of *A* is evident by the fact that, *on the average*, subjects in Condition *A*2 had higher scores than subjects in Condition *A*1. The main effect of *B* is shown by the fact that subjects in Condition *B*1 had higher mean scores than those in *B*2.

However, no interaction between *A* and *B* is present. Variable *A* had precisely the same effect for subjects who were in Condition *B*1 as for those who were in *B*2. Similarly, the main effect of *B* occurred for subjects in *A*1 and in *A*2. Although *A* and *B* each affected subjects' responses, they did not interact. When condition means are graphed, as in Figure 9.6(a), parallel lines indicate no interaction.

Look now at Figure 9.6(b). Again we see two main effects. On the average, subjects in *A*2 scored higher than those in *A*1, and subjects in *B*1 scored higher than subjects in *B*2. However, the lines are no longer parallel, indicating an interaction between *A* and *B*. The precise effect that variable *B* had on subjects' responses depends on which level of *A* we consider. For subjects in Condition *A*1, the effect of *B* was small: *B*1 was somewhat higher than *B*2. However, for subjects in *A*2, the effect of *B* was pronounced; the mean for Condition *B*1 is much larger than the mean for Condition *B*2.

Although an interaction is present in Figure 9.6(b), this interaction *does not qualify* the main effects. The main effect of *B* is present under both *A*1 and *A*2; it is simply stronger under *A*2 than *A*1. Given that the main effects are not qualified by the interaction, we can interpret them if we wish, realizing that the effect is stronger for some levels of *A* than others.

Figure 9.6(c) presents a different case, however. Again, we have two main effects (overall, *A*2 > *A*1 and *B*1 > *B*2) as well as an interaction. But in this case the interaction qualifies the main effects. As you can see, although subjects in Condition *B*1 scored higher on average than subjects in *B*2 (i.e., there was a main effect of *B*), the interaction shows that this effect actually occurred only for subjects in Condition *A*2. For subjects in *A*1, *B* had no effect—the means for Conditions *B*1 and *B*2 did not differ. Put another way, the only combination of *A* and *B* that seemed to produce an effect was Condition *A*2*B*1; the mean for Condition *A*2*B*1 was higher than the means of the other three conditions. In a case like this, it would be misleading to interpret the main effect of *B* because variable *B* had an effect only for subjects in Condition *A*2. However, it would be permissible to interpret the main effect of *A* because *A*1 is lower than *A*2 in both Conditions *B*1 and *B*2.

Figure 9.6(d) shows a different case in which the interaction qualifies the main effects. This is a **crossover (or disordinal) interaction** in which one inde-

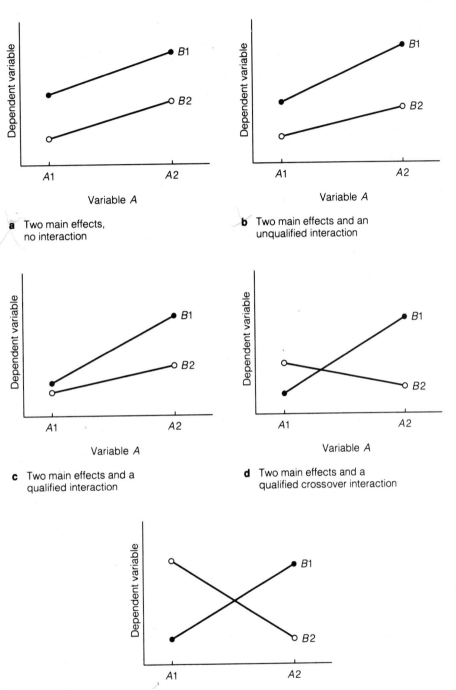

a Two main effects,
no interaction

b Two main effects and an
unqualified interaction

c Two main effects and a
qualified interaction

d Two main effects and a
qualified crossover interaction

e An interaction, but no main effects

Figure 9.6   Interactions

| Table 9.1 | Possible Outcomes of a Two-Way Factorial Experiment | | |

Outcome	Main effect of A?	Main effect of B?	Interaction of A × B?
1	No	No	No
2	Yes	No	No
3	No	Yes	No
4	Yes	Yes	No
5	Yes	No	Yes
6	No	Yes	Yes
7	Yes	Yes	Yes
8	No	No	Yes

pendent variable has opposite effects, depending on the level of the other independent variable. If subjects received A1, B2 resulted in higher scores than B1. If subjects received A2, B2 resulted in lower scores than B1. Given this pattern, the main effects are meaningless. The effects of B reverse depending on which level of A we consider, and the effects of A reverse as a function of B. Crossover interactions qualify main effects, thereby precluding their interpretation.

In Figures 9.6(b), (c), and (d), main effects as well as an interaction were present. In actuality, we may or may not obtain a main effect for one or both variables, and we may or may not obtain a significant interaction. In Figure 9.6(e), for example, the pattern shows an interaction in the absence of any main effects.

Table 9.1 shows the possible outcomes of a two-way factorial experiment. Figure 9.6(a) exemplifies Outcome 4 in Table 9.1 (two main effects, no interaction); the examples in Figures 9.6(b), (c), and (d) are all instances of Outcome 7 (two main effects plus an interaction); Figure 9.6(e) is an example of Outcome 8 (an interaction, but no main effects).

Higher-Order Designs

The examples of factorial designs we have seen so far were two-way designs that involved two independent variables (such as a 2 × 2, a 2 × 3, or a 3 × 5 factorial design). As we noted earlier, factorial designs often have more than two independent variables. Such designs are called **higher-order designs**.

Increasing the number of independent variables in an experiment not only increases the complexity of the design and statistical analyses, but also the complexity of the information that the study provides. As we saw above, a two-way design provides information about two main effects and a two-way interaction.

1. Main effect of *A*
2. Main effect of *B*
3. Interaction of *A* by *B*

A three-way design, such as a $2 \times 2 \times 2$ or a $3 \times 2 \times 4$ design, provides even more information. First, we can examine the effects of each of three independent variables separately.

1. Main effect of *A*
2. Main effect of *B*
3. Main effect of *C*

Second, a three-way design allows us to look at three two-way interactions—interactions of each pair of independent variables while ignoring the third independent variable.

4. Interaction of *A* by *B*
5. Interaction of *A* by *C*
6. Interaction of *B* by *C*

Each two-way interaction tells us whether the effect of one independent variable is different at different levels of another independent variable. For example, testing the *B* by *C* interaction tells us whether variable *B* has a different effect on behavior in Condition *C*1 than in Condition *C*2.

Third, a three-way factorial design gives us information about the combined effects of all three independent variables.

7. Interaction of *A* by *B* by *C*

If statistical tests show that this three-way interaction is significant, it indicates that the effect of one variable differs depending on which combination of the other two variables we examine. For example, perhaps the effect of variable *A* is different in Condition *B*1*C*1 than in Condition *B*1*C*2.

Limitations to the Size of Higher-Order Designs

Logically, factorial designs can have any number of independent variables and thus any number of conditions. For practical reasons, however, researchers seldom design studies with more than three or four independent variables.

For one thing, when a between-subjects design is used, the number of subjects needed for an experiment grows rapidly as we add additional independent variables. For example, a $2 \times 2 \times 2$ factorial design with 15 subjects in each of the eight conditions would require 120 subjects. Adding a fourth independent variable with two levels (creating a $2 \times 2 \times 2 \times 2$ factorial design) would double the number of subjects required to 240. Adding a fifth independent variable with three levels (making the design a $2 \times 2 \times 2 \times 2 \times 3$ factorial design) would require us to collect and analyze data from 720 subjects!

In addition, as the number of independent variables increases, researchers find it increasingly difficult to draw meaningful interpretations from the data. A two-way interaction is much easier to interpret than a four- or five-way interaction, for example.

Mixed Factorial Designs

Behavioral researchers have long recognized that behavior is a function of both situational factors and an individual's personal characteristics. A full understanding of certain behaviors cannot be achieved without taking both these factors into account. Put another way, **subject variables** such as sex, age, intelligence, ability, personality, and attitudes moderate or qualify the effects of situational forces on behavior. Not everyone responds in the same manner to the same situation. For example, people's performance on a test is a function not only of the test itself but of other factors, such as their ability and their level of test anxiety. A researcher interested in determinants of test performance might want to take into account her subjects' levels of anxiety (as indicated by their scores on a measure of test anxiety) as well as the characteristics of the test itself.

Researchers use an **expericorr design** (often called a **mixed factorial design**) to investigate the combined effects of situational factors and subject variables.[1] An expericorr, or mixed factorial design, is a factorial in which one or more factors involve an independent variable that is *manipulated* by the experimenter and one or more factors involve preexisting subject variables that are *measured* rather than manipulated. The label *expericorr* is short for experimental-correlational; such designs combine features of an experimental design in which independent variables are manipulated and features of correlational designs in which subject variables are measured.

Perhaps the most common use of expericorr designs is to look for differences in how male and female subjects respond to an independent variable. For example, to investigate whether men and women respond differently to success and failure, a researcher might use a 2×3 expericorr design such as that shown in Figure 9.7. In this design, one factor involves a subject variable, sex.

---

1. Note that the term *mixed factorial design* is used to refer to two quite different designs. Some use it to refer to designs that include both between-subjects and within-subjects factors—what we have called a between-within or split-plot factorial design. Others use it, as we have here, to refer to designs that include both manipulated independent variables and measured subject variables. Because of this confusion (and because I know of no other widely used term for the latter design), I have coined the term *expericorr design* to refer to designs that involve both manipulated and measured variables.

Figure 9.7   An expericorr or mixed factorial design

Explanation: This 2 × 3 expericorr design has one manipulated independent variable (type of feedback) and one measured subject variable (subject sex).

The other factor is a manipulated independent variable that has three levels: Subjects took a test then received (1) success feedback, (2) failure feedback, or (3) no feedback. When the data have been analyzed, the researcher can examine the main effect of subject sex (overall, did men and women differ?), the main effect of feedback (did subjects respond differently to success, failure, and no feedback?), and most importantly, the interaction of sex and feedback (did men and women respond differently to success, failure, and/or no feedback)?

Classifying Subjects into Groups

Most expericorr designs classify subjects into groups on the basis of a measured subject variable. For discrete subject variables such as sex and race, it is easy to assign subjects into two or more groups.

Sometimes, however, researchers are interested in subject variables that are continuous rather than discrete. For example, a researcher may be interested in how self-esteem moderates reactions to success and failure. Because scores on a measure of self-esteem are continuous, the researcher must decide how to classify subjects into groups. Most researchers use either the median-split procedure or the extreme groups procedure.

In the **median-split procedure,** the researcher identifies the median of the distribution of subjects' scores on the variable of interest (such as self-esteem). You will recall from Chapter 4 that the median is the middle score in a distribution, the score that falls at the 50th percentile. The researcher then classifies subjects with scores below the median as *low* on the variable and those with scores above the median as *high* on the variable. It must be remembered, however, that the designations *low* and *high* are relative to the sample. All subjects could, in fact, be low or high on the attribute in an absolute sense. In a variation of the median-split procedure, some researchers split their sample into three or more groups rather than only two.

Alternatively, some researchers prefer the **extreme groups procedure** for classifying subjects into groups. Rather than splitting the sample at the median, the researcher pretests a large number of potential subjects, then selects subjects for the experiment whose scores are unusually low or high on the variable of interest. For example, the researcher may use subjects whose scores fall in the upper and lower 25% of the distribution, discarding those with scores in the middle.

Uses of Expericorr Designs

Researchers use expericorr designs for three reasons. The first is to investigate the generality of an independent variable's effect. Subjects who possess different characteristics often respond to the same situation in quite different ways. Because of this the effects of certain independent variables may generalize only to subjects with certain characteristics. Expericorr designs permit researchers to determine whether the effects of a particular variable occur for all subjects or only for subjects with certain attributes.

Second, researchers use expericorr designs in an attempt to understand how certain subject variables operate. The emphasis in such studies is on understanding the measured subject variable rather than the manipulated independent variable. For example, a researcher interested in self-esteem might expose persons who were low or high in self-esteem to various experimental conditions. Or a researcher interested in depression might conduct an experiment in which depressed and nondepressed subjects respond to various experimentally manipulated situations. Studying how subjects with different characteristics respond to an experimental manipulation may shed light on that characteristic.

Third, by splitting subjects into groups based on a subject variable, researchers make the subjects within the experimental conditions more homogeneous. This reduces the error variance (the variability within conditions), thereby increasing the power of the study.

B E H A V I O R A L   R E S E A R C H   C A S E   S T U D Y

Hypochondriasis as a Strategy for Protecting Self-Esteem

Smith, Snyder, and Perkins (1983) used an expericorr design to test the hypothesis that hypochondriacs would report more illness symptoms when they thought that illness would serve as an excuse for performing poorly on a test. First, the researchers used the extreme groups procedure to select subjects who were either hypochondriacal or nonhypochondriacal. From an initial sample of 514 subjects, they selected the 60 subjects who scored highest and the 60 subjects who scored lowest on a measure of hypochondriasis.

Subjects then took a test and were assigned randomly to one of three experimental conditions: Some were told that their physical health would have no effect on their test

Table 9.2	**An expericorr design: The hypochondriasis study**

	Health-effect information		
	No effect	No instructions	Nonevaluative
Hypochondriacal	26.6	35.1	30.1
Nonhypochondriacal	20.3	18.2	18.7

From "The Self-Serving Function of Hypochondriacal Complaints: Physical Symptoms as Self-Handicapping Strategies" by T. Smith, C. R. Snyder, and S. C. Perkins, *Journal of Personality and Social Psychology*, 1983, *44*, pp. 787–797. Copyright the American Psychological Association. Adapted by permission of Timothy Smith.

Explanation: In this 2 × 3 expericorr or mixed factorial design, subjects identified as hypochon-driacal or nonhypochondriacal completed a test under one of three sets of information. Hypo-chondriasis was a nonmanipulated subject variable, whereas the information was manipulated as an independent variable. The numbers in the table reflect the average number of symptoms reported by subjects in each of the six conditions. See the text for full details.

performance (no-effect condition), some were not told anything about the effects of health on performance (no-instructions condition), and the rest were told the test would not be scored (nonevaluative control condition). All were asked to complete a question-naire on which they indicated how many physical symptoms they were currently experi-encing. The researchers expected that hypochondriacal subjects would report more symp-toms than nonhypochondriacal subjects to provide an excuse for possible poor performance. However, they would do so only if such an excuse was viable—that is, when they had *not* been told that health would not affect test scores.

This was a 2 × 3 expericorr design: (hypochondriacal versus nonhypochondriacal) by (health has no effect versus no instructions versus nonevaluative). Hypochondriasis was a subject variable measured before the study began, and the information given to subjects about the test was an independent variable manipulated by the researcher.

As the data in Table 9.2 show, subjects who scored high in hypochondriasis reported fewer symptoms when the instructions told them that health would have no effect on their test performance than when they had received no instructions about the effects of health. Low hypochondriacal subjects reported roughly the same number of symptoms regardless of whether they thought health might affect performance. These results sup-ported the authors' hypothesis that hypochondriacs report being ill when they think their symptoms may provide a good excuse for poor performance.

Cautions in Interpreting Results of an Expericorr Design

Although data from an expericorr design are analyzed in the same way as in all other factorial designs, results from such designs must be interpreted with care. Specifically, a researcher can draw causal inferences only about the true independent variables in the experiment—those that were manipulated by the researcher. As always, if effects are obtained for a manipulated independent variable, we can conclude that the independent variable *caused* changes in the dependent variable.

When effects are obtained for the measured subject variable, however, the researcher cannot conclude that the subject variable caused changes in the dependent variable. Because the subject variable is measured rather than manipulated, the results are essentially correlational. And recall from Chapter 6 that we cannot infer causality from a correlation.

If a main effect of the subject variable is obtained, we can conclude that the two groups differed on the dependent variable, but we cannot conclude that the subject variable *caused* the difference. For example, if low and high hypochondriacal subjects differ in how many symptoms they report, we can't infer that hypochondriasis caused them to report more symptoms. In the case of any subject variable, many other things undoubtedly differ between the groups. For example, the highly hypochondriacal subjects may also be more anxious or lower in self-esteem than the low group. Thus, the difference may be due to other factors that correlate with hypochondriasis rather than to hypochondriasis itself.

When a significant interaction is obtained between a manipulated independent variable and a measured subject variable, we say that the subject variable *moderated* subjects' reactions to the independent variable and that the subject variable is a **moderator variable**. In the study by Smith et al. (1983), hypochondriasis moderated reactions to the test. We cannot say, however, that the subject variable caused the observed effects.

SUMMARY

1. In many ways, factorial designs are the mainstay of experimental psychology. The vast majority of experiments involve factorial designs.

2. Factorial designs are experimental designs that include two or more independent variables.

3. There are four types of factorial design: randomized groups, matched-subjects, repeated measures, and split-plot.

4. Factorial designs provide information not only about the effects of each independent variable but also information about the combined effects of the variables.

5. An interaction is present if the effect of a variable is different under one level of another variable than it is under another level of that variable.

6. Expericorr or mixed factorial designs combine manipulated independent variables and measured subject variables. Such designs are often used to identify subject variables that qualify or moderate the effects of the independent variables.

KEY TERMS

factorial design

factor

randomized groups factorial
  design

matched-subjects factorial design

repeated measures factorial design

split-plot factorial design

between-within design

main effect

interaction

crossover interaction

higher-order design

subject variable

expericorr design

mixed factorial design

median-split procedure

extreme groups procedure

moderator variable

REVIEW QUESTIONS

1. Describe a 2 × 3 × 2 factorial design. How many independent variables are involved? How many levels are there of each variable? How many experimental conditions are there?

2. Distinguish between randomized groups, matched-subjects, and repeated measures factorial designs.

3. Describe a split-plot factorial design. The split-plot design is a combination of what two other designs?

4. Describe the main effects and interactions that can be tested in (a) a 2 × 3 factorial design and (b) a 3 × 3 × 3 factorial design.

5. What are the circumstances under which a researcher may and may not interpret the main effects if a significant interaction is present?

6. What are expericorr factorial designs and why are they used?

10

Analyzing Complex Experiments: The Analysis of Variance

L et's return for a moment to the experiment we discussed in Chapter 8 that involved the effectiveness of various strategies for losing weight (Mahoney et al., 1973). In this study, obese adults were assigned randomly to one of five conditions: self-reward only, self-punishment only, self-reward and self-punishment, self-monitoring of weight, and a control condition. At the end of the experiment, the researchers wanted to know whether subjects lost more weight in some conditions than in others. Given the data shown in Table 10.1, how would you determine whether the various weight-reduction strategies were differentially effective in helping subjects in the five groups to lose weight? Put differently, how would you determine whether subjects in some groups lost significantly more weight than subjects in other groups?

One possibility would be to conduct 10 *t*-tests, comparing the mean of each experimental group to the mean of every other group: Group 1 vs Group 2, Group 1 vs Group 3, Group 1 vs Group 4, Group 1 vs Group 5, Group 2 vs Group 3, Group 2 vs Group 4, Group 2 vs Group 5, Group 3 vs Group 4, Group 3 vs Group 5, and Group 4 vs Group 5. If you performed all 10 of these *t*-tests, you could tell which means differed significantly from the others and determine whether the different strategies affected the amount of weight that subjects lost.

The Problem: Inflated Type I Error

Although one could use several *t*-tests to analyze these data, such an analysis creates a serious problem. Recall that when a researcher sets the alpha level at .05, he or she recognizes that a Type I error will occur on 5% of the statistical tests he or she conducts (see Chapter 8). In other words, 5% of the effects that

Table 10.1	**Average Weight Loss in the Mahoney et al. Study**

Group	Condition	Mean pounds lost
1	Self-reward	6.4
2	Self-punishment	3.7
3	Self-reward and self-punishment	5.2
4	Self-monitoring of weight	0.8
5	Control group	1.4

are statistically significant will actually be the result of error variance rather than caused by the independent variable.

If only one *t*-test is conducted, we know we have a 5% chance of making a Type I error. But what if we conduct 10 *t*-tests? Or 25? Or 100? Although the likelihood of making a Type I error on any particular *t*-test is .05, the overall Type I error becomes compounded as we perform an increasing number of tests. As a result, the more *t*-tests we conduct, the more likely it is that one or more of our significant findings will reflect a Type I error.

For example, imagine that we conducted six *t*-tests. What is the likelihood that we will make at least one Type I error? The answer is obtained from the formula

$$1 - (1 - \text{alpha})^c,$$

where *c* equals the number of tests (or comparisons) performed. Thus, the likelihood of making at least one Type I error on six *t*-tests, each with an alpha level of .05,

$$= 1 - (1 - .05)^6$$
$$= 1 - .95^6$$
$$= 1 - .74$$
$$p = .26.$$

In other words, the probability of making a Type I error (that is, rejecting the null hypothesis when it is true) on at least one of the six *t*-tests is .26—more than 1 out of 4. This is considerably higher than the alpha level for each individual *t*-test we conducted, which was .05.

The same problem occurs when we analyze data from factorial designs. To analyze the interaction from a 3×2 design requires several *t*-tests to examine differences between each pair of means. As a result, we increase the probability of making at least one Type I error during the analysis.

Because Type I error becomes inflated when many *t*-tests are conducted, researchers generally don't use *t*-tests when testing differences among more than two means. When we conduct more than one *t*-test, we increase the risk of committing a Type I error and of concluding that we have a significant effect when it is in fact due to error variance. The problem of inflated Type I error emerges both with multilevel designs and with factorials because, in both instances, differences between more than two means are tested.

The solution to this problem is **analysis of variance**, a statistical procedure used to analyze data from multilevel and factorial designs. Analysis of variance—often abbreviated **ANOVA**—analyzes differences between all group means in an experiment *simultaneously*. Rather than testing the difference between each pair of means, ANOVA determines whether *any* of a set of means differs from another using a single statistical test that holds the alpha level at .05 (or whatever level the researcher chooses) regardless of how many group means are involved in the test. For example, rather than conducting six *t*-tests among all pairs of four means (with the likelihood of a Type I error being .26), ANOVA performs a single, simultaneous test on all condition means with only a .05 chance of making a Type I error.

In the remainder of this chapter, we will examine the rationale behind ANOVA. We'll look at the one-way ANOVA, then turn our attention to how ANOVA is used to analyze the data from factorial designs. My purpose here is not so much to show you how to perform an ANOVA as to show you how ANOVA works. In fact, the formulas I will use are for demonstrational purposes; they show what an ANOVA does, but researchers use other forms of these formulas to actually compute an ANOVA. The computational formulas for ANOVA appear in Appendix B.

The Rationale Behind ANOVA

Although the rationale behind the analysis of variance is in most respects identical to that for *t*-tests (Chapter 8), you may find it useful to look at ANOVA in a slightly different way.

Recall that the total variance in a set of experimental data can be broken into two parts: systematic variance (which reflects differences among the experimental conditions) and unsystematic or error variance (which reflects differences among subjects within the experimental conditions). Recall also that even if the independent variable had no effect, we generally find slight differences among condition means (and thus some systematic variance) because of error variance in the data. Random differences among subjects can create between-group differences.

Imagine for a moment that we conducted a multilevel or factorial experiment in which *we knew* the independent variable(s) had *absolutely no effect*. In such a case, we could estimate the amount of error variance in the data in one of two ways: We could actually calculate the error variance by looking at the variability among the subjects within each of the conditions. Or, we could estimate the error variance by looking at the differences between the condition means; *if we knew* the independent variable had no effect (and that there was no confounding), the only source of variability among the condition means would be error variance. I hope you can see, then, that when the independent variable has no effect, the variability among condition means and the variability within groups are two reflections of precisely the same thing—error variance.

To the extent that the independent variable affected subjects' responses and created differences between the conditions, however, the variability among condition means should be larger than if only error variance were operating. Thus, if we find that the variance between conditions is markedly greater than the variance within conditions, we have evidence that the independent variable caused the difference (again assuming no confounds).

As we will see below, in an analysis of variance, we calculate an *F*-test, which is the ratio of variance among conditions (called between-groups variance) to variance within conditions (within-groups or error variance). The larger the between-groups variance relative to the within-groups variance, the larger the calculated value of *F*, and the more likely it is that the independent variable created differences between condition means. By testing this ratio, we can determine the likelihood that the differences between the conditions are due to error variance. If any of this seems confusing, I think it will become clearer as we look more closely at the simplest case of ANOVA.

The One-Way ANOVA

As its name implies, ANOVA analyzes variance in the data. Recall that the total variance in a set of data can be partitioned into two components:

$$\text{Total variance} = \text{systematic variance} + \text{error variance}$$

In a one-way design with a single independent variable, ANOVA breaks the total variance into these two components—systematic variance (presumably due to the independent variable) and error variance. In the case of factorial designs, the systematic variance can be partitioned further into several components to test for the presence of different main effects and interactions.

Total Sum of Squares

We learned in Chapter 2 that the sum of squares reflects the total amount of variability in a set of data. We learned also that the total sum of squares is calculated by (1) subtracting the mean from each score, (2) squaring these differences, and (3) adding them up.

We used this formula for the total sum of squares, which we'll abbreviate SS_{total}:

$$SS_{total} = \Sigma(x_i - \bar{x})^2$$

SS_{total} expresses the total amount of variability in a set of data. ANOVA breaks down, or partitions, this total variability. One part—the sum of squares between groups—involves systematic variance that, assuming confounding is not present, reflects the influence of the independent variable. The other part—the sum of squares within groups—reflects error variance:

$$\text{Total sum of squares} \rightarrow SS_{total} \begin{cases} \rightarrow \text{sum of squares between-groups} \\ \qquad\qquad SS_{bg} \\ \\ \rightarrow \text{sum of squares within-groups} \\ \qquad\qquad SS_{wg} \end{cases}$$

By the way, if we divide SS_{total} by $n - 1$, the result is the variance of the data (see Chapter 2). In ANOVA, this quantity is sometimes called the **total mean square** or MS_{total}.

Sum of Squares Within-Groups

To determine whether differences between condition means reflect only error variance, we need to know how much error variance exists in the data. In an ANOVA, this is estimated by the **sum of squares within-groups** (abbreviated SS_{wg}).

SS_{wg} is equal to the sum of the sums of squares for each of the experimental groups. In other words, if we calculate the sum of squares separately for each experimental group, then add these group sums of squares together, we obtain SS_{wg}:

$$SS_{wg} = \Sigma(x_1 - \bar{x}_1)^2 + \Sigma(x_2 - \bar{x}_2)^2 + \cdots + \Sigma(x_k - \bar{x}_k)^2$$

Think for a moment what SS_{wg} represents. Because all subjects in a particular condition receive the same level of the independent variable, none of the variability within any of the groups can be due to the independent variable. Thus, when we add the sums of squares across all conditions, SS_{wg} expresses the amount of variability that is not due to the independent variable. This, of course, is precisely what error variance is.

We then divide SS_{wg} by the **within-group degrees of freedom** or df_{wg}. This is equal to $(n_1 - 1) + (n_2 - 1) + \cdots + (n_k - 1)$, which is the sum of the individual degrees of freedom for each of the conditions. Identically, $df_{wg} = n - k$, where n is the total number of subjects and k is the number of experimental groups. For example, if our experiment involved 45 subjects who had been assigned randomly to one of three conditions, $df_{wg} = 45 - 3 = 42$.

By dividing SS_{wg} by df_{wg}, we are dividing the total of the within-groups variance by the total within-group degrees of freedom, which gives us an estimate of the average variance within the experimental conditions. This quantity is called the **mean square within-groups** or MS_{wg}:

$$MS_{wg} = SS_{wg}/df_{wg}$$

Again, MS_{wg} provides us with an estimate of the within-groups variance, disregarding the effects of the independent variable. We'll return to MS_{wg} in a moment.

Sum of Squares Between-Groups

Ultimately, we want to know whether the differences between condition means are due only to error variance. Thus, now that we've estimated the error variance from the variability within the groups, we need to calculate the systematic variability between the groups. To estimate the amount of systematic variance, ANOVA uses the **sum of squares between-groups** (sometimes called the *sum of squares for treatment*).

The calculation of the sum of squares between-groups (which we'll abbreviate SS_{bg}) is based on a simple rationale. If the independent variable had no effect, we would expect all of the group means to be roughly equal, aside from whatever differences are due to random error variance. Because all of the means are the same, we would also expect each condition mean to be approximately equal to the mean of all the group means (the **grand mean**). However, if the independent variable caused the means of some conditions to be larger or smaller than the means of others, the condition means will not only differ among themselves but will differ from the grand mean.

Thus, to calculate between-groups variance we first subtract the grand mean from each of the group means. Small differences indicate that the means don't differ very much (and thus the independent variable had little, if any, effect). Large differences, on the other hand, indicate large differences between the groups and, assuming that confound variance was eliminated, suggest that the independent variable caused the means to differ.

Thus, to obtain SS_{bg}, we

1. Subtract the grand mean (GM) from the mean of each group ($\bar{x}_k - GM$).
2. Square these differences ($\bar{x}_k - GM$)^2.
3. Multiply each squared difference by the size of the group $n_k(\bar{x}_k - GM)^2$.
4. Then sum across groups.

This can be expressed by the formula

$$SS_{bg} = n_1(\bar{x}_1 - GM)^2 + n_2(\bar{x}_2 - GM)^2 + \cdots + n_k(\bar{x}_k - GM)^2$$

We then divide SS_{bg} by the quantity $k - 1$, where k is the number of group means that went into the calculation of SS_{bg}. This quantity ($k - 1$) is the **between-group degrees of freedom**. When SS_{bg} is divided by its degrees of freedom ($k - 1$), the resulting number is called the **mean square between-**

groups (or MS_{bg}):

$$MS_{bg} = SS_{bg}/df_{bg}$$

The *F*-test

So far, we have seen how ANOVA partitions the total variance (MS_{total}) into two components—within-groups variance (MS_{wg}) and between-groups variance (MS_{bg}). All that's left is to test whether the between-groups variance is larger than we would expect based on the amount of within-groups (that is, error) variance.

To do this, the analysis of variance relies on a statistical test known as the **F-test**. To obtain the calculated value of *F*, we calculate the ratio of between-groups variability to within-groups variability by dividing MS_{bg} by MS_{wg}:

$$F = MS_{bg}/MS_{wg}$$

Then, just as with the *t*-test, we compare the calculated value of *F* to a critical value in an *F*-table (Appendix A-3).

To find the critical value of *F* in Appendix A-3, we specify three things. First, we set the alpha level (usually .05). Second, we calculate the degrees of freedom for the between-groups variance, which we saw is $k - 1$ (that is, number of groups − 1). Third, we calculate the degrees of freedom for the within-groups variance, which we saw is $n - k$ (that is, number of subjects − number of groups). With these numbers in hand, we can find the critical value of *F* in Appendix A-3 (page 321). For example, if alpha is .05, the degrees of freedom for treatment is 2, and the degrees of freedom for error is 30, the critical value of *F* is 3.32.

If the value of *F* obtained when we divide MS_{bg} by MS_{wg} exceeds the critical value of *F* obtained from the table, we conclude that *at least one of the group means differs from the others* and, thus, that the independent variable had an effect. More formally, if the calculated value of *F* exceeds the critical value, we reject the null hypothesis that the condition means do not differ from one another.

If the calculated value of *F* is less than the critical value, the differences among the group means are no greater than we would expect on the basis of error variance alone. Thus, we fail to reject our null hypothesis and conclude that the independent variable did not have an effect.

In the experiment involving weight loss (Mahoney et al., 1973), the calculated value of *F* was 4.49. The critical value of *F* when $df_{bg} = 4$ and $df_{wg} = 48$ is 2.75. Given that the calculated value exceeded the critical value, the authors rejected the null hypothesis and concluded that the five weight-loss strategies were differentially effective.

Often, the numbers relevant to calculating an ANOVA are listed in an ANOVA table such as that shown in Table 10.2. An ANOVA table shows the sum of squares, degrees of freedom, and mean square for the between-groups and within-groups portions of the variance, as well as the calculated value of *F*.

Table 10.2   **An ANOVA Table**

Source	SS	df	MS	F
Between-groups	SS_{bg}	$k - 1$	$MS_{bg} = SS_{bg}/df_{bg}$	MS_{bg}/MS_{wg}
Within-groups	SS_{wg}	$n - k$	$MS_{wg} = SS_{wg}/df_{wg}$	
Total	SS_{total}	$n - 1$	$MS_{total} = SS_{total}/df_{total}$	

In a real ANOVA table the SS, df, MS, and F columns contain numbers calculated from the formulas above.

IN DEPTH

Calculational Formulas for a One-Way ANOVA

The formulas used in the preceding explanation of the one-way ANOVA are intended to show conceptually how ANOVA works. When actually calculating an ANOVA, however, researchers use formulas that although conceptually identical to those you have just seen, are easier to use. These formulas, along with a numerical example, are in Appendix B-1. I did not use these calculational formulas to explain ANOVA in this chapter, because although efficient for calculational purposes, these formulas do not convey as clearly what the various components of ANOVA really reflect.

Follow-up Tests

When an F-test is statistically significant (that is, when the calculated value of F exceeds the critical value), we know that at least one of the group means differs from one of the others. However, because the ANOVA tests all condition means simultaneously, a significant F-test does not tell us precisely which means differ: Perhaps all of the means differ from each other. Or, maybe only one mean differs from the rest. Or, some of the means may differ significantly from each other, but not from other means.

To identify precisely which means differ significantly (and thus determine the precise effect of the independent variable), researchers use **follow-up tests**, often called **post hoc tests** or **multiple comparisons**.

Several statistical procedures have been developed for this purpose. Some of the more commonly used are the least significant difference (LSD) test, Tukey's test, Scheffe's test, and Newman–Keuls test. Although differing in specifics, each of these tests is used after a significant F-test to determine precisely which condition means differ.

After obtaining a significant *F*-test in their study of weight loss, Mahoney and his colleagues used the Newman–Keuls test to determine which weight-loss strategies were more effective. Refer to the means in Table 10.1 as you read their description of the results of this test:

Newman–Keuls comparisons of treatment means showed that the self-reward *S*'s had lost significantly more pounds than either the self-monitoring ($p < .025$) or the control group ($p < .025$). The self-punishment group did not differ significantly from any other.

Follow-up tests may be conducted *only if the F-test is statistically significant*. If the *F*-test in the ANOVA is not statistically significant, we must conclude that the independent variable had no effect (that is, we fail to reject the null hypothesis) and may not test differences between specific pairs of means.

CONTRIBUTORS TO BEHAVIORAL RESEARCH

Fisher, Experimental Design, and the Analysis of Variance

No other person has contributed more to the design and analysis of experimental research than the English biologist Ronald A. Fisher (1890–1962). After early jobs with an investment company and as a public school teacher, Fisher became a statistician for the experimental agricultural station at Rothamsted, England.

Agricultural research relies heavily upon experimental designs in which growing conditions are manipulated and their effects on crop quality and yield are assessed. In this context, Fisher developed many statistical approaches that have spread from agriculture to behavioral science, the best known of which is the analysis of variance. In fact, the *F*-test was named for Fisher.

In 1925, Fisher wrote one of the first books on statistical techniques, *Statistical Methods for Research*. Despite the fact that Fisher was a poor writer (someone once said that no student should try to read his book unless he or she has read it before), *Statistical Methods* became a classic in the field. Ten years later, Fisher published *The Design of Experiments*, a landmark in research design. These two books raised the level of sophistication in our understanding of research design and analysis and paved the way for contemporary behavioral science (Kendall, 1970).

The Analysis of Factorial Designs

As we've seen, a one-way ANOVA partitions the variability in the dependent variable into two components: between-groups (systematic) variance and within-groups (error) variance. Put differently, in a one-way ANOVA, SS_{total} has two sources of variance: SS_{bg} and SS_{wg}.

In factorial designs, such as those we discussed in Chapter 9, we are able to identify other sources of variability we observe in subjects' responses. Not only can we examine the effects of more than one independent variable on behavior, but we can test whether or not the independent variables have a combined or interactive effect on the dependent variable. Thus, SS_{total} may be partitioned into several sources of variance. In the simplest two-way, A-by-B factorial design, SS_{total} is composed of four components: variance due to A, variance due to B, variance due to the interaction of A and B, and within-groups variance.

The analysis of factorial designs involves a straightforward extension of the one-way ANOVA approach we discussed above. But rather than conducting one F-test for the effect of a single independent variable, we conduct F-tests to examine all possible main effects and interactions.

In a factorial ANOVA, we calculate how much of the total variability in subjects' scores is associated with each of the main effects and interactions. We then compare this variability to the amount of variability we would expect to be present if the independent variables had no effects (either singly or in interaction) and the variability was due only to error variance. If the amount of variance exceeds what we would expect on the basis of error variance alone, we reject the null hypothesis and conclude that the main effect or interaction being tested is statistically significant.

In this section we'll examine the rationale behind a factorial ANOVA, using the simplest case—a two-way factorial. As before, my goal is to show you how a factorial ANOVA works, and the formulas I use are for demonstrational purposes.

Within-Groups Variance

As with the t-test and the one-way ANOVA, we are interested in knowing whether the differences we observe among the condition means (the between-groups variance) are significantly greater than we would expect given the variability within the conditions (error or within-groups variance).

We calculate the amount of error variance by first computing SS_{wg}. As with the one-way ANOVA, SS_{wg} is equal to the sum of the sums of squares for all of the experimental conditions. And as before, we may obtain SS_{wg} by adding the sums of squares for each of the k conditions in the design:

$$SS_{wg} = \Sigma(x_1 - \bar{x}_1)^2 + \Sigma(x_2 - \bar{x}_2)^2 + \cdots + \Sigma(x_k - \bar{x}_k)^2$$

We then divide SS_{wg} by df_{wg}, which equals

$$(j \times k)(n - 1),$$

where j = number of conditions of A, k = number of conditions of B, and n = number of subjects in each condition. For example, in a 3×2 factorial design that involved 15 subjects in each condition, $df_{wg} = (3 \times 2)(15 - 1) = 84$. Dividing SS_{wg} by df_{wg} gives us the mean square within-groups, or MS_{wg}. As with the one-way ANOVA, MS_{wg} reflects the amount of variability *not* due to the independent variable. We'll use MS_{wg} as the denominator of the *F*-tests we conduct to test each main effect and interaction.

Main Effects

In the one-way ANOVA discussed above, all of the between-groups variance was due to the single independent variable. In a factorial ANOVA, however, the between-groups variance may have several sources. One source of between-groups variance is the main effect of each independent variable.

In a factorial design, we use a separate *F*-test to test the main effect for each independent variable. In the case of a two-way design, there are two main effects, one for *A* and one for *B*.

Main effect of A   First, we'll examine the main effect of variable *A*. Testing the main effect of *A* answers the question, Do the means of the conditions of *A* (in a 2 × 2 design, the means of *A*1 and *A*2) differ significantly?

To begin, we compute the sum of squares for *A* (SS_A). In essence, we ignore variable *B* for the moment and determine how much of the variance in the dependent variable is associated with *A* alone. In other words, we disregard the fact that variable *B* even exists and compute SS_{bg} for variable *A*. Figure 10.1 portrays what I mean.

The rationale for testing the main effect of *A* is identical to that for testing the effects of the independent variable in a one-way ANOVA. If the independent variable had no effect, we would expect the means for the various levels of *A* to be roughly equal to the mean of all of the group means (the grand mean). However, if *A* caused the means of some conditions to be larger or smaller than the means of others, we would expect the means to differ among themselves and the group means to differ from the grand mean.

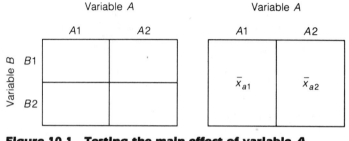

Figure 10.1   Testing the main effect of variable A

Explanation: Imagine we have conducted the 2 × 2 factorial experiment shown on the left. When we test for the main effect A, we temporarily ignore the fact that variable B was included in the design, as in the diagram on the right. The calculation for the sum of squares for A (SS_A) is based on the means for Conditions A1 and A2, disregarding variable B.

To test the effects of A, then, we subtract the grand mean from the mean of each condition of A ($\bar{x}_{ak}$), *ignoring variable B* (see Figure 10.1). SS_A is the sum of these deviations of the condition means from the grand mean (GM) squared:

$$SS_A = n_{a1}(\bar{x}_{a1} - GM)^2 + n_{a2}(\bar{x}_{a2} - GM)^2 + \cdots + n_{aj}(\bar{x}_{aj} - GM)^2$$

SS_A reflects the degree to which the condition means for A differ from the grand mean. If they differ from the GM a great deal, SS_A will be large, indicating that A may have caused the conditions to differ. If they do not differ from the GM, SS_A will be small, indicating that A had little if any effect.

We then compute the degrees of freedom for the main effect of A:

$$df_A = j - 1$$

Recall that j is the number of levels of A.

Then, to obtain the mean square for the main effect of A—MS_A—we divide SS_A by df_A:

$$MS_A = SS_A/df_A$$

Just as with the one-way ANOVA, we perform an F-test for the main effect of A by dividing MS_A by MS_{wg} obtained earlier:

$$F_A = MS_A/MS_{wg}$$

To determine whether this calculated value of F is statistically significant, we refer to the table of critical values of F in Appendix A-3. Armed with alpha (usually .05), df_A ($j - 1$), and df_{wg} ($j \times k$)($n - 1$), we locate the critical value of F in the table.

If our calculated value of F exceeds the critical value, we reject the null hypothesis that variable A had no effect and declare that we have a significant main effect of variable A. If the F-test is significant, we must interpret the main effect of A, but I'll postpone that step for a moment. If the calculated F does not exceed the critical F, we fail to reject the null hypothesis for variable A.

Main effect of B   The rationale behind testing the main effect of B is the same. To test the main effect of B, we subtract the grand mean from the mean of each condition of B, ignoring variable A. SS_B is the sum of these squared deviations of the condition means from the grand mean (GM):

$$SS_B = n_{b1}(\bar{x}_{b1} - GM)^2 + n_{b2}(\bar{x}_{b2} - GM)^2 + \cdots + n_{bk}(\bar{x}_{bk} - GM)^2$$

Remember that in computing SS_B we ignore variable A, pretending for the moment that the only independent variable in the design is variable B (see Figure 10.2).

We then compute the degrees of freedom for B:

$$df_B = k - 1,$$

where k is the number of conditions of variable B.

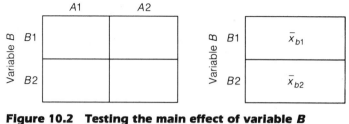

Figure 10.2   Testing the main effect of variable B

Explanation: To test the main effect of B in the design on the left, ANOVA disregards the presence of A (as if the experiment looked like the design on the right). The difference between the mean of B1 and the mean of B2 is tested without regard to variable A.

Then, to obtain MS_B, we divide SS_B by df_B:

$$MS_B = SS_B/df_B$$

We perform an F-test for the main effect of B by dividing MS_B by the MS_{wg} we obtained earlier:

$$F_B = MS_B/MS_{wg}$$

To determine whether this calculated value of F_B is statistically significant, we look up the critical value of F (Appendix A-3), using alpha, df_B $(k - 1)$, and df_{wg} $(j \times k)(n - 1)$. If our calculated value of F exceeds the critical value, we reject the null hypothesis that variable B had no effect.

Interactions

We now conduct an F-test for each possible interaction. In a two-way design, only one interaction—the A by B interaction—is possible. As we learned in Chapter 9, an interaction is present if the effects of one independent variable differ as a function of the other independent variable.

In an ANOVA, the presence of an interaction is indicated if there is variance in subjects' responses that can't be accounted for by the sum of SS_A, SS_B, and SS_{wg}. If no interaction is present, then $SS_A + SS_B + SS_{wg} = SS_{total}$. All of the variance in subjects' responses can be accounted for by the individual main effects of A and B, as well as error variance. However, if the sum of $SS_A + SS_B + SS_{wg}$ is less than SS_{total}, we know that the individual effects of A and B don't account for all of the systematic variance in the dependent variable. And we know that A and B combine in a nonadditive fashion—that is, they interact.

Thus, $SS_{A \times B}$ can be obtained through subtraction (although researchers generally calculate it directly; see Appendix B-2):

$$SS_{A \times B} = SS_{total} - SS_A - SS_B - SS_{wg}$$

After calculating the sum of squares for the interaction ($SS_{A \times B}$), we obtain $MS_{A \times B}$ by dividing $SS_{A \times B}$ by $df_{A \times B}$, which equals

$$(j - 1)(k - 1),$$

where j = number of levels of A and k = number of levels of B. As before, $SS_{A \times B}/df_{A \times B} = MS_{A \times B}$.

We conduct yet another F-test by dividing $MS_{A \times B}$ by MS_{wg}:

$$F = MS_{A \times B}/MS_{wg}$$

As before, we compare this calculated value of F with the appropriate critical value in Appendix A-3. If the calculated value exceeds the critical value, we conclude that a significant interaction is present. Whenever an F-test reveals a significant interaction, additional tests are needed to describe the interaction precisely. I'll return to these follow-up tests in a moment.

The ANOVA Table

When we analyzed data from a one-way design earlier in the chapter, we found it useful to enter the results of our calculations into an ANOVA table that showed the different sources of variability in the data. We use a similar ANOVA table when we analyze factorial designs. The primary difference between these tables is that because we can identify more sources of variability in a factorial design (that is, both main effects and interactions), the table for a factorial ANOVA contains more entries.

For a two-way factorial design, the ANOVA table looks like this:

Source	SS	df	MS	F
Variable A	SS_A	$j - 1$	$MS_A = SS_A/df_A$	MS_A/MS_{wg}
Variable B	SS_B	$k - 1$	$MS_B = SS_B/df_B$	MS_B/MS_{wg}
$A \times B$	$SS_{A \times B}$	$(j - 1)(k - 1)$	$MS_{A \times B} = SS_{A \times B}/df_{A \times B}$	$MS_{A \times B}/MS_{wg}$
Within-groups	SS_{wg}	$(j \times k)(n - 1)$	$MS_{wg} = SS_{wg}/df_{wg}$	
Total	SS_{total}	$n - 1$	$MS_{total} = SS_{total}/df_{total}$	

As you compute an ANOVA, it is helpful to enter the results in the appropriate places in the ANOVA table.

Summary

The rationale for a factorial ANOVA is straightforward, if not downright intuitive. The total variance in subjects' responses is broken down into components that reflect main effects, interaction(s), and error variance. Then, the amount of variance due to each main effect and interaction is compared with the amount of variance for each effect one might expect if the independent variable(s) had no effect.

IN DEPTH

Calculational Formulas for a Two-Way ANOVA

As with the one-way ANOVA we discussed earlier in the chapter, the formulas used in this chapter to describe factorial ANOVA are for demonstrational purposes. The calculational formulas—those you would use when actually conducting a factorial analysis of variance—may be found in Appendix B-2.

Follow-up Tests to a Factorial ANOVA

When we obtain significant effects in an ANOVA, we know that *something* happened in our experiment—that certain means differ significantly from certain other means and that one or more independent variables influenced subjects' responses. However, because ANOVA often tests differences within a set of several means simultaneously, a significant *F*-test does not always indicate the precise effect of the independent variable. Thus, as with one-way ANOVAs, when we obtain a significant *F*-test in analyzing a factorial ANOVA, we must often conduct follow-up tests.

The first step in interpreting the results of any experiment is to calculate the means for the significant effects. For example, if the main effect of *A* is found to be significant, you would calculate the means for the conditions of *A*, ignoring variable *B*. If the main effect of *B* is significant, you would examine the means for the various conditions of *B*. If the interaction of *A* and *B* is significant, you would calculate the means for all combinations of *A* and *B*.

Significant Main Effects

Main effects with two levels   When a main effect involves an independent variable that has only two levels, no follow-up tests are necessary. If the *F*-test shows that the means of two conditions are significantly different, there is nothing more to be done to clarify the effect other than to inspect the means themselves to identify the direction of the effect. In a 2×3 factorial, for example, a significant main effect of *A*, which has two levels, would not require a follow-up test.

Main effects involving more than two levels When an *F*-test reveals a significant main effect for a variable that has more than two levels, follow-up tests are necessary. For example, suppose that a significant main effect involves an independent variable that has three levels. The main effect indicates that a difference exists between at least two of the three condition means, but does not indicate which means differ from which. To determine which means differ, researchers use the same kinds of follow-up tests that they use following a significant one-way ANOVA—LSD, Tukey's, Newman–Keuls, Scheffe's, and the like.

Significant Interactions

If an interaction is statistically significant, we know that the effects of one independent variable differ depending on the level of another independent variable. To describe the precise nature of the interaction, researchers examine the simple main effects.

Tests the difference between *A1B1* and *A2B1*

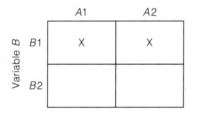

a Simple main effect of *A* at *B1*

Tests the difference between *A1B2* and *A2B2*

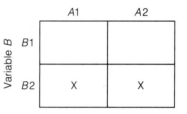

b Simple main effect of *A* at *B2*

Tests the difference between *A1B1* and *A1B2*

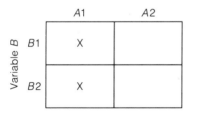

c Simple main effect of *B* at *A1*

Tests the difference between *A2B1* and *A2B2*

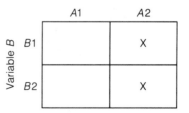

d Simple main effect of *B* at *A2*

Figure 10.3   Simple effects tests

Explanation: A simple main effect is the effect of one independent variable at only one level of another independent variable. If the interaction in a 2 × 2 design such as this is found to be significant, four possible simple main effects are tested to determine precisely which condition means differ.

A **simple main effect** is the effect of one independent variable at a particular level of the other independent variable. It is, in essence, a *main effect* of the variable, but a main effect that occurs *under only one level* of the other variable. If we obtained a significant $A \times B$ interaction, we could examine four simple main effects, which are shown in Figure 10.3:

a. The simple main effect of A at B1. (Do the means of Conditions A1 and A2 differ for subjects who received Condition B1?) See Figure 10.3(a).

b. The simple main effect of A at B2 (Do the means of Conditions A1 and A2 differ for subjects who received Condition B2?) See Figure 10.3(b).

c. The simple main effect of B at A1. (Do the means of Conditions B1 and B2 differ for subjects who received Condition A1?) See Figure 10.3(c).

d. The simple main effect of B at A2. (Do the means of Conditions B1 and B2 differ for subjects who received Condition A2?) See Figure 10.3(d).

Testing the simple main effects shows us precisely which condition means differ from each other.

IN DEPTH

The Relationship Between *t* and *F*

Although their calculational formulas differ, *t*-tests and *F*-tests are based on precisely the same rationale. Each involves a comparison of the variance that is associated with differences between group means to variance within the experimental groups. If the difference or differences between group means exceed what would be expected on the basis of the error variance in the data, those differences are statistically significant—that is, unlikely to be due to error variance alone.

What may not be obvious is that in the case of a two-group design in which only two means are being tested, a *t*-test and an *F*-test are precisely the same statistical test. In fact, if we performed both a *t*-test and an *F*-test on the same two-group experiment, our calculated value of *F* would equal the square of our calculated value of *t* (that is, $F = t^2$). And whether we use a *t*-test or an *F*-test in this instance, we would make precisely the same decision whether to reject the null hypothesis.

Between-Subjects and Within-Subjects ANOVAs

Each of the formulas and examples in this chapter involved using ANOVA to analyze *between-subjects* designs—experiments in which subjects are randomly assigned to experimental conditions (see Chapter 7). Although the rationale is the same, slightly different computational procedures are used for within-subjects and between-within designs in which each subject serves in more than one experimental condition. Just as we use a paired t-test to analyze data from a within-subjects two-group experiment (Chapter 8), we use within-subjects ANOVA for multilevel and factorial within-subjects designs and split-plot ANOVA for between-within designs. Like the paired t-test, these variations of ANOVA capitalize on the fact that we have repeated measures on each subject to reduce the estimate of error variance, thereby providing a more powerful statistical test. Full details regarding these analyses take us beyond the scope of this book but may be found in most introductory statistics books, such as those listed at the end of Chapter 8.

SUMMARY

1. Analysis of variance is the most commonly used statistical procedure for analyzing experimental data.
2. Whether the experiment involves a one-way or a factorial design, ANOVA partitions the total variability in subjects' responses into between-groups variance and within-groups variance. Then an F-test is conducted to determine whether the between-groups variance exceeds the amount we would expect based on the within-groups variance.
3. In a one-way design, a single F-test is used to test the effects of the lone independent variable. A calculated value of F (the ratio of MS_{bg}/MS_{wg}) is compared to a critical value of F. If the calculated value exceeds the critical value, we know that at least one condition mean differs from the others.
4. In a factorial design, three or more F-tests are conducted to test all possible main effects and interactions. For each, a calculated value of F is obtained and compared to a critical value.
5. If the F-tests show that the main effects or interactions are statistically significant, follow-up tests are often needed to elucidate the precise effect of the independent variable. Main effects that involve more than two levels require post hoc tests, whereas interactions are decomposed using simple effects tests.

KEY TERMS

analysis of variance (ANOVA)
total mean square (MS_{total})
sum of squares within-groups
(SS_{wg})

within-group degrees of freedom
(df_{wg})
mean square within-groups
(MS_{wg})

sum of squares between-groups
   (SS_{bg})
grand mean
between-group degrees of freedom
   (df_{bg})
mean square between-groups

F-test
follow-up tests
post hoc tests
multiple comparisons
ANOVA table
simple main effect

REVIEW QUESTIONS

1. Why do researchers use ANOVA rather than t-tests to analyze data from experiments that have more than two groups?
2. If a researcher conducts 10 t-tests, each with an alpha level of .05, what is the likelihood that he or she will make at least one Type I error?
3. An ANOVA for a one-way design partitions the total variance in a set of data into two components. What are they?
4. What variance does the sum of squares within-groups (SS_{wg}) reflect?
5. The sum of squares between-groups (SS_{bg}) represents the degree to which the condition means vary around _____.
6. What is the formula for the F-test?
7. Assuming that the calculated value of F is found to be significant, what tests does the researcher then conduct? Why?
8. Who developed the rationale and computations for the analysis of variance?
9. In an experiment with two independent variables, an ANOVA partitions the total variance into four components. What are they? Draw an ANOVA table for a two-way design, showing all necessary information.
10. When are tests of simple main effects used, and what do researchers learn from them?
11. Imagine that you conducted a two-group experiment that you later analyzed with a t-test. The calculated value of t was 3.00. If you reanalyzed the same dating using an F-test, what value of F should you obtain?

11

Quasi-Experimental Designs

To reduce the incidence of fatal traffic accidents, many states have passed laws requiring passengers in automobiles to wear seat belts. Proponents of such laws claim that wearing seat belts significantly decreases the likelihood that passengers will be killed or seriously injured in a traffic accident. Opponents of these laws argue that wearing seat belts does not decrease traffic fatalities. Instead, they say, it poses an increased risk because seat belts may trap passengers inside a burning car. Furthermore, they argue that such laws are useless because they are difficult to enforce and few people actually obey them anyway. Who is right? Do laws that require people to wear seat belts actually reduce traffic fatalities?

This question seems simple enough until we consider the kind of study that would be needed to show that such laws actually *cause* a decrease in traffic fatalities. To answer such a question would require an experimental design such as those we've been discussing in the past few chapters. We would have to randomly assign passengers to either wear or not wear safety belts, then measure the fatality rate for these two groups.

The problems of doing such a study should be obvious. First, we would find it very difficult to randomly assign people to wear or not wear seat belts and to ensure that our subjects actually followed our instructions. Second, the incidence of serious traffic accidents is so low, relative to the number of drivers, that we would need a gigantic sample to obtain even a few serious accidents within a reasonable period of time. A third problem is an ethical one: Would we want to randomly assign some people to *not* wear seat belts, with the possibility that we would cause them to be killed or injured if they have an accident? I hope you can see that it would not be feasible to design a true experiment to determine whether seat belts are effective in reducing traffic injuries and fatalities.

From the earliest days of psychology, behavioral researchers have shown a distinct preference for experimental designs over other approaches to doing research. This is because, by manipulating the independent variables and carefully controlling other factors that might affect the outcome of the study, experiments allow us to draw relatively confident conclusions about whether the independent variable caused changes in the dependent variable.

However, many real-world questions, such as whether seat-belt legislation reduces traffic fatalities, can't always be addressed within the narrow strictures of experimentation. Often, researchers do not have sufficient control over their subjects to randomly assign them to experimental conditions. In other cases, they may be unable or unwilling to manipulate the independent variable of interest.

In such instances, researchers often use **quasi-experimental designs**. Unlike true experiments, quasi-experiments do not involve randomly assigning subjects to conditions. Instead, comparisons are made between people in groups that already exist (such as those who live in states with and without seat-belt laws) or within a single group of subjects before and after an experimental treatment has occurred (such as examining injuries before and after a seat-belt law is passed).

Because such designs do not involve random assignment of subjects to conditions, the researcher is not able to determine which subjects will receive the various levels of the independent variable. In fact, in many studies the researcher does not manipulate the independent variable at all. Few researchers have the power to introduce legislation regarding seat-belt use, for example. In such cases, the term **quasi-independent variable** is sometimes used to indicate that the variable was not actually manipulated by the researcher but instead occurred for other reasons.

The strength of the experimental designs we examined in the preceding few chapters lies in their ability to demonstrate that the independent variables caused changes in the dependent variables. As we saw, experimental designs do this by eliminating alternative explanations for the findings that are obtained. Experimental designs generally have high internal validity; researchers can conclude that the observed effects were due to the independent variables rather than to other, extraneous factors (see Chapter 7).

Generally speaking, quasi-experimental designs do not possess the same degree of internal validity as experimental designs. Because subjects are not randomly assigned to conditions and the researcher may have no control over the independent variable, potential threats to internal validity are present in most quasi-experiments. Even so, a well-designed quasi-experiment that eliminates as many threats to internal validity as possible can provide strong circumstantial evidence about cause-and-effect relationships.

The quality of a quasi-experimental design depends on how many threats to internal validity it eliminates. As we will see, quasi-experimental designs differ in the degree to which they control threats to internal validity. Needless to say, the designs that eliminate most of the threats to internal validity are preferable to those that eliminate only a few threats. In this chapter we will discuss several basic quasi-experimental designs. We will begin with the weakest, least preferable designs in terms of their ability to eliminate threats to internal validity, then move to stronger quasi-experimental designs.

IN DEPTH

The Internal Validity Continuum

Most researchers draw a sharp distinction between experimental designs (in which the researcher controls both the assignment of subjects to conditions and the independent variable) and quasi-experimental designs (in which the researcher lacks control over one or both of these aspects of the design). However, this distinction should not lead us to hastily conclude that experimental designs are unequivocally superior to quasi-experimental designs. Although this may be true in a very general sense, both experimental and quasi-experimental designs differ widely in terms of their internal validity. Indeed, some quasi-experiments are more internally valid than some true experiments.

A more useful way of conceptualizing research designs is along a continuum of low to high internal validity. At the low validity pole of the continuum are studies that lack the necessary controls to draw any meaningful conclusions about the effects of the independent variable. As we move up the continuum, studies have increasingly tighter experimental control and hence higher internal validity. At the high validity pole of the continuum are studies in which exceptional design and tight control allow us to rule out every reasonable alternative explanation for the findings.

There is no point on this continuum on which we can unequivocally draw a line that separates studies that are acceptable from the standpoint of internal validity from those that are unacceptable. Virtually all studies—whether experimental or quasi-experimental—possess some potential threats to internal validity. The issue in judging the quality of a study is whether the most serious threats have been eliminated, thereby allowing a reasonable degree of confidence in the conclusions we draw. As we will see, well-designed quasi-experiments can provide rather conclusive evidence regarding the effects of quasi-independent variables on behavior.

Pretest–Posttest Designs

As we said, researchers do not always have the power to assign subjects to experimental conditions. This is particularly true when the research deals with the effects of an intervention on a group of people in the real world. For example, a junior high school may introduce a schoolwide program to educate students about the dangers of drug abuse, and the school board may want to know whether the program is effective in reducing drug use among the students. In this instance, random assignment is impossible because *all* students in the school were exposed to the program. If you were hired as a behavioral researcher to evaluate the effectiveness of the program, what kind of a study would you design?

How NOT to Do a Study: The One-Group Pretest–Posttest Design

One possibility would be to measure the students' drug use before the antidrug program and again afterwards to see whether drug use decreased. Such a design could be portrayed as

$$O1 \quad X \quad O2$$

where $O1$ is a pretest measure of drug use, X is the introduction of the antidrug program (the quasi-independent variable), and $O2$ is the posttest measure of drug use 1 year later. (O stands for observation.)

I hope you can see immediately that this design, the **one-group pretest–posttest design**, is a very poor research strategy. It is a poor strategy because it fails to eliminate most threats to internal validity. Many other plausible reasons exist to explain any change in drug use we might observe. If you observe a change in students' drug use between $O1$ and $O2$, how sure are you that the change was due to the antidrug program as opposed to some other factor?

Several other factors could have contributed to the change. For example, the students may have matured from the pretest to the postttest (maturation). In addition, many things other than the program occurred between $O1$ and $O2$ (history). Perhaps a popular rock musician died of an overdose, the principal started searching students' lockers for drugs, or the local community started a citywide Just Say No to Drugs campaign. Another possibility is that the first measurement of drug use ($O1$) may have started students thinking about drugs, resulting in lower use independently of the antidrug program (testing effect). Extraneous factors such as these may have occurred at the same time as the antidrug education program and may have been responsible for decreased drug use.

In addition, the internal validity of one-group pretest–posttest designs may be threatened by **regression to the mean**—the tendency for extreme scores in a distribution to move, or regress, toward the mean of the distribution with repeated testing (Neale & Liebert, 1980). In some studies, subjects are selected because of their extreme scores on some variable of interest. For example, we may want to examine the effects of a drug education program on students who are heavy drug users. Or, perhaps we are examining the effects of a remedial reading program on students who are poor readers. In cases such as this, a researcher may select subjects who have extreme scores on a pretest (of drug use or reading ability, for example), expose them to the quasi-independent variable (the antidrug or reading program), then remeasure them to see whether their scores changed (drug use declined or reading scores improved, for example).

The difficulty with this approach is that when subjects are selected because they have extreme scores on the pretest, their scores may change from pretest to posttest because of a statistical artifact called regression to the mean. As we learned in Chapter 3, all scores contain measurement error that causes subjects' *observed* scores to differ from their *true* scores. Overall, measurement error produces random fluctuations in subjects' scores from one measurement to the next; thus, if we test a sample of subjects twice, subjects' scores are as likely to increase as decrease from the first to the second test.

However, although the general effect of measurement error on the scores in a distribution is random, the measurement error present in extreme scores tends to bias the scores in an extreme direction—that is, away from the mean. For example, if we select a group of subjects with very low reading scores, these subjects are much more likely to have observed scores that were *deflated* by measurement error (because they were tired or ill, for example) than to have observed scores that were higher than their true scores. When subjects who scored in an extreme fashion are retested, many of the factors that contributed to their artificially extreme scores on the pretest are unlikely to be present; for example, students who performed poorly on a pretest of reading ability because they were ill are likely to be healthy at the time of the posttest. As a result, their scores on the posttest are likely to be more moderate than they were on the pretest; that is, their scores are likely to regress toward the mean of the distribution. Unfortunately, a one-group pretest–posttest design does not allow us to determine whether changes in subjects' scores are due to the quasi-independent variable or to regression to the mean.

The one-group pretest–posttest design is called a **preexperimental design** rather than a quasi-experimental design because it lacks control, has little internal validity, and thereby fails to meet any of the basic requirements for a research design at all. Many alternative explanations of observed changes in subjects' scores can be suggested, undermining our ability to document the effects of the quasi-independent variable itself. As a result, such designs should rarely be used.

Nonequivalent Control Group Design

One partial solution to the weaknesses of the one-group design is to obtain one or more control groups for comparison purposes. Because we can't randomly assign students to participate or not participate in the antidrug program, a *true* control group is not possible. However, the design would benefit from adding a *nonequivalent* control group. In a **nonequivalent control group design**, the researcher looks for another group of subjects that appears to be reasonably similar to the group that received the treatment. A nonequivalent control group design comes in two varieties, one that involves only a posttest and another than involves both a pretest and a posttest.

Nonequivalent groups posttest-only design   One option is to measure both groups after one of them has received the experimental treatment. For example, you could assess drug use among students at the school that used the antidrug program and among students at another, roughly comparable school that did not use drug education. This design, the **nonequivalent groups posttest-only design** (or static group comparison) can be diagrammed like this:

Experimental group: X O
Nonequivalent control: — O

Unfortunately, this design also has several weaknesses. Perhaps the most troublesome is that we have no way of knowing whether the two groups were actually similar *before* the experimental group received the treatment. If the two groups differ at time O, we don't know whether the difference was caused by variable X or whether the groups differed even before the experimental group received X (this involves biased assignment of subjects to conditions or the **selection bias**). Because we have no way of being sure that the groups were equivalent before subjects received the quasi-independent variable, the nonequivalent control group posttest-only design is very weak in terms of internal validity and should rarely, if ever, be used.

Nonequivalent groups pretest–posttest design   Some of the weaknesses of this design are eliminated by measuring the two groups twice, once before and once after the treatment. The **nonequivalent groups pretest–posttest design** can be portrayed as follows:

Experimental group: $O1$ X $O2$
Nonequivalent control: $O1$ — $O2$

First, this design lets us see whether the two groups scored similarly on the dependent variable (for example, drug use) before the introduction of the treatment. Even if the pretest scores at $O1$ aren't identical for the two groups, they provide us with baseline information that we can use to determine whether the groups changed from $O1$ to $O2$. If the scores change between the two testing times for the experimental group, but *not* for the nonequivalent control group, we have somewhat more confidence that the change was due to the quasi-independent variable.

For example, to evaluate the antidrug program, you might obtain a nonequivalent control group from another junior high school that does not have an antidrug program under way. If drug use changes from pretest to posttest for the experimental group but not for the nonequivalent control group, we might assume the program had an effect.

Even so, the nonequivalent groups pretest–posttest design does not eliminate all threats to internal validity. For example, a **local history effect** may occur. Something may happen to one group that does not happen to the other (Cook & Campbell, 1979). Perhaps some event occurred in the experimental school, but not in the control school, that affected students' attitudes toward drugs—a popular athelete was kicked off the team for using drugs, for example. If this happens, what appears to be an effect of the antidrug program may actually be due to a local history effect. This confound is sometimes called a **selection-by-history interaction.**

In brief, although the nonequivalent groups design eliminates some threats to internal validity, it doesn't eliminate all of them. Even so, with proper controls and measures, this design can provide useful information on real-world problems.

BEHAVIORAL RESEARCH CASE STUDY

A Nonequivalent Control Group Design

The elderly often decline in physical health and psychological functioning after they are placed in a nursing home. Langer and Rodin (1976) designed a study to test the hypothesis that a portion of this decline is due to the loss of control the elderly often feel when they move from their own homes to an institutional setting.

The subjects in their study were 91 elderly people, from 65 to 90 years old, who lived in a Connecticut nursing home. In designing their study, Langer and Rodin were concerned about the possibility of **experimental contamination.** When subjects in different conditions of a study interact with one another, the possibility exists that they may talk about the study among themselves and that one experimental condition becomes contaminated by the other. To minimize the likelihood of contamination, the researchers decided not to randomly assign residents in the nursing home to the two experimental conditions. Rather, they randomly selected two floors in the facility, assigning residents of one floor to one condition and those on the other floor to the other condition. Residents on different floors interacted very little with one another, so this procedure minimized contamination. However, the decision not to randomly assign subjects to conditions resulted in a quasi-experimental design—specifically, a nonequivalent control group design.

An administrator gave different talks to the residents on the two floors. One talk emphasized the residents' responsibility for themselves and encouraged them to make their own decisions about their lives in the facility. The other talk emphasized the staff's responsibility for the residents. Thus, one group was made to feel a high sense of responsibility and control, whereas the other group experienced lower responsibility and control. In both cases, the responsibilities and options stressed by the administrator were already available to all residents, so the groups differed chiefly in the degree to which their freedom, responsibility, and choice were explicitly stressed.

The residents were assessed on a number of measures a few weeks after hearing the talk. Compared with the other residents, those who heard the talk that emphasized their personal control and responsibility were more active and alert, happier, and more involved in activities within the nursing home. In addition, the nursing staff rated them as more interested, sociable, self-initiating, and vigorous than the other residents. In fact, follow-up data collected 18 months later showed long-term psychological and physical effects of the intervention, including a lower mortality rate among subjects in the high-responsibility group (Rodin & Langer, 1977).

The implication is, of course, that giving elderly residents greater choice and responsibility *caused* these positive changes. However, in considering these results, we must remember that this was a quasi-experimental design. Not only were subjects not assigned randomly to conditions, but they lived on different floors of the facility. To some extent, subjects in the two groups were cared for by different members of the nursing home staff and lived in different social groups. Perhaps the nursing staff on one floor was more helpful than that on another floor, or social support among the residents was greater on one floor than another. Because of these differences, we cannot eliminate the possibility that the obtained differences between the two groups were due to other variables that differed systematically between the groups.

I should note that most psychologists do not view these alternative explanations to Langer and Rodin's findings as particularly plausible. (Indeed, their study is highly regarded in the field.) Even so, the fact that it is a quasi-experiment should make us less confident of the findings than we might be had a true experimental design been used.

Time Series Designs

Some of the weaknesses of the nonequivalent control group designs are further eliminated by a set of procedures known as time series designs. **Time series designs** measure the dependent variable on several occasions before and on several occasions after the quasi-independent variable occurs. By measuring the target behavior on several occasions, further threats to internal validity can be eliminated, as we'll see.

Simple Interrupted Time Series Design

The **simple interrupted time series design** involves taking several pretest measures before introduction of the independent (or quasi-independent) variable, then taking several posttest measures afterwards. This design can be diagrammed as

$$O1 \quad O2 \quad O3 \quad O4 \quad X \quad O5 \quad O6 \quad O7 \quad O8$$

As you can see, the measurement of the dependent variable has been interrupted by the occurrence of the quasi-independent variable (X). For example, we could measure drug use every 3 months for a year before the program, then every 3 months for a year afterward. If the program had an effect on drug use, we should see a marked change between O4 and O5.

The rationale behind this design is that by taking multiple measures both before and after the quasi-independent variable, we can examine the possible effects of the quasi-independent variable against the backdrop of other changes that may be occurring in the dependent variable. For example, using this design, we should be able to distinguish changes due to aging or maturation from changes due to the quasi-independent variable. If drug use is declining because of changing norms or because the subjects are maturing, we should see gradual changes in drug use from one observation to the next, not just between the first four and the last four observations.

To see what I mean, compare the two graphs in Figure 11.1. Which of the graphs seems to show that the drug education program lowered drug use? In

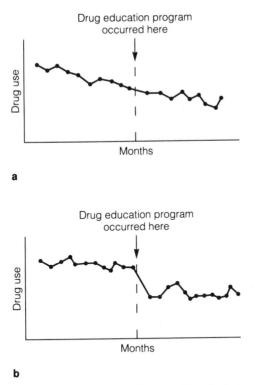

a

b

Figure 11.1   Results from a simple interrupted time series design

Explanation: It is difficult to determine from Figure 11.1(a) whether the drug education program reduced drug use or whether the lower use after the program was part of a general decline in drug use that started before the program. The pattern in Figure 11.1(b) is much clearer. Because the decrease in drug use occurred immediately after the program, we have greater confidence that the change was due to the program.

Figure 11.1(a), drug use is lower after the program than before it, but it is unclear whether the decline was associated with the program or was part of a downward pattern that began *before* the initiation of the program. In Figure 11.1(b), on the other hand, the graph shows that a marked decrease in drug use occurred immediately after the program. Although we can't conclude for certain that the program was, in fact, responsible for the change in drug use, the evidence is certainly stronger in (b) than in (a).

The central threat to internal validity with a simple interrupted time series design is contemporary *history*. We cannot rule out the possibility that the observed effects were due to another outside event that occurred at the same time as the quasi-independent variable. If a rock star died from drugs or an athlete was barred from the team at about the time of the antidrug program, we would not know whether the change between O4 and O5 was due to the program or to the outside influence.

BEHAVIORAL RESEARCH CASE STUDY

A Simple Interrupted Time Series Design: The Effects of No-Fault Divorce

Traditionally, for a married couple to obtain a divorce, one member of the couple had to accuse the other of failing to meet the obligations of the marriage contract (by claiming infidelity or mental cruelty, for example). More recently, many states have passed no-fault divorce laws in which a couple can end a marriage simply by agreeing to and without one partner having to sue the other.

Critics maintain that no-fault divorce laws make it too easy to obtain a divorce and contribute to the rising number of divorces in this country. To examine this question, Mazur-Hart and Berman (1977) used an interrupted time series analysis to study the effects of the passing of a no-fault divorce law in Nebraska in 1972.

Mazur-Hart and Berman obtained the number of divorces in Nebraska from 1969 to 1974. As in all interrupted time series analyses, these years were interrupted by the introduction of the quasi-independent variable (the new no-fault divorce law). Their results are shown in Figure 11.2. This figure shows the number of divorces per month for each of the 6 years of the study, as well as the point at which the new law went into effect.

On first glance, one might be tempted to conclude that divorces did increase after the law was passed. The number of divorces was greater in 1973 and 1974 than in 1969, 1970, and 1971. However, if you look closely, you can see that the divorce rate was increasing even *before* the new law was passed; there is an upward slope to the data for 1969–72. The data for 1973–74 continues this upward trend, but there is no evidence that the number of divorces increased an unusual amount after the law went into effect. In fact, statistical analyses showed that there was no discontinuity in the slope of the line after the introduction of the law. As the authors concluded, "during the period of time studied

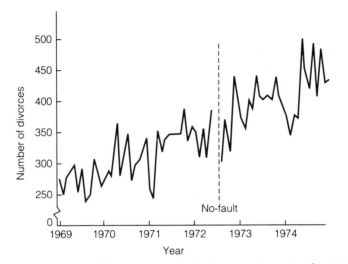

Figure 11.2   Effects of no-fault divorce laws on the number of divorces

From "Changing from Fault to No-Fault Divorce: An Interrupted Time Series Analysis" by S. F. Mazur-Hart and J. J. Berman, 1977, *Journal of Applied Social Psychology, 7,* p. 306.

Explanation: This graph shows the results of an interrupted time series analysis of divorce rates before and after the Nebraska no-fault divorce law. Although the divorce rate was higher after the law went into effect than before, the increase was clearly part of a general upward trend that started before the law went into effect. Thus, the law appears not to have affected the divorce rate.

divorces did systematically increase but . . . the intervention of no-fault divorce had no discernible effect on that increase."

This is one advantage of a time series design over designs that compare only two groups or only two points in time. Had the researchers analyzed data for only 1971 and 1973 (the years before and after the new law), they probably would have concluded that the law increased the divorce rate. By taking several measures before and after the new law went into effect, they were able to tell that the increase in divorces after the new legislation was part of an upward trend that had begun at least 3 years before the law went into effect.

Interrupted Time Series with a Reversal

In special instances, the influence of extraneous *historical* factors may be discounted by observing what happens to behavior when the quasi-independent variable or treatment is first introduced, then removed. The **interrupted time series design with a reversal** may be portrayed like this:

O1   O2   O3   O4   X   O5   O6   O7   O8   −X   O9   O10   O11   O12

You can think of this as two interrupted time series designs in succession. The first examines the effects of the quasi-independent variable (X) on changes in the target behavior (O). As before, we can see whether X is associated with an unusual increase or decrease in the dependent variable (O) between O4 and O5. Then, after X has been in place for a while, we can remove it (at point $-X$) and observe what happens to O. Under some circumstances, we would expect the behavior to return to its pre-X level.

If this occurs, we are more confident that X produced the observed changes. It would be unlikely that some external, historical influence occurred with X, then disappeared when X was removed. Of course, such an effect is logically possible, but in most instances it is unlikely.

To further increase our confidence that the quasi-independent variable, and not outside historical events, created the observed changes at X and $-X$, we could then *reintroduce* the independent variable, observe its effects, then remove it a second time. This is known as an **interrupted time series design with multiple replications** and can be diagrammed as follows:

O1 O2 O3 X O4 O5 O6 $-X$ O7 O8 O9 X O10 O11 O12 $-X$ O13 O14 O15

Quasi-experimental designs where the variable of interest is introduced and then removed have three major limitations. The first is that researchers often do not have the power to remove the quasi-independent variable—to repeal new seat-belt laws or no-fault divorce laws, for example. Second, the effects of some quasi-independent variables remain even after the variable itself is removed. For example, the effects of a community-wide program to reduce racial prejudice should linger even after the program itself is discontinued. Third, the removal of a quasi-independent variable may produce changes that are not due to the effects of the variable per se. For example, if we were interested in the effects of a new incentive system on employee morale, removing work incentives might dampen morale because the employees would be angry about having the system removed (Cook & Campbell, 1979).

Control Group Interrupted Time Series Design

So far, we have discussed time series designs that measure a single group of subjects before and after the quasi-independent variable. Adding comparison groups strengthens these designs by eliminating additional threats to internal validity. By measuring more than one group on several occasions, only one of which receives the quasi-independent variable, we can minimize the plausibility of certain alternative interpretations of the results. For example, we could perform an interrupted time series analysis on the group that received the quasi-independent variable and on a nonequivalent control group that did not receive the quasi-independent variable:

Experimental:	O1	O2	O3	O4	X	O5	O6	O7	O8
Nonequivalent control:	O1	O2	O3	O4	—	O5	O6	O7	O8

This design helps us rule out certain history effects. If both groups experience the same outside events, but a change is observed only for the experimental group, we can be more certain (though not positive) that the change was due to X rather than to an outside influence. Of course, local history effects are possible in which the experimental group experiences extraneous events that the nonequivalent control group does not.

"Patched-up" Quasi-Experimental Designs

In most instances where researchers use quasi-experimental designs, they do not have the necessary control over the environment to structure the research setting precisely as they would like. In many cases, quasi-experimentation involves a pragmatic approach to research—one that attempts to collect the most meaningful data under circumstances than are often less than ideal (Condray, 1986).

The best quasi-experiments are those in which the researcher uses whatever procedures are available to devise a reasonable test of the research hypotheses. Thus, rather than adhering blindly to one particular design, quasi-experimentalists creatively "patch up" basic designs to provide the most meaningful and convincing data possible.

For example, researchers often measure not only the effects of the quasi-independent variable on the outcome behavior, but assess the *processes* assumed to mediate their relationship. Given the absence of random assignment, simply showing that a particular quasi-independent variable was associated with changes in the dependent variable may not convince us that the quasi-independent variable caused the dependent variable to change. However, if the researcher can also demonstrate that the quasi-independent variable was associated with changes in processes assumed to mediate the change in the dependent variable, more confidence is warranted.

For example, rather than simply measuring students' drug use to evaluate the effects of a school's antidrug campaign, a researcher might also measure other variables that should mediate changes in drug use, such as students' knowledge about and attitudes toward drugs. Unlike some extraneous events (such as searches of students' lockers by school authorities), the program should affect not only drug use, but also knowledge and attitudes. Thus, if changes in knowledge and attitudes are observed at the experimental school (but not at a nonequivalent control school), the researcher has more confidence that the antidrug program, and not other factors, produced the change.

By patching up basic quasi-experimental designs with additional quasi-independent variables, comparison groups, and dependent measures, researchers increase their confidence in the inferences they draw about the causal link between the quasi-independent and dependent variables. Such patched-up designs are inelegant and may not conform to any formal design shown in research methods books. But they epitomize the way scientists can structure their collection of data to draw the most accurate conclusions possible (Condray, 1986). And they show that researchers should never hesitate to invent creative strategies for analyzing whatever problem is at hand.

Evaluating Quasi-Experimental Designs

For many years, most behavioral scientists held a well-entrenched bias against quasi-experimental designs. For many, the tightly controlled experiment was the benchmark of behavioral research, and anything less than a true experiment was regarded with suspicion. Most contemporary behavioral researchers tend not to share this bias against quasi-experimentation, recognizing that the limitations of quasi-experimental designs are compensated by some notable advantages.

The first advantage is a pragmatic one. True experimentation—that involving random assignment and researcher-manipulated independent variables—is limited in the questions it can address. Often we want to study the effects of certain variables on behavior, but are unable or unwilling to conduct a true experiment that will allow unequivocal conclusions about causality. Faced with the limitations of the true experiment, we have a choice. We can abandon the topic, leaving potentially important questions unanswered, or we can conduct quasi-experimental research that provides us with tentative answers. Without quasi-experimental research, we would have no way of addressing many important questions.

Second, to suggest that quasi-experimental designs are inherently invalid is fallacious. As we saw earlier, studies fall along a continuum of internal validity. Although no one doubts that studies high in internal validity are to be preferred over those low in internal validity, alternative explanations may be raised about the results of experiments and quasi-experiments alike. In many instances, we must be satisfied with making well-informed decisions on the basis of the best available evidence, while acknowledging that a certain degree of uncertainty exists. Although all of science involves a mixture of objective methods and human judgment, the role of judgment is perhaps more pronounced in quasi-experimental research (Condray, 1986).

Third, our confidence in the conclusions we draw from empirical research comes from two sources. When experiments are conducted, we have confidence in our findings because our study was tightly designed, eliminating most possible threats to internal validity. Even when a particular study cannot eliminate all threats to internal validity, however, we can increase our confidence on the basis of the results of accumulated evidence that demonstrates the same general effect. Thus, rather than reaching conclusions on the basis of a single study, researchers often piece together many strands of information that were accumulated by a variety of methods, much the way Sherlock Holmes would piece together evidence in breaking a case (Condray, 1986). For example, although the results of a single quasi-experimental investigation of an antidrug program at one school may be open to criticism, demonstrating the effects of the program at 10 schools gives us considerable confidence in concluding that the program was effective.

Because our confidence about causal relationships increases as we integrate many diverse pieces of evidence, quasi-experimentation is enhanced by **critical multiplism** (Shadish, Cook, & Houts, 1986). The critical multiplist perspective argues that researchers should critically consider many ways of obtaining evidence relevant to a particular hypothesis, then employ several different approaches in the same study. In quasi-experimental research, no single research approach can yield unequivocal conclusions. However, evidence from multiple approaches may converge to yield conclusions that are as concrete as those obtained in experimental research. Like a game of chess in which each piece has its strengths and weaknesses and in which no piece can win the game alone, quasi-experimentation requires the coordination of several different pieces of research strategy (Shadish et al., 1986). Although any single piece of evidence may be suspect, the accumulated results may be quite convincing.

Thus, do not be misled into thinking that the data provided by quasi-experimental designs are worthless. Rather, we must generally interpret such data with greater caution. Quasi-experimentation provides an important set of research strategies for the behavioral researcher.

IN DEPTH

Evaluating Quasi-Experimentation

One way to evaluate the usefulness of quasi-experimental research is to consider what is required to establish that a particular variable *causes* changes in behavior. To infer causality, we must be able to show that

1. The presumed causal variable preceded the effect in time
2. The cause and the effect covary
3. All other alternative explanations of the results are eliminated through randomization or experimental control.

Quasi-experimental designs meet the first two criteria. First, even if we did not experimentally manipulate the quasi-independent variable, we usually know when it occurred. Thus, we can establish that the presumed cause preceded the presumed effect. Second, it is easy to determine whether two variables covary. A variety of statistical techniques, including correlation and ANOVA, allow us to demonstrate that variables are related to one another. Covariance can be demonstrated just as easily whether the research design is correlational, experimental, or quasi-experimental. Thus, a quasi-experimental design is as strong on this count as any other design.

The primary weakness in quasi-experimental designs is the degree to which they eliminate the effects of extraneous variables on the results. Such designs seldom allow random assignment or control over extraneous variables. As a result, we can never rule out all alternative rival explanations of the findings. As we have seen, however, a well-designed quasi-experiment that eliminates as many threats to internal validity as possible can provide important, convincing information. Furthermore, evidence accumulated from a number of studies can lead to relatively clear-cut conclusions.

Doing Quasi-Experimental Research

Quasi-experimental designs are used most commonly in the context of program evaluation research. **Program evaluation** uses research methods to assess the effects of programs on behavior. A program is any intervention designed to influence behavior. For example, a program may involve a new educational intervention designed to raise students' achievement test scores, a new law intended to increase seat belt use, an incentive program designed to increase employee morale, or a marketing campaign implemented to affect the public's image of a company.

Although program evaluations often contribute to basic knowledge about human behavior, their primary goal is usually to provide information to those who must make decisions about the target programs. Typically, the primary audience for a program evaluation is not the scientific community (as is the case with basic research), but decision makers such as government administrators, legislators, school boards, and company executives. Such individuals need information about program effectiveness to determine whether program goals are being met, to decide whether to continue certain programs, to consider how programs might be improved, and to allocate money and other resources to programs.

In some instances, program evaluators use true experimental designs to assess program effectiveness. Sometimes they are able to randomly assign people to one program or another and have control over the implementation of the program (which is, in essence, the independent variable). In educational settings, for example, new curricula and teaching methods are often tested using true experimental designs.

More commonly, however, program evaluators have little or no control over the programs they evaluate. When evaluating the effects of new legislation, such as the effects of no-fault divorce laws or seat-belt laws, researchers cannot use random assignment or control the independent variable. In industrial settings, researchers have little control over new policies regarding employees. Even so, companies often want to know whether new programs and policies are effective in reducing absenteeism, increasing morale, or bolstering productivity. By necessity, then, program evaluation involves the use of quasi-experimental designs, and increasing numbers of behavioral researchers are using quasi-experimental methods to provide valuable information to decision makers.

SUMMARY

1. Many important research questions are not answered easily using true experimental designs. Quasi-experimental designs are used when researchers cannot control the assignment of subjects to conditions. Instead, comparisons are made between people in groups that already exist or within one or more existing groups of subjects before and after a quasi-independent variable has occurred.

2. The quality of a quasi-experimental design depends on its ability to minimize threats to internal validity.

3. One-group pretest–posttest designs possess little internal validity and should seldom be used.

4. In the nonequivalent control group designs, an experimental group that receives the quasi-independent variable is compared with a nonequivalent comparison group that does not receive the quasi-independent variable. The effectiveness of this design depends on the degree to which the groups can be assumed to be equivalent and the degree to which local history effects can be discounted.

5. In time series designs, one or more groups are measured on several occasions both before and after the quasi-experimental variable is introduced.

6. Although quasi-experimental designs do not allow the same degree of certainty about cause-and-effect relationships as an experiment does, a well-designed quasi-experiment can provide convincing circumstantial evidence regarding the effects of one variable on another.

KEY TERMS

quasi-experimental design
quasi-independent variable
one-group pretest–posttest design
regression to the mean
preexperimental design

nonequivalent control group
  design
nonequivalent groups
  posttest-only design
selection bias

nonequivalent groups
  pretest–posttest design
local history effect
selection-by-history interaction
experimental contamination
time series design
simple interrupted time series
  design

interrupted time series design with
  a reversal
interrupted time series design with
  multiple replications
critical multiplism
program evaluation

REVIEW QUESTIONS

1. How do quasi-experimental designs differ from true experiments?

2. Under what sets of circumstances would a researcher use a quasi-experimental rather than an experimental design?

3. Why should researchers never use the one-group pretest–posttest design?

4. What threats to internal validity are present when the nonequivalent control group posttest-only design is used? Which of these threats are eliminated by the pretest–posttest version of this design?

5. Explain the rationale behind time series designs.

6. Describe the simple interrupted time series design. Discuss how the interrupted time series design with a reversal and the interrupted time series design with multiple replications improves on the simple interrupted time series design.

7. Why does quasi-experimentation sometimes require the use of "patched-up" designs?

8. Discuss the philosophy of critical multiplism as it applies to quasi-experimental research.

9. What three criteria must be met to establish that one variable causes changes in behavior? Which of these criteria are met by quasi-experimental designs? Which of these criteria are not met, and why?

10. What is program evaluation? Why do program evaluators rely heavily on quasi-experimental designs in their work?

QUESTIONS FOR THOUGHT AND DISCUSSION

1. Although quasi-experimental designs are widely accepted in behavioral science, some researchers are troubled by the fact that the evidence provided by quasi-experiments is seldom as conclusive as that provided by true experiments. Imagine you are trying to convince a dubious experimentalist of the merits of quasi-experimental research. What arguments would you use to convince him or her of its value?

2. Imagine that your town or city has increased its nighttime police patrols to reduce crime. Design two quasi-experiments to determine whether this intervention has been effective, one that uses some variation of a non-equivalent control group design and one that uses some variation of a time series design. For each design, discuss the possible threats to internal validity, as well as ways in which the design could be patched-up to provide more conclusive evidence.

12

Single-Subject Designs

In each of the experimental and quasi-experimental designs we have discussed so far, researchers assess the effects of variables on behavior by comparing the average responses of two or more groups of subjects. In these designs, the unit of analysis is always grouped data. In fact, in analyzing the data obtained from these designs, information about the responses of individual participants is usually ignored.

Group designs, such as those we have been discussing, reflect the most common approach to experimentation in behavioral science. Most experiments and quasi-experiments conducted by behavioral scientists involve group designs. Even so, group designs have their critics, some as notable as B. F. Skinner, who offer an alternative approach to experimental research.

In this chapter we will examine a very different kind of experiment—the **single-subject design**. In single-subject research, the unit of analysis is not the experimental group as in group designs, but the individual participant. Often, more than one subject participates in the experiment, but each subject's responses are analyzed separately and the data from individual subjects are never averaged. Because averages are not used, the data from single-subject experiments cannot be analyzed using inferential statistics such as *t*-tests and *F*-tests.

At first, the single-subject approach may strike you as an odd, if not ineffective way to conduct and analyze behavioral research. However, before you pass judgment, let's examine several criticisms of group experiments and how they may be resolved using single-subject designs.

Criticisms of Group Designs and Analyses

Proponents of single-subject research have suggested that group experimental designs fail to adequately handle three research issues—error variance, generality, and reliability.

Error Variance

We saw earlier that all data contain error variance—the results of unidentified factors that affect subjects' responses in an unsystematic fashion. We also learned that researchers must minimize error variance because error variance masks the effects of the independent variable (see Chapter 7 for a review).

Group experimental designs, such as those we've been discussing, provide two partial solutions to the problem of error variance. First, although the responses of any particular subject are contaminated by error variance in unknown ways, *averaging* the responses of several subjects should provide a more accurate estimate of the typical effect of the independent variable. In essence, many of the idiosyncratic sources of error variance cancel each other out when we calculate a group mean. Presumably, then, the mean for a group of subjects is a better estimate of the typical subject's response to the independent variable than the score of any particular subject.

Second, by using groups of subjects we can estimate the amount of error variance in our data. This is what we did when we calculated the within-subjects mean square (MS_{wg}) in Chapter 10. With this estimate, we can use inferential statistics to test whether the differences among the means of the groups are greater than we would expect if the differences were due only to error variance. Indeed, the purpose of using inferential statistics is to separate error variance from systematic variance to determine whether the differences among the group means are significant.

Although group data provide these two benefits, proponents of single-subject designs criticize the way group designs and inferential statistics handle the problem of error variance. They argue that, first, much of the error variance in group data does not reflect variability in behavior per se, but is *created* by the group itself, and second, researchers who use group designs accept the presence of error variance too blithely.

As we noted in Chapter 7, much of the error variance in a set of data is due to individual differences among the subjects. However, in one sense, this **intersubject variance** is *not* the kind of variability that behavioral researchers are usually trying to explain. Error variance resulting from individual differences among subjects is an artificial creation of the fact that, in group designs, we pool the responses of many subjects.

Single-subject researchers emphasize the importance of studying **intrasubject variance**—variability in *an individual's* behavior when he or she is in the same situation on different occasions. This is true behavioral variability that demands our attention. What we typically call error variance is, in one sense, partly a product of individual differences rather than real variations in a subject's behavior.

Because data are not aggregated across subjects in single-subject research, individual differences do not contribute to error variance. Error variance in a single-subject design shows up when a particular participant responds differently under various administrations of the same experimental condition, and reflects, in most instances, inadequate experimental control.

Most researchers who use group designs ignore the fact that their data contain a considerable amount of error variance, as long as they obtain a significant effect of the independent variable. Ignoring error variance is, for single-subject researchers, tantamount to being content with sloppy experimental design and one's ignorance (Sidman, 1960). After all, error variance is the result of factors that have remained unidentified and, thus, uncontrolled by the researcher. Proponents of single-subject designs maintain that rather than accepting error variance, researchers should design studies in a way that allows them to seek out its causes and eliminate it. Through tighter and tighter experimental control, more and more error variance can be eliminated. And in the process, we can learn more and more about the factors that influence behavior.

Generality

In the eyes of researchers who use group designs, averaging across subjects serves an important purpose. By pooling the scores of several participants, the researcher minimizes the impact of the idiosyncratic responses of any particular subject. They hope that by doing so they can identify the general, overall effect of the independent variable, an effect that should generalize to most of the subjects most of the time.

Single-subject researchers argue, however, that the data from group designs do not permit us to identify the general effect of the independent variable as many researchers suppose. Rather than reflecting the typical effect of the independent variable on the average subject, results from group designs represent an average of many individuals' responses that may not accurately portray the response of *any* particular subject. I read recently, for example, that Americans are having an average of 2.1 children. Although we all understand what this statistic tells us about childbearing in this country, it clearly does not reflect the behavior of any family I know!

Given that group averages may not represent any particular subject's responses, attempts to generalize from overall group results may be misleading. Put differently, group means may have no counterpart in the behavior of individual subjects (Sidman, 1960). This point is demonstrated in the accompanying box, How Group Data Misled Us About Learning Curves.

In addition, exclusive reliance on group summary statistics may obscure the fact that the independent variable affected the behavior of some subjects but had no effect (or even opposite effects) on other subjects. Researchers who use group designs rarely examine their raw data to see how many subjects in the group showed the effect and whether some subjects showed opposite effects.

Reliability

A third criticism of group designs is that, in most cases, they demonstrate the effect of the independent variable a single time, and no attempt is made to determine whether the observed effect is reliable—whether it can be obtained again. Of course, researchers may replicate their and others' findings in later studies, but replication *within a single experiment* is rare.

Typically, single-subject experiments replicate the effects of the independent variable in two ways. As I will describe below, some designs introduce an independent variable, remove it, then reintroduce it. This procedure involves **intrasubject replication**—replicating the effects of the independent variable with a single subject.

In addition, most single-subject research involves more than one subject, typically three to five. Studying the effects of the independent variable on more than one subject involves **intersubject replication**. Through intersubject replication, the researcher can determine whether the effects obtained on one subject generalize to other subjects. Keep in mind that even though multiple subjects are used, their data are examined individually. In this way, researchers can see whether all subjects responded similarly to the independent variable.

IN DEPTH

How Group Designs Misled Us About Learning Curves

On certain kinds of tasks, learning is an all-or-none process (Estes, 1964). During early stages of learning, people thrash around in a trial-and-error fashion. However, once they hit upon the correct answer or solution, they subsequently give the correct response every time. Thus, their performance jumps from *incorrect* to *correct* in a single trial.

The performance of a single subject on an all-or-none learning task can be graphed as shown here.

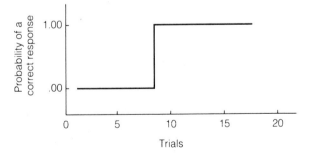

This subject got the answer wrong for seven trials, then hit upon the correct response on trial 8. Of course, after obtaining the correct answer, the subject got it right on all subsequent trials.

Different subjects will hit upon the correct response on different trials. Some will get it right on the first trial, some on the second trial, some on the third trial, and so on. In light of this, think for a moment of what would happen if we averaged the responses of a large number of subjects on a learning task such as this. What would the graph of the data look like?

Rather than showing the all-or-none pattern we see for each subject, the graph of the averaged group data will show a smooth curve like this one:

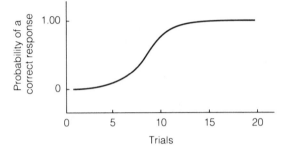

On the average, the probability of getting the correct response starts low, then gradually increases until virtually every subject obtains the correct answer on every trial. However, using group data obscures the fact that at the level of the individual subject, the learning curve was discontinuous rather than smooth. In fact, the results from the averaged, group data *do not reflect the behavior of any subject.* In instances such as this, group data can be quite misleading, whereas single-subject designs show the true pattern.

Basic Single-Subject Designs

ABA Designs

The most common single-subject research designs involve variations of what is known as the **ABA design**. (This is sometimes called a *reversal design.*) The researcher who uses these designs attempts to demonstrate that an independent variable affects behavior—first by showing that the variable causes a target behavior to occur, and then by showing that removal of the variable causes the behavior to cease.

In ABA designs, the subject is first observed in the absence of the independent variable (the baseline or control condition). Many measures of behavior are taken during this phase to establish an adequate baseline for comparison. Then, after the target behavior is seen to be relatively stable, a level of the independent variable is introduced and the behavior is observed again. In many ways the ABA design is a time series design performed on a single subject (see Chapter 11 for time series designs).

If the independent variable influences behavior, we should see a change in behavior from the baseline to the treatment period. However, even if such a change is observed, the researcher should not be too hasty in concluding that the effect was caused by the independent variable. Just as in the time series designs we discussed in Chapter 11, some other event occurring at the same time as the treatment could have produced the observed effect.

To reduce this possibility, the independent variable is then withdrawn. If the independent variable is in fact maintaining the behavior, the behavior may return to its baseline level. The researcher can further increase his or her confidence that the observed behavioral changes were due to the independent variable by replicating the study on other subjects.

The design just described is an example of an *ABA design*, the simplest single-subject design. In this design, A represents a baseline period in which the independent variable is not present, and B represents an experimental period. So, the ABA design involves a baseline period (A), followed by introduction of a level of the independent variable (B), followed by removal of the independent variable (A).

Many variations and elaborations of the basic ABA design are possible. To increase our confidence that the changes in behavior were due to the independent variable, a researcher may decide to introduce the same level of the independent variable a second time. This design would be labeled an *ABAB design*.

Logically, a researcher could reintroduce then remove a level of the independent variable again and again, as in an ABABABA or ABABABABA design. Each successive intrasubject replication of the effect increases our confidence that the independent variable is causing the observed effects.

Multiple-I Designs

ABA-type designs compare the presence of a nonzero level of an independent variable (during B) with the absence of the independent variable (during A). However, other single-subject designs test differences among *levels* of an independent variable, similar to the one-way group designs we discussed in Chapter 8. Single-subject designs that present varying nonzero levels of the independent variable are called **multiple-I designs**.

In one such design, the **ABC design**, the researcher obtains a baseline (A), then introduces one level of the independent variable (B) for a certain period of time. Then, this level is removed and another level of the independent variable is introduced (C). Of course, we could continue this procedure to create an ABCDEFG . . . design.

Often, researchers insert a baseline period between each successive introduction of a level of the independent variable, resulting in an *ABACA design*. After obtaining a baseline (A), the researcher introduces one level of the independent variable (B), then withdraws it as in an ABA design. Then a second level of the independent variable is introduced (C), then withdrawn (A). We could continue to manipulate the independent variable by introducing new levels of it, returning to baseline each time.

Such designs are commonly used in research that investigates the effects of drugs on behavior. Subjects are given different dosages of a drug, with baseline periods occurring between the successive dosages. In one such study, Dworkin, Bimle, and Miyauchi (1989) tested the effects of cocaine on how rats respond to punished and nonpunished responding. Over several days, four different dosages of cocaine were administered to five pairs of rats, with baseline sessions scheduled between each administration of the drug. While under the influence of the drug, one rat in each pair received punishment, whereas the other did not. We'll return to the results of this experiment in a moment.

Multiple Baseline Designs

In some instances, the effects of an independent variable do not disappear when the variable is removed. For example, if a clinical psychologist teaches a client a new way to cope with stress, it is difficult to "unteach" it. When this is so, an ABA design is of limited usefulness. How then can we be sure the obtained effects are due to the independent variable as opposed to some extraneous factor?

One way is to use a multiple baseline design. In a **multiple baseline design**, two or more behaviors are studied simultaneously. After obtaining baseline data on all behaviors, levels of an independent variable are introduced that are hypothesized to affect *only one of the behaviors*. In this way, the selective effects of a variable on a specific behavior can be documented.

By measuring several behaviors, the researcher can show that the independent variable caused the target behavior to change, but did not affect other behaviors. If the effects of the independent variable can be shown to be specific to certain behaviors, the researcher has increased confidence that the obtained effects were, in fact, due to the independent variable.

Data from Single-Subject Designs

As we noted earlier, researchers who use single-subject designs resist summarizing their results in the forms of means, standard deviations, and other forms of *group* data. Furthermore, because they object to averaging data across subjects, those who use such designs do not use inferential statistics, such as *t*-tests and *F*-tests, to test whether the differences between experimental conditions are significant.

The preferred method of presenting the data from single-subject designs is with graphs that show the results individually for each subject. Figure 12.1 shows the results from two subjects in the study of the effects of cocaine on reactions to punishment described above (Dworkin et al., 1989).

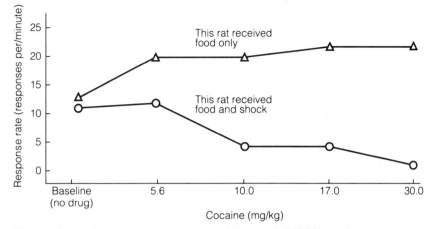

Figure 12.1   Results from the Dworkin et al. (1989) study

Adapted from "Differential Effects of Pentobarbital and Cocaine on Punished and Nonpunished Responding" by S. I. Dworkin, C. Bimle, and T. Miyauchi, 1989, *Journal of the Experimental Analysis of Behavior, 51*, p. 182. Used with permission of the Society for the Experimental Analysis of Behavior.

Explanation: This graph shows the behavior of two rats in the Dworkin et al. study. One rat received only food when it pressed a bar (nonpunished); the other rat received food and shock (punished). The graph shows that increasing dosages of cocaine had quite different effects on the response rates for these two animals. Increasing dosages resulted in increased responding for the nonpunished rat, but in decreased responding for the punished rat. Dworkin et al. replicated this pattern on four other pairs of rats, thereby demonstrating the intersubject generalizability of their findings.

Rather than testing the significance of the experimental effects, single-subject researchers employ **graphic analysis** (also known as **criterion by inspection**). Put simply, the single-subject researcher judges whether or not the independent variable affected behavior by visually inspecting graphs of the data for individual subjects, such as those depicted in Figure 12.1. If the behavioral changes are pronounced enough to be discerned through a visual inspection of such graphs, the researcher concludes that the independent variable affected the subject's behavior. If the pattern is not clear enough to conclude that a behavioral change occurred, the researcher concludes that the independent variable did not have an effect. In the case of the Dworkin et al. study (Figure 12.1), graphic analysis revealed marked differences in how subjects responded under different dosages of cocaine.

Ideally, the researcher would like to obtain results like those shown in Figure 12.2. As you can see in this ABA design, the behavior was stable during the baseline period, changed quickly when the independent variable was introduced, then returned immediately to baseline when the independent variable was removed.

Unfortunately, the results are not always this clear-cut. Look, for example, at the data in Figure 12.3. During the baseline period, the subject's responses were fluctuating somewhat. Thus, it is difficult to tell whether the

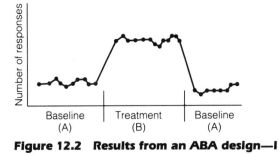

Figure 12.2   Results from an ABA design—I

Explanation: In this ABA design, the effect of the independent variable is clear-cut. The number of responses increased sharply when the treatment was introduced, then returned to baseline when it was withdrawn.

independent variable caused a change in behavior during the treatment period, or whether the observed change was a random fluctuation such as those that occurred during baseline. (This is why single-subject researchers try to establish a stable baseline before introducing the independent variable.) Furthermore, when the independent variable was removed, the subject's behavior changed but did not return to the original baseline level. Did the independent variable cause changes in behavior? In the case of Figure 12.3, the answer to this question is equivocal.

Compared to the complexities of inferential statistics, graphic analysis may appear, on the surface, to be astonishingly straightforward and simple. However, many researchers are disturbed by the looseness of using visual inspection to assess whether or not an independent variable influenced behavior; eyeballing, they argue, is not sufficiently sensitive or objective as a means of data analysis. Specifically, many researchers criticize graphic analysis be-

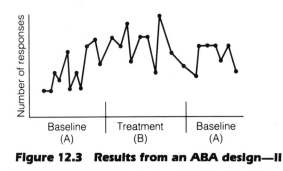

Figure 12.3   Results from an ABA design—II

Explanation: In this ABA design, whether or not the independent variable affected the number of responses is unclear. Because responding was not stable during the baseline (A), it is difficult to determine the extent to which responding changed when the treatment was introduced (B). In addition, responding did not return to the baseline level when the treatment was withdrawn.

cause there is no widely accepted criterion for determining whether or not an effect of the independent variable was obtained.

Proponents of single-subject research counter that, on the contrary, visual inspection is *preferable* to inferential statistics. Because graphic analysis is admittedly a relatively insensitive way to examine data, only the strongest effects will be accepted as real. This is in contrast to group data, in which very weak effects may be found to be statistically significant.

Uses of Single-Subject Designs

During the earliest days of psychology, single-subject research was the preferred research strategy. Many of the founders of behavioral science—Weber, Wundt, Pavlov, Thorndike, Ebbinghaus, and others—relied heavily on single-subject approaches. Today, the use of single-subject designs is closely wedded to the study of operant conditioning. Indeed, B. F. Skinner has been among the most outspoken proponents of single-subject research. Virtually all of Skinner's influential research has involved single-subject designs.

Single-subject designs have been used to study operant processes on both humans and nonhumans, including rats, pigeons, mice, dogs, fish, monkeys, and cats. They have been used both in laboratory research to study basic behavioral processes and in applied settings, such as classrooms, factories, and mental institutions.

In basic research, single-subject designs have been used most commonly to study the effects of various schedules of reinforcement and punishment on behavior. Virtually the entire research literature involving schedules of reinforcement is based on single-subject designs, for example. Similarly, psychophysicists, who study basic processes of sensation and perception, sometimes use single-subject designs.

In applied research, single-subject designs have been used most frequently to study the effects of behavior modification—techniques for changing problem behaviors that are based on the principles of operant conditioning. Such designs have been used widely, for example, in the context of therapy to study the effects of behavior modification on phenomena as diverse as bed-wetting, delinquency, catatonic schizophrenia, aggression, self-injurious behavior, and shyness. Single-subject research has also been used widely in industrial settings (to study the effects of various treatments on a worker's performance, for example) and in schools (to study the effects of token economies on learning).

Finally, single-subject designs are sometimes used for demonstrational purposes simply to show that a particular behavioral effect can be obtained. For example, developmental psychologists have been interested in whether young children can be taught to use memory strategies to help them remember better. Using a single-subject design to show that five preschool children learned to use memory strategies would demonstrate that young children can, in fact, learn such strategies. The causal inferences one can draw from such demonstrations are often weak and the effects are of questionable generalizability, but such studies can provide indirect, somewhat anecdotal evidence that particular effects can be obtained.

Critique of Single-Subject Designs

Well-designed single-subject experiments can provide convincing evidence regarding the causal effects of independent variables on behavior. They have been used quite effectively in the study of many phenomena, particularly the study of basic learning processes.

Despite their obvious uses, single-subject designs have certain limitations. First, because the reversal of treatment effects is important to the logic of the ABA designs, these designs are most useful in cases in which the effects of the independent variable reverse quickly. They are less useful when the independent variable produces permanent changes in behavior.

Second, despite the argument that the results of single-subject studies are more generalizable than the results of group designs, single-subject experiments do not inherently possess greater external validity. Generalizability depends heavily on the manner in which subjects are selected. Even when strong experimental effects are obtained across all subjects in a single-subject experiment, these effects may still be limited to others who are like one's subjects. It is certainly true, however, that single-subject designs permit researchers to see how well the effects of the independent variable generalize across subjects.

Third, single-subject designs are not well suited for studying *interactions* among variables. Although one could logically test a subject under all possible combinations of the levels of two or more independent variables, such studies are often difficult to implement (see Kratochwill, 1978).

Finally, ethical issues arise when ABA designs are used to assess the effectiveness of clinical interventions. Is it ethical to withdraw a potentially helpful treatment from a troubled client to assure the researcher that the treatment was, in fact, effective? For example, we might be hesitant to withdraw the treatment that was introduced to reduce depression in a suicidal patient simply to convince ourselves that the treatment did, in fact, ameliorate the client's depression.

SUMMARY

1. Single-subject designs investigate the effects of independent variables on individual research participants. Unlike group designs, in which data are averaged across subjects for analysis, each subject's responses are analyzed separately and the data from individual subjects are not averaged.

2. Because averages are not used, the data from single-subject experiments cannot be analyzed using inferential statistics. Rather, effects of the independent variable on behavior are detected through graphic analysis.

3. The most common single-subject designs, variations of the ABA design, involve a baseline period, followed by a period in which the independent variable is introduced. Then, the independent variable is withdrawn or transferred to another behavior.

4. More complex designs may involve several successive periods in which the independent variable is reintroduced, then withdrawn.

5. In multiple-I designs, several levels of the independent variable are administered in succession, often with a baseline period between each administration.

6. Behavioral researchers tend to feel strongly about single-subject designs. Either they argue that they are the preferred method of research in psychology or they reject them as being of limited usefulness. There can be little doubt, however, that these designs have been very useful in the study of operant processes. Furthermore, proponents of single-subject designs have provided important insights regarding the drawbacks of group designs and inferential statistics. Even researchers who prefer group designs are well advised to acknowledge the limitations of their methodologies.

KEY TERMS

group design
single-subject design
intersubject variance
intrasubject variance
intrasubject replication
intersubject replication
ABA design

multiple-I design
ABC design
ABACA design
multiple baseline design
graphic analysis
criterion by inspection

REVIEW QUESTIONS

1. Discuss the common criticisms of group designs that are leveled by the proponents of single-subject designs.

2. What is the rationale behind the ABA design?

3. Can single-subject designs be used to test among various levels of an independent variable (as in a one-way group design)?

4. When are multiple baseline designs typically used?

5. How do single-subject researchers analyze their data?

6. Discuss the advantages and disadvantages of single-subject designs, relative to group designs.

QUESTIONS FOR THOUGHT AND DISCUSSION

1. You have learned in this chapter that single-subject designs are somewhat controversial. Many researchers argue that they are the preferred method of experimental research, but others reject them as being of limited usefulness. Part of this disagreement seems to involve the researchers' areas of interest. Single-subject designs lend themselves to certain areas of investigation, whereas they are difficult, if not impossible, to use in other areas. Given your knowledge of psychology, what do you see as the topics for which single-subject designs might be quite useful? In what areas of psychology are such designs more difficult to use, and why?

2. Which side of the controversy regarding single-subject designs do you find most convincing? What is your position regarding single-subject designs?

3. Locate a published experiment that used a group design, and redesign it using a single-subject approach. Remember that many group designs do not convert easily to single-subject designs.

CHAPTER 13

An Overview of Advanced Designs and Analyses

Until the 1970s, most behavioral research involved relatively straightforward correlational, experimental, or quasi-experimental designs such as those discussed in Chapters 6 through 12. And the primary statistical analyses were ones you are already familiar with—correlation, regression, *t*-tests, analysis of variance, and the like. During the past 15 years or so, however, behavioral scientists have begun to use increasingly complex research designs and statistical analyses. As a group, these are called **multivariate techniques** because they permit researchers to examine relationships among many variables at once.

Most of the techniques we have discussed allow researchers to examine relationships between only two dependent variables (as with correlation) or between one or more independent variables and one dependent variable (*t*-tests and ANOVA). Multivariate procedures allow researchers to examine relationships between or within *sets* of variables. Multivariate techniques have by no means replaced the designs and analyses you are already familiar with. Rather, advanced techniques are used when the complexity of a researcher's hypotheses calls for them.

Three factors have contributed to the increased use of complex designs and analyses in recent years. Perhaps the most important factor is a pragmatic one. Most multivariate statistical analyses are difficult, if not nearly impossible, to perform by hand. However, the increased availability of computers and software to conduct these analyses has put advanced statistical analyses within easy grasp of any researcher who has access to a computer (which today includes virtually all researchers in this country). Analyses that once took many hours (or even days!) to conduct by hand can now be performed in a few seconds by a computer.

Second, behavioral scientists' views of behavioral processes have become increasingly complex. In the early days of psychology, hypotheses and the studies designed to test them were usually quite simple and involved only a few variables. Today, however, researchers sometimes test hypotheses that involve many variables. Such complex models of behavior cannot be analyzed easily using simple correlations or *t*-tests, but require multivariate analytic techniques.

The third factor contributing to the increased use of multivariate designs and analyses involves advances in our knowledge of research design and statistics. Analyses are available today that had not been invented or refined several years ago. Furthermore, increasing statistical sophistication has led behavioral researchers to recognize the limitations of many commonly used analyses— limitations that can be overcome through more advanced techniques.

In this chapter we will examine four multivariate techniques: multivariate analysis of variance, discriminant function analysis, canonical correlation, and factor analysis. My purpose in this chapter is not to teach you how to use these procedures. Because of their complexity, such in-depth coverage would require an entire book in its own right. (Those of you who plan to go on to advanced study in psychology have this to look forward to!) Rather, my purpose will be to explain when and why these procedures are used and, in a general sense, how they work. This way, you will understand these techniques when you encounter them in the future. As I mentioned, multivariate techniques are being used with increasing frequency, and you are likely to come across these techniques in your coursework and reading. If you would like more information about these techniques, I recommend the books listed at the end of this chapter.

MANOVA and Discriminant Function Analysis

In previous chapters we discussed two techniques often used to analyze differences among groups of subjects: the *t*-test (to test differences between two groups) and the analysis of variance (ANOVA) (to test differences between more than two groups). The *t*-test and ANOVA are very useful and widely used analyses, but both have a limitation: They allow us to test differences between groups on only one dependent variable at a time.

For reasons that I'll explain in a moment, researchers sometimes want to test differences between groups on *several* dependent variables *simultaneously*. Because *t*-tests and ANOVAs cannot do this, researchers turn to one of two multivariate procedures: multivariate analysis of variance (MANOVA) and discriminant function analysis (DFA).

Multivariate Analysis of Variance

Whereas an analysis of variance tests differences among the means of two or more groups on one dependent variable, a **multivariate analysis of variance,** or

MANOVA, tests differences between the means of two or more groups on two or more dependent variables simultaneously.

A reasonable question at this point is why anyone would want to test group differences on *several* dependent variables at the same time. Why not simply perform several ANOVAs—one on each dependent variable? Researchers turn to MANOVA rather than ANOVA for two reasons.

Conceptually related dependent variables One reason for using MANOVA arises when a researcher has measured several dependent variables, all of which tap into the same general construct. When several dependent variables measure different aspects of the same construct, the researcher may wish to analyze the variables as a set rather than individually.

Suppose you were interested in determining whether a marriage enrichment program improved married couples' satisfaction with their relationships. You conducted an experiment in which couples were randomly assigned to one of three groups. One group of couples participated in a structured marriage enrichment activity for 2 hours, one group participated for 2 hours in unstructured conversations of their own choosing, and a third group participated in no activity together. (I hope you recognize this as a one-way randomized groups design with three conditions; see Chapter 8.)

One month after the program, members of each couple were asked to rate their marital satisfaction on six dimensions involving satisfaction with finances, communication, ways of dealing with conflict, sexual relations, social life, and recreation.

If you wanted to, you could analyze these data by conducting six ANOVAs—one on each dependent variable. However, because all six of your dependent variables reflect various aspects of general marital satisfaction, you might want to know whether the program affected satisfaction *in general* across all of the dependent measures. If this were your goal, you might use MANOVA to analyze your data. MANOVA combines the information from all six dependent variables into a new composite variable, then analyzes whether subjects' scores on this new composite variable differ among the experimental groups.

Inflation of Type I error A second use of MANOVA is to minimize Type I error. As you learned earlier, when we perform many statistical comparisons on many pairs of group means, the probability of obtaining a difference that is due only to error variance increases with the number of tests we perform. For this reason, we used ANOVA rather than *t*-tests when our experimental design involved more than two conditions (and thus more than two means). ANOVA allowed us to test all mean differences while holding the Type I error at whatever alpha level we chose.

In Chapter 10 we saw that Type I error becomes inflated when we test differences among many pairs of means on a single dependent variable. A similar problem arises when we conduct *t*-tests or ANOVAs *on many dependent variables*. The more dependent variables we analyze in a study, the more likely we are to obtain significant differences that are due solely to Type I error.

To use an extreme case, imagine we conducted a two-group study in which we measured 100 dependent variables, then tested the difference between the two group means on each of these variables with 100 *t*-tests. Assuming that the independent variable had absolutely no effect on the dependent variable, on how many variables would you expect to find significant differences?

You should be able to see that if we set our alpha level at .05, we would expect to obtain five significant *t*-tests (that is, 5 out of 100) even though our independent variable had absolutely no effect. Although few researchers use as many as 100 dependent variables in a single study, Type I error increases whenever we analyze more than one dependent variable.

Because MANOVA allows a researcher to test differences among the means of the groups *across all dependent variables simultaneously*, the overall alpha level is held at .05 (or whatever level the researcher chooses) no matter how many tests are conducted. Although most researchers don't worry about analyzing a few variables one by one, many use MANOVA to guard against Type I error whenever they analyze many dependent variables.

How MANOVA works   In the first step of a MANOVA, a weight or coefficient is calculated for each of the original dependent variables. These weights are chosen mathematically according to how important each variable is in differentiating among the various groups. For example, aspects of marital satisfaction that were most affected by the 2-hour marriage enrichment program (and thus that differed most among the groups) would receive greater weights than aspects of marital satisfaction that were less affected by the program. Put differently, dependent variables that were most affected by the manipulation would be weighted more heavily than variables that were less affected.

Then, a new composite variable is calculated by multiplying each dependent variable by its weight and then summing. This composite variable, called the **canonical variable**, is a weighted sum of the original dependent variables *that includes all of the variance in the original variables*. Thus, it provides us with a single index of our variable of interest (such as marital satisfaction) in which the more important aspects of satisfaction have been weighted more heavily.

In the second step of the MANOVA; a multivariate version of the *F*-test is performed to determine whether subjects' scores on this new canonical variable differ among the experimental conditions. If the multivariate *F*-test is significant, we can conclude that the experimental manipulation affected the *set* of dependent variables as a whole.

In cases in which all of the variables measure aspects of the same construct, the researcher may stop at this point, knowing that the composite variable differs significantly among the groups. For example, in our study of marriage enrichment, we would conclude that the marriage enrichment workshop created significant differences in the overall satisfaction in the three experimental groups.

In cases in which MANOVA is being used to limit Type I errors and the dependent variables are not necessarily conceptually related, obtaining a significant multivariate *F*-test allows the researcher to then conduct ANOVAs on each variable separately. Having been assured by the MANOVA that the groups differ significantly on *something*, the researcher may then perform additional analyses without risking an increased chance of Type I error. However, if the MANOVA is not significant, the researcher is not allowed to examine the individual dependent variables using ANOVAs. To do so would run the risk of increasing Type I errors.

BEHAVIORAL RESEARCH CASE STUDY

Effects of Having a Disabled Sibling: An Example of MANOVA

McHale and Gamble (1989) interviewed 62 children between the ages of 8 and 14, half of whom had a younger brother or sister who was mentally retarded. The remaining children had a younger sibling with no disability. Among the data they collected were six ratings relevant to the children's adjustment. They measured each child's self-esteem on four dimensions (academics, social acceptance, conduct, and general self-worth), as well as depression and anxiety.

The researchers conducted a multivariate analysis of variance on these six scores. As explained above, the MANOVA tested whether the two groups of children differed on the weighted sum of these six dependent variables (the canonical variable). The MANOVA revealed a significant difference between the two groups, showing that children with disabled siblings had lower overall adjustment scores than those without disabled siblings. Put differently, the significant MANOVA showed that the two groups differed on the canonical variable which, remember, involved all six of the variables related to adjustment.

Because the MANOVA was statistically significant, the researchers were permitted to analyze each dependent variable separately using ANOVA. These analyses revealed significant differences between the groups on four of the six dependent variables. Specifically, compared with children without disabled brothers or sisters, children who had a disabled sibling were more depressed, more anxious, and had lower self-esteem relevant to social acceptance and conduct.

Discriminant Function Analysis

Discriminant function analysis, or DFA, is used to identify variables that differ or discriminate among two or more groups. Whereas MANOVA is used to answer the question, Do the means of the groups differ on the set of dependent variables?, DFA is used to answer, Which of the dependent variables discriminate subjects in the groups?

For example, a researcher might be interested in knowing what variables discriminate between two groups of patients in a mental hospital—those patients who are able to leave the hospital within 6 weeks after admission and those who must stay longer than 6 weeks. She might measure 15 different variables, then use DFA to determine the variables on which these two groups of patients differ.

You may be able to see that MANOVA and DFA are actually two sides of the same analytic coin. If a difference is obtained between groups (in MANOVA), that variable can be used to discriminate between the groups (DFA). Indeed, MANOVA and DFA are essentially the same analysis mathematically, but because they are used for different purposes, the information each provides to the researcher is somewhat different. Researchers use MANOVA to test whether groups differ on the set of dependent variables. DFA, on the other hand, is used to identify variables that discriminate between groups.

BEHAVIORAL RESEARCH CASE STUDY

Predictors of Drug Use: An Example of Discriminant Function Analysis

Curtis and Simpson (1977) used discriminant function analysis (DFA) to examine predictors of opioid drug use (opioids are drugs such as heroin that are derived from opium). They identified three groups of subjects: those who used opioid drugs on a daily basis, those who used opioid drugs less than daily, and those who did not use opioid drugs. To identify variables that discriminated among these groups, they measured 13 variables on their subjects and entered these into a DFA.

Their results showed that of these variables, five distinguished between the heavy opioid users and the other two groups. The discriminating variables included age, race, length of time the person had used illicit drugs, family size, and kind of drug the person used the first time he or she took illicit drugs.

Canonical Correlation

In Chapter 6, we learned that the Pearson correlation coefficient describes the relationship between any two variables, and that multiple correlation is used to describe the relationship between one variable and a set of variables.

Sometimes researchers are interested not in relationships between two variables or between one variable and a set, but in the relationship between two *sets* of variables. To examine the relationship between two sets of variables, researchers use **canonical correlation**. (*Canonical* is a mathematical term that refers to a formula expressed in its most basic or general form.) Like most multivariate statistical procedures, the mathematical details of canonical correlation are complex and don't really concern us here.

In a general sense, canonical correlation analysis forms two canonical variables such as those calculated in MANOVA. The original dependent variables in each set are weighted, then added to create two canonical variables that contain all of the variance in the two original sets of variables. Then a correlation coefficient is calculated between these two canonical variables.

Just as a Pearson correlation coefficient can be squared to indicate the percentage of variance in one variable that is accounted for by the other, a canonical correlation can be squared to show the percentage of variance in one set of variables that can be accounted for by the other set.

If the two sets of variables correlate significantly, subsequent analyses are conducted to examine precisely how the variables within one set are related to the variables in the other.

BEHAVIORAL RESEARCH CASE STUDY

Information Use Among School Administrators: An Example of Canonical Correlation

One would think that executives and administrators intent on making good administrative decisions would regularly seek data regarding the performance of their organizations. On the contrary, many managers rely on objective information only rarely, depending instead on their intuition and others' opinions in making decisions.

McColskey, Altschuld, and Lawton (1985) were interested in understanding why some administrators do not seek and use objectively obtained information in managing their organizations. Using high school principals as subjects, these researchers measured two sets of variables. One set (the predictor variables) involved factors that might be expected to lead principals to rely more heavily on formal, objective sources of data: their leadership orientation (the degree to which the principal viewed his or her role as that of an active leader), the degree of freedom the principal felt in making decisions (principals who felt no autonomy or freedom might see little need to obtain information with which to make decisions), the principal's experience with research methodology (principals with more research experience might be more data oriented), and open-mindedness (open-minded principals might be less threatened by data).

The second set of variables involved two measures of the degree to which the principal relied on formal sources of information. One measured the degree to which the principal used data to monitor his or her school, and the other assessed the degree to which the principal used data to report to superiors and subordinates.

The researchers then conducted a canonical correlation analysis on these two sets of variables. The canonical correlation between the two sets of variables was .59, which was statistically significant. In other words, the set of predictor variables was significantly related to the variables that measured information use. Indeed, approximately 36% of the variance ($.59^2$) in principals' information use could be accounted for by the set of predictor variables. Subsequent analyses showed that the best predictor of formal information use was the principal's leadership orientation.

Factor Analysis

Factor analysis refers to a class of multivariate statistical techniques used to analyze the interrelationships among a large number of variables. Its purpose is to identify the underlying dimensions or factors that account for the relationships that are observed among the variables.

If we look at the correlations among a large set of variables, we will see that certain variables correlate highly among themselves, but weakly with other variables. Presumably, these patterns of correlations occur because the highly correlated variables measure the same general construct, but the uncorrelated variables measure different constructs. Put another way, the presence of correlations among several variables suggests that the variables are each related to aspects of a more basic underlying factor. Factor analysis is used to identify the underlying factors that account for the observed patterns of relationships among a set of variables.

An Intuitive Approach

Suppose for a moment that you obtained subjects' scores on five variables that we'll call A, B, C, D, and E. When you calculated the correlations among these five variables, you obtained the following correlation matrix:

	A	B	C	D	E
A	1.00	.78	.85	.01	−.07
B	—	1.00	.70	.09	.00
C	—	—	1.00	−.02	.04
D	—	—	—	1.00	.86
E	—	—	—	—	1.00

Look closely at the pattern of correlations. Based on the pattern, what conclusions would you draw about the relationships among variables A, B, C, D, and E? Which variables seem to be related to each other?

As you can see, variables A, B, and C correlate highly with each other, but each correlates weakly with variables D and E. Variables D and E, on the other hand, are highly correlated. This pattern suggests that these five variables may be measuring only two different constructs: A, B, and C seem to measure aspects of one construct, whereas D and E measure something else. In the language of factor analysis, two **factors** underlie these data and account for the observed pattern of relationships among the variables.

Basics of Factor Analysis

Although identifying the factor structure may be relatively easy with a few variables, imagine trying to identify the factors in a data set that contained 20 or 30 or even 100 variables! Factor analysis identifies and expresses the factor structure using mathematical procedures, rather than by eyeballing the data as we have just done.

The mathematical details of factor analysis are complex and don't concern us here, but let us look briefly at how factor analyses are conducted. The grist for the factor analytic mill consists of correlations among a set of variables. Factor analysis attempts to identify the minimum number of factors that will do a reasonably good job of accounting for the observed relationships among the variables. At one extreme, if all of the variables are highly correlated with one another, the analysis will identify a single factor. In essence, all of the observed variables are measuring aspects of the same thing. At the other extreme, if the variables are totally uncorrelated, the analysis will identify as many factors as there are variables. This makes sense; if the variables are not at all related, there are no underlying factors that account for their interrelationships. Each variable is measuring something different, and there are as many factors as variables.

The solution to a factor analysis is presented in a **factor matrix**. Table 13.1 shows the factor matrix for the variables we examined in the correlation matrix above. Down the left column of the factor matrix are the original variables—A, B, C, D, and E. Across the top are the factors that have been

Table 13.1 **A Factor Matrix**

Variable	Factor	
	1	2
A	.97	−.04
B	.80	.04
C	.87	.00
D	.03	.93
E	−.01	.92

Explanation: This is the factor matrix for a factor analysis of the correlation matrix above. Two factors were obtained, suggesting that these five variables measure two underlying factors. A researcher would interpret the factor matrix by looking at the variables that loaded highest on each factor. Factor 1 is defined by variables A, B, and C. Factor 2 is defined by variables D and E.

identified from the analysis. The numerical entries in the table are **factor loadings**. Factor loadings are the correlations of the variables with the factors. A variable that correlates with a factor is said to *load* on that factor.

Researchers use these factor loadings to interpret and label the factors. By seeing which variables load on a factor, the researcher can usually identify the nature of a factor. In interpreting the factor structure, researchers typically consider variables that load at least ±.30 with each factor. That is, they look at the variables that correlate at least ±.30 with a factor and try to discern what those variables have in common. By examining the variables that load on a factor, they can usually determine the nature of the underlying construct.

For example, as you can see in Table 13.1, variables *A*, *B*, and *C* each load greater than .30 on factor 1, whereas the factor loadings of variables *D* and *E* with factor 1 are quite small. Factor 2, on the other hand, is defined primarily by variables *D* and *E*. This pattern indicates that variables *A*, *B*, and *C* reflect aspects of a single factor, whereas *D* and *E* reflect aspects of a different factor. In a real factor analysis, we would know what the original variables were measuring, and we would use that knowledge to identify and label the factors we obtained. For example, we might find that variables *A*, *B*, and *C* were measures of verbal ability, whereas variables *D* and *E* were measures of conceptual ability.

Uses of Factor Analysis

Factor analysis has two basic uses. First, it is used to study the underlying structure of psychological constructs. Many questions in psychology involve the structure of behavior and experience. How many distinct mental abilities are there? What are the basic traits that underlie human personality? What are the primary emotional expressions? What factors underlie job satisfaction? Factor analysis is used to answer such questions, thereby providing a framework for understanding behavioral phenomena. This use of factor analysis is portrayed in the accompanying Behavioral Research Case Study.

Researchers also use factor analysis to reduce a large number of variables to a smaller, more manageable set of data. Often, a researcher measures a large number of variables, knowing that these variables measure only a few basic constructs. For example, subjects may be asked to rate their current mood on 80 mood-relevant adjectives (such as happy, hostile, pleased, nervous). Of course, these do not reflect 80 distinct moods; instead, several items are used to measure each mood. So, a factor analysis may be performed to reduce these 80 scores to a small number of factors that reflect basic emotions. Once the factors are identified, common statistical procedures may be performed on the factors themselves rather than on the original items. Not only does this approach eliminate the redundancy involved in analyzing many measures of the same thing, but analyses of factors are usually more powerful and reliable than measures of individual items.

BEHAVIORAL RESEARCH CASE STUDY

The Five-Factor Model of Personality: An Example of Factor Analysis

How many basic personality traits are there? Obviously, people differ on dozens, if not hundreds, of attributes, but presumably many of these variables are aspects of broader and more general traits.

Factor analysis has been an indispensible tool in the search for the basic dimensions of personality. By factor-analyzing people's ratings of themselves, researchers have been able to identify the basic dimensions of personality and to see which specific traits load on these basic dimensions. In several studies of this nature, factor analyses have obtained five personality factors: extraversion, agreeableness, conscientiousness, emotional stability, and openness.

In a variation of this work, McCrae and Costa (1987) asked whether the same five factors would be obtained if we analyzed others' ratings of an individual rather than the individual's self-reports. Some 274 subjects were rated on 80 adjectives by a person who knew them well, such as a friend or co-worker. When these ratings were factor analyzed, five factors were obtained that closely mirrored the factors obtained when people's self-reports were analyzed.

A portion of the factor matrix is shown below. (Although the original matrix contained factor loadings for all 80 dependent variables, the portion shown below involves only 15 variables.) Recall that the factor loadings in the matrix are correlations between each item and the factors.

Based on the factor loadings, how would you interpret each of the five factors? Remember that factors are interpreted by looking for items that load at least $\pm.30$ with a factor; factor loadings meeting this criterion are highlighted.

Adjectives	Factor				
	I	II	III	IV	V
Calm–worrying	**.79**	.05	−.01	−.20	.05
At ease–nervous	**.77**	−.08	−.06	−.21	−.05
Relaxed–high-strung	**.66**	.04	.01	**−.34**	−.02
Retiring–sociable	−.14	**.71**	.08	.08	.08
Sober–fun-loving	−.08	**.59**	.12	.14	−.15
Aloof–friendly	−.16	**.58**	.02	**.45**	.06
Conventional–original	−.06	.12	**.67**	.08	−.04
Uncreative–creative	−.08	.03	**.56**	.11	.25
Simple–complex	.16	−.13	**.49**	−.20	.08
Irritable–good-natured	−.17	**.34**	.09	**.61**	.16
Ruthless–soft-hearted	.12	.27	−.01	**.70**	.11
Selfish–selfless	−.07	−.02	.04	**.65**	.22
Negligent–conscientious	−.01	.02	.08	.18	**.68**
Careless–careful	−.08	−.07	−.01	.11	**.72**
Undependable–reliable	−.07	.04	.05	.23	**.68**

On the basis of their examination of the entire factor matrix, McCrae and Costa (1987) labeled five factors:

I   Neuroticism
II   Extraversion
III   Openness
IV   Agreeableness
V   Conscientiousness

These five factors, obtained from peers' ratings of subjects, mirror closely the five factors obtained from factor analyses of subjects' self-reports and lend further support to the five-factor model of personality.

SUMMARY

1. Multivariate techniques have become increasingly common in behavioral research during the past 10–15 years. Researchers use multivariate procedures to study the relationships between many variables simultaneously, thereby allowing them to test relationships between and within large sets of variables.

2. Multivariate analysis of variance (MANOVA) is used to test the differences among two or more groups on a set of dependent variables. MANOVA is used in two general cases: when the dependent variables all measure aspects of the same construct (and thus lend themselves to analysis as a group) and when the researcher is concerned that performing analyses on many dependent variables will inflate the possibility of Type I error.

3. Discriminant function analysis (DFA), which is conceptually and mathematically related to MANOVA, is used to identify variables that discriminate among two or more groups of subjects.

4. Canonical correlation provides a measure of the degree of relationship between two sets of variables.

5. Factor analysis is used to reveal the factors that underlie the relationships within a set of variables. Starting with the matrix of correlations among a set of variables, factor analysis helps researchers identify the basic factors. Factor analysis is used to test hypotheses about the structure of behavior and personality, as well as to reduce a large set of data to a small number of factors for use in other analyses.

KEY TERMS

multivariate technique
multivariate analysis of variance
   (MANOVA)

canonical variable
discriminant function analysis
   (DFA)

canonical correlation
factor analysis
factor

factor matrix
factor loading

REVIEW QUESTIONS

1. When do researchers use multivariate techniques?
2. Why are multivariate techniques used more often today than they were in the past?
3. When would you use a multivariate analysis of variance?
4. How does a MANOVA combine all of a researcher's dependent variables into a single variable for purposes of analysis?
5. In what way are discriminant function analysis and MANOVA closely related techniques?
6. Imagine you are examining the correlation between two sets of variables. How could you determine the percentage of variance in one set of variables that can be accounted for by the other set?
7. What does the factor matrix tell us?

QUESTIONS FOR THOUGHT AND DISCUSSION

For each of the research questions below, tell which multivariate technique you would use.

1. A researcher asks 500 married persons to rate their satisfaction on 35 aspects of their marriages. The researcher wants to reduce these 35 aspects down to a few basic dimensions of marital satisfaction.
2. A college administrator wants to find a way of identifying students who have a high probability of dropping out of college during their freshman year. All incoming freshmen complete a battery of 15 tests (ability, motivation, personality, etc.). At the end of the year, the administrator wants to identify tests that can be used to distinguish between students who did and did not drop out during the year.
3. A counselor is interested in the relationship between self-esteem and reckless behavior. He administers four measures of self-esteem and seven measures of reckless behavior (for example, drunk driving, fighting, playing with guns) to 700 eighth-graders. He wants to know whether self-esteem and reckless behavior are related.
4. An experimental psychologist is interested in the effects of temperature on office workers. In a true experiment, office workers go about their daily jobs in offices in which the temperature is 60°, 70°, or 80°F. The dependent variables include three measures of mood (anxiety, depression, hostility), a measure of job satisfaction, and a test of work motivation. The researcher wants to see whether temperature affected this set of measures.

FOR MORE INFORMATION

Many books on multivariate techniques require advanced knowledge of mathematics or statistics. The two books below present multivariate analyses in a more conceptual fashion:

Hair, Jr., J. F., Anderson, R. E., & Tatham, R. L. (1987). *Multivariate data analysis* (2nd ed). New York: Macmillan.

Tabachnick, B. G., & Fidell, L. S. (1989). *Using multivariate statistics* (2nd ed). New York: Harper & Row.

14

Ethical Issues in Behavioral Research

Imagine you are a student in an introductory psychology course. One of the course requirements is that you participate in research being conducted by faculty in the psychology department. When the list of available studies is posted, you sign up for a study titled "Decision Making."

When you report to a laboratory in the psychology building, you are met by a researcher who tells you that the study in which you will participate involves how people make decisions. You will work with two other research participants on a set of problems, then complete questionnaires about your reactions to the task. The study sounds innocuous and mildly interesting, so you agree to participate.

You and the other two participants then work together on a set of difficult problems. As the three of you reach agreement on an answer to each problem, you give your team's answer to the researcher. After your group has answered all of the problems, the researcher says that if you wish, he'll tell you how well your group performed on the problems. The three of you agree, so the researcher gives you a score sheet that shows that your group scored in the bottom 10% of all groups he has tested. Nine out of every 10 groups of subjects performed better than your group! Not surprisingly, you're somewhat deflated by this feedback.

Then, to make things worse, one of the other subjects off-handedly remarks to the researcher that the group's poor performance was mostly *your* fault. Now, you're not only depressed about the group's performance, but embarrassed and angry as well. The researcher, clearly uneasy about the other subject's accusation, escorts you to another room where you complete a questionnaire on which you give your reaction to the problem-solving task and the other two participants.

When you finish the questionnaire, the researcher says, "Before you go, let me tell you more about the study you just completed. The study was *not*, as I told you earlier, about decision making. Rather, we are interested in how people respond when they are blamed for a group's failure by other members of the group." The researcher goes on to tell you that your group did *not* really perform poorly on the decision problems; in fact, he did not even score your group's solutions. Your group was assigned randomly to the failure condition of the experiment, so you were told your group had performed very poorly. Furthermore, the other two subjects were not subjects at all, but confederates—accomplices of the researcher—who were instructed to blame you for the group's failure.

This example, which is similar to some studies in psychology, raises a number of ethical questions. Was it ethical:

- For you to be required to participate in a study to fulfill a course requirement?
- For the researcher to mislead you regarding the purpose of the study? (After all, your agreement to participate in the experiment was based on false information about its purpose.)
- For you to be led to think that the other participants were subjects, when they were actually confederates?
- For the researcher to lie about your performance on the decision-making test, telling you that your group performed very poorly?
- For the confederate to blame you for the group's failure?

In brief, you were lied to and humiliated as part of a study in which you had little choice but to participate. As a subject who participated in this study, how would you feel about how you were treated? As an outsider, how do you evaluate the ethics of this study? Should people be required to participate in research? Is it acceptable to mislead and deceive subjects if necessary to obtain needed information? How much distress, psychological or physical, may researchers cause subjects in a study?

Behavioral scientists have wrestled with ethical questions such as these for many years. In this chapter, we'll examine many of the ethical issues that behavioral researchers address each time they design and conduct a study. After an overview of the approaches people take to making ethical decisions, we'll devote most of the chapter to ethical issues in research involving human participants. Later in the chapter, we'll look also at the ethics of research involving nonhuman animals.

Approaches to Ethical Decisions

Most ethical issues in research arise because behavioral scientists have two sets of obligations that sometimes conflict. On the one hand, the behavioral researcher's job is to provide information that enhances our understanding of behavioral processes and leads to the improvement of human or animal welfare. This obligation requires scientists to pursue research they believe will be useful in extending knowledge or solving problems. On the other hand, behavioral scientists also have an obligation to protect the rights and welfare of the people or animals who participate in their research.

When these two obligations coincide, few ethical issues arise. However, when the researcher's obligations to science and society conflict with obligations to protect the rights and welfare of research participants, the researcher faces an ethical dilemma.

The first step in understanding ethical issues in research is to recognize that well-meaning people may disagree, sometimes strongly, about the ethics of particular research procedures. Not only do people disagree over specific research practices, but they also often disagree over the fundamental ethical principles that should be used to make ethical decisions. Ethical conflicts often reach an impasse because of basic disagreements regarding how ethical decisions should be made and, indeed, whether they can be made at all.

People tend to adopt one of three general approaches to resolving ethical issues about research. These three approaches differ in terms of the criteria that people use to make decisions regarding what is right and wrong (Schlenker & Forsyth, 1977).

Deontology

An individual operating from a deontological position maintains that ethics must be judged in light of a universal moral code. Certain actions are inherently unethical and should never be performed regardless of the circumstances. A researcher who operates from a deontological perspective might argue, for example, that lying is immoral in all situations regardless of the consequences, and thus that deception in research is always unethical.

Skepticism

Ethical skepticism asserts that concrete and inviolate moral codes such as those proclaimed by the deontologist cannot be formulated. Given the diversity of opinions regarding ethical issues and the absence of consensus regarding ethical standards, skeptics resist those who claim to have an inside route to moral truth. Skepticism does not deny that ethical principles are important, only that ethical rules are, by their nature, arbitrary and relative to culture and time.

One skeptical approach, ethical egotism, argues that ethical decisions must be a matter of the individual's conscience: One should do what one thinks is right and refrain from doing what one thinks is wrong. The final arbiter on ethical questions is the individual him- or herself. Thus, an ethical egotist would claim that research ethics cannot be imposed from the outside but are a matter of the individual researcher's conscience.

Teleology

The teleological approach to ethical decisions is a utilitarian one. It argues that judgments regarding the ethics of a particular action depend on the consequences of that action. An individual operating from a teleological perspective would argue that the potential benefits of a particular action should be weighed against the potential costs. If the benefits are sufficiently large relative to the costs, the action is ethically permissible. A researcher who operates from a teleological perspective would argue that whether or not a particular research procedure is ethical depends on the benefits and costs associated with using the procedure. As we will discuss below, the official guidelines for research enforced by the federal government and most professional organizations (including the American Psychological Association), are essentially teleological.

When Ideologies Clash

People with different ethical ideologies often have a great deal of difficulty agreeing on which research procedures are permissible and which are not. As you can see, these debates involve not only the ethics of particular research practices, such as deception, but also disagreements about the fundamental principles that should guide ethical decisions. Thus, we should not be surprised that well-meaning people sometimes disagree about the acceptability of certain research methods.

IN DEPTH

What Is Your Ethical Ideology?

To what extent do you agree or disagree with the following statements?

1. Weighing the potential benefits of research against its potential harm to participants could lead to sacrificing the participants' welfare and hence is wrong.
2. Scientific concerns sometimes justify potential harm to research participants.
3. If a researcher can foresee any type of harm, no matter how small, he or she should not conduct the study.
4. What is ethical varies from one situation and society to the next.
5. Lying to participants about the nature of a study is always wrong, irrespective of the type of study or the amount of information to be gained.
6. It is possible to develop codes of ethics that can be applied without exception to all psychological research.

A deontologist would agree with statements 1, 3, 5, and 6, and disagree with statements 2 and 4. A skeptic would agree with statement 4 and disagree strongly with statements 5 and 6. How a skeptic would respond to statements 1, 2, and 3 would depend on his or her personal ethics. A teleologist would agree with statements 2, 4, and 6, and disagree with statements 1, 3, and 5.

From Schlenker & Forsyth (1977), *Journal of Experimental Social Psychology*. Reprinted with permission of Barry R. Schlenker and Academic Press.

Basic Ethical Guidelines

Whatever their personal feelings about such matters, all behavioral researchers are bound by two sets of ethical guidelines. The first involves principles set forth by the American Psychological Association. The APA has published a set of guidelines for research that involves human participants, as well as regulations for the use and care of animals in research. In addition, the division of the APA for specialists in developmental psychology has set additional standards for research involving children.

Behavioral researchers are also bound by regulations set forth by the federal government. Concerned about the rights of research participants, the Surgeon General of the United States issued a directive in 1966 that required federally supported research to be reviewed to ensure the welfare of human research participants. Later, specific regulations were adopted by the Department of Health and Human Services to protect human subjects (U.S. Department of Health and Human Services, 1983). Recently, the U.S. Department of Agriculture proposed additional regulations for the care of research animals. We'll elaborate on important aspects of these regulations below.

The official approach to research ethics in both the APA principles and federal regulations is essentially a teleological one. Rather than specifying a rigid set of dos and don'ts, these guidelines require researchers to weigh potential benefits of the research against its potential costs and risks. Thus, in determining whether or not to conduct a piece of research, researchers must consider the likely benefits and costs of a particular study. Weighing the pros and cons of a study is called a **cost–benefit analysis**.

Potential Benefits

Behavioral research has five potential benefits.

Basic knowledge   The most obvious benefit of research is that it enhances our understanding of behavioral processes. Of course, studies differ in the degree to which they are expected to enhance knowledge. In a cost–benefit analysis, greater potential costs are considered permissible when the contribution of the research is expected to be high.

Improvement of research or assessment techniques   Some research is conducted to improve the techniques that researchers use to measure and study behavior. The benefit of such research is not to extend knowledge directly, but to improve the research enterprise itself. Of course, such research has an indirect effect on knowledge by providing more reliable, valid, useful, or efficient research methods.

Practical outcomes   Some studies provide practical benefits by directly improving human or animal welfare. For example, research in clinical psychology may improve the quality of psychological assessment and treatment, studies of educational processes may enhance learning in schools, tests of experimental drugs may lead to improved drug therapy, and investigations of prejudice may reduce racial tensions.

Benefits for researchers   Those who conduct research usually stand to gain from their research activities. First, research serves an important educational function. Through conducting research, students gain first-hand knowledge about the research process and about the topic they are studying. Indeed, students are often required to conduct research in the form of class projects, senior research, theses, and dissertations. Fully trained scientists also benefit from research. Not only does it fulfill an educational function for them as it does for students, but many researchers must conduct research to maintain their jobs and advance in their careers.

Benefits for research participants   The people who participate in research may also benefit from their participation. Such benefits are most obvious in clinical research in which subjects receive experimental therapies that may help them with a particular problem. Research participation also can serve an educational function as subjects learn about behavioral science and its methods. Finally, some studies may, in fact, be enjoyable to participants.

Potential Costs

Benefits such as these must be balanced against potential risks and costs of the research. Some of these costs are relatively minor. For example, research participants invest a certain amount of time and effort into a study; their time and effort should not be squandered on research that has limited value.

　　More serious are risks to participants' mental or physical welfare. Sometimes, in the course of a study, participants may suffer social discomfort, threats to their self-esteem, stress, boredom, anxiety, pain, or other aversive states. Participants may also suffer if the confidentialty of their data is compromised and others learn about their responses. Most serious are studies in which human and nonhuman animals are exposed to conditions that may threaten their health or lives. We'll return to these kinds of costs and how we protect subjects against them in a moment.

In addition to costs to the research participants, research has other costs. Conducting research costs money in terms of salaries, equipment, and so forth, and researchers must determine whether their research is justified financially. In addition, some research practices may be detrimental to the profession or to society at large. For example, the use of deception may promote a climate of distrust toward behavioral research.

Balancing Benefits and Costs

The issue facing the researcher, then, is whether the benefits expected from a particular study are sufficient to warrant the expected costs. A study with only limited benefits warrants only minimal costs and risks, whereas a study that may make a potentially important contribution may permit greater costs.

Of course, the researcher him- or herself may not be the most objective judge of the merits of a piece of research. For this reason, federal guidelines require that research be approved by an Institutional Review Board.

The Institutional Review Board

Many years ago, decisions regarding research ethics were left to the conscience of the individual investigator. However, after several cases in which the welfare of human and nonhuman subjects was compromised (most of these cases were in medical rather than psychological research), the U.S. Department of Health and Human Services ordered all research involving human participants to be reviewed by an **Institutional Review Board** (IRB) at the investigator's institution. All institutions that receive federal funds (which includes virtually every college and university in the United States) must have an IRB that reviews all research conducted with human participants.

To ensure maximum protection for subjects, an institution's IRB must have a minimum of five members who come from a variety of both scientific and nonscientific disciplines. In addition, at least one member of the IRB must be a member of the community who is not associated with the institution in any way.

Researchers who use human participants must submit a written proposal to their institution's IRB for approval. This proposal describes the purpose of the research, the procedures that will be used, and the potential risks to research participants. Often researchers submit research materials, such as questionnaires that subjects will complete. Although the IRB may exempt certain pieces of research from consideration by the board, all research involving human participants should be submitted for consideration.

Five issues dominate the discussion of ethical issues in research that involves human participants: lack of informed consent (including invasion of privacy), coercion to participate, potential physical or mental harm, deception, and violation of confidentiality. In the following sections we will discuss each of these issues.

IN DEPTH

The Ten Commandments of Behavioral Research Ethics

The American Psychological Association has published its guidelines for research involving human subjects in a book entitled *Ethical Principles in the Conduct of Research with Human Participants* (1982). In addition to discussing how researchers should make decisions regarding research ethics, this book presents the following 10 basic ethical principles.

A. In planning a study the investigator has the responsibility to make a careful evaluation of its ethical acceptability. To the extent that the weighing of scientific and human values suggests a compromise of any principle, the investigator incurs a correspondingly serious obligation to seek ethical advice and to observe stringent safeguards to protect the rights of human participants.

B. Considering whether a participant in a planned study will be a "subject at risk" or a "subject at minimal risk," according to recognized standards, is of primary ethical concern to the investigator.

C. The investigator always retains the responsibility for ensuring ethical practice in research. The investigator is also responsible for the ethical treatment of research participants by collaborators, assistants, students, and employees, all of whom, however, incur similar obligations.

D. Except in minimal-risk research, the investigator establishes a clear and fair agreement with research participants, prior to their participation, that clarifies the obligations and responsibilities of each. The investigator has the obligation to honor all promises and commitments included in that agreement. The investigator informs the participants of all aspects of the research that might reasonably be expected to influence willingness to participate and explains all other aspects of the research about which the participants inquire. Failure to make full disclosure prior to obtaining informed consent requires additional safeguards to protect the welfare and dignity of the research participants. Research with children or with participants who have impairments that would limit understanding and/or communication requires special safeguarding procedures.

E. Methodological requirements of a study may make the use of concealment or deception necessary. Before conducting such a study, the investigator has a special responsibility to (1) determine whether the use of such techniques is justified by the study's prospective scientific, educational, or applied value; (2) determine whether alternative procedures are available that do not use concealment or deception; and (3) ensure that the participants are provided with sufficient explanation as soon as possible.

F. The investigator respects the individual's freedom to decline to participate or to withdraw from the research at any time. The obligation to protect this freedom requires careful thought and consideration when the investigator is in a position of authority or influence over the participant. Such positions of authority include, but are not limited to, situations in which research participation is required as part of employment or in which the participant is a student, client, or employee of the investigator.

G. The investigator protects the participant from physical and mental discomfort, harm, and danger that may arise from research procedures. If risks of such consequences exist, the investigator informs the participant of that fact. Research procedures likely to cause serious and lasting harm to a participant are not used unless the failure to use these procedures might expose the participant to the risk of greater harm, or unless the research has great potential benefit and fully informed and voluntary consent is obtained from each participant. The participant should be informed of procedures for contacting the investigator within a reasonable time period following participation should stress, potential harm, or related questions or concerns arise.

H. After the data are collected, the investigator provides the participant with information about the nature of the study and attempts to remove any misconceptions that may have arisen. Where scientific or humane values justify delaying or withholding this information, the investigator incurs a special responsibility to monitor the research and to ensure that there are no damaging consequences for the participant.

I. Where research procedures result in undesirable consequences for the individual participant, the investigator has the responsibility to detect and remove or correct these consequences, including long-term effects.

J. Information obtained about a research participant during the course of an investigation is confidential unless otherwise agreed upon in advance. When the possibility exists that others may obtain access to such information, this possibility, together with the plans for protecting confidentiality, is explained to the participant as part of the procedure for obtaining informed consent.

From *Ethical Principles in the Conduct of Research with Human Participants* (pp. 5–7), 1982, Washington, DC: American Psychological Association. Copyright 1982 by the American Psychological Association. Reprinted by permission.

The Principle of Informed Consent

A primary responsibility of any researcher is to obtain the **informed consent** of the individuals who participate in his or her research. Not only does obtaining informed consent ensure that researchers do not violate people's privacy but it ensures that prospective research participants are given enough information about the nature of a study that they can make a reasoned decision regarding whether they want to participate.

Problems with Obtaining Informed Consent

Although few would quarrel in principle with the notion that subjects be informed about a study and allowed to choose whether or not to participate, several considerations may make researchers hesitant to use informed consent or may preclude informed consent altogether.

Compromising the validity of the study   The most common difficulty arises when fully informing an individual about a study would compromise the validity of the data. People often act quite differently when they are under scrutiny than when they don't think they are being observed. Furthermore, divulging the nature of the study may sensitize subjects to aspects of their behavior of which they normally are not aware. It would be fruitless, for example, for a researcher to tell subjects, "This is a study of nonverbal behavior. During the next 5 minutes, researchers will be rating your expression, gestures, body position, and movement. Please act naturally." Thus, researchers sometimes wish to observe people in natural settings without revealing to the participants that they are being observed.

Subjects who are incompetent to give informed consent   Certain classes of people are unable to give valid consent. Children, for example, are neither cognitively nor legally able to make such informed decisions. Similarly, individuals who are mentally retarded or who are out of touch with reality (such as psychotics) cannot be expected to give informed consent. When one's research calls for participants who cannot provide valid consent, consent must be obtained from the parent or legal guardian of the participant.

Ludicrous cases of informed consent   Some uses of informed consent would be ludicrous because obtaining participants' consent would pose a greater burden than not obtaining it. For a researcher who was counting the number of people riding in cars that passed a particular intersection, obtaining informed consent would be both impossible and unnecessary.

Guidelines for Informed Consent

What must subjects be told?   Special cases such as these present researchers with an ethical dilemma. Under what circumstances may a researcher withhold information relevant to informed consent? The accepted general principal governing informed consent states that

> The investigator informs the participants of all aspects of the research that might reasonably be expected to influence willingness to participate and explains all other aspects of the research about which the participants inquire (American Psychological Association, 1982, pp. 5–6).

Note that this principle does not require the investigator to divulge everything about the study. The only requirement is that features be divulged that might influence the subject's willingness to participate. Thus, a researcher may withhold the hypotheses of the study, but he or she cannot fail to tell participants that they will experience pain or discomfort.

Whenever a researcher chooses to be less than fully candid with a subject, he or she is obligated not only to later inform the subject of all relevant details but to be sure the subject understands why certain information was initially withheld.

When may informed consent be waived? An Institutional Review Board may waive or modify the normal requirements for informed consent when certain conditions are met (U.S. Department of Health and Human Services, 1983):

- The research involves no more than minimal risk to participants;
- The waiver of informed consent will not adversely affect the rights and welfare of subjects; and
- The research could not practically be carried out if full informed consent were required.

For example, a researcher observing patterns of seating on public buses would probably not be required to obtain participants' informed consent. This is because the risk to participants is minimal, failure to obtain their consent would not adversely affect their welfare and rights, and the research could not be carried out if people riding buses were informed in advance that their choice of seats was being observed.

Invasion of privacy The right to privacy is a person's right to decide "when, where, to whom, and to what extent his or her attitudes, beliefs, and behavior will be revealed" to others (Singleton, Straits, Straits, & McAllister, 1988, p. 454). The APA's book *Ethical Principles* does not include explicit guidelines regarding **invasion of privacy**, noting only that "the ethical investigator will assume responsibility for undertaking a study involving covert investigation in private situations only after very careful consideration and consultation" (1982, p. 39). Thus, the circumstances under which researchers may collect data without participants' knowledge is left to the investigator's judgment.

Federal guidelines state that research involving the observation of people in *public* places (shopping or eating, for example) need not be reviewed by an IRB. However, if people are to be observed under circumstances in which they reasonably expect privacy, IRB approval is required.

DEVELOPING YOUR RESEARCH SKILLS

You Be The Judge: What Constitutes Invasion of Privacy?

In your opinion, which, if any, of these actual studies constitute an unethical invasion of privacy?

Men using a public restroom are observed surreptitiously by a researcher hidden in a toilet stall, and the time they take to urinate is recorded (Middlemist, Knowles, & Matter, 1976).

A researcher pretends to be a lookout for gay men having sex in a public restroom. On the basis of the men's car license plates, the researcher tracks down the subjects through the Department of Motor Vehicles. Then, under the guise of another study, he interviews them in their homes (Humphreys, 1975).

Researchers covertly film people who strip the parts from seemingly abandoned cars (Zimbardo, 1969).

Subjects waiting for an experiment are videotaped without their prior knowledge or consent. However, they are given the option of erasing the tapes if they do not want their tapes to be used for research purposes (Ickes, 1982).

Shoppers in a drugstore are exposed to a shoplifting confederate, and their reactions are observed (Gelfand, Hartmann, Walder, & Page, 1973).

Researchers hide under dormitory beds and eavesdrop on college students' conversations (Henle & Hubbell, 1938).

What criteria did you use to decide which, if any, of these studies were acceptable to you?

Freedom from Coercion to Participate

All ethical guidelines insist that potential subjects not be coerced into participating in research. **Coercion** occurs when subjects agree to participate because of real or implied pressure from an individual who has authority or influence over them. The most common example involves cases in which professors require their students to serve as research subjects. Other examples include employees in business and industry who are asked to participate in research by their employers, military personnel who are required to serve as subjects, prisoners who are asked to volunteer for research, and clients who are asked to provide data by their therapists or physicians. What all of these classes of subjects have in common is that they may believe, correctly or incorrectly, that refusing to participate will have negative consequences for them—a lower course grade, putting one's job in jeopardy, reprimands from one's superiors, or simply displeasing an important person.

Ethical Principles states that researchers must respect an individual's freedom to decline to participate in research or to discontinue participation at any time. Most colleges and universities who use students as research participants now offer students who do not wish to participate an alternative way of fulfilling the course requirement.

Minimizing Physical and Mental Stress

Most behavioral research is innocuous. However, because many important topics in behavioral science involve how people or animals respond to unpleasant physical or psychological events, it is important that we understand the effects of unpleasant events such as stress, failure, fear, and pain. Researchers find it difficult to study such topics if they are prevented from exposing their subjects to at least small amounts of physical or mental stress. But how much discomfort may a researcher inflict on participants?

According to the applicable principle,

> The investigator protects the participant from physical and mental discomfort, harm, and danger that may arise from research procedures. If risks of such consequences exist, the investigator informs the participant of that fact. Research procedures likely to cause serious and lasting harm to a participant are not used unless the failure to use these procedures might expose the participant to the risk of greater harm, or unless the research has great potential benefit and fully informed and voluntary consent is obtained from each participant.

At the extremes, most people tend to agree regarding the amount of discomfort that is permissible. For example, most people agree that an experiment that leads subjects to think they are dying is highly unethical. One study did just that by injecting subjects, without their knowledge, with a drug that caused them to stop breathing temporarily (Campbell, Sanderson, & Laverty, 1964). Similarly, few people object to studies that involve only minimal risk. **Minimal risk** is "risk that is no greater in probability and severity than that ordinarily encountered in daily life or during the performance of routine physical or psychological examinations or tests" (*Official IRB Guidebook*, 1986).

Between these extremes, however, considerable controversy arises regarding the amount of physical and mental distress that is permitted in research. In large part, the final decision must be left to the individual investigator and the IRB at his or her institution.

Deception in Research

Perhaps no research practice has evoked as much controversy among behavioral researchers as **deception**. Thirty years ago methodological deception was rare, but the use of deception increased dramatically during the 1960s (Christensen, 1988). Although some areas of behavioral research use deception rarely if at all, it is common in other areas. A survey of 691 studies in social psychology—the area in which deception is most common—showed that, of articles published in leading journals between 1965 and 1979, 58% used some form of deception technique (Gross & Fleming, 1982).

Uses of Deception

Behavioral scientists use deception for a number of reasons. The most common one is to prevent subjects from learning the true purpose of a study so that their behavior will not be artificially affected. Other uses include

- Presenting subjects with a false purpose of the study
- Using an experimental confederate who poses as another subject or as an uninvolved bystander
- Providing false feedback to subjects

"They discovered that your research is fraudulent, so your grant will be funded in conterfeit bills."

© 1990 by Sidney Harris, *American Scientist* Magazine.

- Involving subjects without their knowledge
- Presenting two related studies as unrelated
- Giving incorrect information regarding stimulus materials

In each instance, researchers use deception because they believe it is necessary for studying the topic of interest.

Objections to Deception

Many objections have been raised regarding the use of deception; these can be classified roughly into two basic categories.

The most obvious objection is a strictly ethical one—that lying and deceit are immoral and reprehensible acts, even when they are used for good purposes such as research. Baumrind (1971) argued, for example, that "fundamental moral principles of reciprocity and justice are violated" when research psychologists use deception. She added that "scientific ends, however laudable they may be, do not themselves justify the use of means that in ordinary transactions would be regarded as reprehensible" (p. 890). This objection is obviously a deontological one, based on the violation of moral rules.

The second objection is pragmatic. Even if deception can be justified on the grounds that it leads to positive outcomes (the teleological perspective), it may lead to undesirable consequences. For example, because of widespread deception, research participants may enter research studies already suspicious of what the researcher tells them. In addition, subjects who learn that they have been deceived may come to distrust psychologists and the research process in general, undermining the public's trust in behavioral science.

Although the first objection is a purely ethical one for which there is no objective resolution, the second concern has been examined empirically. Several studies have tested how research participants react when they learn they have been deceived by the researcher. In most studies that assessed reactions to deception, the vast majority of subjects (usually over 90%) say they realize that deception is sometimes necessary for methodological reasons and report positive feelings about their participation in the study. Even Milgram (1963), who has been soundly criticized for his use of deception, found that less than 2% of his subjects reported having negative feelings about their participation in his experiment on obedience.

In general, as long as they are informed about details of the study afterward, subjects appear not to mind being misled for good reasons (Christensen, 1988). Put differently, research participants do not seem to regard deception in research settings in the same way they view lying in everyday life. Instead, they view it as a necessary aspect of certain research (Smith & Richardson, 1983). In fact, research shows that, assuming they are properly debriefed, subjects report *more positive* reactions to their participation and higher ratings of a study's scientific value if the study included deception (Smith & Richardson, 1983; Straits, Wuebben, & Majka, 1972).

Findings such as these should not be taken to suggest that deception is necessarily an acceptable practice. However, they do show that, when properly handled, deception per se need not have negative consequences for research participants.

Debriefing

APA guidelines require that research participants be debriefed.

> After the data are collected, the investigator provides the participant with information about the nature of the study and attempts to remove any misconceptions that may have arisen (American Psychological Association, 1982, p. 6).

A **debriefing** accomplishes four goals. First, the debriefing clarifies the nature of the study for participants. Although the researcher may have withheld certain information at the beginning of the study, the participant should be more fully informed after it is over. This does not require that the researcher give a lecture regarding the area of research, only that the participant leave the study with a sense of what was being studied and how his or her participation contributed to knowledge in an area.

Occasionally, subjects are angered or embarrassed when they find they were fooled by the researcher. Of course, the more smug a researcher is about the deception, the more likely the subject is to react negatively. Thus, researchers should be sure to explain the reasons for the deception, express their apologies for misleading the subject, and allow the participant to express his or her feelings about being deceived.

The second goal of debriefing is to remove any stress or other negative consequences. For example, if subjects were provided with false feedback about their performance on a test, the deception should be explained. In cases in which subjects have been led to perform embarrassing or socially undesirable actions, researchers must be sure that participants leave with no bad feelings about what they have done.

A third goal of the debriefing is for the researcher to obtain subjects' reactions to the study itself. Often, if carefully probed, participants will reveal that they didn't understand part of the instructions, were suspicious about aspects of the procedure, were disturbed by the study, or had heard about the study from other people. Such revelations may require modifications in the procedure.

The fourth goal of a debriefing is more intangible. Subjects should leave the study feeling good about their participation. Researchers should convey their genuine appreciation for subjects' time and cooperation, and give subjects the sense that their participation was important.

Confidentiality in Research

The information obtained about research participants in the course of a study is **confidential.** This means that such information may be used only for purposes of the research and may not be divulged to others. When others have access to participants' data, their privacy is invaded.

The easiest way to maintain confidentiality is to ensure that subjects' responses are *anonymous.* If no information is collected that can be used to identify the subject, confidentiality will not be a problem.

In many instances, however, researchers need to know the identity of a research participant. For example, they may need to collate data collected in two different research sessions. To do so, they must know which subjects' data is which.

Several practices are used to solve this problem. Sometimes subjects are given codes to use on their data that allow researchers to connect their data without divulging their identity. In cases in which the data are in no way potentially sensitive or embarrassing, names may be collected. In such cases, however, researchers should remove all information that might identify a subject after the identifying information is no longer needed.

BEHAVIORAL RESEARCH CASE STUDY

The Milgram Experiments

Perhaps no research has been the center of as much ethical debate as Stanley Milgram's (1963) studies of obedience to authority. Milgram was interested in factors that affect the degree to which people obey an authority's orders, even when those orders lead them to harm another person. To examine this question, he tested subjects' reactions to an experimenter who ordered them to harm another subject.

The Study

Subjects were recruited by mail to participate in a study of memory and learning. Upon arriving at a laboratory at Yale University, the subject met an experimenter and another subject who was participating in the same experimental session.

The experiment was described as a test of the effects of punishment on learning. Based on a drawing, one subject was assigned the role of teacher and the other subject was assigned the role of learner. The teacher watched as the learner was led to an adjoining room, strapped into a chair, and had an electrode placed on his wrist. The teacher was then seated in front of an imposing shock generator that would deliver shocks to the other subject. The shock generator had a row of 30 switches, each of which was marked with a voltage level, beginning with 15 volts and proceeding in 15-volt increments to 450 volts.

The experimenter told the teacher to read the learner a list of word pairs, such as *blue–box* and *wild–duck*. After reading the list, the teacher would test the learner's memory by giving him the first word in each pair. The learner was then to give the second word in the pair. If the learner remembered the word correctly, the teacher was to go to the next word on the list. However, if the learner remembered the word incorrectly, the teacher was to deliver a shock by pressing one of the switches. The teacher was to start with the switch marked *15 volts*, then increase the voltage one level each time the learner missed a word.

Once the study was under way, the learner began to make a number of errors. At first, he didn't react to the shocks, but as the voltage increased, he began to object. When the learner received 120 volts, he simply complained that the shocks were painful. As the voltage increased, he first asked, then demanded that the experimenter stop the study. However, the experimenter told the teacher that "the experiment requires that you continue." With increasingly strong shocks, the learner began to yell, then pound on the wall, and after 300 volts, scream in anguish. Most of the teachers were reluctant to continue, but the experimenter insisted that the subject continue with the experimental procedure. After 330 volts, the learner stopped responding altogether; the teacher was left to imagine that the subject had fainted or, worse, died. Even then, the experimenter instructed the teacher to treat no response as a wrong answer and to deliver the next shock.

As you probably know (or have guessed), the learner was in fact a confederate of the experimenter, and he received no shocks. The real subjects, of course, thought they were actually shocking another person. Even so, 65% of the subjects delivered all 30 shocks—up to 450 volts—even though the learner had protested, then fallen silent. This level of obedience was entirely unexpected and attests both to the power of authority figures to lead people to perform harmful actions and to the compliance of research subjects.

The Ethical Issues

Milgram's research raised a number of ethical issues and stimulated an intense debate on research ethics that continues today. Milgram's study raises virtually every ethical question that can be raised.

> Subjects were misled about the purpose of the study.
> A confederate posed as another subject.
> Subjects were led to believe they were shocking another person.
> Subjects were led to perform a behavior that, in retrospect, may have been very disturbing to them.
> Subjects experienced considerable stress as the experiment continued. They sweated, trembled, stuttered, swore, and laughed nervously as they delivered increasingly intense shocks.
> Subjects' attempts to withdraw from the study were discouraged by the experimenter's insistence that they continue.

What is your reaction to Milgram's experiment? Did Milgram violate basic ethical principles in this research?

The Informed Consent Form

One of the primary ways of ensuring that many of the subject's rights have been protected is to use an informed consent form. Federal guidelines require that such forms be used except in special cases.

As its name implies, an **informed consent form** informs the research participant of the nature of the study and obtains his or her agreement to participate. As we discussed above, the principle of informed consent requires that the nature of the subject's participation be described and that all aspects of the study that might reasonably affect his or her willingness to participate be presented.

Beyond a simple description of the study, federal guidelines require that an informed consent form

- Mention any "reasonable foreseeable" risks or discomforts to the subject, as well as possible benefits that may occur because of the research.
- Clarify the extent to which the data will be confidential.
- Assure the subject that participation is fully voluntary, and that refusal to participate will not result in any penalties or loss of benefits to which the subject is otherwise entitled.
- Inform the subject that he or she may withdraw from the study at any time for any reason without penalty.
- Notify the subject who to contact for answers to questions about the research, and who to contact should a research-related injury occur.

To document that an informed consent form was used, the form must be signed by the subject or by the subject's legally authorized representative (such as parents in the case of children). A copy of the form must be given to the person who signs it. In some cases, informed consent may be given orally, but only if a witness is present to attest that informed consent occurs.

Common Courtesy

Aside from the formal guidelines, ethical research requires a large dose of common courtesy. The people who participate in research are contributing their time and energy, often without compensation, to your research. They deserve the utmost in common courtesy.

A few years ago I conducted an informal survey of students who had participated in research as part of their course in introductory psychology. In this survey I asked what problems they had encountered in their participation. The vast majority of their responses did not involve violations of basic ethical principles involving coercion, harm, deception, or violation of confidentiality. Rather, their major complaints had to do with how they were treated *as people* during the course of the study.

Their chief complaints were that

- The researcher failed to show up or was late.
- The researcher was not adequately prepared.
- The researcher was cold, abrupt, or downright rude.
- The researcher failed to show appreciation for the subject.

Subjects must be treated with common courtesy and respect at all times.

Ethics in Research with Animals

In 1985, the American Psychological Association approved the most recent version of its *Guidelines for Ethical Conduct in the Care and Use of Animals.* These guidelines are noticeably less detailed than those involving human subjects, but they are no less explicit regarding the importance of treating nonhuman animals in a humane and ethical fashion.

These guidelines stipulate that all research that uses nonhuman animals must be monitored closely by a person who is experienced in the care and use of laboratory animals and that a veterinarian be available for consultation. Furthermore, all personnel who are involved in animal research, including students, must be familiar with these guidelines and adequately trained regarding the use and care of animals. Thus, if you should become involved with such research, you are obligated to aquaint yourself with these guidelines and abide by them at all times.

The facilities in which laboratory animals are housed are closely regulated by the National Institutes of Health, as well as federal, state, and local laws. Obviously, animals must be housed under humane and healthful conditions. According to the *Guidelines*, the facilities should be inspected by a veterinarian at least twice a year.

Advocates of animal rights are most concerned, of course, about the experimental procedures to which the animals are subjected during research. The APA *Guidelines* require the investigator to justify the use of all procedures that involve more than momentary or slight pain to the animal.

> The scientific purpose of the research should be of sufficient potential significance as to outweigh any harm or distress to the animals used (APA, *Guidelines*, 1985, p. 5).

Procedures that involve more than minimal pain or distress require strong justification.

The APA regulations also provide guidelines for the use of surgical procedures, the study of animals in field settings, the use of animals for educational (as opposed to research) purposes, and the disposition of animals.

IN DEPTH

Behavioral Research and Animal Rights

During the 1980s several animal rights organizations were formed to protest the use of animals for research purposes. Although the protests were aimed initially at medical researchers, behavioral researchers have also been accused of misusing and mistreating the animals they use in their research. Some animal rights groups have simply pressured researchers to treat animals more humanely, whereas others have demanded that the practice of using animals in research be stopped entirely. (Members of some such groups have burglarized animal research laboratories and released the animals.)

Like most ethical issues in research, debates involving the use of animals in research arise because of the competing pressures to advance knowledge and improve welfare on the one hand and to protect animals on the other. Undoubtedly, animals have been occasionally mistreated, either by being housed under inhumane conditions or by being subjected to unnecessary pain or distress during the research itself. However, researchers who conduct research on animals argue that such unfortunate abuses should not blind us to the value of behavioral research on animals.

In the address he delivered upon receiving the APA's Award for Distinguished Professional Contributions, Neal Miller (1985) chronicled the significant contributions of animal research. In defending the use of animals in behavioral research, Miller noted that animal research has contributed to the rehabilitation of neuromuscular disorders, to understanding and reducing stress and pain, to developing drugs for the treatment of various human and animal problems, to processes involved in substance abuse, to improving memory deficits in the elderly, to improving the survival rate for premature infants, and to the development of behavioral approaches in psychotherapy. Miller's list involves only the contributions of *behavioral* research, and does not include the advances in medicine and other fields that came about through the use of animals.

To some animal rights activists, the benefits of the research are beside the point. They argue that, like people, animals have certain moral rights, and that human beings have no right to subject nonhuman animals to pain, stress, and often death, for their own purposes.

In an ideal world we would be able to solve problems of human suffering without using animals in research. But in our less than perfect world most behavioral researchers subscribe to the teleological view that the potential benefits of most animal research outweigh its potential costs.

The Importance of Common Sense

By and large, the guidelines discussed in this chapter provide only a framework for making ethical decisions about research practices. Rather than specifying a universal code of dos and don'ts, they present the principles by which researchers should resolve ethical issues. No unequivocal criteria exist by which researchers can decide how much stress is too much, when deception is and is not appropriate, or whether data may be collected without subjects' knowledge in a particular study. As a result, knowledge of APA principles and federal regulations must be accompanied by a good dose of common sense.

SUMMARY

1. Ethical issues arise in virtually every study of human or animal behavior. Usually the issues are minor ones, but often they involve the fundamental conflict between the scientific search for knowledge and the welfare of research participants.

2. Researchers sometimes disagree, not only regarding the ethicality of specific research practices but also regarding how ethical decisions should be made. Researchers operating from the deontological, skeptical, and teleological perspectives use very different standards for judging the ethical acceptability of research procedures.

3. Professional organizations and the federal government have provided regulations for the protection of human and animal subjects.

4. Five issues must be considered when human participants are used: informed consent (including invasion of privacy), coercion to participate, potential physical or psychological harm, deception, and confidentiality. Although APA and federal guidelines provide general guidance regarding these issues, in the last analysis individual researchers must weigh the potential benefits of their research against its potential costs.

5. Federal regulations require an Institutional Review Board (IRB) at an investigator's institution to approve research involving humans to protect research participants.

6. Professional and governmental regulations also govern the use and care of nonhuman animals in research.

KEY TERMS

deontology
skepticism
teleology

cost–benefit analysis
Institutional Review Board
(IRB)

*Ethical Principles in the Conduct
    of Research with Human
    Participants*
informed consent
invasion of privacy
coercion to participate
minimal risk

deception
debriefing
confidentiality
Milgram study (1963)
informed consent form
*Guidelines for Ethical Conduct in
    the Care and Use of Animals*

REVIEW QUESTIONS

1. Distinguish between deontology, skepticism, and teleology as approaches to making decisions.
2. Which of these three ethical philosophies comes closest to the official ethical guidelines expressed by federal regulatory agencies and the American Psychological Association?
3. What factors should be considered when doing a cost–benefit analysis of a proposed study?
4. What is the purpose of the Institutional Review Board?
5. According to the principle of informed consent, what must subjects be told before soliciting their agreement to participate in a study?
6. When is it not necessary to obtain informed consent?
7. In general, how much mental or physical risk is permissible in research?
8. Why do researchers use deception?
9. What are some methods researchers use to maintain the confidentiality of subjects' responses?
10. Describe the Milgram (1963) study and discuss the ethical issues it raised.
11. What are the basic ethical principles that animal researchers must follow?

QUESTIONS FOR THOUGHT AND DISCUSSION

1. In your view, when is deception permissible in research?
2. Milgram conducted his experiments on obedience in the days before all research was scrutinized by an Institutional Review Board. Imagine, however, that Milgram had submitted his research to an IRB of which you were a member. What ethical issues would you raise as a member of the board? Would you have voted to approve Milgram's research? In thinking about this, keep in mind that before the study was conducted no one expected subjects to obey the researcher as strongly as they did (see Schlenker & Forsyth, 1977).
3. To gain practice writing an informed consent form, write one for the Milgram study described in this chapter.

15

Disseminating Research Findings

As a system for enhancing knowledge, science requires that every investigator share his or her findings with the rest of the scientific community. Only if one's findings are made public can knowledge accumulate as researchers build upon and refine one another's work. As we discussed in Chapter 1, a defining characteristic of science is that, over the long haul, it is self-correcting. But self-correction can occur only if research findings are widely disseminated. To this end, informing others of the outcome of one's work is a critical part of the research process.

In this chapter we will examine how researchers distribute their work—to other scientists, to students, and to the general public. Because the effective communication of one's research nearly always involves writing, much of this chapter will be devoted to scientific writing. We will discuss the criteria of good scientific writing and along the way help you to improve your own writing. We'll also examine the guidelines that behavioral researchers use to prepare their research reports, a system of rules often called **APA style**. To begin, however, we'll take a look at the three main routes by which behavioral scientists disseminate their research to others.

How Scientific Findings Are Disseminated

Researchers disseminate the results of their investigations in three ways: journal publications, presentations at professional meetings, and personal contact.

Journal Publication

Journal publication is the primary route by which research findings are disseminated to the scientific community. Scientific journals serve not only as a means of communication among researchers (most researchers subscribe to one or more journals in their fields), but journals serve as the basis for the permanent storage of research findings in library collections.

Before most journals will publish a research paper, it must undergo the process of **peer review**. In peer review, a paper is evaluated by other scientists who have expertise in the topic under investigation. Although different journals use slightly different systems of peer review, the general process is as follows.

1. The author submits copies of his or her paper to the editor of a relevant journal. (The editor's name and address typically appear on the inside front cover of the journal.) Authors are permitted to submit a particular piece of work to only one journal at a time.

2. The editor then sends a copy of the paper to two or more peer reviewers who are known to be experts in the area of the paper. Each of the reviewers reads and evaluates the paper, addressing its conceptualization, methodology, analyses, and implications. Each reviewer decides whether the paper, considered in its entirety, warrants publication in the journal.

3. The reviewers then send written reviews, typically a page or two in length, to the journal editor, along with their recommendations regarding whether or not the paper should be published.

4. Having received the reviewers' comments, suggestions, and recommendations, the editor considers all of their input and usually reads the paper him- or herself. The editor then makes one of four editorial decisions. First, he or she may decide to publish the paper as is. Editors rarely make this decision, however; even if the paper is exceptional, the reviewers virtually always suggest ways in which it can be improved. Second, the editor may accept the paper for publication contingent upon the author making certain changes and clarifications. Third, the editor may decide *not* to accept the paper for publication in the journal, but will ask the authors to revise the paper in line with the reviewers' recommendations and to resubmit it for reconsideration. Editors make this decision when they think the paper has potential merit, but see too many problems in the paper to warrant publication in its original form. The fourth decision an editor may make is to reject the paper, with no opportunity for the author to resubmit the paper to that particular journal. However, once the manuscript is rejected, the author may submit it for consideration at another journal.

The most common editorial decision is the fourth one—rejection. In the leading journals in behavioral science, between 70% and 90% of the submitted manuscripts are rejected for publication (*Summary report of journal operations*, 1989).

Even if they are ultimately accepted for publication, most submitted papers undergo one or more rounds of reviews and revisions before they are published. In all, from the initial submission of the paper to final publication, the process typically takes a year or two.

Presentations at Professional Meetings

The second route by which scientific findings are distributed is through presentations at professional meetings. Most behavioral researchers belong to one or more professional organizations, such as the American Psychological Association, the American Psychological Society, the American Educational Research Association, the Psychonomic Society, regional organizations (such as the Southeastern, Midwestern, and Western Psychological Associations), and a number of other groups that cater to specific areas of behavioral science (such as psychophysiology, law and psychology, social psychology, health psychology, and so on). Most of these organizations hold annual meetings at which researchers present their latest work.

In most instances, researchers who wish to present their research submit a proposal that is peer reviewed by other researchers. However, the acceptance rate for professional meetings is much higher than that for journal publication.

Depending on the specific organization and on the researcher's preference, the presentation of a paper at a professional meeting can take one of two forms. The traditional manner involves a verbal presentation to an audience. Typically, papers on related topics are included in the same **paper session,** in which each speaker has 15 or 20 minutes to present his or her research and to answer questions from the audience.

A second mode of presentation that has become increasingly popular is the poster session. In a **poster session,** researchers display summaries of their research on poster boards, then stand beside their posters to answer questions and discuss their work with interested persons. (These poster sessions somewhat resemble the format of a high school science fair.) Although some researchers view poster sessions as somehow less professional than verbal presentations, many prefer poster sessions. Not only do more people typically attend a particular poster session than a paper session (thus, the research gets wider exposure) but poster sessions allow more one-on-one interactions between researchers.

Personal Contact

A great deal of communication among scientists occurs through informal channels, such as personal contact. After researchers have been actively involved in an area of investigation for a few years, they get to know others who are interested in the same topic. Not only do they talk with one another at professional meetings, sharing their latest ideas and findings, but they often send prepublication drafts of their latest papers to these individuals. This network, which has been called the hidden university, is an important channel of scientific communication that allows researchers to stay informed regarding the latest advances in their fields. Researchers who are linked into these informal networks often become aware of advances in their fields a year or more before those advances are published in scientific journals.

Elements of Good Scientific Writing

Good writing skills are essential for researchers. No matter how insightful, creative, or well designed particular studies may be, they are unlikely to have an impact on behavioral science if researchers do not convey their ideas and findings in a clear, accurate, and engaging manner. Unfortunately, good writing can not be taught as easily as experimental design or the calculation of a correlation coefficient. It develops only through conscious attention to the details of good writing, coupled with practice and feedback from others.

Thus, I know I cannot teach you to be an effective writer in the next few pages. However, I can offer some suggestions that will set you on the way toward developing your own writing skills. Specifically, I will focus in this section on the importance of organization, clarity, and conciseness, and offer you hints on how to achieve them.

Organization

The first prerequisite for clear writing is organization, the order in which one's ideas are expressed. The general organization of research reports in behavioral science is dictated by guidelines established by the American Psychological Association. Among other things, these guidelines stipulate the order in which sections of a paper must appear. In light of these guidelines (which we will examine in detail later in this chapter), you will have few problems with the general organization of a research paper.

Problems are more likely to arise in the organization of ideas *within* sections of the paper. If the order in which ideas are expressed is faulty, readers are likely to become confused. Someone once said that good writing is like a good road map; the writer should take the reader from point A to point B— from the beginning to the end—in the straightest possible route, without backtracking, without detours, and without getting the reader lost along the way. To do this, you must present your ideas in an orderly and logical progression. One thought should follow from and build on another in a manner that will be easily grasped by the reader.

Before you start writing, make a rough outline of the major points you wish to express. This doesn't necessarily need to be one of those detailed, multilevel outlines you learned to make in high school. Just a list of major points will usually suffice. Be sure the major points in your outline progress in an orderly fashion. Starting with an outline may alert you to the fact that your ideas do not flow coherently or that you need to add certain points to make them progress more smoothly.

As you write, be sure that the transitions between one idea and another are clear. If you move from one idea to another too abruptly, the reader may miss the connection between them and lose your train of thought. Pay particular attention to the transitions from one paragraph to another. Often, you'll need to write transition sentences that explicitly lead the reader from one paragraph to the next.

Clarity

Perhaps the fundamental requirement of scientific writing is clarity. Unlike some forms of fiction in which vagueness enhances the reader's experience, the goal of scientific writing is to communicate information. It is essential, then, that the information be conveyed in a clear, articulate, and unclouded manner.

This is a very difficult task, however. You don't have to read many articles published in scientific journals to know that not all scientific writers express themselves clearly. Often, writers find it difficult to step outside themselves and imagine how a reader will interpret their words. Even so, clarity must be a writer's first and foremost goal.

Two primary factors contribute to the clarity of one's writing: sentence construction and word choice.

Sentence construction The best way to enhance the clarity of your writing is to pay close attention to how you construct your sentences. Awkwardly constructed sentences distract and confuse the reader.

First, state your ideas in the most explicit and straightforward manner possible. One way to do this is to avoid the passive voice. For example, compare the following sentences:

> The subjects were told by the experimenter to press the button when they were finished (passive voice).

> The experimenter told the subjects to press the button when they finished (active voice).

I think you can see that the second sentence, which is written in the active voice, is the better of the two.

Second, avoid overly complicated sentences. Be *economical* in the phrases you use. For example, the sentence, There were several different subjects who had not previously been told what their IQ scores were, is terribly convoluted. It can be streamlined to, Several subjects did not know their IQ scores. In a moment, I'll share with you one method I use for identifying awkwardly constructed sentences in my own writing.

Word choice Another way to enhance the clarity of one's writing is to choose one's words carefully. Choose words that convey *precisely* the idea you wish to express. Say what you mean, and mean what you say, is the scientific writer's dictum.

In everyday language, we often use words in ways that are discrepant from their true dictionary definition. For example, we tend to use *theory* and *hypothesis* interchangably in everyday language, but they mean different things to researchers. Similarly, people talk informally about seeing a therapist or counselor, but psychologists draw a distinctions between therapists and counselors. Can you identify the problem in this sentence?

> Many psychologists feel that the conflict between psychology and psychiatry is based on fundamental differences in their theoretical assumptions.

In everyday language, we loosely interchange *feel* for *think*; but in this sentence, *feel* is the wrong choice.

Use specific terms. When expressing quantity, avoid loose approximations such as *most* and *very few*. Be careful with words, such as *significant*, that can be interpreted in two ways (i.e., *important* versus *statistically significant*). Use verbs that convey precisely what you mean. The sentence, Smith *argued* that earlier designs were flawed, connotes greater animosity on Smith's part than does the sentence, Smith *suggested* that earlier designs were flawed. Use the most accurate word.

There is no way that I can identify for you all of the pitfalls of poor word choice. I simply want to encourage you to consider your words carefully to be sure you "say what you mean."

Finally, avoid excessive jargon. As in every discipline, psychology has a specialized vocabulary for the constructs it studies—such as operant conditioning, cognitive dissonance, and preoperational stage—constructs without which behavioral scientists would find it difficult to communicate. However, refrain from using jargon when a more common word that conveys the desired meaning exists. In other words, don't use jargon when everyday language will do the job.

Conciseness

A third important consideration in scientific writing is *conciseness*. Say what you are going to say as economically as possible. Like you, readers are busy people. Think how you feel when you must read a 26-page journal article that could have conveyed all of its points in only 15 pages. Have mercy on your readers! Conciseness is also important for practical reasons. Scientific journals publish a limited number of pages each year. As a result, papers that are unnecessarily long rob the field of badly needed journal space.

However, do not use conciseness as an excuse for skimpy writing. Research papers *must* contain all necessary information. Ideas must be fully developed, methods described in detail, results examined carefully, and so on. The advice to "be concise" should be interpreted as an admonition to include only the necessary information and to express it as succinctly (yet clearly) as possible.

DEVELOPING YOUR RESEARCH SKILLS

What's Wrong with These Sentences?

Each of the sentences below contains one or more common writing or grammatical errors. Can you spot them? (Answers are at the end of the chapter.)

1. Since this finding was first obtained on male subjects, several researchers have questioned its generalizability.
2. This phenomena has been widely studied.
3. While most researchers have found a direct relationship between incentives and performance, some studies have obtained a curvilinear relationship.
4. Twenty females were used as subjects.
5. After assigning subjects to conditions, subjects in the experimental group completed the first questionnaire.
6. The data was analyzed with a 2 × 2 ANOVA.

Proofreading and Rewriting

Good writers are *rewriters*. Writers whose first draft is ready for public distribution are rare, if they exist at all. Most researchers revise their papers several times before they allow anyone else to see them (unlike the students I've known who hand in their first draft!).

When you reread your own writing, do so with a critical eye. Have you included everything necessary to make your points effectively? Is the paper organized? Are ideas presented in a logical and orderly progression, and are the transitions between them clear? Is the writing clear and concise? Have you used precise vocabulary throughout?

When you proofread your paper, *read it aloud*. I often imagine that I am a television newscaster and that my paper is the script of a documentary I am narrating. (If you feel silly pretending to be a newscaster, read your paper aloud and imagine how it would sound coming from the mouth of your favorite commentator—Dan Rather, Barbara Walters, Jane Pauley, Peter Jennings, or whoever.) Reading a paper aloud is the best way I know to spot awkward constructions. Sentences that look fine on paper often sound stilted or convoluted when they are spoken.

If time permits, write and revise your paper, then set it aside for a few days. After a period away from the paper, I am always able to see weaknesses that I had missed earlier.

Many researchers also seek feedback from colleagues and students. They ask others to critique a polished draft of the paper. Typically, other people will find areas of confusion, awkwardness, poor logic, and other problems. If you ask for others' feedback, be prepared to accept their criticisms and suggestions gracefully. After all, that's what you asked them to give you!

Whatever tactics you use, proofread and revise your writing not once but several times, until it reads smoothly from beginning to end.

Using Nonsexist Language

Consider for a moment the following sentence: The therapist who owns his own practice is as much a businessman as a psychologist. Many people regard such writing as unacceptable because it involves *sexist language*—language that reinforces sexism by treating men and women differently. In the sentence above, the use of *he* and *businessman* seems to imply that all therapists are men.

In the 1970s, the American Psychological Association was one of several organizations and publishers to adopt guidelines for the use of **nonsexist**, or **gender-neutral language**. Using nonsexist language is important for two reasons. First, careless use of gender-related language may promote sexism. For example, consider the sentence, Fifty fraternity men and 50 sorority girls were recruited to serve in the study. The use of the nonparallel phrase *men and girls* reinforces stereotypes about and status differences between men and women.

Second, sexist language can create ambiguity. For example, does the sentence, Policemen experience a great deal of job-related stress, refer only to police*men* or to both male and female police officers?

The APA discusses many variations of sexist language and offers suggestions on how to use nonsexist substitutes in your writing ("Guidelines for Nonsexist Language," *Publication Manual*, 1983, pp. 43–49). I'll discuss three of the more common cases of sexist language below.

He/Him/His

Historically, writers have used generic pronouns such as *he*, *him*, and *his* to refer to both men and women, as in the sentence, Every citizen should exercise his right to vote. However, the use of generic masculine pronouns to refer to people of both sexes is problematic on two counts.

First, using masculine pronouns can create ambiguity and confusion. Consider the sentence, After each subject completed his questionnaire, he was debriefed. Were the subjects described here both men and women, or men only? Second, many have argued that the use of generic masculine pronouns is inherently male centered and sexist (see Pearson, 1985). What is the possible justification, they ask, for using masculine pronouns to refer to both sexes?

Writers deal with the problem of generic pronouns in one of two ways. On one hand, phrases that include both *he or she* or *his or her* can be used:

"After each subject completed his or her questionnaire, he or she was debriefed." However, the endless repetition of *he or she* in a paper can become tiresome. A second, preferred way to avoid sexist language is to use plural nouns and pronouns; the plural form of generic pronouns, such as they, them, and theirs are gender-free: After subjects completed their questionnaires, they were debriefed. Incidentally, APA style discourages use of the form *s/he* to refer to both sexes.

Man

Similar problems arise when the word *man* and its variations (e.g., mankind, the average man, manpower, businessman, policeman, mailman) are used to refer to both men and women. Not only do man-linked words foster confusion, but, again, we should ask ourselves why we use words such as *policeman* to refer to female police officers.

In most instances, other gender-neutral words can be substituted for man-linked words. For example, terms such as *police officer, letter carrier, chairperson*, and *supervisor* are preferable to *policeman, mailman, chairman*, and *foreman*.

Nonequivalent Forms

Other instances of sexist language involve words that are not used equivalently for women and men. The earlier example involving "fraternity men and sorority girls" is an example of this. Furthermore, some words that would seem structurally equivalent for men and women have different connotations. For example, a person who *mothered* a child did something quite different from the person who *fathered* a child. If caretaking behavior is meant, words such as *parenting* or *nurturing* are preferred over mothering. Other words, such as *coed*, have no equivalent form for the other gender (i.e., what is a *male coed* called?) and should be avoided.

IN DEPTH

Sexist Language: Does It Really Matter?

Some writers object to being forced to use nonsexist language. Some argue that so-called sexist language is really immaterial, maintaining that everyone knows that *he* refers to both men and women and that *mankind* includes everybody. Others point out that nonsexist language leads to awkwardly constructed sentences and distorts the English language.

At one level, the arguments for and against nonsexist language are philosophical or political: Should we write in ways that discourage sexism and promote egalitarianism? At another level, however, the debate regarding nonsexist language can be examined empirically. Several researchers have investigated the effects of sexist and nonsexist language on readers' comprehension.

Kidd (1971) examined the question of whether readers interpret the word *man* to refer to everyone as opponents of nonsexist language maintain. In her study, subjects read sentences that used the word *man* or a variation, then answered questions in which they identified the gender of the person referred to in each sentence. Although the word *man* was used in the generic sense, subjects interpreted it to refer to men 86% of the time.

In another study, Stericker (1981) studied the effects of gender-relevant pronouns on students' attitudes toward jobs. Subjects read descriptions of several jobs (such as lawyer, interior decorator, high school teacher). In these descriptions, Stericker manipulated whether the job descriptions used *he, he or she*, or *they*. Her results showed that female subjects were more interested in the jobs when *he or she* was used in the description than when only *he* was used, but that male subjects' preferences were unaffected by which pronoun was used.

In brief, several studies have shown that whether writers use sexist or gender-neutral language *does* make a difference in the inferences readers draw (see Adams & Ware, 1989; Pearson, 1985). In the eyes of most readers, *man, he,* and other masculine pronouns are not generic, gender-neutral designations that refer to men and women equally.

APA Style

In 1929, the American Psychological Association adopted a set of guidelines regarding the preparation of research reports. This first set of guidelines, which was only seven pages long, was subsequently revised and expanded several times. The most recent edition of these guidelines—the **Publication Manual of the American Psychological Association**, 3rd edition—was published in 1983 and runs over 200 pages.

Most journals that publish behavioral research—not only in psychology but in other areas such as sociology and communication—require that manuscripts conform to APA style. In addition, most colleges and universities insist that students use APA style as they write theses and dissertations, and many professors ask that their students write class papers in APA style. Thus, a basic knowledge of APA style is an essential part of the behavioral researcher's toolbox.

The guidelines in the *Publication Manual* serve three purposes. First, many of the guidelines are intended to help authors write more effectively. Thus the manual includes discussions of grammar, clarity, word usage, punctuation, and so on. Second, some of the guidelines are designed to make published research articles uniform in certain respects. For example, the manual specifies the sections that every paper must include, the style of reference citations, and the composition of tables and figures. When writers conform to a single style, readers are spared from a variety of idiosyncratic styles that may distract them from the content of the paper itself. Third, some of the guidelines are designed to facilitate the conversion of typewritten (or, more likely, word-processed) manuscripts into printed journal articles. Certain style conventions assist the editors, proofreaders, and typesetters who prepare manuscripts for publication.

The APA *Publication Manual* specifies the parts that every research report must have, as well as the order in which they appear. Generally speaking, a research paper should have a minimum of seven sections:

> Title page
> Abstract
> Introduction
> Method
> Results
> Discussion
> References

In addition, papers may have sections for author notes, footnotes, tables, figures, and/or appendixes, all of which appear at the end of the typed manuscript. Each of these sections is briefly discussed below.

Title Page

The title page of a research paper should include four pieces of information: the title, the authors' names, the authors' affiliation, and a running head.

The title should state the central topic of the paper clearly, yet concisely. As much as possible, it should mention the major variables under investigation. Titles of research reports are generally less than 15 words long. The title is centered near the top of the first page of the manuscript.

Good titles

Effects of caffeine on the acoustic startle response
Parenting styles and children's ability to delay gratification
Probability of relapse after recovery from an episode of depression

Poor titles

A study of memory
Effects of feedback, anxiety, cuing, and gender on semantic and episodic memory under two conditions of threat: A test of competing theories

In the examples of poor titles, the first is not sufficiently descriptive, and the phrase "A study of" is unnecessary. The second title is too long and involved.

Directly beneath the title are the author's name and affiliation. Most authors use their first name, middle initial, and last name; nicknames should be avoided. The affiliation identifies the institution where the research was conducted.

At the bottom of the title page is the running head, an abbreviated form of the title. For example, the title "Effects of social exclusion on dysphoric emotions" could be reduced to "Effects of exclusion." When an article is typeset for publication, the running head appears at the top of every page of the printed article.

Abstract

The second page of a manuscript consists of the abstract. The **abstract** is a brief summary of the content of the paper. The abstract should describe, in 150 words or less,

- The problem under investigation
- The subjects used in the study
- The research procedures
- The findings
- The conclusions or implications of the study

Because this is a great deal of information to convey in so few words, many researchers find it difficult to write an accurate and concise abstract that is coherent and readable. In some ways, the abstract is the single most important part of a journal article. Most readers decide whether or not to read an article on the basis of its abstract. Furthermore, the abstract is published in *Psychological Abstracts* and is retrieved by many computerized literature search services. Although the abstract is usually the last part of a paper to be written, it is by no means the least important section.

Introduction

The body of a research report begins on page 3 of the manuscript. The title of the paper is repeated at the top of page 3, followed by the introduction itself. (The heading *Introduction* does *not* appear, however.)

The introduction describes for the reader the problem under investigation and presents a background context in which the problem can be understood. The author discusses aspects of the existing research literature that pertain to the study. This by no means involves an exhaustive review of all research that has been conducted on the topic. Rather, the introduction should selectively review previous work that deals specifically with the topic under investigation.

After discussing the problem and previous research, state the purpose and rationale of your research. Typically, this is done by stating explicit hypotheses that were examined in the study.

The introduction should proceed in an organized and orderly fashion.

You are presenting, systematically and logically, the conceptual background that provides a rationale for your particular study. In essence, you are building a case for why your study was conducted and what you expected to find.

Throughout the paper, but particularly in the introduction, you will cite previous research conducted by others. I'll return below to how one cites previous studies using APA style.

After writing the introduction, ask yourself:

- Did I adequately orient the reader to the purpose of the study?
- Did I review the literature adequately, using appropriate, accurate, and complete citations?
- Did I deal with both theoretical and empirical issues relevant to the topic?
- Did I clearly state the research question or hypothesis?

Method

The method section describes precisely how the study was conducted. A well-written method allows readers to judge the adequacy of the procedures that were used and provides a context for them to interpret the findings. A complete description of the method is essential so that readers may assess what a study does and does not demonstrate. In addition, the method section allows other researchers to replicate the study if they wish. Thus, the method should describe, as concisely and clearly as possible, precisely how the study was conducted.

Typically, the method is subdivided into three sections, labeled Subjects, Apparatus (or Materials), and Procedure.

Subjects   The subjects section describes the subjects and how they were selected. If human subjects were used, researchers typically report the number, sex, and age of the subjects, along with their general demographic characteristics. In many cases, the manner in which the subjects were obtained is also included. If nonhuman animals were used, researchers report the number, genus, species, and strain, as well as their sex and age. Often, relevant information regarding the housing, nutrition, and other treatment of the animals is included as well.

Apparatus or materials   If special equipment or materials were used in the study, they are described in a section labeled *Apparatus* or *Materials*. For example, sophisticated equipment for presenting stimuli or measuring responses should be described, as well as special instruments or inventories.

Procedure   The procedure section describes in a step-by-step fashion precisely how the study was conducted. Included here is information regarding experimental manipulations, instructions to the subjects, and all experimental procedures.

After writing the method, ask youself:

- Did I describe the method adequately and clearly, including all information that would be needed for another investigator to replicate the study?
- Did I fully identify the subjects who participated?
- Did I describe the apparatus and materials fully?
- Did I report fully on the research procedure in a step-by-step fashion?

Results

The results section reports the statistical analyses of the data obtained in the study. Generally, writers begin by reporting the most important results, then work their way to secondary findings. Researchers are obligated to describe all relevant results, even those that are contrary to their predictions. However, you should not feel compelled to include every piece of data obtained in the study. Often, researchers collect and analyze more data than what is needed to make their points.

When reporting the results of statistical tests, such as t-tests or F-tests, include information about the kind of analysis that was conducted, the degrees of freedom for the test, the calculated value of the statistic, and an indication of its significance or nonsignificance. If an experimental design was involved, also include the means for the effect. (Because it is difficult to type the conventional symbol for the mean, $\bar{x}$, on a typewriter, the symbol M is used for the mean.) The results of statistical analyses are typically separated from the rest of the sentence by commas, as in the following sentence:

> A t-test revealed that subjects exposed to uncontrollable noise made more errors ($M = 7.5$) than subjects who were exposed to controllable noise ($M = 4.3$), $t(39) = 4.77$, $p < .05$.

Note that this sentence includes the name of the analysis, the condition means, the degrees of freedom (39), the calculated value of t (4.77), and the significance level of the test (.05).

When you need to report a large amount of data—many correlations or means, for example—consider putting some of the data in tables or in figures (graphs). APA style requires that tables and figures be appended to the end of the manuscript, with indicators in the results section saying where the table or figure should appear when the article is printed.

Tables and figures are often useful, but they should be used only when the results are too complex to describe in the text itself. Furthermore, avoid repeating the same data in both the text and in a table or figure. Remember to be economical.

The results should be reported as objectively as possible with minimal interpretation, elaboration, or discussion. The material included in the results section should involve what your data showed, *not* your interpretation of the data.

After writing the results, ask yourself:

- Did I clearly describe how the data were analyzed?
- Did I include all results that bear on the original purpose of the study?
- Did I include all necessary information when reporting statistical tests?
- Did I describe the findings objectively, with minimal interpretation and discussion?

Discussion

Having described the data, you are free in the discussion to interpret, evaluate, and discuss your findings. As a first step, discuss the results in terms of the original purpose or hypothesis of the study. Most researchers begin the discussion with a statement of the central findings and how they relate to the hypotheses under investigation. You then move on to discuss other major findings in the study.

As you do, integrate your results with existing theory and previous findings, referencing others' work where appropriate. Be sure to note inconsistencies between your results and those of other researchers, and mention qualifications and limitations of your study. However, do not feel compelled to dwell on every possible weakness or flaw in your research. All studies have shortcomings; it is usually sufficient simply to note yours in passing.

After writing the discussion, ask yourself:

- Did I state clearly what I believe are the major contributions of my research?
- Did I integrate my findings with both theory and previous research, citing others' work where appropriate?
- Did I note possible qualifications and limitations of my findings?

References

Throughout the text of the paper, you will cite previous work that is relevant to your study. APA guidelines specify the form that such references should take.

Citations in the text of the paper   If you are like most students, you have probably learned to use footnotes to cite others' work. Rather than using footnotes, APA style uses the author–date system in which others' work is cited by inserting the last name of the author and the year of publication at the appropriate point in the text. The book you are reading uses the author–date system.

The author–date system allows you to cite a reference in one of two ways. In the first, the author's last name, followed by the date of publication in parentheses, is included as part of the sentence, as shown in the following examples:

> Jones (1980) showed that subjects . . .
> In a recent review of the literature, Jones (1980) concluded . . .
> This finding was replicated by Jones (1980).

If the work being cited has two authors, cite both names each time:

> Jones and Williams (1980) showed . . .
> In a recent review of the literature, Jones and Williams (1980) concluded . . .

If the work has more than two authors, but fewer than six, cite all authors the *first* time you use the reference. Then, if the reference is cited again, include only the first author, followed by *et al.* and the year:

> Jones, Williams, Smith, Cutlip, Anderson, and Bell (1980) showed that subjects who . . . (first citation)
> Jones et al. (1980) revealed . . . (subsequent citations)

The second way of citing references in the text is to place the authors' last names, along with the year of publication, within parentheses at the appropriate point:

> Several studies have obtained similar results (Jones & Smith, 1980).

If several works are cited in this fashion, alphabetize them by the last name of the first author and separate them by semicolons:

> The effects of stress on decision making have been investigated in several studies (Anderson, 1987; Cohen & Bourne, 1978; Smith, Havert, & Menken, 1980; Williams, 1974).

The reference list   All references cited in the text must appear in a reference list that begins on a new page immediately after the discussion section. References are listed in alphabetical order by the first author's last name. The APA *Publication Manual* presents 63 variations of reference style, depending on whether the work being referenced is a book, journal article, newspaper article, dissertation, film, or whatever.

However, the vast majority of citations are to journal articles, books, and papers presented at professional meetings, so I'll limit my examples to these three types of references.

The reference to a *journal article* includes, in this order,

1. Author's last name(s) and initials
2. Year of publication (in parentheses)
3. Title of the article, with only the first word capitalized

4. Name of the journal (all important words in the title are capitalized, and the title is underlined) (Words underlined in a manuscript will be typeset in italic.)
5. Volume number of the journal (underlined)
6. Page numbers of the article

Smith, M. B. (1980). The effects of research methods courses on student depression. *Journal of Cruelty to Students, 15*, 67–78.

Smith, M. B., Jones, H. H., & Long, I. M. (1978). The relative impact of *t*-tests and *F*-tests on student mental health. *American Journal of Unfair Teaching, 7*, 235–240.

Note that the second line of each reference is indented three spaces. References to *books* include, in this order,

1. Author's last name(s) and initial(s)
2. Year of publication (in parentheses)
3. Title of the book (only the first word of the title is capitalized, and the title is underlined)
4. City and state in which the book was published (followed by a colon)
5. Name of the publisher

Leary, M. R. (1991). *Introduction to behavioral research methods.* Belmont, CA: Wadsworth.

References to a *paper presented at a professional meeting* include, in this order,

1. Author's last name(s) and initial(s)
2. Year and month in which the paper was presented (in parentheses)
3. Title of the paper (underlined)
4. Phrase "Paper presented at the meeting of . . ." following by the name of the organization
5. City and state in which the meeting occurred

Wilson, H. K., & Miller, F. M. (1988, April). *Research methods, existential philosophy, schizophrenia, and the fear of death.* Paper presented at the meeting of the Society for Undergraduate Teaching, Dallas, TX.

Optional Sections

In addition to the title page, abstract, introduction, method, results, discussion, and references, which are required in all research reports, most papers include one or more of the following sections.

Author notes   Often, a page labeled *Author Notes* directly follows the references. In the author notes, the author(s) thank those who helped with the study, acknowledge grants and other financial support for the research, and give an address where they may be contacted for additional information or for copies of the paper. Although the author notes are inserted at the end of a typed manuscript, they typically appear at the bottom of the first page of the published article.

Footnotes In APA style, footnotes are used rarely. They are used to present ancillary information and are typed at the end of the paper. In the published article, however, they appear at the bottom of the page on which the footnote superscript appears.

Tables and figures As I noted above, tables and figures are often used to present the results. In the typed manuscript they appear at the end of the paper. In the published article, they are inserted at the point indicated in the text.

Appendixes Appendixes are rarely included in published journal articles. Occasionally, however, authors wish to include detailed information that does not easily fit into the text itself. If so, the appendix appears at the end of the manuscript and at the end of the article.

Headings, Spacing, and Pagination

Headings With the exception of the introduction, each section we have discussed is labeled. For the other major sections of the paper—abstract, method, results, discussion, and references—the heading is centered in the middle of the page. For subsections of these major sections (such as the subsections for subjects, apparatus, and procedure), a side head is used. A side head is typed flush with the left margin and is underlined. For example, the headings for the method section typically look like this:

The title and abstract appear on the first two pages of every manuscript. The introduction then begins on page 3. The method section does *not* start on a new page, but begins directly beneath wherever the introduction ends. Similarly, the results and discussion sections begin immediately after the method and results sections, respectively. Thus, the text begins with the introduction on page 3, but the next three sections do not start on a new page. However, the references, author notes, footnotes, tables, figures, and appendixes each begins on a new page.

Spacing   Research reports written in APA style are double-spaced from start to finish—no single spacing or triple spacing is permitted. Set your typewriter or word processor on double spacing and leave it there.

Pagination   Pages are numbered in the upper right corner, starting with the title page as page 1. In APA style, a short title, consisting of the first two or three words of the title, is also typed in the upper right corner of each page, just above the page number. Often, the pages of a manuscript become separated or scrambled during the editorial and publication process; this short title allows the editor or typesetter to identify which pages go with which manuscript.

Sample Manuscript

To the new researcher, APA style is complex and confusing; indeed, few veteran researchers are familiar with every detail in the APA *Publication Manual*. Even so, the guidelines contained in this manual are designed to enhance effective communication among researchers, and behavioral researchers are expected to be familiar with the basics of APA style.

What follows is an example of a short research report that has been prepared according to APA style. This is a typewritten manuscript that an author might submit for publication; the published article would, of course, look very different. I've annotated this manuscript to point out some of the basic guidelines that we have discussed above.

Hindsight Distortion

and the 1980 Presidential Election

Mark R. Leary

Wake Forest University

The title page includes the title, the author's name, and the author's institutional affiliation. At the bottom is the running head—the short title that appears at the top of each page of a published article.

Running head: HINDSIGHT DISTORTION

Abstract

The tendency for people retrospectively to overestimate the degree to which they expect events to occur was examined in the context of the 1980 presidential election. Previous research has concluded that distorted hindsight occurs because people have difficulty reconstructing prior probabilities for an event after it has occurred, but the possible mediation of motivational factors, specifically self-esteem and self-presentation, has not been adequately examined. Two-hundred seventy-five subjects were asked either before or after the 1980 presidential election, and under public or private response conditions, to predict the outcome of the election (preelection) or to indicate what they would have predicted the outcome to be had they been asked before the election (postelection). In addition, subjects were classified as being either high or low in ego involvement regarding knowledge of politics. Results showed clear evidence of hindsight distortion: Subjects asked after the election said they would have predicted an outcome closer to the results of the election than those asked before, but there was no evidence of mediation by self-esteem or self-presentation concerns.

The Abstract appears on page 2 and summarizes the study in 100 to 150 words.

Hindsight Distortion

and the 1980 Presidential Election

> The introduction starts on Page 3 with the title of the paper centered at the top of the page.

Although the magnitude of Ronald Reagan's victory over Jimmy Carter in the 1980 presidential election took all but professional political observers by surprise, a great deal of postelection commentary focused retrospectively on preelection signs that a Republican victory was in the works (see "Carter Post-Mortem," 1980). The tone of many of these analyses suggested that the writers were not, after all, particularly surprised by Carter's defeat and that the election outcome was easily understandable in terms of certain critical events during the Carter administration, particularly during the campaign itself. These commentaries make one forget that the election was too close to call until the last few days of the campaign, and appear to reflect the general tendency for people retrospectively to overestimate the degree to which they could have predicted the outcomes of certain events.

> The paper starts with a general introduction to the topic under investigation—distorted hindsight. This is followed by a brief review of previous research on this topic.

Research has repeatedly demonstrated that people overestimate the prior probability of events they believe have occurred. For example, Fischhoff (1975b) asked subjects to read about a historical incident and estimate how likely various outcomes had been at the time the incident occurred.

> The preceding sentence contains a reference citation that uses the author–date format. In this instance, the author's name is incorporated into the sentence.

Subjects who thought they knew the outcome of the event considered that outcome to have been more probable than subjects who did not know the outcome. Even when subjects were instructed to respond as if they did not know the actual outcome of the event, they were unable to ignore this information and continued to overestimate the prior probabilities of events they believed had occurred (see also Fischhoff & Beyth, 1975).

More recently, Fischhoff (1977) and Wood (1978) showed that people also overestimate the degree to which they had known answers to questions of fact, even when warned of potential bias in their responses and admonished to be as accurate as possible in recalling what they had known before being told the correct answer.

In attempting to explain the occurrence of distorted hindsight, also known as the "knew-it-all-along" effect, Fischhoff (1975a, 1975b) suggested that once they know the outcome of an event, people find it difficult to reconstruct what they actually knew prior to the event. By reasoning backward from the event to its possible causes, the individual may see relationships among factors that were not obvious before the event took place. Factors that are clearly associated with the event in some way are recalled more easily, while factors unrelated to the observed outcome are rendered less salient. Conflicting information that does not fit into the reconstruction of the factors leading up to the event is either ignored or reinterpreted in light of what has subsequently happened.

It is possible, however, that distorted hindsight may arise due to motivational, rather than informational, processes. First, people may retrospectively claim they "knew it would happen" to enhance their self-esteem. The conclusion that one was adequately intelligent, perceptive, and/or farsighted to anticipate an event may rightfully result in a positive self-evaluation. Such an effect would be more likely with individuals who take pride in their knowledge of such events because the failure to predict accurately would be more threatening to their self-image (see Walster, 1967).

Alternatively, people may distort their public statements regarding the event as a self-presentation strategy (Goffman, 1959; Schlenker, 1980), expecting to gain social rewards by demonstrating their perceptiveness to others.

In this sentence, reference citations appear in parentheses.

Fischhoff (1977) and Wood (1978) dismissed a self-presentation explanation of the hindsight phenomenon because distorted hindsight has been obtained despite nonevaluative instructions that deemphasized subjects' performance, admonitions to work hard to accurately recall predictions, and warnings to beware of potential hindsight distortion in one's responses. However, previous studies have not completely eliminated factors that may motivate subjects to claim that they knew more than they actually did for self-presentational purposes. If distorted hindsight were obtained even when subjects' responses were entirely anonymous, thus affording them no opportunity to impress others with their perceptiveness, we would have a stronger case for dismissing self-presentation as a mediating factor.

In an initial test of these motivational hypotheses, Leary (1981) asked subjects to predict the score of a football game (pregame) or to state what they would have predicted the score to be had they been asked before the game (postgame). Subjects responded either publicly or privately and were asked the degree to which their knowledge of football was important to them. Consistent with Fischhoff's information-processing hypothesis, subjects asked after the game said they would have predicted a score that was significantly closer to the actual score than subjects who made predictions before the game, but this was not qualified by ego involvement in sports knowledge or response publicness, demonstrating that distorted hindsight may occur in the absence of motivational effects.

> The final paragraph of the introduction states the objectives of the study.

In the present study, the role of information processing, self-esteem, and self-presentation factors in distorted hindsight were reexamined while attempting to increase the strength of the motivational factors used by Leary (1981). An attempt was made to reduce the plausibility of alternative explanations for previous results by rendering subjects' responses more anonymous in the private response condition than was possible in the milling throng of a football game, devising a better measure of ego involvement in knowledge of the target event, and utilizing a potentially more involving event (the 1980 presidential election).

> The method begins immediately following the end of the introduction, with the heading Method centered on the page. The subheadings for subjects and procedure appear as side heads. Because no specialized materials or apparatus were used in this study, an apparatus/materials section is not included.

Method

Subjects

Subjects were 134 male and 141 female university students between the ages of 18 and 22. They were randomly assigned to experimental conditions before the start of the study.

> The number, sex, and age of the subjects are given.

Procedure

Subjects were contacted in their living quarters on either the Monday before or the Wednesday after the 1980 presidential election and asked to participate in an "election survey." In the public response condition, subjects were asked to sign their names on the questionnaires, complete them as the experimenter watched, then return them directly to him or her. In the private response condition, subjects were asked not to sign their names, were assured that their responses would be completely anonymous, completed the questionnaires out of sight of the experimenter, and returned them to the experimenter in a sealed envelope.

The first two questions were designed to ascertain the degree to which subjects' knowledge of politics was important to their self-esteem. It was reasoned that ego involvement in knowledge of a topic is a joint function of how knowledgeable individuals believe themselves to be regarding the topic and how important they consider such knowledge to be. Thus, subjects answered questions to assess these two factors on 12-point Likert scales. Their responses on these items were later multiplied and the product taken as an index of ego involvement in knowledge of politics.

Subjects were then asked to indicate the percentage of the popular vote that they believed each of the three major candidates (Anderson, Carter, and Reagan) would receive in the election (preelection condition) or the percentage they would have predicted the candidates would receive had they been asked before the election (postelection condition). Subjects were told that their estimates for the three candidates should add to 100%.

> The method provides sufficient detail for other investigators to replicate the study if they wish. The results begin immediately after the method.

Results

Subjects' responses to the items assessing self-reported knowledge about the election and the importance they placed on such knowledge were multiplied, and subjects classified as either low or high in ego involvement regarding knowledge of politics (median = 71). The ego-involvement factor was then entered with timing (before or after election) and response publicness (public or private) into a $2 \times 2 \times 2$ ANOVA for each candidate.

> A median split procedure was used to classify subjects as low or high in ego involvement regarding politics. Subjects' scores on the measure of ego involvement in politics were ranked. Subjects with scores above the median were classified as high in ego involvement and those with scores below the median were classified as low in ego involvement.
>
> Because one factor in this design—ego involvement—was a subject variable, whereas the other two factors were manipulated, this is an example of the expericorr design we discussed in Chapter 9. Note that the analyses were described very explicitly.

Only a main effect of timing, $F(1, 267) = 4.89$, $p < .03$, was obtained on subjects' estimates of the percentage of votes Ronald Reagan would obtain in the election. Examination of means (see Table 1) reveals that, consistent with past research, subjects who knew the outcome of the election said they would have predicted an outcome signifi-

----

Insert Table 1 about here

> This statement designates where the table is to be placed when the article is typeset for publication. In the typed manuscript, the table appears at the end of the paper.

cantly closer to the actual outcome than subjects who made their predictions before the election. Like the media, subjects asked before the election underestimated how well Reagan would perform; those asked after the election revised their "predictions" upward. No effects of response publicness or ego involvement were obtained, either singly or in interaction with other variables.

Both a main effect of timing, $F(1, 267) = 11.86$, $p < .001$, and a main effect of ego involvement in knowledge of politics, $F(1, 267) = 7.71$, $p < .01$, were obtained on estimates of the percentage of the vote John Anderson would receive.

Note that in describing the results of the F-tests, the degrees of freedom, the calculated value of F, and the probability level are included. The means appear in the table.

First, subjects asked before the election (see Table 1) greatly overestimated how well Anderson would do, while those asked afterward, although still too high, were significantly closer to the actual outcome, again demonstrating hindsight distortion. Second, the main effect of ego involvement shows that subjects classified as high in ego involvement in knowledgeability of politics ($M = 10.8$) were significantly more accurate in assessing Anderson's vote-getting power than those low in ego involvement ($M = 13.6$).

No effects of the independent or subject variables were obtained on subjects' estimates of how well Carter would perform in the election. Examination of means (see Table 1) for the pre- and postelection conditions reveals why. Subjects' preelection estimates of the percentage of votes Carter would obtain were quite close to the percentage Carter actually received. There is no way in which hindsight distortion can occur when people's preevent predictions are accurate.

Discussion

Consistent with previous research, subjects' postelection recall of how well they had expected the candidates to fare in the election was more closely in line with the actual results of the election than subjects' preelection estimates. Yet, despite clear evidence of hindsight distortion, there was no evidence of mediation by either self-esteem or self-presentation factors.

The discussion begins with a general statement of the study's findings.

Thus the present results are consistent with those obtained previously that supported an information-processing explanation of distorted hindsight (Fischhoff, 1975b, 1977; Fischhoff & Beyth, 1975; Leary, 1981; Wood, 1978). Subjects' knowledge of the election outcome appears to have hindered their cognitive reconstruction of the information that was actually available prior to the election. Subjects asked after the election seemed to believe, if not that they had foreseen the outcome, that their preelection expectancies were less discrepant from the election results than they really were.

Although postelection recall was distorted toward the actual election results, post-election estimates were still somewhat discrepant from the final vote. This suggests that certain factors constrained the degree of hindsight distortion that occurred. Preevent predictions may serve as an anchor that prevents people from claiming post facto that they had made a perfectly accurate prediction. Although one's initial expectancies cannot be perfectly reconstructed once an outcome is known, enough information is available to hold postevent recall in check. Subjects appeared unable to accurately recall their preelection predictions, but they knew, for example, that few people had expected Reagan to do as well as 51% of the vote and thus could not, in retrospect, claim that they had known he would do that well.

> The paper concludes with recommendations for future research.

Given the ubiquitousness of distorted hindsight, additional research is needed that examines the conditions under which it does and does not occur, and the behavioral consequences of overestimating one's accuracy in judging events. For example, attributions of blame are often predicated on the belief that the consequences of certain decisions and actions were potentially foreseeable (Shaw & Sulzer, 1964), so that distorted hindsight may lead individuals to unjustifiably blame others for failing to see what was "foreseeable" only in retrospect (Fischhoff, 1975a). Similarly, since disconfirmed expectancies and observed incongruences often serve to facilitate learning and adjustment, the failure to be surprised by certain occurrences may interfere with experience-based learning and lead people to underestimate what may be learned from the past (Fischhoff, 1975a, 1977). In short, the "Monday morning quarterback" in us all warrants future research attention.

> The references begin on a new page.

References

Carter post-mortem: Debate hurt, but it wasn't only case of defeat. (1980, November 9).

New York Times, pp. 1, 18.

> This is the reference format for a newspaper article with no author listed.

Fischhoff, B. (1975a, April). The silly certainty of hindsight. Psychology Today, pp. 71-

76.

> This is the reference format for a magazine article.

Fischhoff, B. (1975b). Hindsight is not equal to foresight: The effect of outcome knowl-

edge on judgment under uncertainty. Journal of Experimental Psychology: Human

Perception and Performance, 1, 288-299.

Fischhoff, B. (1977). Perceived informativeness of facts. Journal of Experimental Psy-

chology: Human Perception and Performance, 3, 349-358.

> This reference for a journal article includes the author's name, the year of
> publication (in parentheses), the title of the article, the name of the journal
> (underlined), the volume number (underlined), and the page numbers.

Fischhoff, B., & Beyth, R. (1975). "I knew it would happen"—Remembered probability of

once-future things. Organizational Behavior and Human Performance, 13, 1-16.

Goffman, E. (1959). The presentation of self in everyday life. Garden City, NY: Doubleday.

> This reference to a book includes the author's name, the year of publication,
> the title (underlined), the city of publication, and the publisher.

Leary, M. R. (1981). The distorted nature of hindsight. Journal of Social Psychology, 115,

25-29.

Schlenker, B. R. (1980). Impression management: The self-concept, social identity, and

interpersonal relations. Pacific Grove, CA: Brooks/Cole.

Shaw, M. E., & Sulzer, J. L. (1964). An empirical test of Heider's levels in attribution of

responsibility. Journal of Abnormal and Social Psychology, 69, 39-46.

Walster, E. (1967). Second-guessing important events. Human Relations, 20, 239-249.

Wood, G. (1978). The knew-it-all-along effect. Journal of Experimental Psychology: Hu-

man Perception and Performance, 4, 345-353.

> Remember that only references cited in the text appear in the reference list.

Author's Note

This is an edited and revised version of an article that was published in the Person-

ality and Social Psychology Bulletin. At the time the experiment was conducted, the

author was at Denison University. The author would like to thank the members of

Psychology 201 who helped with the study, and Wendy McColskey for her comments on

an earlier version of this article. Requests for reprints should be sent to Mark R. Leary,

Department of Psychology, Wake Forest University, Winston-Salem, NC 27109.

The author's notes report information about the execution of the study, express acknowledgments, and provide an address where the author may be
reached. Although they are typed on a separate page at the end of the manuscript, in a published article the author's notes appear at the bottom of the first
page.

Table 1

Pre- and Postelection Estimates of the Percentage of the Vote Obtained by Each Candidate

Candidate	Preelection	Postelection	Actual Percentage
Reagan	44.3	46.6	51.0
Anderson	14.1	10.5	7.0
Carter	41.7	42.9	41.0

Note. The differences between the preelection means and the postelection means are significant for Reagan and Anderson, but not for Carter.

Tables appear at the end of the manuscript.

KEY TERMS

APA style   paper session   nonsexist language
peer review   poster session   abstract

REVIEW QUESTIONS

1. What are the three primary ways that scientists share their work with the scientific community?
2. When an author submits a manuscript to a journal, by what general process is the decision made whether or not to publish the paper?
3. What are the three central characteristics of good writing?
4. Why do authors avoid using sexist language?
5. List in order the major sections of all research papers.
6. What is the purpose of the introduction of a paper?
7. What information should be included in the method section of a paper?
8. When presenting the results of statistical analyses, what information should be presented?
9. Show the proper form (APA style) for the reference citation to (1) a journal article and (2) a book.

ANSWERS TO "WHAT'S WRONG WITH THESE SENTENCES?"

1. According to APA style, the preferred meaning of *since* is "between a particular past time and the present," and it should not be used as a synonym for *because*. In this example, the meaning of *since* is ambiguous—does it mean "because" or "in the time since?"
2. *Phenomena* is plural; the singular form is *phenomenon*.
3. *While* should be used to mean *during the same time as*. The proper word here is *whereas* or *although*.
4. APA style specifies that *female* (and *male*) are to be used only as adjectives. As such, they must modify a noun (female students, female employees, for example).
5. The phrase *after assigning subjects to conditions* is a dangling modifier that has no referent in the sentence. One possible remedy would be to write, "After the experimenter assigned subjects to conditions, subjects in the experimental group completed the first questionnaire."
6. *Data* is plural; *datum* is singular. Thus, the sentence should be, "The data *were* analyzed . . ."

Statistical Tables

Appendix A-1   Table of Random Numbers

54	83	80	53	90	50	90	46	47	12	62	68	30	91	21	01	37	36	20	95	56	44
36	85	49	83	47	89	46	28	59	02	87	98	10	47	22	67	27	33	13	60	56	74
60	98	76	53	02	01	82	77	45	12	68	13	09	20	73	07	92	53	45	42	88	00
62	79	39	83	88	02	60	92	82	00	76	30	77	98	45	00	97	78	16	71	80	25
43	32	31	21	10	50	42	16	85	20	74	29	64	72	59	58	96	30	73	85	50	54
04	06	78	46	48	03	45	42	29	96	84	39	43	11	45	33	29	98	73	24	85	16
88	92	41	05	15	27	96	28	95	35	89	35	37	97	32	63	45	83	48	12	13	86
77	55	21	12	47	48	36	64	45	52	23	47	98	27	08	63	26	05	45	12	02	89
66	56	61	47	78	76	79	71	47	80	14	78	01	33	00	87	07	02	71	28	22	87
07	52	33	33	62	64	27	52	21	08	39	74	15	66	41	04	93	20	49	23	83	91
91	56	78	63	85	29	88	09	97	30	55	53	68	48	85	52	90	80	11	88	29	84
02	71	28	22	87	97	19	42	21	03	50	39	80	61	30	80	12	75	84	32	76	33
15	50	42	16	66	78	90	11	23	45	52	62	69	79	86	96	03	13	19	82	22	93
64	65	33	97	30	74	07	40	84	27	60	94	31	93	76	97	31	47	65	23	98	32
66	00	19	89	62	32	37	74	85	50	78	76	20	87	25	94	03	46	77	47	97	32
53	88	67	43	29	16	24	91	62	49	04	17	76	79	81	18	41	15	88	62	62	28
23	89	00	30	81	69	80	17	50	48	85	68	27	33	93	45	99	79	48	60	02	82
78	32	26	30	92	41	33	82	88	50	08	53	43	51	78	88	83	77	67	98	07	35
57	84	36	18	38	52	30	76	32	85	42	93	87	61	95	04	53	18	34	29	23	23
58	20	13	24	27	27	19	39	57	30	56	82	24	06	89	96	38	30	58	74	14	95
13	39	15	65	09	20	71	01	53	11	40	99	63	36	39	43	82	77	37	40	23	29
89	62	56	22	12	56	34	46	73	32	50	91	48	19	54	54	07	31	05	60	35	89
95	01	61	16	96	94	44	43	80	69	84	95	14	93	57	48	61	36	15	26	65	10
87	07	15	56	09	36	90	74	78	28	97	82	45	36	11	82	02	13	72	70	13	45
14	65	89	78	52	33	02	05	97	32	13	07	47	21	51	61	44	38	68	01	25	04
63	25	42	44	14	27	77	78	56	91	39	37	19	60	17	99	68	76	14	16	24	34
89	40	87	73	19	90	15	27	68	93	76	95	45	41	41	34	37	92	68	60	27	37
91	71	57	46	17	64	98	17	15	64	36	83	22	97	58	80	97	45	39	90	83	96
19	55	28	47	72	56	17	10	51	31	30	43	15	46	41	38	66	23	62	46	42	46
16	67	20	88	26	82	94	22	57	52	91	24	92	31	38	98	32	62	09	76	88	39
26	55	42	12	15	77	06	08	55	86	68	56	74	06	23	01	35	16	20	58	61	93
07	41	37	55	67	62	77	83	26	25	49	35	18	09	18	92	30	76	44	89	66	22
49	97	63	88	58	07	94	08	07	83	59	99	67	35	95	83	67	28	71	67	04	77
63	41	65	82	12	58	31	76	14	02	36	32	82	30	84	67	13	98	14	90	07	44
46	49	86	69	62	09	45	07	66	69	82	10	06	85	64	37	24	50	37	76	66	13
07	83	36	27	20	35	63	17	32	08	93	87	51	18	01	75	72	46	28	88	34	86
14	08	64	69	40	98	03	39	03	21	82	36	96	19	15	20	06	62	19	90	80	37
63	33	98	17	10	72	17	96	96	03	97	00	07	26	74	63	47	73	73	11	62	78
47	37	57	04	14	46	07	06	86	67	96	68	35	80	34	17	75	33	63	57	25	90
08	84	98	27	72	48	10	48	84	30	28	24	74	96	78	40	41	74	45	41	40	51
03	91	76	37	27	35	31	42	97	76	41	66	30	17	20	92	00	01	01	58	72	05
46	42	60	16	64	82	85	99	15	81	74	16	61	42	71	40	30	17	79	71	37	49
57	68	54	54	74	25	07	47	34	88	15	95	89	79	26	15	19	36	55	22	37	10

Appendix A-2   Critical Values of *t*

1-tailed	0·25	0·1	0·05	0·025	0·01	0·005	0·001	0·0005
2-tailed	0·5	0·2	0·1	0·05	0·02	0·01	0·002	0·001
df 1	1·000	3·078	6·314	12·706	31·821	63·657	318·31	636·62
2	0·816	1·886	2·920	4·303	6·965	9·925	22·327	31·598
3	·765	1·638	2·353	3·182	4·541	5·841	10·214	12·924
4	·741	1·533	2·132	2·776	3·747	4·604	7·173	8·610
5	0·727	1·476	2·015	2·571	3·365	4·032	5·893	6·869
6	·718	1·440	1·943	2·447	3·143	3·707	5·208	5·959
7	·711	1·415	1·895	2·365	2·998	3·499	4·785	5·408
8	·706	1·397	1·860	2·306	2·896	3·355	4·501	5·041
9	·703	1·383	1·833	2·262	2·821	3·250	4·297	4·781
10	0·700	1·372	1·812	2·228	2·764	3·169	4·144	4·587
11	·697	1·363	1·796	2·201	2·718	3·106	4·025	4·437
12	·695	1·356	1·782	2·179	2·681	3·055	3·930	4·318
13	·694	1·350	1·771	2·160	2·650	3·012	3·852	4·221
14	·692	1·345	1·761	2·145	2·624	2·977	3·787	4·140
15	0·691	1·341	1·753	2·131	2·602	2·947	3·733	4·073
16	·690	1·337	1·746	2·120	2·583	2·921	3·686	4·015
17	·689	1·333	1·740	2·110	2·567	2·898	3·646	3·965
18	·688	1·330	1·734	2·101	2·552	2·878	3·610	3·922
19	·688	1·328	1·729	2·093	2·539	2·861	3·579	3·883
20	0·687	1·325	1·725	2·086	2·528	2·845	3·552	3·850
21	·686	1·323	1·721	2·080	2·518	2·831	3·527	3·819
22	·686	1·321	1·717	2·074	2·508	2·819	3·505	3·792
23	·685	1·319	1·714	2·069	2·500	2·807	3·485	3·767
24	·685	1·318	1·711	2·064	2·492	2·797	3·467	3·745
25	0·684	1·316	1·708	2·060	2·485	2·787	3·450	3·725
26	·684	1·315	1·706	2·056	2·479	2·779	3·435	3·707
27	·684	1·314	1·703	2·052	2·473	2·771	3·421	3·690
28	·683	1·313	1·701	2·048	2·467	2·763	3·408	3·674
29	·683	1·311	1·699	2·045	2·462	2·756	3·396	3·659
30	0·683	1·310	1·697	2·042	2·457	2·750	3·385	3·646
40	·681	1·303	1·684	2·021	2·423	2·704	3·307	3·551
60	·679	1·296	1·671	2·000	2·390	2·660	3·232	3·460
120	·677	1·289	1·658	1·980	2·358	2·617	3·160	3·373
∞	·674	1·282	1·645	1·960	2·326	2·576	3·090	3·291

Note. From Table 12 of *Biometrika Tables for Statisticians* (Vol. 1, ed. 1) by E. S. Pearson and H. O. Hartley, London: Cambridge University Press, 1966, p. 146. Adapted by permission of the publisher and the Biometrika Trustees.

Appendix A-3 Critical Values of F

Values of F (for alpha level = .05)

df associated with the numerator (df_{bg})

df associated with the denominator (df_{wg})

	1	2	3	4	5	6	7	8	9	10	12	15	20	24	30	40	60	120	∞
1	161.4	199.5	215.7	224.6	230.2	234.0	236.8	238.9	240.5	241.9	243.9	245.9	248.0	249.1	250.1	251.1	252.2	253.3	254.3
2	18.51	19.00	19.16	19.25	19.30	19.33	19.35	19.37	19.38	19.40	19.41	19.43	19.45	19.45	19.46	19.47	19.48	19.49	19.50
3	10.13	9.55	9.28	9.12	9.01	8.94	8.89	8.85	8.81	8.79	8.74	8.70	8.66	8.64	8.62	8.59	8.57	8.55	8.53
4	7.71	6.94	6.59	6.39	6.26	6.16	6.09	6.04	6.00	5.96	5.91	5.86	5.80	5.77	5.75	5.72	5.69	5.66	5.63
5	6.61	5.79	5.41	5.19	5.05	4.95	4.88	4.82	4.77	4.74	4.68	4.62	4.56	4.53	4.50	4.46	4.43	4.40	4.36
6	5.99	5.14	4.76	4.53	4.39	4.28	4.21	4.15	4.10	4.06	4.00	3.94	3.87	3.84	3.81	3.77	3.74	3.70	3.67
7	5.59	4.74	4.35	4.12	3.97	3.87	3.79	3.73	3.68	3.64	3.57	3.51	3.44	3.41	3.38	3.34	3.30	3.27	3.23
8	5.32	4.46	4.07	3.84	3.69	3.58	3.50	3.44	3.39	3.35	3.28	3.22	3.15	3.12	3.08	3.04	3.01	2.97	2.93
9	5.12	4.26	3.86	3.63	3.48	3.37	3.29	3.23	3.18	3.14	3.07	3.01	2.94	2.90	2.86	2.83	2.79	2.75	2.71
10	4.96	4.10	3.71	3.48	3.33	3.22	3.14	3.07	3.02	2.98	2.91	2.85	2.77	2.74	2.70	2.66	2.62	2.58	2.54
11	4.84	3.98	3.59	3.36	3.20	3.09	3.01	2.95	2.90	2.85	2.79	2.72	2.65	2.61	2.57	2.53	2.49	2.45	2.40
12	4.75	3.89	3.49	3.26	3.11	3.00	2.91	2.85	2.80	2.75	2.69	2.62	2.54	2.51	2.47	2.43	2.38	2.34	2.30
13	4.67	3.81	3.41	3.18	3.03	2.92	2.83	2.77	2.71	2.67	2.60	2.53	2.46	2.42	2.38	2.34	2.30	2.25	2.21
14	4.60	3.74	3.34	3.11	2.96	2.85	2.76	2.70	2.65	2.60	2.53	2.46	2.39	2.35	2.31	2.27	2.22	2.18	2.13
15	4.54	3.68	3.29	3.06	2.90	2.79	2.71	2.64	2.59	2.54	2.48	2.40	2.33	2.29	2.25	2.20	2.16	2.11	2.07
16	4.49	3.63	3.24	3.01	2.85	2.74	2.66	2.59	2.54	2.49	2.42	2.35	2.28	2.24	2.19	2.15	2.11	2.06	2.01
17	4.45	3.59	3.20	2.96	2.81	2.70	2.61	2.55	2.49	2.45	2.38	2.31	2.23	2.19	2.15	2.10	2.06	2.01	1.96
18	4.41	3.55	3.16	2.93	2.77	2.66	2.58	2.51	2.46	2.41	2.34	2.27	2.19	2.15	2.11	2.06	2.02	1.97	1.92
19	4.38	3.52	3.13	2.90	2.74	2.63	2.54	2.48	2.42	2.38	2.31	2.23	2.16	2.11	2.07	2.03	1.98	1.93	1.88
20	4.35	3.49	3.10	2.87	2.71	2.60	2.51	2.45	2.39	2.35	2.28	2.20	2.12	2.08	2.04	1.99	1.95	1.90	1.84
21	4.32	3.47	3.07	2.84	2.68	2.57	2.49	2.42	2.37	2.32	2.25	2.18	2.10	2.05	2.01	1.96	1.92	1.87	1.81
22	4.30	3.44	3.05	2.82	2.66	2.55	2.46	2.40	2.34	2.30	2.23	2.15	2.07	2.03	1.98	1.94	1.89	1.84	1.78
23	4.28	3.42	3.03	2.80	2.64	2.53	2.44	2.37	2.32	2.27	2.20	2.13	2.05	2.01	1.96	1.91	1.86	1.81	1.76
24	4.26	3.40	3.01	2.78	2.62	2.51	2.42	2.36	2.30	2.25	2.18	2.11	2.03	1.98	1.94	1.89	1.84	1.79	1.73
25	4.24	3.39	2.99	2.76	2.60	2.49	2.40	2.34	2.28	2.24	2.16	2.09	2.01	1.96	1.92	1.87	1.82	1.77	1.71
26	4.23	3.37	2.98	2.74	2.59	2.47	2.39	2.32	2.27	2.22	2.15	2.07	1.99	1.95	1.90	1.85	1.80	1.75	1.69
27	4.21	3.35	2.96	2.73	2.57	2.46	2.37	2.31	2.25	2.20	2.13	2.06	1.97	1.93	1.88	1.84	1.79	1.73	1.67
28	4.20	3.34	2.95	2.71	2.56	2.45	2.36	2.29	2.24	2.19	2.12	2.04	1.96	1.91	1.87	1.82	1.77	1.71	1.65
29	4.18	3.33	2.93	2.70	2.55	2.43	2.35	2.28	2.22	2.18	2.10	2.03	1.94	1.90	1.85	1.81	1.75	1.70	1.64
30	4.17	3.32	2.92	2.69	2.53	2.42	2.33	2.27	2.21	2.16	2.09	2.01	1.93	1.89	1.84	1.79	1.74	1.68	1.62
40	4.08	3.23	2.84	2.61	2.45	2.34	2.25	2.18	2.12	2.08	2.00	1.92	1.84	1.79	1.74	1.69	1.64	1.58	1.51
60	4.00	3.15	2.76	2.53	2.37	2.25	2.17	2.10	2.04	1.99	1.92	1.84	1.75	1.70	1.65	1.59	1.53	1.47	1.39
120	3.92	3.07	2.68	2.45	2.29	2.17	2.09	2.02	1.96	1.91	1.83	1.75	1.66	1.61	1.55	1.50	1.43	1.35	1.25
∞	3.84	3.00	2.60	2.37	2.21	2.10	2.01	1.94	1.88	1.83	1.75	1.67	1.57	1.52	1.46	1.39	1.32	1.22	1.00

Appendix A-3 (Continued)

df associated with the numerator (df_{bg})

	1	2	3	4	5	6	7	8	9	10	12	15	20	24	30	40	60	120	∞
1	4052	4999.5	5403	5625	5764	5859	5928	5981	6022	6056	6106	6157	6209	6235	6261	6287	6313	6339	6366
2	98.50	99.00	99.17	99.25	99.30	99.33	99.36	99.37	99.39	99.40	99.42	99.43	99.45	99.46	99.47	99.47	99.48	99.49	99.50
3	34.12	30.82	29.46	28.71	28.24	27.91	27.67	27.49	27.35	27.23	27.05	26.87	26.69	26.60	26.50	26.41	26.32	26.22	26.13
4	21.20	18.00	16.69	15.98	15.52	15.21	14.98	14.80	14.66	14.55	14.37	14.20	14.02	13.93	13.84	13.75	13.65	13.56	13.46
5	16.26	13.27	12.06	11.39	10.97	10.67	10.46	10.29	10.16	10.05	9.89	9.72	9.55	9.47	9.38	9.29	9.20	9.11	9.02
6	13.75	10.92	9.78	9.15	8.75	8.47	8.26	8.10	7.98	7.87	7.72	7.56	7.40	7.31	7.23	7.14	7.06	6.97	6.88
7	12.25	9.55	8.45	7.85	7.46	7.19	6.99	6.84	6.72	6.62	6.47	6.31	6.16	6.07	5.99	5.91	5.82	5.74	5.65
8	11.26	8.65	7.59	7.01	6.63	6.37	6.18	6.03	5.91	5.81	5.67	5.52	5.36	5.28	5.20	5.12	5.03	4.95	4.86
9	10.56	8.02	6.99	6.42	6.06	5.80	5.61	5.47	5.35	5.26	5.11	4.96	4.81	4.73	4.65	4.57	4.48	4.40	4.31
10	10.04	7.56	6.55	5.99	5.64	5.39	5.20	5.06	4.94	4.85	4.71	4.56	4.41	4.33	4.25	4.17	4.08	4.00	3.91
11	9.65	7.21	6.22	5.67	5.32	5.07	4.89	4.74	4.63	4.54	4.40	4.25	4.10	4.02	3.94	3.86	3.78	3.69	3.60
12	9.33	6.93	5.95	5.41	5.06	4.82	4.64	4.50	4.39	4.30	4.16	4.01	3.86	3.78	3.70	3.62	3.54	3.45	3.36
13	9.07	6.70	5.74	5.21	4.86	4.62	4.44	4.30	4.19	4.10	3.96	3.82	3.66	3.59	3.51	3.43	3.34	3.25	3.17
14	8.86	6.51	5.56	5.04	4.69	4.46	4.28	4.14	4.03	3.94	3.80	3.66	3.51	3.43	3.35	3.27	3.18	3.09	3.00
15	8.68	6.36	5.42	4.89	4.56	4.32	4.14	4.00	3.89	3.80	3.67	3.52	3.37	3.29	3.21	3.13	3.05	2.96	2.87
16	8.53	6.23	5.29	4.77	4.44	4.20	4.03	3.89	3.78	3.69	3.55	3.41	3.26	3.18	3.10	3.02	2.93	2.84	2.75
17	8.40	6.11	5.18	4.67	4.34	4.10	3.93	3.79	3.68	3.59	3.46	3.31	3.16	3.08	3.00	2.92	2.83	2.75	2.65
18	8.29	6.01	5.09	4.58	4.25	4.01	3.84	3.71	3.60	3.51	3.37	3.23	3.08	3.00	2.92	2.84	2.75	2.66	2.57
19	8.18	5.93	5.01	4.50	4.17	3.94	3.77	3.63	3.52	3.43	3.30	3.15	3.00	2.92	2.84	2.76	2.67	2.58	2.49
20	8.10	5.85	4.94	4.43	4.10	3.87	3.70	3.56	3.46	3.37	3.23	3.09	2.94	2.86	2.78	2.69	2.61	2.52	2.42
21	8.02	5.78	4.87	4.37	4.04	3.81	3.64	3.51	3.40	3.31	3.17	3.03	2.88	2.80	2.72	2.64	2.55	2.46	2.36
22	7.95	5.72	4.82	4.31	3.99	3.76	3.59	3.45	3.35	3.26	3.12	2.98	2.83	2.75	2.67	2.58	2.50	2.40	2.31
23	7.88	5.66	4.76	4.26	3.94	3.71	3.54	3.41	3.30	3.21	3.07	2.93	2.78	2.70	2.62	2.54	2.45	2.35	2.26
24	7.82	5.61	4.72	4.22	3.90	3.67	3.50	3.36	3.26	3.17	3.03	2.89	2.74	2.66	2.58	2.49	2.40	2.31	2.21
25	7.77	5.57	4.68	4.18	3.85	3.63	3.46	3.32	3.22	3.13	2.99	2.85	2.70	2.62	2.54	2.45	2.36	2.27	2.17
26	7.72	5.53	4.64	4.14	3.82	3.59	3.42	3.29	3.18	3.09	2.96	2.81	2.66	2.58	2.50	2.42	2.33	2.23	2.13
27	7.68	5.49	4.60	4.11	3.78	3.56	3.39	3.26	3.15	3.06	2.93	2.78	2.63	2.55	2.47	2.38	2.29	2.20	2.10
28	7.64	5.45	4.57	4.07	3.75	3.53	3.36	3.23	3.12	3.03	2.90	2.75	2.60	2.52	2.44	2.35	2.26	2.17	2.06
29	7.60	5.42	4.54	4.04	3.73	3.50	3.33	3.20	3.09	3.00	2.87	2.73	2.57	2.49	2.41	2.33	2.23	2.14	2.03
30	7.56	5.39	4.51	4.02	3.70	3.47	3.30	3.17	3.07	2.98	2.84	2.70	2.55	2.47	2.39	2.30	2.21	2.11	2.01
40	7.31	5.18	4.31	3.83	3.51	3.29	3.12	2.99	2.89	2.80	2.66	2.52	2.37	2.29	2.20	2.11	2.02	1.92	1.80
60	7.08	4.98	4.13	3.65	3.34	3.12	2.95	2.82	2.72	2.63	2.50	2.35	2.20	2.12	2.03	1.94	1.84	1.73	1.60
120	6.85	4.79	3.95	3.48	3.17	2.96	2.79	2.66	2.56	2.47	2.34	2.19	2.03	1.95	1.86	1.76	1.66	1.53	1.38
∞	6.63	4.61	3.78	3.32	3.02	2.80	2.64	2.51	2.41	2.32	2.18	2.04	1.88	1.79	1.70	1.59	1.47	1.32	1.00

df associated with the denominator (df_{wg})

Note. From Table 18 of Biometrika Tables for Statisticians (Vol. 1, ed. 1) by E. S. Pearson and H. O. Hartley, London: Cambridge University Press, 1966, pp. 171–173.

Statistical Formulas

Appendix B-1 Calculational Formulas for One-Way ANOVA

Appendix B-2 Calculational Formulas for Factorial ANOVA

Appendix B-1

Calculational Formulas for a One-Way ANOVA

The demonstrational formulas for one-way ANOVA presented in Chapter 10 help to convey the rationale behind ANOVA, but they are unwieldy for computational purposes. Appendix B-1 presents the calculational formulas for performing a one-way ANOVA on data from a between-groups (completely randomized) design.

The data used in this example are from a hypothetical study of the effects of physical appearance on liking. In this study, subjects listened to another subject talk about him- or herself over an intercom for 5 minutes. Subjects were led to believe that the person they listened to was either very attractive, moderately attractive, or unattractive. To manipulate perceived attractiveness, the researcher gave each subject a Polaroid photograph that was supposedly a picture of the other subject. In reality, the pictures were prepared in advance and were *not* of the person who talked over the intercom.

After listening to the other person, subjects rated how much they liked him or her on a 7-point scale (where 1 = disliked greatly and 7 = liked greatly). Six subjects participated in each of the three conditions. The ratings for the 18 subjects are shown below.

Attractive Picture	Unattractive Picture	Neutral Picture
7	4	5
5	3	6
5	4	6
6	4	4
4	3	5
6	5	5

STEP 1   For each condition, compute

1. The sum of all of the scores in each condition (Σx)
2. The mean of the condition ($\bar{x}$)
3. The sum of the squared scores (Σx^2)
4. The sum of squares ($\Sigma x^2 - [(\Sigma x)^2/n]$)

You'll find it useful to enter these quantities into a table such as the following:

	Attractive Picture	Unattractive Picture	Neutral Picture
Σx	33	23	31
$\bar{x}$	5.5	3.8	5.2
Σx^2	187	91	163
SS	5.50	2.83	2.83

$\bar{x}_T = 4.833$

Steps 2–4 calculate the within-groups portion of the variance.

STEP 2   Compute SS_{wg}—the sum of the SS of each condition:

$$SS_{wg} = SS_{a1} + SS_{a2} + SS_{a3}$$
$$= 5.50 + 2.83 + 2.83$$
$$= 11.16$$

STEP 3   Compute df_{wg}:

$$df_{wg} = N - k, \qquad \text{where } n = \text{total number of subjects and}$$
$$k = \text{number of conditions}$$
$$= 18 - 3$$
$$= 15$$

STEP 4   Compute MS_{wg}:

$$MS_{wg} = SS_{wg}/df_{wg}$$
$$= 11.16/15$$
$$= .744$$

Set MS_{wg} aside momentarily as you calculate SS_{bg}.

Steps 5–7 calculate the between-groups portion of the variance.

Between Subjects?

STEP 5   Compute SS_{bg}:

$$SS_{bg} = \frac{(\Sigma x_{a1})^2 + (\Sigma x_{a2})^2 + \cdots + (\Sigma x_{ak})^2}{n} - \frac{(\Sigma x)^2}{N}$$
$$= \frac{(33)^2 + (23)^2 + (31)^2}{6} - \frac{(33 + 23 + 31)^2}{18}$$
$$= \frac{1089 + 529 + 961}{6} - \frac{(87)^2}{18}$$
$$= 429.83 - 420.50$$
$$= 9.33$$

STEP 6   Compute df_{bg}:

$$df_{bg} = k - 1, \qquad \text{where } k = \text{number of conditions}$$
$$= 3 - 1$$
$$= 2$$

STEP 7   Compute MS_{bg}:

$$MS_{bg} = SS_{bg}/df_{bg}$$
$$= 9.33/2$$
$$= 4.67$$

STEP 8   Compute the calculated value of F:

$$F = MS_{bg}/MS_{wg}$$
$$= 4.67/.744$$
$$= 6.28$$

STEP 9   Determine the critical value of F using Appendix A-3. For example, the critical value of F when $df_{bg} = 2$, $df_{wg} = 15$, and alpha $= .05$ is 3.68.

STEP 10   If the calculated value of F (step 8) is equal to or greater than the critical value of F (step 9), we reject the null hypothesis and conclude that at least one mean differed from the others. In our example, 6.28 was greater than 3.68. Thus, we reject the null hypothesis and conclude that at least one mean differed from the others. Looking at the means, we see that subjects who received attractive pictures liked the other person most ($\bar{x} = 5.5$), those who received moderately attractive photos were second ($\bar{x} = 5.2$), and those who received unattractive pictures liked the other person least ($\bar{x} = 3.8$). We would need to conduct post hoc tests to determine which means differed significantly (see Chapter 10).

If the calculated value of F (step 8) is less than the critical value (step 9), we fail to reject the null hypothesis and conclude that the independent variable had no effect on subjects' responses.

Appendix B-2

Calculational Formulas for a Two-Way Factorial ANOVA

The conceptual rationale and demonstrational formulas for factorial analysis of variance are discussed in Chapter 10. The demonstrational formulas in Chapter 10 help to convey what each aspect of factorial ANOVA reflects, but they are unwieldy for computational purposes. Appendix B-2 presents the calculational formulas for performing factorial ANOVA on data from a between-groups factorial design.

The data are from a hypothetical study of the effects of audience size and composition on speech disfluencies, such as stuttering and hesitations. Twenty subjects told the story of Goldilocks and the Three Bears to a group of elementary school children or to a group of adults. Some subjects spoke to an audience of 5; others speak to an audience of 20. This was a 2×2 factorial design, the two independent variables being audience composition (children versus adults) and audience size (5 versus 20). The dependent variable was the number of speech disfluencies—stutters, stammers, misspeaking, and the like—that the subject displayed while telling the story.

The data were as follows:

		B AUDIENCE SIZE	
		Small (b_1)	Large (b_2)
		3	7
		1	2
	Children (a_1)	2	5
		5	3
A AUDIENCE COMPOSITION		4	4
		3	13
		8	9
	Adults (a_2)	4	11
		2	8
		6	12

STEP 1 For each condition (i.e., each combination of a and b), compute

1. The sum of all of the scores in each condition (Σx)
2. The mean of the condition ($\bar{x}$)
3. The sum of the squared scores (Σx^2)
4. The sum of squares ($\Sigma x^2 - [(\Sigma x)^2/n]$)

You'll find it useful to enter these quantities into a table such as that given below:

		B: b_1	b_2
a_1	Σx	15	21
	$\bar{x}$	3.0	4.2
	Σx^2	55	103
	SS	10	14.8
A: a_2	Σx	23	53
	$\bar{x}$	4.6	10.6
	Σx^2	129	579
	SS	23.2	17.2

Also, calculate $\Sigma(\Sigma x)^2/N$—the square of the sum of the condition totals divided by the total number of subjects:

$$\begin{aligned}\Sigma(\Sigma x)^2/N &= (15 + 21 + 23 + 53)^2/20 \\ &= (112)^2/20 \\ &= 12544/20 \\ &= 627.2\end{aligned}$$

This quantity appears in several of the formulas below.

Steps 2–4 compute the within-groups portion of the variance.

STEP 2 Compute SS_{wg}:

$$\begin{aligned}SS_{wg} &= SS_{a1b1} + SS_{a1b2} + SS_{a2b1} + SS_{a2b2} \\ &= 10 + 14.8 + 23.2 + 17.2 \\ &= 65.2\end{aligned}$$

STEP 3 Compute df_{wg}:

$df_{wg} = (j \times k)(n - 1)$, where j = levels of A
k = levels of B
n = subjects per condition

$$\begin{aligned}&= (2 \times 2)(5 - 1) \\ &= 16\end{aligned}$$

STEP 4 Compute MS_{wg}:

$$\begin{aligned}MS_{wg} &= SS_{wg}/df_{wg} \\ &= 65.2/16 \\ &= 4.075\end{aligned}$$

Set MS_{wg} aside for a moment. You will use it in the denominator of the F-tests you perform to test the main effects and interaction below.

Steps 5–8 calculate the main effect of A.

STEP 5   Compute SS_A:

$$SS_A = \frac{(\Sigma x_{a1b1} + \Sigma x_{a1b2})^2 + (\Sigma x_{a2b1} + \Sigma x_{a2b2})^2}{(n)(k)} - \frac{[\Sigma(\Sigma x)]^2}{N}$$

$$= \frac{(15 + 21)^2 + (23 + 53)^2}{(5)(2)} - 627.2$$

$$= \frac{(36)^2 + (76)^2}{10} - 627.2$$

$$= \frac{1296 + 5776}{10} - 627.2$$

$$= 707.2 - 627.2$$

$$= 80.0$$

STEP 6   Compute df_A:

$$df_A = j - 1, \text{ where } j = \text{levels of } A$$

$$= 2 - 1$$

$$= 1$$

STEP 7   Compute MS_A:

$$MS_A = SS_A/df_A$$

$$= 80.0/1$$

$$= 80.0$$

STEP 8   Compute F_A:

$$F_A = MS_A/MS_{wg}$$

$$= 80.0/4.075$$

$$= 19.63$$

STEP 9   Determine the critical value of F using Appendix A-3. The critical value of F (alpha level $= .05$) when $df_A = 1$ and $df_{wg} = 16$ is 4.49.

STEP 10   If the calculated value of F (step 8) is equal to or greater than the critical value of F (step 9), we reject the null hypothesis and conclude that at least one mean differed from the others. In our example, 19.63 was greater than 4.49, so we reject the null hypothesis and conclude that a_1 differed from a_2. To interpret the effect, we would inspect the means of a_1 and a_2 (averaging across the levels of B). When we do this, we find that subjects who spoke to adults ($\bar{x} = 7.6$) emitted significantly more disfluencies than those who spoke to children ($\bar{x} = 3.6$).

If the calculated value of F (step 8) is less than the critical value (step 9), we fail to reject the null hypothesis and conclude that the independent variable had no effect on subjects' responses.

Steps 11–14 calculate the main effect of B.

STEP 11   Compute SS_B:

$$SS_B = \frac{(\Sigma x_{a1b1} + \Sigma x_{a2b1})^2 + (\Sigma x_{a1b2} + \Sigma x_{a2b2})^2}{(n)(j)} - \frac{[\Sigma(\Sigma x)]^2}{N}$$

$$= \frac{(15 + 23)^2 + (21 + 53)^2}{(5)(2)} - 627.2$$

$$= \frac{(38)^2 + (74)^2}{10} - 627.2$$

$$= \frac{1444 + 5476}{10} - 627.2$$

$$= 692 - 627.2$$

$$= 64.8$$

STEP 12   Compute df_B:

$$df_B = k - 1$$

$$= 2 - 1$$

$$= 1$$

STEP 13   Compute MS_B:

$$MS_B = SS_B/df_B$$

$$= 64.8/1$$

$$= 64.8$$

STEP 14   Compute F_B:

$$F_B = MS_B/MS_{wg}$$

$$= 64.8/4.075$$

$$= 15.90$$

STEP 15   Determine the critical value of F using Appendix A-3. The critical value of $F(1, 16) = 4.49$.

STEP 16   If the calculated value of F (step 14) is equal to or greater than the critical value of F (step 15), we reject the null hypothesis and conclude that at least one mean differed from the others. In our example, 15.90 was greater than 4.49, so the main effect of B—audience size—was significant. Looking at the means for b_1 and b_2 (averaged across levels of A), we find that subjects emitted more speech disfluencies when they spoke to large audiences than when they spoke to small audiences; the means for the large and small audiences were 7.4 and 3.8, respectively.

If the calculated value of F (step 14) is less than the critical value (step 15), we fail to reject the null hypothesis and conclude that the independent variable had no effect on subjects' responses.

Steps 17–23 calculate the $A \times B$ interaction.

The simplest way to obtain $SS_{A \times B}$ is by subtraction. If we subtract SS_A and SS_B from SS_{bg} (the sum of squares between-groups), we get $SS_{A \times B}$.

STEP 17   Compute SS_{bg}:

$$SS_{bg} = \frac{(\Sigma x_{a1b1})^2 + (\Sigma x_{a1b2})^2 + (\Sigma x_{a2b1})^2 + (\Sigma x_{a2b2})^2}{n} - \frac{\Sigma(\Sigma x)^2}{N}$$

$$= \frac{(15)^2 + (21)^2 + (23)^2 + (53)^2}{5} - 627.2$$

$$= \frac{225 + 441 + 529 + 2809}{5} - 627.2$$

$$= 800.8 - 627.2$$

$$= 173.6$$

STEP 18   Compute $SS_{A \times B}$:

$$SS_{A \times B} = SS_{bg} - SS_A - SS_B$$

$$= 173.6 - 80.0 - 64.8$$

$$= 28.8$$

STEP 19   Compute $df_{A \times B}$:

$$df_{A \times B} = (j - 1)(k - 1)$$

$$= (2 - 1)(2 - 1)$$

$$= (1)(1)$$

$$= 1$$

STEP 20   Compute $MS_{A \times B}$:

$$MS_{A \times B} = SS_{A \times B}/df_{A \times B}$$

$$= 28.8/1$$

$$= 28.8$$

STEP 21   Compute $F_{A \times B}$:

$$F_{A \times B} = MS_{A \times B}/MS_{wg}$$
$$= 28.8/4.075$$
$$= 7.07$$

STEP 22   Determine the critical value of F using Appendix A-3. We've seen already that for F (1, 16), the critical value is 4.49.

STEP 23   If the calculated value of F (step 21) is equal to or greater than the critical value of F (step 22), we reject the null hypothesis and conclude that at least one mean differed from the others. In our example, 7.07 was greater than 4.49, so we conclude that the $A \times B$ interaction was significant.

Looking at the means we calculated in step 1, we see that subjects who spoke to a large audience of adults emitted a somewhat greater number of speech disfluencies than those in the other three conditions.

Audience composition	Audience size	
	Small	Large
Children	3.0	4.2
Adults	4.6	10.6

To determine precisely which means differed from one another, we would conduct tests of simple main effects.

If the calculated value of F (step 21) is less than the critical value (step 22), we fail to reject the null hypothesis and conclude that variables A and B (audience composition and size) did not interact.

Glossary

ABA design a single-subject design in which baseline data are obtained (A), the independent variable is introduced and behavior is measured again (B), then the independent variable is withdrawn and behavior is observed a third time (A)

ABC design a multiple-I single-subject design that contains a baseline period (A), followed by the introduction of one level of the independent variable (B), followed by the introduction of another level of the independent variable (C)

acquiescence response set the tendency for some people to agree with statements regardless of their content

alpha level the maximum probability that researcher is willing to make a Type I error; typically, the alpha level is set at .05

analysis of variance (ANOVA) an inferential statistical procedure used to test differences between means

ANOVA table a table that shows the results of an analysis of variance, including the sum of squares (SS), degrees of freedom (df), mean squares (MS), and F-values for all effects

APA style guidelines set forth by the American Psychological Association for preparing research reports; these guidelines may be found in the *Publication Manual of the American Psychological Association* (3rd ed.)

applied research research aimed toward solving real-world problems or improving the quality of life

a priori prediction a prediction that is made about the outcome of a study before data are collected

archival research research in which data are analyzed from existing records, such as census reports, court records, or personal letters

attrition the loss of subjects during a study

basic research research aimed toward basic understanding without regard for whether that understanding will be immediately applicable in solving real-world problems

behavioral coding system a procedure for converting observed behaviors to numerical data for purposes of analysis

behavioral measure the direct observation of a particular behavior

beta the probability of committing a Type II error

between-groups design an experimental design in which each subject serves in only one condition of the experiment

between-groups variance the portion of the total variance in a set of scores that reflects systematic differences between the experimental groups

between-within design an experimental design that combines one or more between-subjects factors with one or more within-subjects factors; a split-plot design

biased assignment a threat to internal validity that occurs when subjects are assigned to conditions in a nonrandom manner, producing systematic differences among conditions prior to introduction of the independent variable

canonical correlation a multivariate statistical procedure that examines the relationship between two sets of variables

canonical variable in many multivariate techniques, a composite variable that is calculated by summing two or more dependent variables that have been weighted according to their ability to differentiate among groups of subjects

carryover effects a situation in within-subjects designs in which the effects of one level of the independent variable are still present when another level of the independent variable is introduced

class interval a subset of a range of scores; in a grouped frequency distribution, the number of subjects who fall into each class interval is shown

cluster sampling a sampling procedure in which the researcher first samples clusters or groups of participants, then samples participants from the selected clusters

coefficient of determination the square of the correlation coefficient; indicates the proportion of variance in one variable that can be accounted for by the other variable

conceptual definition an abstract, dictionary-type definition

concurrent validity a form of criterion-related validity that reflects the extent to which a measure allows a researcher to distinguish between respondents at the time the measure is taken

condition one level of an independent variable

confederate an accomplice of an experimenter whom subjects assume to be another subject or an uninvolved bystander

confounding a condition that exists when something other than the independent variable differs systematically among the experimental conditions

confound variance the portion of the total variance in a set of scores that is due to extraneous variables that differ systematically between the experimental groups; also called secondary variance

construct validity the degree to which a measure of a particular construct correlates with measures of related constructs as one would expect

control group subjects who receive a zero level of the independent variable

convenience sample a nonprobability sample that includes whatever subjects are readily available

correlation coefficient an index of the direction and magnitude of the relationship between two variables; the value of a correlation coefficient ranges from -1.00 to $+1.00$

correlational research research designed to examine the nature of the relationship between two naturally occurring variables

cost–benefit analysis a method of making decisions in which the potential costs and risks of a study are weighed against its likely benefits

counterbalancing a procedure used in within-subjects designs in which different subjects receive the levels of the independent variable in different orders; counterbalancing is used to avoid systematic order effects

criterion by inspection the practice in single-subject research of analyzing the effects of an independent variable by visually inspecting the data for individual subjects; also called graphic analysis

criterion-related validity the extent to which a measure allows a researcher to distinguish among respondents on the basis of some behavioral criterion

criterion variable the variable being predicted in a regression analysis; the dependent variable

critical multiplism the philosophy that researchers should use many ways of obtaining evidence regarding a particular hypothesis rather than relying on a single approach

cross-lagged panel correlational design a research design in which two variables are measured at two points in time and correlations between the variables across time are examined

crossover interaction an interaction in which one independent variable has opposite effects, depending on the level of another independent variable

debriefing the procedure through which research participants are told about the nature of a study after it is completed

deception the practice of misleading or lying to subjects for research purposes

deduction the process of reasoning from a general proposition to a specific implication of that proposition; for example, hypotheses are often deduced from theories

demand characteristics aspects of a study that indicate to subjects how they are expected to respond

dependent variable the response measured in a study, typically a measure of subjects' thoughts, feelings, behavior, or physiological reactions

descriptive research research designed to describe the behavior, thoughts, or feelings of a group of subjects

descriptive statistics numbers that summarize and describe the behavior of subjects in a study; the mean and standard deviation are descriptive statistics, for example

differential attrition the loss of subjects during a study in a manner such that the loss is not randomly distributed across conditions

discriminant function analysis (DFA) a multivariate statistical procedure that identifies variables that differ or discriminate between two or more groups

double-blind procedure the practice of concealing the purpose and hypotheses of a study both from the participants and from the researchers who have direct contact with the participants

economic sample a sample that provides a reasonable degree of accuracy at a reasonable cost in terms of money, time, and effort

empiricism the practice of relying on observation to draw conclusions about the world

environmental manipulation an independent variable that involves the experimental modification of the subject's physical or social environment

epsem design a sampling procedure in which all cases in the population have an equal probability of being chosen for the sample; epsem stands for equal-probability selection method

error of estimation the degree to which data obtained from a sample are expected to deviate from the population as a whole; also called the margin of error

error variance that portion of the total variance in a set of data that remains unaccounted for after systematic variance is removed; variance that is unrelated to the variables under investigation in a study; within-groups variance

expericorr design an experimental design that includes one or more manipulated independent variables and one or more preexisting subject variables that are measured rather than manipulated; a mixed factorial design

experiment a study in which the researcher assigns subjects to conditions and manipulates at least one independent variable

experimental contamination a situation that occurs when subjects in one experimental condition are indirectly affected by the independent variable in another experimental condition because they interacted with subjects in the other condition

experimental control the practice of eliminating or holding constant extraneous variables that might affect the outcome of an experiment

experimental group subjects who receive a nonzero level of the independent variable

experimental hypothesis the hypothesis that the independent variable did have an effect; equivalently, the hypothesis that the means of the various experimental conditions will differ from one another

experimental research research designed to test whether certain variables cause changes in behavior, thoughts, or feelings

experimenter expectancy effect the influence of the researcher's hypotheses on the outcome of a study; also called the Rosenthal effect

experimenter's dilemma the fact that, generally speaking, the greater the internal validity of an experiment, the lower its external validity, and vice versa

external validity the degree to which the results obtained in one study can be replicated or generalized to other samples, research settings, and procedures

extreme groups procedure creating two groups of subjects with unusually low or unusually high scores on a particular variable

face validity the extent to which a measurement procedure appears to measure what it is supposed to measure

factor (1) in experimental designs, an independent variable; (2) in factor analysis, the underlying dimension that is assumed to account for observed relationships among variables

factor analysis a class of multivariate statistical techniques that are used to identify the underlying dimensions (factors) that account for the observed relationships among a set of measured variables

factorial design an experimental design in which two or more independent variables are manipulated

factor loading in factor analysis, the correlation between a variable and a factor

factor matrix a table that shows the results of a factor analysis; in this matrix the rows are variables and the columns are factors

failing to reject the null hypothesis concluding on the basis of statistical evidence that the null hypothesis is true—that the independent variable did not have an effect

falsifiability the requirement that a hypothesis must be capable of being falsified

follow-up tests inferential statistics that are used after a significant *F*-test to determine which means differ from which; also called post hoc tests or multiple comparisons

frequency the number of subjects who obtained a particular score

frequency distribution a table that shows the number of subjects who obtained each possible score on a measure

frequency polygon a form of line graph

F-test an inferential statistical procedure used to test for differences among condition means; the *F*-test is used in ANOVA

grand mean the mean of all of the condition means in an experiment

graphic analysis in single-subject research, the visual inspection of graphs of the data to determine whether or not the independent variable affected the subject's behavior

group design an experimental design in which several subjects serve in each condition of the design and the data are analyzed by examining the average responses of subjects in these conditions

grouped frequency distribution a table that indicates the number of subjects who obtained each of a range of scores

halo bias the tendency for observers' ratings of a subject to be distorted by their overall evaluation of the subject

histogram a form of bar graph

history effects changes in subjects' responses between pretest and posttest that are due to an outside, extraneous influence rather than to the independent variable

homogeneous sample a sample in which the subjects are very similar to one another; data from homogeneous samples tend to have lower error variance than data from heterogenous samples

hypothesis a proposition that follows logically from a theory; also, a prediction regarding the outcome of a study

hypothetical construct an entity that cannot be directly observed but that is inferred on the basis of observable evidence; intelligence, status, and anxiety are examples of hypothetical constructs

independent variable in an experiment, the variable that is varied or manipulated by the researcher to assess its effects on subjects' behavior

induction the process of reasoning from specific instances to a general proposition about those instances; for example, hypotheses are sometimes induced from observed facts

inferential statistics mathematical analyses that allow researchers to draw conclusions regarding the reliability and generalizability of their data; *t*-tests and *F*-tests are inferential statistics, for example

informed consent the practice of informing participants regarding the nature of their participation in a study and obtaining their written consent to participate

informed consent form a form that describes the nature of subjects' participation in a study (including all possible risks) and provides a place for subjects to indicate their willingness to participate

Institutional Review Board (IRB) a committee mandated by federal regulations that must evaluate the ethics of research conducted at institutions that receive federal funding

instructional manipulation an independent variable that is varied through verbal information that is provided to subjects

interaction the combined effect of two or more independent variables such that the effect of one independent variable differs across the levels of the other independent variable(s)

interitem reliability the consistency of respondents' scores on a set of conceptually related items; the degree to which a set of items that ostensibly measure the same construct are intercorrelated

internal validity the degree to which a researcher draws accurate conclusions about the effects of an independent variable

interrater reliability the degree to which the observations of two independent raters or observers agree; also called interjudge or interobserver reliability

interrupted time series design a study in which the dependent variable is measured several times, the independent variable is introduced, and then the dependent variable is measured several more times

intersubject replication in single-subject research, the attempt to document the generalizability of an experimental effect by demonstrating the effect on other participants

interval scale a measure on which equal distances between scores represent equal differences in the property being measured

interview schedule the series of questions and accompanying response formats that guides an interviewer's line of questioning during an interview

intrasubject replication in single-subject research, the attempt to repeatedly demonstrate an experimental effect on a single participant by alternatively introducing and withdrawing the independent variable

invasion of privacy violation of research participants' rights to determine how, when, or where they will be studied

invasive manipulation an independent variable that directly alters the participant's body, such as surgical procedures or the administration of chemical substances

item-total correlation the correlation between respondents' scores on one item from a scale and the sum of their responses on the remaining items; an index of interitem reliability

knowledgeable informant someone who knows a subject well enough to report on his or her behavior

level one value of an independent variable

linear regression analysis a statistical procedure in which an equation is developed to predict scores on one variable from scores on another variable

local history effect a threat to internal validity in which some extraneous event happens to one experimental group that does not happen to the other groups

main effect the effect of a particular independent variable, ignoring the effects of other independent variables in the experiment

matched random assignment a procedure for assigning subjects to experimental conditions in which subjects are first matched into homogeneous blocks, then subjects within each block are assigned randomly to conditions

matched-subjects design an experimental design in which subjects are matched into homogeneous blocks, and subjects in each block are randomly assigned to the experimental conditions

maturation changes in subjects' responses between pretest and posttest that are due to the passage of time rather than to the independent variable; aging, fatigue, and hunger may produce maturation effects, for example

mean the mathematical average of a set of scores; the sum of a set of scores divided by the number of scores

mean square between-groups a measure of between-groups variance calculated by dividing the sum of squares between-groups by the between-groups degrees of freedom

mean square within-groups the average variance within experimental conditions; the sum of squares within-groups divided by the degrees of freedom within-groups

measurement error the deviation of a subject's observed score from its true score

measures of central tendency descriptive statistics that convey information about the average or most typical score in a distribution; the mean, median, and mode are measures of central tendency

measures of variability descriptive statistics that convey information about the spread or variability of a set of data; the range, variance, and standard deviation are measures of variability

median the score that falls at the 50th percentile in a rank-ordered distribution; the middle score in a distribution

median-split procedure assigning subjects to two groups depending on whether their scores on a particular variable fall below or above the median of that variable

minimal risk risk to research participants that is no greater than they would be likely to encounter in daily life or during routine physical or psychological examinations

mixed factorial design (1) an experimental design that includes one or more manipulated independent variables and one or more preexisting subject variables that are measured rather than manipulated; an expericorr design; (2) the term is also used by some researchers to refer to between-within designs

mode the most frequent score in a distribution

moderator variable a variable that qualifies or moderates the effects of another variable on behavior

multilevel design a one-way design with more than two levels of the independent variable

multiple baseline design a single-subject design in which two or more behaviors are studied simultaneously

multiple comparisons inferental statistics that are used after a significant *F*-test to determine which means differ from which; also called post hoc tests or follow-up tests

multiple correlation coefficient the correlation between one variable and a set of other variables

multiple-I design a single-subject design in which levels of an independent variable are introduced one at a time

multiple regression analysis a statistical procedure in which an equation is derived by which one variable (the criterion variable) can be predicted from a set of other variables (the predictor variables)

multistage sampling a variation of cluster sampling in which large clusters of subjects are sampled, followed by smaller clusters from within the larger clusters, followed by still smaller clusters, until subjects are sampled from the small clusters

multivariate analysis of variance (MANOVA) a multivariate statistical procedure that simultaneously tests differences among the means of two or more groups on two or more dependent variables

multivariate technique a class of statistical procedures that allows the examination of relationships among many variables simultaneously; MANOVA, factor analysis, and canonical correlation are examples of multivariate techniques

negative correlation an inverse relationship between two variables such that subjects with high scores on one variable tend to have low scores on the other variable, and vice versa

negatively skewed distribution a distribution in which there are more high scores than low scores

nominal scale a measure on which the numbers assigned to subjects' characteristics are merely labels; subject sex is on a nominal scale, for example

nonequivalent groups posttest-only design a quasi-experimental design in which two preexisting groups are studied—one that has received the quasi-independent variable and one that has not

nonequivalent groups pretest–posttest design a quasi-experimental design in which two preexisting groups are tested—one that has received the quasi-independent variable and one that has not; each group is tested twice—once before and once after one group receives the quasi-independent variable

nonprobability sample a sample selected in such a way that the likelihood of any member of the population being chosen for the sample cannot be determined

normal distribution a distribution of scores that rises to a rounded peak in the center with symmetrical tails descending to the left and right of the center

null finding obtaining no significant differences among condition means; concluding that the independent variable did not have an effect

null hypothesis the hypothesis that the independent variable will not have an effect; equivalently, the hypothesis that the means of the various experimental conditions will not differ

one-group pretest–posttest design a preexeperimental design in which one group of subjects is tested both before and after a quasi-independent variable has occurred; because it fails to control for nearly all threats to internal validity, this design should never be used

one-way design an experimental design with a single independent variable

operational definition a definition that defines a construct by specifying precisely how it is measured or manipulated in a particular study

operationism the philosophy that says that only operational definitions may be used in science

order effects an effect on behavior produced by the specific order in which levels of the independent variable are administered in a within-subjects design

ordinal scale a measure on which the numbers assigned to subjects' responses reflect the rank order of subjects from highest to lowest

outlier an extreme score; typically scores that fall farther than ± 3 standard deviations from the mean are considered outliers

paired *t*-test a *t*-test performed on a repeated measures two-group design

partial correlation the correlation between two variables with the influence of one or more other variables removed

Pearson correlation coefficient the most commonly used measure of correlation

perfect correlation a correlation of -1.00 or $+1.00$, indicating that two variables are so closely related that one can be perfectly predicted from the other

physiological measure a measure of bodily activity; in behavioral research, physiological measures generally are used to assess processes within the nervous system

placebo control group subjects who receive an ineffective treatment; this is used to identify and control for placebo effects

placebo effect a physiological or psychological change that occurs as a result of mere suggestion that the change will occur

positive correlation a direct relationship between two variables such that subjects with high scores on one variable also tend to have high scores on the other variable, whereas low scorers on one variable tend to also score low on the other

positively skewed distribution a distribution in which there are more low scores than high scores

post hoc explanation an explanation offered for a set of findings after the data are collected and analyzed

post hoc tests inferental statistics that are used after a significant *F*-test to determine which means differ; also called follow-up tests or multiple comparisons

posttest-only design an experiment in which subjects' responses are measured only once—after introduction of the independent variable

power the degree to which a research design is sensitive to the effects of the independent variable; powerful designs are able to detect effects of the independent variable more easily than less powerful designs

predictive validity a form of criterion-related validity that reflects the extent to which a measure allows a researcher to distinguish between respondents at some time in the future

predictor variable in a regression analysis, the variables that are used to predict scores on the criterion or dependent variable

preexperimental design a design that lacks the necessary controls to minimize threats to internal validity; typically preexperimental designs do not involve adequate control or comparison groups

pretest-posttest design an experiment in which subjects' responses are measured twice—once before and once after introduction of the independent variable

pretest sensitization the situation that occurs when being pretested affects subjects' responses on the posttest

primary variance that portion of the total variance in a set of scores that is due to the independent variable; also called treatment variance

probability sample a sample selected in such a way that the likelihood of any individual in the population being selected can be specified

program evaluation the use of behavioral research methods to assess the effects of programs on behavior

pseudoscience claims of knowledge that are couched in the trappings of science but that violate the central criteria of scientific investigation, such as systematic empiricism, public verification, and solvability

psychometrics the field devoted to the study of psychological measurement; experts in this field are known as *psychometricians*

purposive sample a sample selected on the basis of the researcher's judgment regarding the "best" subjects to select for research purposes

quasi-experimental design a research design in which the researcher cannot assign subjects to conditions and/or manipulate the independent variable; instead, comparisons are made between groups that already exist or within a single group before and after a quasi-experimental treatment has occurred

quasi-independent variable the independent variable in a quasi-experimental design; the designator *quasi-independent* is used when the variable was not manipulated by the researcher

quota sample a sample selected to include specified proportions of certain kinds of subjects

randomized groups design an experimental design in which each subject serves in only one condition of the experiment; a between-groups design

range a measure of variability that is equal to the difference between the largest and smallest scores in a set of data

ratio scale a measure on which scores possess all of the characteristics of real numbers

raw data matrix a table of the original data collected on a sample of subjects; in this table, each subject is represented by a row and each dependent variable is represented by a column

regression coefficient the slope of a regression line

regression constant the y-intercept in a regression equation; the value of y when $x = 0$

regression equation an equation from which one can predict scores on one variable from one or more other variables

regression to the mean the tendency for subjects who are selected on the basis of their extreme scores on some measure to obtain less extreme scores when they are retested

rejecting the null hypothesis concluding on the basis of the statistical evidence that the null hypothesis is false—that the independent variable did have an effect

relative frequency distribution a table that indicates the proportion of subjects who fell in each class interval

reliability the consistency or dependability of a measuring technique

repeated measures design an experimental design in which each subject serves in more than one condition of the experiment; a within-subjects design

representative sample a sample from which one can draw accurate, unbiased estimates of the characteristics of a larger population

response format the manner in which respondents indicate their answers to questions

Rosenthal effect see experimenter expectancy effect

sample a subset of a population; the group of subjects who are selected to participate in a research study

sampling the process by which a sample is chosen from a population to participate in a research study

sampling error the difference between scores obtained on a sample and the scores that would have been obtained if the entire population had been studied

sampling frame a listing of the members of a population

scatter plot a graphical representation of subjects' scores on two variables; the values of one variable are plotted on the x-axis and those of the other variable are plotted on the y-axis

secondary variance that portion of the total variance in a set of scores that is due to extraneous variables that differ systematically between the experimental groups; also called confound variance

selection bias a threat to internal validity that involves experimental groups not being equivalent before the manipulation of the independent or quasi-independent variable

selection-by-history interaction see local history effect

self-report measure a measure on which subjects provide information about themselves, on a questionnaire or in an interview, for example

simple frequency distribution a table that indicates the number of subjects who obtained each score

simple interrupted time series design a quasi-experimental design in which subjects are tested on many occasions—several before and several after the introduction of the quasi-independent variable

simple main effect the effect of one independent variable at a particular level of another independent variable

simple random assignment placing subjects in experimental conditions in such a way that every subject has an equal chance of being placed in any condition

simple random sample a sample selected in such a way that every possible sample of the desired size has the same chance of being selected from the population

single-subject design an experimental design in which the unit of analysis is the individual participant rather than the experimental group

social desirability bias the tendency for some people to distort their responses in a manner that portrays them in a positive light

split-half reliability the correlation between respondents' scores on two halves of a single instrument; an index of interitem reliability

split-plot factorial design an experimental design that combines one or more between-subjects factors with one or more within-subjects factors; also called a between-within design

standard deviation a measure of variability that is equal to the square root of the variance

statistical significance a finding that is very unlikely to be due to error variance

stratified random sampling a sampling procedure in which the population is divided into strata, then subjects are sampled randomly from each stratum

stratum a subset of a population that shares a certain characteristic; for example, a population could be divided into the strata of men and women

subject variable a personal characteristic of research participants, such as age, self-esteem, or extraversion

sum of squares the sum of the squared deviations from the mean

sum of squares between-groups the total variance in a set of scores that is associated with the independent variable; the sum of the squared differences between each condition mean and the grand mean

sum of squares within-groups the sum of the variances of the scores within particular experimental conditions

systematic sampling a sampling procedure in which every nth name is selected from a list

systematic variance that portion of the total variance in a set of scores that is related in an orderly, predictable fashion to the variables the researcher is investigating

table of random numbers a table containing numbers that occur in a random order; such a table appears in Appendix A-1

test–retest reliability the consistency of respondents' scores on a measure across time

testing practice effect the situation that arises when taking a test once (during a pretest, for example) improves subjects' performance on subsequent administrations of the test

theory a set of propositions that attempt to specify the interrelationships among a set of constructs

time series design a class of quasi-experimental designs in which subjects are tested on many occasions—several before and several after the introduction of the quasi-independent variable

total mean square the variance of a set of data; the sum of squares divided by its degrees of freedom

treatment variance that portion of the total variance in a set of scores that is due to the independent variable; also called primary variance

true score the hypothetical score that a subject would have obtained if the attribute being measured could be measured without error

*t***-test** an inferential statistical procedure used to test the difference between two means

two-group experimental design an experiment with two conditions; the smallest possible experiment

Type I error erroneously rejecting the null hypothesis; concluding that an independent variable had an effect when, in fact, it did not

Type II error erroneously failing to reject the null hypothesis; concluding that the independent variable did not have an effect when, in fact, it did

unobtrusive measure a dependent variable that can be measured without affecting subjects' responses

validity the extent to which a measurement procedure actually measures what it is intended to measure

variance a numerical index of the variability in a set of data

within-groups variance the variability among scores within a particular experimental condition

within-subjects design an experimental design in which each subject serves in more than one condition of the experiment; a repeated measures design

*z***-score** an indication of how much a particular subject's score varies from the mean in terms of standard deviations; also called a standard score

References

Adams, K. L., & Ware, N. C. (1989). Sexism and the English language: The linguistic implications of being a woman. In J. Freeman (Ed.), *Women: A feminist perspective* (pp. 470–484). Mountain View, CA: Mayfield.

American Psychological Association. (1982). *Ethical principles in the conduct of research with human participants*. Washington, DC: Author.

American Psychological Association. (1983). *Publication manual of the American Psychological Association* (3rd ed.). Washington, DC: Author.

American Psychological Association. (1985). *Guidelines for ethical conduct in the care and use of animals*. Washington, DC: Author.

Anderson, C. A. (1989). Temperature and aggression: Ubiquitous effects of heat on occurrence of human violence. *Psychological Bulletin, 106,* 74–96.

Bales, R. F. (1970). *Personality and interpersonal behavior*. New York: Holt, Rinehart & Winston.

Baron, R. A., & Bell, P. A. (1976). Aggression and heat: The influence of ambient temperature, negative affect, and a cooling drink on physical aggression. *Journal of Personality and Social Psychology, 33,* 245–255.

Baumrind, D. (1971). Principles of ethical conduct in the treatment of subjects: Reactions to the draft report of the committee on ethical standards in psychological research. *American Psychologist, 26,* 887–896.

Bell, C. R. (1962). Personality characteristics of volunteers for psychological studies. *British Journal of Social and Clinical Psychology, 1,* 81–95.

Berman, W. H. (1988). The role of attachment in the post-divorce experience. *Journal of Personality and Social Psychology, 54,* 496–503.

Blumenthal, T. D., & Gescheider, G. A. (1987). Modification of the acoustic startle response by a tactile prepulse: Effects of stimulus onset asynchronicity and prepulse intensity. *Psychophysiology, 24,* 320–327.

Bower, G. H., Karlin, M. B., & Dueck, A. (1975). Comprehension and memory for pictures. *Memory and Cognition, 3,* 216–220.

Bringmann, W. (1979). Wundt's lab: "humble . . . but functioning" (letter to the editor). *APA Monitor* (Sept/Oct), 13.

Brown, A. S. (1988). Encountering misspellings and spelling performance: Why wrong isn't right. *Journal of Educational Psychology, 80,* 488–494.

Campbell, D., Sanderson, R. E., & Laverty, S. G. (1964). Characteristics of a conditioned response in human subjects during extinction trials following a single traumatic conditioning trial. *Journal of Abnormal and Social Psychology, 68,* 627–639.

Campbell, D. T., & Stanley, J. C. (1966). *Experimental and quasi-experimental designs for research.* Skokie, IL: Rand McNally.

Campbell, P. B. (1983). The impact of societal biases on research methods. In B. L. Richardson & J. Wirtenberg (Eds.), *Sex role research* (pp. 197–214). New York: Praeger.

Carlson, R. (1971). Where is the person in personality research? *Psychological Bulletin, 75,* 203–219.

Cheek, J. M. (1982). Aggregation, moderator variables, and the validity of personality tests: A peer-rating study. *Journal of Personality and Social Psychology, 43,* 1254–1269.

Christensen, L. (1988). Deception in psychological research: When is its use justified? *Personality and Social Psychology Bulletin, 14,* 664–675.

Cialdini, R. B., Vincent, J. E., Lewis, S. K., Catalan, J., Wheeler, D., & Darby, B. L. (1975). Reciprocal concessions procedure for inducing compliance: The door-in-the-face technique. *Journal of Personality and Social Psychology, 31,* 206–215.

Cochran, W. G.; Mosteller, F., & Tukey, J. W. (1953). Statistical problems in the Kinsey report. *Journal of the American Statistical Association, 48,* 673–716.

Condray, D. S. (1986). Quasi-experimental analysis: A mixture of methods and judgment. In W. M. K. Trochim (Ed.), *Advances in quasi-experimental design and analysis* (pp. 9–28). San Francisco: Jossey-Bass.

Cook, T. D., & Campbell, D. T. (1979). *Quasi-experimentation.* Boston: Houghton Mifflin.

Cordaro, L., & Ison, J. R. (1963). Psychology of the scientist: X. Observer bias in classical conditioning of the planaria. *Psychological Reports, 13,* 787–789.

Cronbach, L. J. (1970). *Essentials of psychological testing* (3rd ed.). New York: Harper & Row.

Cronbach, L. J., & Meehl, P. E. (1955). Construct validity in psychological tests. *Psychological Bulletin, 52,* 281–302.

Crowne, D. P., & Marlowe, D. (1964). *The approval motive: Studies in evaluative dependence.* New York: John Wiley.

Curtis, B., & Simpson, D. D. (1977). Differences in background and drug use history among three types of drug users entering drug therapy programs. *Journal of Drug Education, 7,* 369–379.

Dworkin, S. I., Bimle, C., & Miyauchi, T. (1989). Differential effects of pentobarbital and cocaine on punished and nonpunished responding. *Journal of the Experimental Analysis of Behavior, 51,* 173–184.

Eron, L. D., Huesmann, L. R., Lefkowitz, M. M., & Walder, L. O. (1972). Does television violence cause aggression? *American Psychologist, 27,* 253–263.

Estes, W. K. (1964). All-or-none processes in learning and retention. *American Psychologist, 19,* 16–25.

Feyerabend, P. K. (1965). Problems of empiricism. In R. Colodny (Ed.), *Beyond the edge of certainty.* Englewood Cliffs, NJ: Prentice-Hall.

Fiedler, F. E. (1967). *A theory of leadership effectiveness.* New York: McGraw-Hill.

Freedman, J. L. (1975). *Crowding and behavior.* San Francisco: W. H. Freeman.

Gelfand, D. M., Hartmann, D. P., Walder, P., & Page, B. (1973). Who reports shoplifters: A field-experimental study. *Journal of Personality and Social Psychology, 25,* 276–285.

Gottschalk, L. A., Uliana, R., & Gilbert, R. (1988). Presidential candidates and cognitive impairment measured from behavior in campaign debates. *Public Administration Review, 48,* 613–618.

Grady, K. E. (1981). Sex bias in research design. *Psychology of Woman Quarterly, 5,* 628–636.

Gross, A. E., & Fleming, I. (1982). Twenty years of deception in social psychology. *Personality and Social Psychology Bulletin, 8,* 402–408.

Hair, Jr., J. F., Anderson, R. E., & Tatham, R. L. (1987). *Multivariate data analysis* (2nd ed.). New York: Macmillan.

Hansel, C. E. M. (1980). *ESP and parapsychology: A critical re-evaluation.* Buffalo, NY: Prometheus Books.

Hart, E. A., Leary, M. R., & Rejeski, W. J. (1989). The measurement of social physique anxiety. *Journal of Sport and Exercise Psychology, 11,* 94–104.

Hempel, C. G. (1966). *Philosophy of natural science.* Englewood Cliffs, NJ: Prentice-Hall.

Henle, M., & Hubbell, M. B. (1938). "Egocentricity" in adult conversation. *Journal of Social Psychology, 9,* 227–234.

Huck, S. W., & Sandler, H. M. (1979). *Rival hypotheses: Alternative explanations of data based conclusions.* New York: Harper & Row.

Huff, D. (1954). *How to lie with statistics.* New York: W. W. Norton.

Humphreys, L. (1975). *Tearoom trade: Impersonal sex in public places.* Chicago: Aldine.

Hunt, M. (1974). *Sexual behavior in the 1970s.* Chicago: Playboy Press.

Ickes, W. (1982). A basic paradigm for the study of personality, roles, and social behavior. In W. Ickes & E. S. Knowles (Eds.), *Personality, roles and social behavior* (pp. 305–341). New York: Springer-Verlag.

Janis, I. L. (1982). *Groupthink.* Boston: Houghton Mifflin.

Jung, J. (1971). *The experimenter's dilemma.* New York: Harper & Row.

Kaplan, R. M. (1982). Nader's raid on the testing industry. *American Psychologist, 37,* 15–23.

Kendall, M. G. (1970). Ronald Aylmer Fisher, 1890–1962. In E. S. Pearson & M. G. Kendall (Eds.), *Studies in the history of probability and statistics* (pp. 439–453). London: Charles Griffin.

Kidd, V. (1971). A study of the images produced through the use of the male pronoun as the generic. *Moments in Contemporary Rhetoric and Communication, 1,* 25–30.

Kinsey, A. C., Pomeroy, W. B., & Martin, C. E. (1948). *Sexual behavior in the human male.* Philadelphia: Saunders.

Kinsey, A. C., Pomeroy, W. B., Martin, C. E., & Gebhard, P. H. (1953). *Sexual behavior in the human female.* Philadelphia: Saunders.

Kirby, D. (1977). The methods and methodological problems of sex research. In J. S. DeLora & C. A. B. Warren (Eds.), *Understanding sexual interaction.* Boston: Houghton Mifflin.

Kratochwill, T. R. (1978a). *Single subject research.* New York: Academic Press.

Kuhn, T. S. (1962). *The structure of scientific revolutions.* Chicago: University of Chicago Press.

Langer, E. J., & Rodin, J. (1976). The effects of choice and enhanced personal responsibility for the aged: A field experiment in an institutional setting. *Journal of Personality and Social Psychology, 34,* 191–198.

Levin, I., & Stokes, J. P. (1986). An examination of the relation of individual difference variables to loneliness. *Journal of Personality, 54,* 717–733.

Mahoney, M. J., Moura, N. G. M., & Wade, T. C. (1973). Relative efficacy of self-reward, self-punishment, and self-monitoring techniques for weight loss. *Journal of Consulting and Clinical Psychology, 40,* 404–407.

Masters, W. H., & Johnson, V. (1966). *Human sexual response.* Boston: Little, Brown.

Mazur-Hart, S. F., & Berman, J. J. (1977). Changing from fault to no-fault divorce: An interrupted time series analysis. *Journal of Applied Social Psychology, 7,* 300–312.

McClelland, D. C., Atkinson, J. W., Clark, R. A., & Lowell, E. L. (1953). *The achievement motive.* New York: Appleton–Century–Crofts.

McColskey, W. H., Altschuld, J. W., & Lawton, R. W. (1985). Predictors of principals' reliance on formal and informal sources of information. *Educational Evaluation and Policy Analysis, 7,* 427–436.

McCrae, R. R., & Costa, P. T., Jr. (1987). Validation of the five-factor model of personality across instruments and observers. *Journal of Personality and Social Psychology, 52,* 81–90.

McHale, S. M., & Gamble, W. C. (1989). Sibling relationships of children with disabled and nondisabled brothers and sisters. *Developmental Psychology, 25,* 421–429.

Middlemist, R. D., Knowles, E. S., & Matter, C. F. (1976). Personal space invasion in the lavatory: Suggestive evidence for arousal. *Journal of Personality and Social Psychology, 35,* 541–546.

Milgram, S. (1963). Behavioral study of obedience. *Journal of Abnormal and Social Psychology, 67,* 371–378.

Miller, N. E. (1985). The value of behavioral research on animals. *American Psychologist, 40,* 423–440.

Mook, D. G. (1983). In defense of external invalidity. *American Psychologist, 38,* 379–387.

Moscowitz, D. S. (1986). Comparison of self-reports, reports by knowledgeable informants, and behavioral observation data. *Journal of Personality, 54,* 294–317.

Neale, J. M., & Liebert, R. M. (1980). *Science and behavior.* Englewood Cliffs, NJ: Prentice-Hall.

Official IRB guidebook. (1986). Prepared by the President's Commission for the Study of Ethical Problems in Medicine and Biomedical and Behavioral Research. Washington, DC: National Printing Office.

Orne, M. T., & Scheibe, K. E. (1964). The contribution of nondeprivation factors in the production of sensory deprivation effects: The psychology of the "panic button." *Journal of Abnormal and Social Psychology, 68,* 3–12.

Pearson, E. S., & Kendall, M. G. (1970). *Studies in the history of statistics and probability.* London: Griffin.

Pearson, J. C. (1985). *Gender and communication.* Dubuque, IA: Wm. C. Brown.

Popper, K. R. (1959). *The logic of scientific discovery.* New York: Basic Books.

Radner, D., & Radner, M. (1982). *Science and unreason.* Belmont, CA: Wadsworth.

Reardon, P., & Prescott, S. (1977). Sex as reported in a recent sample of psychological research. *Psychology of Women Quarterly, 2,* 57–61.

Rodin, J., & Langer, E. J. (1977). Long-term effects of a control-relevant intervention with the institutionalized aged. *Journal of Personality and Social Psychology, 35,* 897–902.

Rosen, L. A., Booth, S. R., Bender, M. E., McGrath, M. L., Sorrell, S., & Drabman, R. S. (1988). Effects of sugar (sucrose) on children's behavior. *Journal of Consulting and Clinical Psychology, 56,* 583–589.

Sawyer, H. G. (1961). The meaning of numbers. Speech before the American Association of Advertising Agencies, as cited in E. J. Webb, D. T. Campbell, R. D. Schwartz, & L. Sechrest, *Unobtrusive measures* (1966). Skokie, IL: Rand McNally.

Scarr, S., Webber, P. L., Weinberg, R. A., & Wittig, M. A. (1981). Personality resemblance among adolescents and their parents in biologically related and adoptive families. *Journal of Personality and Social Psychology, 40,* 885–898.

Scheier, M. F., & Carver, C. S. (1985). Dispositional optimism and physical well-being: The influence of generalized outcome expectancies on health. *Journal of Personality, 55,* 169–210.

Schlenker, B. R., & Forsyth, D. R. (1977). On the ethics of psychological research. *Journal of Experimental Social Psychology, 13,* 369–396.

Schuman, H., & Kalton, G. (1985). Survey methods. In G. Lindzey & E. Aronson (Eds.), *Handbook of social psychology* (3rd ed., Vol. 1). New York: Random House.

Shadish, W. R., Cook, T. D., & Houts, A. C. (1986). Quasi-experimentation in a critical multiplist mode. In W. M. K. Trochim (Ed.), *Advances in quasi-experimental design and analysis* (pp. 29–46). San Francisco: Jossey-Bass.

Sidman, M. (1960). *Tactics of scientific research.* New York: Basic Books.

Singleton, Jr., R., Straits, B. C., Straits, M. M., & McAllister, R. J. (1988). *Approaches to social research.* New York: Oxford University Press.

Smith, S. S., & Richardson, D. (1983). Amelioration of deception and harm in psychological research: The important role of debriefing. *Journal of Personality and Social Psychology, 44,* 1075–1082.

Smith, T. W., Snyder, C. R., & Perkins, S. C. (1983). The self-serving function of hypochondriacal complaints: Physical symptoms as self-handicapping strategies. *Journal of Personality and Social Psychology, 44,* 787–797.

Stanovich, K. E. (1986). *How to think straight about psychology.* Chicago: Scott, Foresman.

Stericker, A. (1981). Does "he or she" business really make a difference? The effect of masculine pronouns as generics on job attitudes. *Sex Roles, 7,* 637–641.

Stigler, S. M. (1986). *The history of statistics.* Cambridge, MA: Belknap Press.

Straits, B. C., Wuebben, P. L., & Majka, T. J. (1972). Influences on subjects' perceptions of experimental research situation. *Sociometry, 35,* 499–518.

Summary report of journal operations. (1989). *American Psychologist, 44,* 1070.

Tabachnick, B. G., & Fidell, L. S. (1989). *Using multivariate statistics* (2nd ed.). New York: Harper & Row.

Terkel, J., & Rosenblatt, J. S. (1968). Maternal behavior induced by maternal blood plasma injected into virgin rats. *Journal of Comparative and Physiological Psychology, 65,* 479–482.

Timms, M. W. H. (1980). Treatment of chronic blushing by paradoxical intention. *Behavioral Psychotherapy, 8,* 59–61.

Underwood, B. J. (1957). *Psychological research.* New York: Appleton–Century–Crofts.

U.S. Department of Health and Human Services. (1983). *Code of federal regulations pertaining to the protection of human subjects.* Washington, DC: Government Printing Office.

von Daniken, E. (1970). *Chariots of the Gods?* New York: Bantam.

Walk, R. D. (1969). Two types of depth discrimination by the human infant with five inches of visual depth. *Psychonomic Society, 14,* 251–255.

Watson, R. I. (1978). *The great psychologists* (4th ed.). Philadelphia: J. B. Lippincott.

Wundt, W. (1874). *Principles of physiological psychology.* Leipzig: Engelmann.

Zimbardo, P. G. (1969). The human choice: Individuating reason, and order versus deindividuation, impulse, and chaos. In W. J. Arnold & D. Levine (Eds.), *Nebraska symposium on motivation, 1969.* Lincoln, NE: University of Nebraska Press.

Name Index

Subject Index

ABA design, 236–237, 240, 333
ABC design, 237, 333
Abstract, 293
Acquiescence response set, 63, 333
Alpha coefficient, 56
Alpha level, 162, 165, 194, 200,
  205–207, 248, 333
American Psychological Association,
  ethical principles of
  animal subjects, 278–279
  human subjects, 263, 266–267
Analysis of variance (ANOVA),
  196–211, 333
  factorial, 202–208
  follow-up tests and, 201–202, 208
  invention of, 202
  and MANOVA, 246–247
  one-way, 197–201, 324–326
  rationale for, 196–197
  relationship to *t*, 210
  two-way, 327–332
  within-subjects, 210–211
Animal subjects, 278–279
APA style, 19–20, 291–300, 333
Applied research, 3, 4, 333
A priori prediction, 12–13, 333
Archival research, 49, 334
Attrition, 136, 334
Author-date system, 19, 296–297
Author notes, 298

Bar graph, 71–74
Baseline, 124, 237, 240
Basic research, 3, 4, 334
Behavioral coding system, 43, 334
Behavioral measure, 42, 334
Behavioral research
  costs of, 264–265
  founding of, 5–6
  goals of, 2–4
  types of, 17–18

value of, 4–5, 263–264
variability and, 24–26
Beta, 162, 334
Between-groups design, 126, 334
Between-groups variance, 334. *See
  also* systematic variance
Between-subjects design, 126
Between-within design, 180–181,
  334
Bias
  demand characteristics and, 138–
    140
  experimenter, 138
  observer, 63
  selection, 135, 218, 345
  social desirability, 62–63, 346
Biased assignment, 135, 334

Canonical correlation, 250–252, 334
Canonical variable, 248, 334
Carryover effects, 128–129, 334
Case study, 15
Causality, 15, 111–114, 121, 226–
  228
Central tendency, 75
Class interval, 70–71, 334
Cluster sampling, 86–87, 334
Coefficient of determination, 102–
  104, 334
Coercion to participate, 270–271
Conceptual definition, 13–14, 334
Conciseness, 68
Concurrent validity, 61, 334
Condition, 122, 125, 335
Confederate, 123, 335
Confidentiality, 275
Confounding, 130–131, 133–138,
  158, 335
Confound variance, 130–133, 158,
  335
Construct, 60

Construct validity, 60, 335
Contamination, 219
Control group, 123–124, 141, 152,
  217–220, 224, 335
Convenience sample, 90, 92, 335
Correlation, 18, 37, 67, 97–117, 121
  as a measure of linear relation-
    ships, 107–108, 115
  causality and, 111–114
  graphs and, 100–101
  invention of, 106–107
  negative, 100, 101, 107
  partial, 114
  perfect, 100, 101, 103
  positive, 99–100, 101, 102
  regression analysis and, 114–117
  variance and, 102–104
  zero, 100, 101, 103
Correlation coefficient
  coefficient of determination and,
    102–104
  description of, 98–102, 335
  formula for, 104–106
  interpretation of, 107–114
  magnitude of, 100
  multiple, 117
  sign of, 99–100
  outliers and, 110–111
  Pearson, 99, 104–106, 107
  reliability and, 111
  restricted range and, 108–109
Cost-benefit analysis, 263–265, 335
Counterbalancing, 127–128, 153,
  335
Craniotomy, 41
Creationism, 9, 11
Criterion by inspection, 239, 335
Criterion-related validity, 60–61,
  335
Criterion variable, 116, 335
Critical multiplism, 227, 335